Versions of Primary Education

Where has primary education come from? What, once the dust of recent legislation has settled, is the balance of change and continuity? Where, as we approach the millennium, should primary education be heading? The five studies in this book come from the tumultuous period from the mid-1980s to the mid-1990s when the dominant educational ideas and practices of the previous two decades were being questioned and primary teachers were being unceremoniously ejected from the Plowden era into the very different ethos of the National Curriculum. The first four studies portray the ideas, practices and dilemmas of primary teaching at different points during this period. They also exemplify different approaches to classroom research, though all of them stay close to the interactions between teacher and child which are central to learning. These studies therefore raise educational questions which are perennial and fundamental, rather than tied to policy or fashion. The final study uses a broader brush to provide a historical framework for understanding the particular blend of change and continuity which characterises English primary education as a whole. It then offers critical reflections on the capacity of current primary policies and structures to meet the needs of the next century and suggests the kinds of questions which ought to be addressed.

Robin Alexander is Professor of Primary Education at the University of Warwick.

Versions of Primary Education

Robin Alexander

with contributions from John Willcocks,
Kay Kinder and Nick Nelson

London and New York

First published 1995
by Routledge
11 New Fetter Lane, London EC4P 4EE

Simultaneously published in the USA and Canada
by Routledge
29 West 35th Street, New York, NY 10001

©1995 Robin Alexander
The moral rights of the author and contributors
have been asserted.

Typeset in Palatino by
Florencetype Ltd, Stoodleigh, Devon

Printed and bound in Great Britain by
T.J. Press (Padstow) Ltd, Padstow, Cornwall

British Library Cataloguing in Publication Data
A catalogue record for this book is available from the British Library

Library of Congress Cataloguing in Publication Data
A catalogue record for this book has been requested

ISBN 0-415-12838-2

Contents

Illustrations

FIGURES

TABLES

Acknowledgements

Formal thanks are due to those who gave financial support to the research projects which provided some of the material for this book: the University of Leeds, which funded the work described in the second half of Chapter 2; Leeds City Council, which funded the project from which Chapters 3 and 4 are drawn; and the Economic and Social Research Council, whose grant made possible the study reported in Chapter 5. I am also grateful to the publishers of the earlier versions of those chapters which appeared elsewhere: Falmer Press (Chapters 2 and 3) and Trentham Books (the first half of Chapter 6).

Less formally, I hope, I must thank all those who worked with me on these projects, especially Nick Nelson and Elizabeth Willcocks (CICADA), Kay Kinder (the Professional Knowledge and PRINDEP projects), and above all John Willcocks (PRINDEP and CICADA). Three of these colleagues collaborated with me in writing the original versions of the papers which appear, adapted or rewritten, as these chapters, and their contributions are acknowledged on the book's title page and in the text. Any infelicities which have crept in during the editing and rewriting processes are of course my responsibility, not theirs. I am also very grateful to Alison Moore, whose help in preparing text from apparently incompatible software was invaluable.

The work of many teachers and an even larger number of children provided the raw material for some of these studies. Convention requires me to preserve their anonymity, but I hope that if any of them read this book they will recognise what they gave to it and accept my thanks.

Equally, what appears here reflects the no less important benefit I have gained from the work of my fellow-explorers of the complex world of primary education. Of these – and, as the bibliography demonstrates, they are many – I particularly wish to acknowledge my debt over many years to Alan Blyth, Neville Bennett, Jim Campbell, Jennifer Nias and Jim Rose.

Chapter 1

Pluralities

In 1986, when I observed and talked with the teachers who feature in the first of this book's classroom studies, a national curriculum for England and Wales seemed a possibility, though not yet a certainty. It is true that the debate about education was becoming more noisy and polarised, but then that was the by now all-too-familiar face of this decade of conviction politics, and compared with what had happened elsewhere on the political scene – the jingoism of the Falklands war, the violence and despair of the miners' strike, the alarm and dissent over the Reagan-Thatcher nuclear weapons alliance, the growing gulf between rich and poor – talk of tidying up the curriculum seemed very small beer. Thus it was still possible for primary teachers to presume, subject to broad public expectations about the importance of the basics, that the curriculum was theirs to shape, and that questions of educational value and purpose, though in a democratic society of concern to everybody, were principally for professionals to define and respond to.

By 1988, when I and colleagues gathered the material from sixty primary classrooms which formed the basis for Chapters 3 and 4, we knew the government's intentions. The previous April, Secretary of State Kenneth Baker had announced to the Commons Education Committee the imminence of the National Curriculum and related changes, the consultation papers on grant-maintained schools, financial delegation, education in inner London, academic tenure in higher education, collective worship, and of course the National Curriculum, had all been issued, and in between those two events Margaret Thatcher had romped home in the general election for a third successive term, thus making it inevitable that 'consultation' would mean nothing of the sort. And so it turned out: in July 1988 the Education Reform Act received Royal Assent, and the governmment had given hardly any ground on the provisions which provoked such widespread protest during the previous months.

Yet still the enormity of what was to come had not struck home in the primary world. The stock assurance at in-service sessions organised to prepare teachers for the changes was 'Don't worry: you're doing this already', even though the first subject proposals (mathematics and science in August 1988, English and design and technology in November) and the specifications for testing at age 7 issued in December had all indicated otherwise.

Thus it was that the ideas and practices which feature in Chapters 3 and 4 were not much different from those of ten or even twenty years earlier, and a major local education authority remained confident that its vision of primary education, grounded in the certainties of those earlier decades, could and would shape the work of teachers and pupils in its 230 primary schools for many years to come.

By 1992, when the final classroom study in this book (Chapter 5) was undertaken, everything had changed. The National Curriculum had come into force in September 1989. LEAs had submitted their schemes for budgetary delegation that same month and, as these were progressively implemented, so LEA power began to decline. During the next three years the succession of subject interim reports, proposals, consultation reports and draft orders had been translated into statutory orders for all nine subjects at Key Stages 1 and 2, and the assessment procedures for Key Stage 1 had been piloted, trialled, evaluated and implemented. In 1990, ILEA, the country's largest local education authority, had been abolished. In October 1991, consumerism had spawned a Parents' Charter whose various threats and promises included the abolition, after a century and a half, of Her Majesty's Inspectorate, and its replacement by parent-friendly OFSTED, putative sibling to OFGAS and OFTEL. Meanwhile, in its run-up to the 1992 general election the government had turned its attention from curriculum to teaching methods, exploiting in the process the report from the project which gave rise to Chapters 3 and 4 of this book, and a controversial discussion paper on classroom practice at Key Stage 2 had been, in just six weeks, commissioned, written and published. (My own involvement in these two developments is not the issue here: my concern at this point is simply to recall the events and the climate.) At the same time, with HMI neutralised and the LEAs weakened, the government had intensified its assault on what it saw as the last bastion of the 'educational establishment', the teacher training institutions and departments.

These changes – the challenge to the prevailing culture of primary education, the transformation of the primary curriculum, and the assault on established educational thinking – provide one of the contexts for this book.

During the same period, in what used to be thought of as the rarified world of academe (now rudely shakened by government policies on higher education and teacher training), another revolution was taking place. Most researchers being opportunists, change was generating research on change (and Chapter 5 is an example of this) but, more important for this book's concerns, primary schools and classrooms had at last been acknowledged as worthy of researchers' attentions, and a succession of studies focused on teachers and pupils at work. Researchers saw the problems in different ways, came from different research traditions and employed different methods. Thus, all at about the same time, Bennett, Galton, Mortimore and their colleagues were undertaking process-product research which included systematic sampling and a substantial element of quantification with a view to identifying the characteristics of effective teaching; Armstrong was harnessing the intensity of practitioner insight to uncover the processes of learning as it happened; Pollard was using interactionist perspectives to explore the realities of classroom life as these appeared not to external observers but to teachers and children themselves; and Nias was probing ever deeper into the individual and collective psyches of teachers at work.

These are just examples to indicate something of the scope and diversity of the field. By 1988 Alan Blyth, himself arguably the outstanding figure in the post-war development of primary education as a field for serious academic study, mapped out the following areas in which significant research communities were by then at work: child development and learning, philosophical and critical analysis, the sociology of primary schools, organisational and management studies, curriculum studies, pedagogy, and the lives and careers of teachers (Blyth 1989).

The 1988 Education Reform Act gave a boost to some fields of research at the expense of others (as funding for research dried up or was restricted to projects which would advance government policy), especially to work in the fields of curriculum, management, assessment, teacher effectiveness and the impact of policy on teachers and schools. Nevertheless, the territory was by then well staked out and the pre-existing research agendas were maintained. Moreover, just as a war spawns a host of scientific and technological innovations, so policy encouraged attention to areas hitherto not always given the prominence in research which they required – assessment and the use and management of time in schools being two important examples.

These developments in research in primary education, some predating the 1988 Act, some arising as a consequence of it, provide the second context for this book.

Together, the two sets of developments – changes in the rationale, policy and practice of primary education, and changes in the focus and methods of research and study in primary education – combined to suggest the theme of 'versions': the idea that, though there is one legal 'system' of primary education, there are many views of its proper purposes and conduct, many aspects of the work of teachers and pupils which merit study, and many ways these can be viewed and explored. The idea of 'versions' is an important corrective to the unassailable certainties of those, not just in government, who believe that only one model of primary education, and one way of studying it, is possible.

There was a third consideration: born not of the recent past but of the possible future. Millennium studies are currently fashionable, though of course the year 2000 is in reality no more significant for the children who happen to be in our primary schools at that time than the years 1995 or 2005. But it is the symbolic value of the millennium which counts, as we ponder on how far humankind has come since the event which initiated this particular way of defining the passing of the years, and count the costs as well as the benefits of what used to be called 'progress'. The need to reflect on recent developments seemed to prompt an even more pressing need to consider where primary education might or should be heading, and how far the ideas, policies, structures and practices inherited from the past are adequate to meet the needs of the future.

The other 'versions' of primary education, then, have yet to materialise, but the need to identify them is prompted by considerations much more pressing than the imminence of the millennium. First, there is the future itself, in strict terms unknowable and unpredictable, but worthy of the attention of all of us, for it is ours. Especially, it belongs to children in primary schools, now and over the next two or three decades, for assuming that a global catastrophe is avoided, medical advances may enable some of them to live not just well into the next century but possibly beyond. What kinds of lives will they have? What kinds of lives do they deserve? And 'global' rather than 'national' is the operative word here: for, cliché or not, ours is an increasingly interdependent world – morally as well as economically and electronically – and what happens, say, in the fast expanding economies of the Pacific rim or in the overpopulated Indian sub-continent, let alone the European Union, could well have as great an impact on the lives of these children as any national policies.

Second, there is the matter of the National Curriculum: a model imposed by fiat, untried, untested, unjustified except by recourse to the crudest of claims and slogans. Is this really the version of the primary curriculum which should serve us for the start of the next century, as its proponents proudly proclaim? And what of the attendant policies on assessment and finance?

Third, the Dearing reports of 1993 proposed a five-year moratorium on curriculum change. Dearing, the School Curriculum and Assessment Authority (SCAA) and the government may have imagined that this would put a stop to all fond talk of alternatives and encourage teachers to get on with the job of making the 1995 revised model of the National Curriculum work. But making it work does not prove that it is educationally sound, and though one kind of moratorium – on policy made on the hoof and on the deluge of paper from DFE and SCAA – is welcome, that should provide just the opportunity this country needs for asking the questions about education in general and primary education in particular which were pre-empted by government policy in 1987/88 and frustrated by the pace and quantity of change during the years thereafter.

This is the background to the present book. Let us turn now to its structure and content. It draws on four linked empirical studies, together with a fifth study of a historical, analytical and reflective kind which sets both the empirical studies and current developments in a wider perspective and allows us to raise and consider the questions about the future to which I have referred.

Alongside the theme of diversity which is captured in the book's title and which I have elaborated above, there is a second theme: change and continuity. The evolution of the primary curriculum, and of the processes of teaching and learning in primary schools, demonstrate both radical transformation and the abiding influence of long-established structures, ideas and habits. In this respect we can begin to assess in a balanced way the impact of the two post-war 'revolutions' in primary education: that of the 1960s and 1970s, when teachers were on the whole happy to embrace the ideals and practices associated with the Plowden Report, and the traumatic, policy-led changes of the period since 1988 which primary teachers viewed, initially at least, with much less equanimity and with which they are still coming to terms.

The book stays close to the heart of primary education, for the four empirical accounts at its core all draw on systematic classroom observation of children and teachers at work. This observation was undertaken, respectively, in 1986, 1988 and 1992. Thus, the accounts in Chapters 2, 3, 4 and 5 capture and illustrate the nature, condition and problems of primary education first when the Plowden revolution still provided the main reference-point for most primary teachers, next at a time when government sabre-rattling was loudest and teachers were beginning to face the uncomfortable implications of the shift from *laissez-faire* to curriculum centralisation and prescription, and finally at a point when the new order was establishing itself and the impact of the 1988 Act in general, and the National Curriculum in particular, was beginning to be assessed.

Each project was to some extent grounded in its predecessor – and the 1992 study actually draws on and contrasts data from two of the earlier studies – but each also explores territory which is new. Thus, the 1986 study is chiefly concerned to unravel the real-life demands and dilemmas of all that used to be connoted by 'informal' in primary curriculum and teaching. The two 1988 studies together constitute a substantial analysis of teachers at work in sixty classrooms involved in the widely publicised Leeds evaluation, and their focus moves from the broad context of planning and organisation to the fine detail of pupil–teacher interaction. The fourth study, from 1992, starts where the 1988 account leaves off, and looks at interaction much more closely in an attempt to discover more about this critical influence on children's learning and about the extent to which as the content of the curriculum changes so the discourse through which content is mediated to children changes also.

It is important not to overstate the chronology, for this is to imply that a study of primary schooling undertaken before the arrival of the National Curriculum may be of little value to those whose professional world is now rather different. That, manifestly, is not the case. The National Curriculum is a specification of subject matter. There is considerably more to education than this, and if a piece of educational research is worth its salt it should address what is universal as well as what is transitory. Indeed, its very way of addressing the here and now should be such as to offer insights into these perennial aspects and problems of education. Pedagogy, a major theme of Chapters 3, 4 and 5, is one such perennial aspect, and a profoundly significant one, for both children and teachers.

Chapters 2 to 6 are mostly based on material produced previously, though only the smaller part of this has actually appeared in print. In its original form Chapter 2 appeared in a collection of studies assessing the character and impact of 'informal' primary education (Blyth 1988). Chapters 3 and 4 started life as interim evaluation reports from the Primary Needs Independent Evaluation Project (PRINDEP), and were circulated within Leeds but no further afield. The report which provided the basis for Chapter 3 was then re-edited for inclusion in a published collection of documents from that project (Alexander et al. 1988), while Chapter 4, by a long way the most substantial of the project's eleven interim reports, has never before appeared outside Leeds. Chapter 5, from the CICADA project, also appears in print here for the first time. Chapter 6 started life as a public lecture given at the University of Leeds. More or less in that form it was published by the Association for the Study of Primary Education (ASPE) as Alexander (1994a). However, the constraints of the occasion for which it was first prepared were such that the discussion of the future of primary education with which it ended had to be very brief. That discussion has now been totally rewritten as a much expanded second half to the paper which also adopts a somewhat different approach to the question of where primary education might be heading.

Placing the five studies together in this way both demonstrates their affinity and the way that as a sequence they combine to provide a many-sided account of the critical period 1986–92 and the longer historical span – 1840–1995 – in which this period is set. The book also provides four contributions to the now well-established and increasingly influential field of primary classroom research, and five contrasting approaches to that systematic study of primary education with which policy and professional development need to go hand-in-hand if the system is to improve. It also contains abundant illustrative material of teachers and children at work, including transcribed classroom talk.

It is hoped that these many versions of primary education – past, present and future; observational, conversational and historical; quantitative and qualitative; concerned with classrooms, teachers and children; exploring practices and ideas – will demonstrate something of the current richness of primary education and contribute to the debate about its future.

Chapter 2

Garden or jungle?

Our first version of primary education is the one indicated by the word 'informal' – popularly presented as the antithesis of the 'formal' or traditional primary education of regimented classrooms, didactic teaching and a subject-bound curriculum, but in reality something considerably more complex. The study combines historical and classroom-based perspectives to home in on some of the core dilemmas of day-to-day work experienced by a group of experienced teachers in 1986, the year before the National Curriculum was announced. Thus, though the storm clouds are gathering in the educational sky, few working in the education service at this time have any idea of the thunderbolt which, a year later, the government will unleash. For them, the goal of informality remains as central to professional consciousness as the National Curriculum was to become a few years later.

Certain words have acquired a peculiar potency in primary education, and few more so than 'informal'. Never properly defined, yet ever suggestive of ideas and practices which were indisputably right, 'informal' was the flagship of the semantic armada of 1960s Primary-speak, whose vessels, somewhat tattered now, are beginning to disappear over the educational horizon: spontaneity, flexibility, natural-ness, growth, needs, interests, freedom, the whole, the seamless robe, the child's view of the world, thematic work, integration, individualisation, self-expression, discovery ... and many more. On whither they are heading – for immortality, for oblivion, or for a refit – we shall have to await the verdict of history.

It was probably pointless to try, as some did, to define any of these words as exact operational concepts. If, for example, 'informal' indicates (as the dictionary tells us) a situation lacking or eschewing publicly established and agreed norms, forms and conventions, celebrating instead private idiom and idiosyncrasy, then to seek to 'formalise' infor-mality in this way is not so much practically problematical as logically impossible.

Yet the paradox of formalised formlessness was in a sense achieved, at least at the level of the public language of primary education. Primaryspeak became at one and the same time nebulous but normative, obscure but ordained, imprecise but imposed.

For the situation was (and is) about rather more than terminological fuzziness. Primaryspeak was never simply a descriptive or technical language comparable to that used, say, by doctors, though it included a technical element, particularly in relation to children's cognition and learning and to the more highly codified curriculum areas like reading and mathematics. It was a language generated against the historical backdrop of a professional community seeking to distance itself from its Victorian roots: a language of persuasion and solidarity, an ideological shorthand.

It was also a language which served a function in relation to professional hierarchy: it exerted a subtle but irresistible pressure towards consensus, conformity and cohesion; and it strengthened the power base of heads and advisers.

So, what has changed? We know that informality has been on the defensive since the mid-1970s, certainly in the pure form that we used to be told made British primary education, like British democracy, British broadcasting and the Great British Breakfast, the envy of the world. The gulf between the sometimes overblown claims and the classroom realities, the 'myth of progressivism', was confirmed by a succession of empirical studies (for example, Galton et al. 1980, 1980; Bennett et al. 1984; Mortimore et al. 1988; Galton 1989; Alexander 1992). Some of the most strenuously defended tenets of informality were challenged on the grounds of their practical viability as well as their educational effectiveness: the assertion that the class teacher, simply by virtue of being with all the children all the time, knows each of them to the extent necessary for devising curriculum experiences which exactly 'match' their abilities, needs and potentialities; individualised learning and group work; and the belief that the only valid pattern of classroom organisation is one where several different curriculum areas are being pursued simultaneously.

Moreover, as I noted above, the language of informality is of itself on the move. The kind of child-centred sloganising that would have produced a standing ovation only ten years ago is now as likely to make listeners shift uneasily on their chairs. But is the old language being replaced by one which has a greater degree of neutrality, aptness or precision? Somehow, I think not. It is true that where protagonists once espoused 'freedom', 'flexibility', 'spontaneity' and 'discovery' they may now espouse the apparent rigour of 'skills', 'concepts', 'match' and 'standards'. Where they endorsed 'creativity', 'self-expression' and 'making and doing' they may now endorse 'problem-solving' and 'technology'. 'Individualisation' has been replaced by 'collaborative group work'; 'professional autonomy' by 'collegiality'; the 'seamless cloak' of the thematically based curriculum has ceased to be *de rigueur*, and 'subjects' are no longer taboo.

Such terminological adjustments undoubtedly mirror genuine shifts in consciousness and practice. But equally, they may sometimes be little more than a prudent updating of public professional vocabulary, having a fairly tenuous relationship with private classroom practice and allowing the latter to proceed undisturbed. In any event, an activity as complex as teaching, where individual knowledge and skill are built up slowly and sometimes painfully over many years, cannot be transformed as rapidly as these verbal shifts imply, and indeed to claim such overnight trans-formation is to diminish rather than enhance teacher professionality.

Every example above of the updated Primaryspeak is problematic in at least two senses: first, the terms are capable of sustaining any of a large number of meanings, yet they are (as in the 1960s) too seldom defined; and second, even if or when given a stipulative definition each has still to be put into practice. Thus: what *is* a 'skill'? Can one conceive as readily of imaginative skills as one can of manual skills? And if so, which is doubtful, how does one teach them? Or, what kinds of professional relationships and responsibilities are indicated by 'colle-giality'? How do these accommodate to the head's contractual accountability to governors and the LEA? How do they accommodate to the value-divergence which is the essential heart of all educational discourse? What is the right balance between individuality and uniformity in teaching and how is it to be achieved? Is collegiality, in short, as easy, or as cosy, as it sounds? The speed and scale of terminological changes such as these, and the all-too-frequent failure, now as in the 1960s, to treat the terms as conceptually or operationally problematic, suggest to me two themes concerning the professional situation and development of primary teachers which are worth pursuing and which, indeed, will be pursued in this chapter.

'FOR WANT OF WELL PRONOUNCING SHIBBOLETH'

The first theme is the *function* of the public professional language of primary education. If terms manifestly in need of definition are not in fact defined, that suggests either that everyone knows exactly what they mean, which is clearly not the case, or that in the context within which such terms are used their meaning does not much matter.

I have referred elsewhere (Alexander 1984: 210–16) to the contrast between 'academic', 'everyday' and 'ideological' language in primary education, to the dominance of the latter, and to the barriers this dominance can place in the way of meaningful professional discourse. A particular component of ideological language is the recurrence of key words and phrases such as those I have exemplified. Scheffler (1971) characterises these as 'slogans', but this conveys only part of their force; rather, they seem to function as shibboleths:

> In that sore battle when so many died
> Without reprieve adjudged to death
> For want of well pronouncing Shibboleth.
>
> (Milton, *Samson Agonistes*, lines 287–9)

While a slogan, then, fosters collective solidarity among the troops, a shibboleth has a more self-serving function in relation to the recognition and advancement of the individual. Of course, the stakes for primary teachers are not so high as they were for those 42,000 Ephraimites, though there are not a few teachers who can attest to careers frustrated because of their failure to conform to the LEA or school orthodoxies of the day, just as there are a fair number who are seen by less successful colleagues to have gained advancement less by merit than by 'saying what the head/adviser wanted to hear' – and of course the fact that appointments are made on the basis of verbal performance at interview rather than operational performance in the classroom legitimates and indeed celebrates the shibboleth. (It is true that we have witnessed in recent years an encouraging move away from so one-dimensional an approach to appointments, at least where senior posts are concerned, with appointing bodies viewing candidates in action in the classroom, but there too the focus of attention may be less the nature and quality of children's learning than the visual equivalents of verbal shibboleths – what in the trade is so ingenuously but revealingly termed 'display'. Thus, conscious of this, Sue, one of the teachers I refer to in the second half of this chapter: 'Teaching needs to be visible: I play the game.')

So although the power context in which shibboleths operate in primary education is less overtly adversarial, more subtle and indirect, than that portrayed by Milton, it may be none the less as pervasive. We are dealing not so much with an ideological blunderbuss pointed directly at teachers' heads (though even that, both locally and nationally, seems now to be happening) than with what for some may be the inexorably engulfing shroud of pseudo-consensus.

Power changes hands, ideologies are superseded: so too are shibboleths. Primaryspeak has updated itself in keeping with the political climate: the language of educational openness and liberalism has given way to a tougher-sounding language of quasi-instrumentality. But its functions are as before.

PUBLIC LANGUAGE, PRIVATE PRACTICE

The second theme which this consideration of professional language requires me to pursue is rather different. Like the first, it is offered as a hypothesis. It runs as follows. Despite our sometimes ritualistic use of the words 'practice' and 'practical' in ways which suggest that teaching is little more than a simple manual activity, the job does in fact require a high degree of cognitive engagement. If there are such evident discontinuities between public language and classroom practice, and if such public language so obviously and grossly oversimplifies the job the teacher actually does, might this not suggest two other possibilities? The first is fairly readily verified: that until recently, and even today in many schools, the primary teacher's world was a relatively private one, in which there was little incentive and no requirement to explicate to others one's ideas, beliefs and practices except at the deliberately (and maybe necessarily) level of bland and uncontroversial anecdotes over staffroom coffee or the strategic exchange of shibboleths at job interviews. The second is that perhaps there is something about teaching in general, and primary teaching in particular, which makes precision and neutrality in professional discourse difficult to achieve. Might not some of the confusions, paradoxes and contradictions to which commentators can so devastatingly point be not so much failings in teachers as inherent properties of the task to which those teachers are committed? Might not the job of primary teaching be in reality more subtle, complex and sophisticated than either of the public linguistic forms so far available – academic/technical and ideological – can convey?

To answer these latter questions, and to get inside some of the processes and themes identified in this introductory section, we must talk with and examine the activities of teachers themselves, so it is with their work and thoughts that much of this chapter will be concerned. I shall seek to show how some of the problems of discourse and practice raised above manifest themselves as tensions and dilemmas which individual teachers have to confront, resolve or come to terms with during their professional development; how, while some of these tensions and dilemmas are intrinsic to teaching, others are created or at least exacerbated by the grandiloquent vagueness of the language and expectations concerning classroom practice as proclaimed most characteristically by people who do not (or no longer) have to implement them; and how the individual teacher's encounters with such tensions, dilemmas and expectations also mirror – and of course are inevitably tied up casually with – the history and development of primary education as a whole.

We start with the latter – macro, historical – context, entering it (appropriately, in view of the discussion so far) via an update of one of the most hallowed of all metaphors in the lexicon of informality.

OTHER METAPHORS, OTHER REALITIES

Into the garden

One of the abiding characteristics of the language of primary education is its use of metaphors in general and organic metaphors in particular. This is not really surprising, given that the one unalterable fact about primary education, regardless of changing ideologies, priorities and procedures, is its concern with children who are growing and developing.

But for Froebel, and many others for whom his ideas had a particular resonance, 'growth' and 'development' were depicted in botanical rather than zoological terms – hence of course the kindergarten, with children as plants and teacher as gardener, and the associated horticultural imagery with which we are all so familiar – natural, ripening, unfolding, budding points, nurturing and so on (Jenkins 1975; Blyth 1984).

A garden is not, except in so far as it contains plants, a 'natural' environment. Rather, it is a contest, man's taming of nature, in which plants are placed, shaped, bred and cross-bred in accordance with human notions of form and order; most obviously so in the case of Le Nôtre's manicured geometric formalism, more gently so in the English pastoral tradition of Capability Brown. But even in the latter landscape it is a man-made re-ordering of nature, rather than nature untamed, which is on view.

Thus, in the garden metaphor *order* and *authority* are as important as the more familiar notion of growth. The educational garden is enclosed and protected; it is free from weeds and impure strains; it is visually pleasing; it is harmonious; in it everybody and everything knows and accepts its place. There is more than a hint here, as Dearden pointed out many years ago (1968), of authoritarianism – and, one might add, of eugenics.

This is not the digression it may begin to seem. For these kinds of images and associated assumptions are peculiarly pervasive (deeply rooted, one might say) in primary education: not just where teacher–child relationships and the curriculum are concerned, but also in our inherited view of the primary system as a whole, past and present. Notions like 'flexibility', 'spontaneity', 'enrichment' and so on have been treated as self-evident, unproblematic and efficacious, and practices like thematic work, the integrated day and groupwork have been regarded as incontestably 'right' for young children, not because of any conceptual subtlety or operational inviolability (far from it) but because to challenge such specifics was to threaten the whole – the entire inter-connected package or edifice of ideas, practices, institutions and roles, the professional consensus by which these were sustained and, in turn, the professional power structure through which consensus was achieved, enforced and regulated.

There has been, therefore, a tendency to slide from the organic, unifica-tory concept of the young child's education (which may well have a great deal to commend it) to the view that the system as a whole has the same kind of preordained and 'natural' coherence (which is manifestly not the case).

There are many examples of the consequences of failing properly to separate for analytical purposes the educational ideology from the institutional context, and the world of childhood from the world of teacherhood. One such is what one might term the 'correspondence' approach to curriculum preparation in initial teacher education – the notion that the teacher needs to experience in terms of quantity, proportion and character a grown-up version of what is offered to the child. Another example, a different aspect of the same problem, is the almost universal failure to question the existing curriculum pecking order in primary schools, with its dominance of what I call (1984: chap. 3) 'Curriculum I' – the 'basics' of numeracy and literacy – over the 'Curriculum II' of environmental and social, personal and moral, physical, aesthetic and expressive development and understanding. Such questioning as does occur may be more at the level of rhetoric (of course everything is equally important, it is asserted) than at the level of practice, where the discrepancies in time and resource allocation, in teacher expertise and above all in quality of learning and seriousness of profes-sional intention tell a different story. Or there is the matter of the class teacher system, unquestionably the 'best' way of educating children of primary age, we are told, and woe betide anyone who dares to suggest otherwise.[1]

Many of those involved in primary education will confirm how difficult it is to prise open this package of certainties. Yet of course there is nothing inevitable, incontestable, let alone natural, about them. The Curriculum I/II divide and the class teacher system are no more than enduring throwbacks to the ancestors of today's primary schools, the nineteenth-century elementary schools: to the sternly utilitarian '3Rs' curriculum on the one hand, and, on the other, to the form of organi-sation devised to secure delivery of that curriculum as cheaply and efficiently as possible.

Stepping outside the garden

I would suggest that the time has come to re-examine the sanitised, ahistorical, consensual and unproblematic version of primary education as a whole which informal ideology, by a process of hegemony, seems to have generated.

To help us on our way I would suggest that if we must proceed on the basis of metaphor we should at least have some alternatives to enliven the debate and challenge the consensus. My alternative to the ordered garden, for the sake of consistency, would also be botanical, but it would employ the rather more rampant image of the jungle.

The jungle of primary education is vast, dense and rambling. It is at once open and secret. Its sights and sounds invite and welcome, the display of some of its species attract and seduce; yet further in it becomes impenetrable, able to be negotiated only with knowledge of shibboleths and hidden pathways; its surface harmony barely camouflaging on the one hand a surprising diversity, and on the other, myriad struggles for space and survival.

If the metaphor seems extreme, that is only because we have conditioned ourselves to accept metaphors, images, versions of primary reality and history which overstate order, harmony and consensus. The truth lies somewhere in between, but – however portrayed – it must, I suggest, more explicitly acknowledge and accommodate diversity, disagreement and compromise than hitherto. For in primary education, values and beliefs about children, curriculum and pedagogy diverge and compete. The curriculum is at best an uneasy compromise between competing but precariously coexisting values, and at worst (as now) a no-holds-barred political battleground. Children's potentialities, far from being recognised and nurtured by an all-seeing teacher-gardener, may sometimes remain undetected, unaroused, unrealised, suppressed even. Children, as do teachers, evolve or fail to evolve their own strategies for coping, surviving or succeeding. Power and rewards are unevenly distributed and, for many, the pursuit and maintenance of power, influence and status override most other considerations.

The jungle of educational history

The jungle metaphor can prompt an alternative perspective not just on schools and the situations and careers of children and teachers but also on the history and current disposition of the system as a whole. The idea of primary education's encapsulating different and sometimes competing traditions and ideologies is not new. Blyth in 1965 showed how the 'elementary', 'developmental' and 'preparatory' traditions had come together in post-war primary education. Richards (1982) contrasts the ideologies of 'liberal romanticism', 'educational conservatism', 'liberal pragmatism' and 'social democracy'. Golby (1986) replaces the 'preparatory' tradition in Blyth's list by 'technological'.

I suggest that we can now fairly readily identify seven distinct ideologies which have been prominent at different points in the history of primary education and which are all, though to varying and shifting degrees, discernible in current primary discourse and practice. They are presented in the schematic form of Table 2.1 for ease of reference.

Table 2.1 Some dominant ideologies in primary education

Ideology	*Central values in respect of curriculum*
1 Elementary	Curriculum to meet society's economic and labour needs, and to preserve the existing social order. Education as a preparation for working life.
2 Progressive	Curriculum to enable the child to realise his/her full potential as an autonomous individual. Childhood a unique phase of development, not just a preparation for adulthood. Curriculum open, negotiable.
3 Developmental	Curriculum to be structured and sequenced in accordance with the child's psychological and physiological development and learning needs.
4 Behavioural/ mechanistic	Curriculum defined and structured in terms of hierarchies of observable and testable learning outcomes.
5 Classical humanist	Curriculum about initiating the child into the 'best' of the cultural heritage, defined chiefly in terms of disciplines or forms of understanding: the arts, sciences and humanities.
6 Social imperatives: adaptive/utilitarian	Curriculum to meet society's economic, technological and labour needs, to enable the child to adapt to changes in these, and to preserve the existing social order.
7 Social imperatives: reformist/egalitarian	Curriculum to enable the child both to fulfil individual potential and to contribute to societal progress. The latter defined in terms of plurality, democracy and social justice, as well as the economy.

A chronological sequence of sorts can be inferred here. For example, it is clear that the progressive tradition was in part a reaction against the instrumentality and rigidity of elementary education, that it in turn was buttressed by the emergent discipline of developmental psychology, and that by the 1980s the wheel seemed to have come full circle with the Thatcher government's espousal of a utilitarian and cost-cutting ideology which resembled none more than that of elementary education a century earlier. But the sequential analysis should be used with caution, for the important point in the context of the present discussion is this: ideologies do not come in single file, one replacing another, but compete, interact and continue in juxtaposition. Some are modified, some are driven, temporarily or permanently, underground, minority viewpoints become majority ones, and vice versa. Different ideologies continue to influence the system in different ways and to differing degrees.

Thus, the residual but powerful legacy of the elementary system is ever present, as I have already argued, in 'Curriculum I' – the continuing allegiance to a particular (though now expanding) notion of 'basics' – and the class teacher system. The progressive tradition has had a profound impact upon the physical and interpersonal milieu of primary schools which political centralisation and prescription are unlikely to diminish. The developmental tradition, especially through Piaget's work, has transformed our views of children's cognition and of the kinds of learning activities and experiences which are appropriate at different stages of development. Behaviourism, having had minimal impact on primary education when first imported here from the United States, is experiencing a new respectability with the current emphasis upon attainment targets, statements of attainment and national tests. Even classical humanism, a public/grammar-school import, is detectable in HMI's liberal 'areas of learning and experience' approach to the 5–16 curriculum (DES 1985a).[2] And although all political parties at both national and local levels agree on the need for education to be socially relevant and responsive, they differ sharply on how such 'relevance' is to be defined and on which aspects of society and culture demand a curricular response.[3]

So while each of the seven traditions/ideologies above has emerged at different points during the history of primary education, every one of them is detectable to some degree and in some aspect of the system as it now stands. The juxtaposition may in some cases be a trouble-free one (progressivism and developmentalism, for example, have forged a powerful alliance), in which case the garden metaphor will suffice and the process is one of hybridisation: mixed ancestry but a viable organism.[4] But in other cases where the ideologies conflict – most notably perhaps in the 1980s debate about the curriculum, the jungle metaphor is more apt. In such a climate the essential incompatibility of some of the ideologies is exposed; so too are the Darwinistic consequences of their juxtaposition – with the arts, to take just one current example, having to adapt by redefining themselves in accordance with prevailing social relevance criteria (hence the emphasis on 'skills' and 'design' rather than 'self-expression') or face extinction.

Informal education, as a conception, is a progressive/developmental hybrid; but as practice, even in those schools claiming to manifest informality at its purest, it is a considerably more complex mixture.

The current struggle in the primary jungle seems to involve, on the one hand, a rearguard action by grassroots progressivism in the face of government utilitarianism, with behaviourism opportunistically waiting in attendance on the latter and an updated classical humanism available from HMI as a compromise.[5] On the other, it is for many teachers a struggle whose protagonists are less clearly identifiable because the more pressing problems concern time, space, resources, recognition and survival. The language of primary discourse – in any staffroom, on any course, in the educational press – echoes the contest: spontaneity/ planning; openness/aims and objectives; growth/standards; balance/ relevance; themes/subjects; autonomy/accountability; self-expression/ skills; topics/science; life-skills/the world of work; co-operation/ competition . . . and so on. (The pairings are not, I hasten to add, mutually exclusive – as they are sometimes presented – but given their differing genealogies their resolution requires effort.)

LIVING IN THE PRIMARY JUNGLE

The randomness of experience

And so to the teachers, whose individual development, I suggested, while not mirroring exactly the processes and cross-currents explored above, at least offers parallels and counterpoints. It is they who have to make practical sense of the competing ideas and claims and have to come to terms with the jungle – to hack a path through it, to learn to accept and perhaps exploit its confusion and luxuriance, or be overwhelmed by it.

From here on, I shall be drawing on data collected as part of a research project on professional knowledge-in-action which involved an intensive programme of observation, videotaping, individual interviewing and collective discussion with experienced primary teachers in Leeds, Bradford and Calderdale LEAs. Readers will find an account of the project methodology in Appendix 1.

Professional development often tends to be conceived in terms which highlight formal career events and moves – initial training, induction, changes of school, promotion, in-service activities and courses – and which sees these passage rites as what, centrally, 'develops' a teacher. Thus, development becomes first an intermittent succession of events rather than a continuous process, and second something which is handed down by others (advisers, heads, teacher educators) rather than initiated or executed by teachers themselves.

In contrast to this somewhat managerialist view, teachers themselves tend to highlight 'experience' as the main agent in their development, though because experiences are unique and the word itself is so nebulous it tends not to be explicated further and therefore loses ground to what can be formalised. Moreover, everyone is familiar with the adage about 'experience' (is it thirty years' experience or one year repeated thirty times?) which reminds us that learning from experience requires receptivity, predisposition and effort on the part of the learner. Working closely with experienced teachers one becomes aware of how random and serendipitous, in contrast to the tidy and top-down training-to-retirement sequence, professional development actually is – a view charted in some of the recent studies of teacher development (for example, Ball and Goodson 1985; Sikes *et al.* 1985; Nias 1992; Campbell and Neill 1994c). For some teachers, initial training has a major impact; for others, a negligible one. In-service activities, similarly, can inspire or frustrate. But more important than either seem to be the school contexts within which teachers happen to find themselves: the children, heads and fellow-teachers with whom they work and the professional climate and affiliations which such communities engender. Circumstances and outcomes, then, have a large chance element.

Teachers as agents in one another's development

Such influences can be positive or negative. Thus, while Graham attests to the impact of two very different heads on his classroom practice and professional relationships, Peter talks despairingly of having encountered only 'anti-models' during his career so far – teachers whose values he did not share, whose perceived parochialism he despised and from whose practice he wished to distance his own as far as possible.

For all these teachers, colleagueship – day-to-day communion with fellow-teachers whom one likes and respects and from whom one can learn – was something to be prized. Yet all too often, as Nias's work also shows (Nias 1984, 1985, 1992), the individual primary teacher feels isolated and at variance with the prevailing professional culture of a particular school. In such cases, an alternative reference group may be available outside the school, or it may not be, and the teacher's development may be frustrated by the denial of such stimulus and support.

How one learns from others varies, of course. Some blossom in a rebarbative relationship; others may seek the security of consensus or even of paternalism. For professional development is as much about the teacher's personal attributes and capacities as it is about the professional experiences and people encountered. Thus, Sue, from her own schooldays on, has always been intensely competitive, and as a teacher needs colleagues among whom she can shine yet who will also stimulate and encourage her. Jenny, Pam and Graham have a restless, questing mentality which makes them intensely impatient with those who are too easily satisfied. In contrast, Sheila has a more relaxed outlook on colleagues, and values their company for its own sake, exemplifying the kind of tolerance she seeks to foster in her pupils.

Professional development as a personal journey

Equally inseparable are non-professional, particularly family influences. Several teachers' own sometimes traumatic experiences of failure at school seem strongly to have coloured their approach to the children they teach and particularly to those they see as less able, disadvantaged or withdrawn. Several admit to identifying particularly with those children who are 'like me as a child' – whether boisterous and mischievous, or introverted and earnest.

The family is a powerful influence – whether being the child of one's parents and enacting in one's teaching the kinds of relationship and qualities one most valued in them; or being oneself a parent and seeing in the children one teaches resonances of the anxieties, foibles and pleasures of one's own offspring. Equally, it must be said, there are those who never manage to connect their own and others' experiences and situations in this way.

So professional development is less fundamentally an institutional sequence of formally designated activities than a personal journey, in which individual personality, experience and maturation, and teacher growth, are not easily separated and where the key influences extend, contextually and temporally, well beyond the knowledge, let alone the control, of professional development agents or agencies.

Professional development and classroom decision-making

Another way of viewing professional development is as a process of coming to terms with the kinds and contexts of *decision-making* that the job of teaching demands. Calderhead (1984) distinguishes 'immediate', 'routine' and 'reflective' classroom decisions, and Jackson (1968) 'pre-active', 'interactive' and 'postactive' phases of teaching. Putting these together we can see that the interactive phase – that which takes place in the classroom, with the children – has an intensity, complexity and pressure that thinking, planning and talking away from the classroom never have. In a busy primary classroom the teacher certainly reflects in action in the way Schön (1982) argues, though the process is much more concentrated and pressurised than for professionals like town planners or psychotherapists whose reflective processes Schön illustrates in detail: decisions must be taken quickly, and once taken, lived with. By trial and error the teacher learns which decisions work and which do not, so that what start early in one's career as immediate decisions may soon become routine. The teacher also routinises some of the decisions during the preactive and postactive phases, thus allowing more time for reflection on other aspects of the job (or simply for living). Interactive decision-making becomes smoother and less fraught, and time is opened up for immediate decisions, however rapid, to be grounded in some degree of reflection.

That at least is how it looks in theory. In practice, much depends on the teacher's individual skills, attributes, circumstances and commitments. Thus, Bennett *et al.* (1984) noted a tendency towards 'crisis management' in primary classrooms, which he criticised on the grounds that it restricts opportunities for the kinds of careful one-to-one diagnostic interactions that match of learning task to child requires. This in general terms is a just stricture. But for some teachers, queues at their desk are not necessarily a symptom of any kind of organisational crisis, and they may feel no particular lack of diagnostic time or space. For these, the more that is routinised, the easier the job becomes, the less it has to be thought about outside the classroom, and indeed the less incentive there is for such reflection, particularly of a questioning or critical variety, since, in the words of one of our teachers, it only 'makes waves'.

For others, however, the extent of reflection does not diminish, and carries its own impetus, rewards and penalties. For a start, as Graham points out, every situation and encounter in teaching, however familiar, is also unique, and previous experience can never provide a blueprint. Citing what he felt to be his mishandled approach to a child with behavioural problems he said:

> You only progress as a teacher if you take each experience, evaluate it and try to improve upon it ... [yet] no matter how many experiences, no matter what your bank of experiences is ... you're still going to come across [a situation where] you'll never have quite the right answer, and that's where I feel my problems are in professional development. We do want to do things properly, but there's no real yardstick for how you actually deal with any one situation.

For teachers with this kind of reflective commitment, the routinising of some aspects of teaching may actually make the job more rather than less taxing, though in a different way. For the inexperienced teacher, the challenges are immediate and clear-cut: content and control – what shall I teach them and how shall I secure and maintain their co-operation? As through experience one acquires a content and control vocabulary for answering these questions in a variety of circumstances, so one creates cognitive space to re-examine first the very aspects of the job one has routinised and the routines one has adopted, and second, aspects or layers of the task of teaching which hitherto one may have treated as 'givens' and subjected to little thought.

Sue illustrates this graphically. Now with ten years' experience behind her, she has developed a considerable interest in curriculum as a professional issue, and in particular in the need to secure for 'Curriculum II' areas like art and environmental studies the attention to conceptual structure and underlying cognitive processes which she sees as more usually restricted to mathematics and language. She is prepared (in the face of prevailing primary ideologies) to assert that, while she is no less child-centred than her colleagues, she now finds thinking about curriculum matters more challenging and rewarding. But, recalling her first years in teaching:

> My major concern at that time was control. I mean it was a case of 'sod the curriculum' . . . how you're going to cope with the day and make sure these kids don't walk all over you before four o'clock and if you got out at the end of the day and felt reasonable then you'd succeeded.

Learning from experience: does the job get easier or harder?

Sue *had* succeeded, yet now, like Pam, Sheila, Judith and others, she saw the job as getting harder rather than easier. One telling manifestation of this was the way that several of them, for all their accumulated banks of experience, ideas and resources, spent if anything longer in mid-career planning away from the classroom than they had as trainees or probationers. But whereas in the early days the main effort went into producing workcards and other materials to keep the children occupied, now the emphasis was more upon reflecting on individual children, keeping records, devising more and more sophisticated strategies for maximising the time that with a class of thirty could be devoted to each child; engaging with curriculum less in terms of 'What shall they do?', more in terms of 'What precisely do I want each of them to learn? What kinds of concepts and skills? How can I ensure that they do so?'; probing the minefield of 'match', and so on.

For some of our teachers, the associated emotions arising from a combined sense of the problematic nature of the task, once they honestly faced it, and the inevitable shortfall between aspirations and outcomes, could be uncomfortable: words like 'uncertainty', 'pressure', 'responsibility', 'muddle', 'quandary' were common; so too were more self-lacerating terms like 'obsession' and 'guilt'.

As I suggested earlier, the central factor in professional development is the kind of person the teacher is. Teaching becomes harder, more complex and problematic only if one chooses or is disposed to see it that way – as Sue remarked: 'They don't have to be problems. I could just get on and ignore them' – so for many teachers the job does in fact become easier. But it is worth commenting here on another contributory strand too often neglected in discussion of professional development: the teacher's age and life-situation. Our teachers ranged in age from 30 to 50, but most were between 36 and 44, the period during which what

Erikson (1963) terms one's 'ego-identity' begins to be tested, and during which one becomes increasingly conscious of one's shortcomings, of lost opportunities, of failures in relationships, of career frustration, of the mortality of one's parents and hence of oneself, of the end of the generally rewarding intensity of parenting young children . . . and, for some, of the proximity of despair.

The case, however, must not be overstated. Teaching, like many other jobs, is intellectually and situationally demanding. It poses challenges and problems which have to be and in fact are resolved. While with experience and maturity a teacher's apprehension of these challenges and problems may become keener and more subtle, and the focus of their reflection and preparation may shift to deeper levels, and while earlier certainties may begin to be questioned, for many teachers this can fairly readily be accommodated, and nothing detracts from the pleasure, the regenerative power and what Lortie (1975) calls the 'psychic rewards' of being among young children. In any case, an alternative line of professional development is available, that leading to habituation, complacency and intellectual ossification.

Competing imperatives and teacher development

Let us take stock for a moment. The theory being evolved so far is of professional development as in part a deepening consciousness of the problematic nature of teaching. All our teachers, though to varying degrees, were aware of being caught between different versions of how they ought to act, what we came to call *'competing imperatives'*. Some of these competing imperatives were situational – to do with the constraints of a school building and its resources; or the differing and not necessarily compatible or personally acceptable expectations of a head, or an adviser or parents; or the values and styles of the colleagues with whom one is obliged to work; or of course the particular children one teaches and the physical circumstances in which one teaches them. Many of the competing imperatives were value-related – to do with reconciling alternative views of children's needs and capacities or contrasting views of curriculum priorities. Some were uncomfortably pointed up by the professional power context – finding oneself at variance, for example, with school or LEA orthodoxy, but feeling obliged to toe the line or at least to pronounce the shibboleth.

This idea has something in common with the Berlaks' (1981) idea of 'dilemmas' in primary schooling – a set of sixteen 'control', 'curriculum' and 'societal' polarities (for example, public vs personal knowledge, knowledge as content vs knowledge as process, extrinsic vs intrinsic motivation) which they see as underlying the schooling process in general, at the macro, societal level, and therefore confronting and needing to be resolved by each teacher at the micro level of the class-room. There are difficulties here: it could be argued that for a dilemma to exist for a person they must be conscious of it, whereas the Berlaks presented little evidence that this was so in individual cases, seeing the dilemmas as inescapably 'in the situation' as they as outsiders defined it. Moreover, their dilemmas were presented as mutually exclusive polarities, which in real life they rarely are. However, the idea is a potent one, and offers an important bridge between societal values and the situation of the individual teacher. A different notion of professional 'dilemmas' is provided by Argyris and Schön (1974). For them the dilemma is a mismatch within a professional's 'espoused theory' (the ideas 'to which one gives allegiance and which one communicates to others') or between such espoused theory and one's 'theory-in-use' (the ideas which actually, regardless of what one claims to others, govern and inform one's actions). A dilemma in this sense is an intellectual tension or inconsistency, which it may cause discomfort to oneself to acknowledge and which, because of this, one may respond to by any of a number of strategies: keeping the two kinds of theory firmly apart (progressive ideology and shibboleths for others – the staffroom and job interviews – and theory-in-use for oneself); changing the one but not the other; selectively ignoring or suppressing anything that points to such an inconsistency; redirecting blame for such an inconsistency away from oneself to others – parents, children, colleagues for example.

This version of dilemmas is also useful. The idea of an espoused theory/theory-in-use mismatch, given the idealistic nature of some of the former in primary education, is particularly important, and the coping strategies are readily observable.

The present idea of 'competing imperatives' is looser and more eclectic than in either of these models, and tries to capture a sense of tensions, many of which the teacher is well aware of, emanating from and within many sources and levels – primary ideology, central government, HMIs, LEA advisers, parents, head, colleagues, one's particular physical and interpersonal situation as a teacher, and oneself. In this more generalised usage what is being argued is (1) that the teacher is at the intersection of many such competing imperatives; and (2) that teachers may become more conscious of, and indeed conscious of more, such competing imper-atives as they become more experienced and their increased executive competence opens up to them deeper levels of awareness about the nature, and the problems, of the job they are doing.

The link with primary ideology, whether 1960s informality or its 1980s update, should by now be fairly clear. Such ideology is essentially an array of values, beliefs and prescriptions concerning children, knowledge and society and how these should be translated into appropriate curriculum content and teaching strategies. Values are not absolutes.

They are by their nature contestable and contested. They yield, or are generated in deliberate opposition to, alternative values. In the case of primary education, as I showed above, the amalgam of progressive and developmental ideas that has constituted 'informality' is but one of a number of concurrent and perhaps conflicting value systems which generate pressures and demands that the teacher has to reconcile in their practice.

'Competing imperatives' are a more cerebral representation of the primary jungle, and among these imperatives some of the hardest to cope with are those which are especially pervasive in informal ideology – accessible, attractive and indeed irresistible as generalised values, but rather less easy to translate into viable classroom practices. Yet, because of their status as power-backed orthodoxies, they are also difficult for the ordinary teacher to question or resist.

This process can now be illustrated by reference to the four sets of competing imperative which featured most prominently in our data: teachers' response to the generalised sense of an obligation to demonstrate 'flexibility' and 'openness'; their approaches to planning; the question of whether and/or when the teacher should 'intervene' in children's learning; and the organisational devices of grouping and groupwork.

THE IMPERATIVES OF EXPERIENCE: FOUR EXAMPLES

Openness and flexibility: the informal paradox

As so much of the language of informal and post-informal primary education centres on an opposition of 'openness' (desirable) to 'structure' (undesirable), whether in curriculum content, pedagogy or the school building itself, it is not surprising that the imperatives thereby created for teachers can be prominent and problematic. Our teachers fell into three groups: those who espoused flexibility but whose patterns of classroom practice seemed relatively fixed, yet for whom the possible paradox was not an admitted problem; those for whom the paradox was apparent, yet who felt under a sense of obligation to strive for the ever-receding ideal of flexibility and thereby faced an acute sense of the mismatch between ideal and reality; and those who recognised the paradox but had ceased to worry too much about it, had become more accepting and realistic and had thereby achieved flexibility in a rather different sense.

So, for example, Joyce's work with a class of 5–7-year-olds was a highly efficient implementation of a procedure termed the 'flexible day' which she saw as having official endorsement. Flexibility here (as with the integrated day, which it resembled) had two aspects: different

curriculum areas pursued by different groups of children simultaneously, and a degree of individual choice. The procedure was complex
and professionally demanding, and was sustained by very firm teacher
control, and an emphasis upon 'discipline' and 'routines' to which
children were expected to conform and in which they were trained. The
curriculum was divided three ways: language, mathematics and the rest
(art, topic, science and craft) which was designated 'choosing'. Children
spent equal amounts of time, in rotation, on each.

The organisation, therefore, classically reflected the Curriculum I/II
scenario. Flexibility and choice were in fact restricted to Curriculum II
('choosing') while Curriculum I was non-negotiable. Since the three areas
fitted the typical primary school day (three relatively uninterrupted
sessions punctuated by play or dinner-time, and a fourth for PE/
games/story/finishing off/administrative odds and ends) all additional
curriculum demands – science, drama, music and so on – had to be accommodated in the three-way structure. In practice, because of the protected
status of Curriculum I, this meant acute pressure on the one area where
flexibility and choice actually existed, 'choosing' (Curriculum II).

Joyce's situation, operationally impressive though it was, thus
enshrined a paradox which could not really be acknowledged, since both
the term 'flexible day' and this form of organisation – which seemed to
gainsay usual definitions of 'flexible' – had been officially endorsed.

Janet, a teacher of 6–7-year-olds, was well aware of the potential for
this kind of paradox, and such consciousness made her somewhat
uncomfortable, even guilt-ridden. For she had acquired a notion of
'flexibility' not as a specific form of organisation but as a moral absolute
which her teaching must at all costs demonstrate in order to gain
approval (from herself as well as others) as 'good informal practice'.
Janet had learned to treat anything not 'flexible' as 'rigid' – a polarity,
which like so many in primary education, carries a strongly disappro-
batory loading. This meant that, since she had set herself a virtually
unattainable ideal of flexibility, the spectre of 'rigidity' hung (quite unjus-
tifiably for those who observed her) over much of what she did. So, for
example, even a modest degree of subject-separation in the curriculum
opened up the risk of 'little boxes' and 'compartmentalisation', while
putting into operation 'flexibility' through a system of groups undertaking different activities simultaneously the danger she perceived was
that her need closely to monitor children's progress represented some
kind of 'imposition' upon them.

But alongside 'flexibility' as shibboleth – and, except through inflexi-
bility, an unattainable ideal – was another, more personal version. Janet,
as an experienced teacher on the way to headship, was increasingly
conscious of the fact that her abiding anxiety, over many years, to meet
others' expectations of how she should teach, in fact contradicted the

idea of 'flexibility' in its truest sense. Janet, therefore, was moving towards a version of flexibility as being less about conforming to an approved style than about freedom to think and act independently of such preconceptions, to evolve her own version of flexibility.

Such emerging autonomy was always constrained by external require-ments and demands. Janet, like Andy, Jenny and several others, found the ubiquity of published mathematics schemes a distinctly double-edged benefit. On the one hand, they provided a framework and prop in a curriculum area having a high and very public profile in primary education and for which they, like so many primary teachers until recently, lacked the extent of personal proficiency, and therefore, confidence, they wished. On the other hand, such schemes 'imposed' a 'rigid structure' of the very kind that they sought to reject, and in the most prominent area of the curriculum, at that. Since working through the schemes was mandatory, the dilemma seemed unresolvable. Janet's partial resolution was to accept this contradiction and constraint, to identify instead those curriculum areas where she would be free to develop her own style and interests, and there to introduce 'flexibility' in a more individual sense. Topic work provided the required context: it was the area where she could freely enact her own 'personal view of the world . . . views on how to bring up children . . . on what's important in life' free from external expectations and constraints. She, like several others, felt liberated in topic work to an extent which seemed impossible in mathematics and language. Indeed, these teachers accepted that to some extent themes for topic work were often chosen to reflect the teacher's rather than the child's interests. Perhaps, therefore, the case made by HMI in the primary and first school surveys (DES 1978 and 1982) against randomness and repetition in topics is not quite so clear-cut as it seems, for against the apparently inexcusable idiosyncrasy of such arrangements one should maybe set this kind of personal commitment and enthusiasm, from which, surely, children must benefit.

As we worked with Janet, over two terms, we (and she) perceived a gradual loosening of the earlier grip of the shibboleth of 'flexibility'. Janet moved, and felt herself moving, from an outer-directed to an inner-directed approach in this and other respects which made her less educationally fashion-conscious and conformist, more relaxed, less insecure and guilt-ridden. Having admitted to us what she could obviously not admit to the primary hierarchy, that flexibility in teaching, at least in the absolutist, Utopian form presented in the informal rhetoric, was unattainable, she became more realistic and accepting of herself – and thus more truly flexible.

Sheila was also conscious of tension here but had less room for manoeuvre. Teaching in a brand new fully open-plan school, her curriculum and organisation had to reflect in every way not just 'flexibility' (which does at least imply some boundaries) but also 'openness' (which seems to imply none at all). Her recurrent phrase was 'freely-flowing'. Children had to be able to move freely from one part of the building to another and from one kind of learning, unencumbered by subject labels, to the next. Curriculum areas had to merge into one another imperceptibly. The whole had to be thematically unified. Staff relationships had to be open, frank and collaborative. This ideology was one, it should be emphasised, to which she herself was totally committed: it accorded with her personal values, and the consistency made her seem a happy and fulfilled professional.

Yet the now familiar paradox and tensions were evident, for what Sheila sought was what we came to term a 'non-framing framework' or a 'non-structuring structure': some kind of formula for planning and organising children's learning in her section of the school which enabled her to plan, organise and monitor children's programmes in accordance with prior commitments to appropriate experiences in mathematics, language, 'creativity' and 'investigation', but which did not imply acceptance of these, conceptually or organisationally, as subjects.

There was a constant and recurrent tension in Sheila's interviews between 'freely-flowing' as an elusive ideal and 'bittiness' as ever-present danger – the Scylla and Charybdis of competing imperatives in informal primary education, perhaps. For the very procedures which had been designed in order to promote, exemplify and enact flexibility – large open spaces, shared curriculum/resource areas, collaborative teaching – in fact made the open curriculum more rather than less difficult to achieve than for one teacher in a box classroom. The complex logistics of one space, four curriculum areas, three teachers and sixty children dictated considerable forward planning, and, in particular, prior agreement on the use of time and space so that children and curriculum could 'freely flow' without collision. 'Spontaneity', the usual adjunct of 'openness', was therefore ruled out except in a limited sense, and 'flexibility' was somewhat circumscribed.

Sheila was well aware of the challenge of reconciling ideology with physical and professional circumstances, and of the added pressure on her of having to prove, as deputy head, that such physical and organi-sational circumstances, having been designed to deliver flexibility and openness, would do just that, but because she identified so unequivocally with the value-system she accepted both the challenge and the consequent tensions and problems.

Peter, a teacher of 10–11-year-olds, shared Janet's sense of guilt (a word used by several of these teachers) about having or displaying structure in curriculum and pedagogy. Like Janet, too, he had learned to worry less about demonstrating allegiance to textbook informality and those who dictated it, and more about evolving his own style. But he also hinted at the limits to such independence when he suggested that one reason why this issue was less problematic for him now was that 'structure is no longer a dirty word ... we are emerging from the dark days of the polarity between progressive and traditional'. 'Structure', therefore, may well become not just respectable but transmuted into orthodoxy and accorded shibboleth status: as overused and eventually as meaningless as 'informal'. We shall see.

Planning, anti-planning and teacher psyche

The flexibility/openness/structure tension applies at the preactive (planning) as well as at the interactive stage of teaching. Informal ideology dictates to teachers that they avoid what Calderhead (1984) terms 'comprehensive' planning, as incompatible with flexibility and spontaneity. The particular objections seem to be first to writing one's plans down on paper (except in the form of a topic web, since that has the informal virtue of being limited only by the size of paper one writes on and the notional topic web stretching towards infinity is ideologically very sound). Planning in the sense of ongoing reflection away from the classroom about what one has done and what one intends to do – 'one plans (thinks about teaching) all the time' – is accepted as inevitable and proper. The second objection is to the pre-ordinate nature of the written plan, which is seen to 'tie down', 'constrain', 'predetermine' to excess what teacher and children can do. In contrast, writing up what one has done, say at the end of a week, is deemed ideologically acceptable – even though planning after the event, if one thinks about it, is something of a logical curiosity.

Despite all this, however, most of our teachers not only planned in advance but planned in detail and in writing too. Moreover, several of them attested to planning now, in mid-career, in far greater detail than they had as inexperienced teachers (though, as I have mentioned, their focus of attention in such planning had changed). For this sometimes massive task – the number of hours per week for some of them frequently went into double figures – no official guidance was available, for being ideologically suspect, written planning was rarely discussed.

So individuals had to evolve their own planning styles. Some of them imported and applied models they had encountered on courses – topic webs and checklists of skills were common – but such everyday models, like the behavioural objectives model endorsed by academics in the 1960s (and now experiencing a renaissance) are only applicable in certain circumstances, and Calderhead's (1984) assertion that planning is dominated by the particular classroom context and focuses upon learning activities rather than learning outcomes, which our experience supports, underlines the limited usefulness of the few handed-down planning paradigms that teachers encounter. What Calderhead's review of teachers' planning underplays (and the theoretical models themselves ignore) is the impact of factors in addition to those of children, classroom and resources usually included in 'situational analysis' approaches. In particular, planning in primary education varies quite markedly (1) from one curriculum area to another – different paradigms are implied and used for mathematics, art and topic work, for example; and (2) according to teacher personality and development.

Some teachers, therefore, felt a psychological need to plan in great detail in advance (two spoke of their fear of chaos, others of their need for security), while others were happy planning 'incrementally'. For some, even, planning became almost obsessive. But, ideology apart, there seems no good reason why individual teachers should not plan in whatever way, and to whatever level of detail, makes them professionally confident and efficient when they enter the classroom.

It should also be mentioned, because this is where the anti-planning rhetoric is particularly unrealistic, that the comprehensive planners never felt enslaved by their plans. On the contrary, they seemed to be liberated by them. They frequently deviated from them, sometimes to a marked degree, and some of the most relaxed, 'spontaneous' and 'flexible' teaching we saw had been preceded by the most detailed planning. The planning then, does not dictate precisely the form of the action, but it ensures that one thinks through possibilities and contingencies and provides a resource on which one can draw if necessary. There is an analogy with the performing artist's practice and training – the more thorough the preparation, the more confident and apparently effortless is the performance, and the greater the capacity to take those risks which give a performance flair and make it move and excite rather than merely interest its audience. It is an imperfect analogy, but on the other hand the notion of teacher as artist is – in the light of emerging analysis of the way that experienced teachers actually operate – at least as convincing as that of teacher as scientist or even technician.

The relationship of planning style to curriculum areas is also significant, not only in the obvious sense that teachers see mathematics, art and topic as implying different planning paradigms, but also because there may be a direct correspondence between a teacher's knowledge of a curriculum area and the extent of his/her planning. It can cut both ways: the less one knows, the more one needs to plan to ensure security/the more one knows, the less one needs to worry. Or, the more one knows, the more learning possibilities one can envisage and the more one feels the need to structure learning in advance to ensure that these are actually encountered/ the less one knows, the less one can envisage and therefore plan.

Walking the ideological tightrope: the teacher as intervening non-interventionist

Next are some competing imperatives arising in the interactive phase of teaching. It is a measure of the power of informality as a historical phenomenon and as a shaper of teacher consciousness that of all the words in the educational vocabulary even 'teaching' itself should have acquired pejorative overtones in the primary sector ('We mustn't teach: we must let them learn').

Underlying this is a simple confusion of 'teaching' with 'telling', which can readily be sorted out. Once this is done, a genuine pedagogical issue remains: the degree and nature of the teacher's mediation in the child's learning. I use 'mediation' as the most neutral term available because of course the linguistic minefield here is a pretty extensive one and many of the other words in common currency carry a strong adverse loading – 'direction', 'intervention', 'pushing', 'interfering', 'forcing', 'intruding'. The competing imperatives, therefore, are clear and situationally acute. While ideology dictates a teacher role of facilitator and encourager, common sense (not to mention recent classroom research) indicates the benefit for children of purposeful intervention by the teacher, especially of a kind which generates cognitive challenge.

To some degree, there has always been an infant/junior divergence here, with the belief that 'children learn at their own rate and when they are ready ... we shouldn't interfere' more strongly espoused where younger children are concerned (King 1978, 1989). For two of our teachers, this aggravated the problem, therefore.

Sue had worked mainly with juniors but was now deputy head and in charge of infants, with a class of 6–7-year-olds. She was highly ambitious, for herself and the children, and believed firmly both in detailed forward planning on the basis of a clear conceptual map of each curriculum area and in setting up and closely directing experiences to maximise children's learning in accordance with such maps. She was irritated by what she saw as colleagues' rationalising espousal of wait-and-see 'readiness'; was eager to 'push as hard as I can to see what I can get back' and to demonstrate that, given engaged and knowledgeable teaching, some notions of what infants can do (or, perhaps, cannot do) are misconceived. Yet at the same time she was anxious about seeming to 'push' or 'overstretch' the children. Behind this dilemma lay her strong commitment to planning, structure and process in the curriculum. This led her to place high priority on advancing and deepening her own curriculum understanding, to the extent that she had come to the view that the main reason why some colleagues resisted 'intervention' and demanded what she saw as too little from the children was that they had little idea of what to demand.

Pam expressed similar anxieties. As a reception teacher she had imbibed both informality and non-intervention. Her practice, in fact (like that of most of the other teachers in this group), displayed the external characteristics by which 'good informal practice' is usually defined – diversity in activities at any one time, grouping, busyness, display and so on – and indeed she cited the Plowden genealogy of much of her thinking, together with a random array of other influences, which underscores my earlier point about serendipity in professional development. Pam both operated within, yet was profoundly critical of, informality.

Her central aims – of fostering children's independence, their willingness and capacity to ask questions, their positive attitude to learning – were familiar enough. The problem for Pam was that her lively and honest intellect made her constantly aware of the danger that such goals might slide into rhetoric. Yet with a class of twenty-two 'reception' children, some of whom had arrived in September and the rest in February, she felt – for all her considerable experience – that numbers, lack of time and professional isolation would combine to subvert her goals. Watching and listening to colleagues, she was critical of the various coping strategies she felt that they adopted in the face of these constraints, and suspected herself of using such strategies also: undervaluing the capacities and interests that children bring to the classroom; levelling them down to a providable-for mean, and labelling and grouping them accordingly; encouraging passivity and conformity to ensure stability and cohesion; responding disproportionately to the children who are most visible or who demand attention; identifying 'what children cannot do rather than what they can do' in as far as it is easier to remedy a deficit than exploit a strength.

To compensate, Pam invested immense amounts of time and energy in detailed planning – yearly, termly, half-termly, weekly and nightly – then, ever alive to the pervasiveness of informal ideology, was duly defensive about having done so. Apologies for teacher intervention are prominent in her interview transcripts: she worries about 'pushing', 'imposing', 'putting too much in', 'giving too much input', 'intervening', 'over-organising', being 'over-ambitious', entertaining 'over-expectation'. And she was also alive to the possibility – again, perceived as a failing in fellow-teachers – that she might be planning for notional and generalised 'levels' of ability rather than with individual children's capacities in mind: 'All the planning's there before they've considered the children'.

Every organisational challenge honestly confronted raised such tensions, and a feeling that it is actually far easier to survive as a teacher by ignoring them. Thus, to intervene is necessary: but to intervene is to make work for oneself. To match curriculum experiences to a child's abilities and needs requires that one should pitch work above rather than below what one initially diagnoses those abilities and needs to be, and that one should be 'unwilling too readily to accept the children's responses' as they stand: yet to do so is perhaps to make it more likely that children may 'fail' or at least feel themselves doing so. And, Pam believed, children themselves may consciously underachieve in order (1) to attract the approval they need, and (2) to get comfortably by (Becker's 'exchange bargaining' strategy as applied by Galton (1989) to primary classrooms).

It is important to note that this critical analysis was offered not by an academic researcher seeking to demystify or debunk primary teaching and its associated ideologies, but by a committed and talented teacher whose ideas and practice, far from being maverick, were firmly embedded in the progressive/developmental tradition, yet whose experience and personal qualities had increased her pessimism in respect of the actual achievability of that tradition's ideals.

Grouping: simple recipes, complex repercussions

The central pedagogical challenges – of diagnosing children's needs, fostering their learning and monitoring their progress; and of doing so in the context of large numbers and the ambitious curricular and organisational expectations associated with prevailing ideology – provoked different responses and strategies in our twelve teachers, though all were conscious of them as overriding but not easily reconciled imperatives.

The one strategy they did have in common was grouping. The number of groups we saw operating at any one time ranged from three to eleven (in the latter case a 'group' could be two children working together). More often than not, the groups would be working in different curriculum areas. Sometimes groups were relatively fixed and had names or numbers; elsewhere their membership varied according to the nature of the learning task and the needs and characteristics of individuals and/or the dynamics and cohesion of the group as a whole. The groups were, variously, of comparable ability, of mixed ability (that is, less comparable ability – the notion of a 'single ability' group is surely unsustainable), based on friendship or on what the teacher saw as likely, socially, to work. Sometimes, following Tann's (1981) distinction arising from the ORACLE project, children were grouped and sometimes they were doing group work: that is to say, physically grouped and working individually on the one hand, physically grouped and working collaboratively on the other. Most of the teachers had varied combinations of grouping and group-work, though deliberate strategies for actually promoting collaborative activity were less common.

Sometimes groups followed a relatively standard routine of moving from one activity to another in rotation and at more or less fixed intervals, while elsewhere there was less routinisation, and teachers would need to spend some time explaining the procedures for the particular session, day or week to the children. Some teachers delivered these instructions by bringing the whole class together; others went round each group in turn; elsewhere the group's tasks for the day or week were listed on a sheet or the blackboard, or on cards, and the children simply settled themselves down in accordance with such instructions as soon as they arrived in the morning.

And so on. The point demonstrated by this catalogue, arising from the work of a mere twelve teachers, is that the blanket term 'grouping' is capable of being operationalised in a large number of ways, not just across different classrooms, but within a single classroom by one teacher. And yet, considering the ubiquity and diversity of the practice, the term as it is offered to teachers – as shibboleth and quintessential feature of the informal package – is an astonishingly (or typically) unqualified and monodimensional one. There seems simply to be an overriding assumption that grouping is one of the minimum conditions of 'good primary practice' and that no more needs to be said.

As will now be clear from other examples already discussed, I am arguing that this combination of generalised ideological pressure and vagueness about operational detail can generate high levels of anxiety and guilt among teachers and can cause some to place quite unrealistic and inappropriate demands on themselves.

Among our teachers, the perceived imperatives where grouping was concerned were four-fold:

1 Children should be grouped.
2 At any one time each group should be doing something different, and preferably working in different curriculum areas.
3 The teacher should as far as possible give constant and equal attention to each group.

To these, for some of the teachers, was added a more recent imperative:

4 Children in groups should be working co-operatively.

The last of these, of course, was attributed to the ORACLE research (Galton *et al.* 1980a, 1980b). Whatever the intentions of Galton's and Simon's team, the message increasingly being received by teachers, almost certainly via advisers and teacher educators rather than from direct reading of the project's publications, is that unless children are interacting and collaborating within their groups, there is little point in grouping them. This message seems to have been delivered to, or at least received by, teachers working with every age of primary child from reception to top juniors, despite the fact that the children in the ORACLE study were no younger than 8+. It is of course a questionable message in this form. Why shouldn't teachers, when grouping children, have purposes in mind other than to promote co-operative learning?

Taken together, and expressed concisely as in the list above, it will be seen that grouping, so conceived, can never be less than a major challenge to the teacher's skill, particularly where the inexperienced teacher is concerned.

Equally serious is the way that this particular aspect of primary ideology and practice reveals the price teachers have to pay for having their own ideas on such matters ignored. For the ORACLE research, like some other observational research of the past decade or so – and indeed the HMI surveys – takes little account of teachers' intentions in offering its characterisations and critiques of their practices. Yet intentionality in pedagogy is surely of critical importance: first, in the obvious sense that a teacher needs to have good reasons for working in a particular way; and second, because practice can only be fully understood if one engages with the thinking that underlies it (the rationale for the project from which this material is drawn). Practice is not just observable, codable and measurable behaviours but an array of ideas, values and intentions; and, in action, diagnoses, decisions and judgements. Practice is thought and thought is practice.

Grouping: there's still only one teacher

Space does not permit me to portray here the various ways in which our teachers responded to, or liberated themselves from, the established or emergent imperatives associated with grouping, but it is instructive in the present context to draw attention to one issue: that of how they dealt with the need, in the context of a complex pattern of organisation, to give adequate supervision and attention to each child.

Three patterns emerged. At one end of the continuum was the highly routinised and controlled procedure associated with the 'flexible day' arrangements already described. Here the teacher monitored children's progress mostly from a fixed point in the centre of the room which gave her sight-lines to every corner, and circumvented the problem of queues, which diversity in grouping tends to generate, by rules and procedures governing the number of children allowed out at once, how they should wait for attention, what they should do having finished a piece of work, and so on. At the other end of the continuum, a large number of groups undertaking very diverse activities (though all loosely related to a common 'theme') generated a considerable monitoring challenge which could be responded to either by what Andy called 'buzzing around' at a sometimes frantic rate from group to group and child to child, or by an apparently random monitoring of those children who overtly demanded attention. In the latter case, children might wait in queues for some time – not necessarily in the way that Bennett reports, at the teacher's desk – but peripatetically, following the teacher as he or she moved round the room, with attention divided between this moving tail and those children still seated.

At a mid-point in this supervisory continuum, between what we came to call its 'Queen Bee' and 'Bluebottle' poles, were teachers who adopted what we termed a 'high investment/low investment' strategy. That is to say, they set up groups in such a way that, because of the nature of the work being undertaken, one or at the most two groups at any one time required their close attention. So, for example, Judith spent the best part of an hour seated with a mathematics group, interacting with them both collectively in a 'group instructor' mode, and individually, with only occasional forays to other groups. Such movement would be judged necessary on the basis of intermittent scanning.

The argument presented by Judith, Sue and others who adopted this kind of strategy was that such concentrated attention on a relatively small number of children over a sustained period was more productive in terms of both diagnosis/match and children's learning than the brevity and superficiality of the interactions which result from seeking to give all children equal attention. Provided that such a strategy is carefully planned and monitored, the teacher can ensure that over, say, a week, every group and every individual within a group gains a significant amount of undivided and concentrated attention of the kind that can produce the 'higher-order cognitive interactions' that Galton, Mortimore and their colleagues (Galton *et al.* 1980a, 1980b; Mortimore *et al.* 1988) regarded as the prerequisites for purposeful learning. The procedure is comparable to the idea, now, since Bullock, fairly well established, that the ever-nagging primary imperative of 'hearing children read' is best responded to on the basis of 'sustained and occasional' rather than 'little and often'.

There is nothing new or revolutionary about the high/low investment strategy: many teachers of the kind who manage to remain unimpressed by swings in educational fashion regard it as 'just common-sense'. But it is not dilemma-free. There is the initial anxiety that it is manifestly contrary to the 'equal attention' imperative and others out, or up, there might disapprove. Then some felt that the kind of learning activity that could be undertaken with relatively low teacher investment of attention might necessarily be somewhat undemanding for the child, and that this could scarcely be defended. In fact, as we observed and discussed with the teachers who had most extensively developed this strategy, this is not inevitable. On the contrary, an activity which makes little demand on the children often ends up demanding a lot from the teacher because children finish quickly or become bored and restless.

One way through seemed to be to make pupil activities in the low teacher-investment groups to some degree self-monitoring; in other words, to devise tasks for these groups which required and encouraged collective problem-solving and decision-making, so that children would turn to one another rather than to the teacher.

That is easier said than done, however. As Sue commented: 'if the work is high demand cognitively for the children, then it's high investment for me as teacher'. All the same, we believe we saw examples of children who were to a large degree self-directed yet, because of the care taken in devising the learning task, were also working at a high level cognitively.

The other dilemma is more fundamental and takes us back to the question of the curriculum as a whole and the relatively unshakeable nature of the Curriculum I/II structure. As other teachers, not in this group, have commented when discussing the high investment/low investment strategy, 'Well, you'd only do this in maths and language work, wouldn't you?' Our teachers admitted that it was all too easy to respond to the perceived pressure to concentrate on the basics by making these the 'high investment' groups and allowing children undertaking Curriculum II activities like art, craft or topic work to get on more or less unsupervised, perhaps rationalising the lack of teacher investment in terms of the post-ORACLE shibboleth of co-operative groupwork (to which, indeed, topics in an obvious way seem to lend themselves). In this event, lack of teacher expertise would give the differential a further twist. As Graham said, the work in, say, science, might be undemanding simply because the teacher did not know what questions it was possible to ask.[6]

Sue was conscious of this danger, and of what she saw as her not wholly convincing response to it. She had a considerable personal commitment to art, and her teaching in this area was nothing if not demanding of children's intellectual as well as expressive capacities, so that her conceptual and pedagogical framework was one which, ideally, combined high demand for the children with high teacher investment of an interactive kind. But this commitment tended to be overridden by her consciousness of Curriculum I as an irresistible imperative so that, first, children were invariably grouped for mathematics/language but generally not for art, and second, if they were grouped for art as well as for mathematics/language she would tend to concentrate her attention on the latter groups, while feeling guilty, because of the clash with her personal values, for doing so.

One final point needs to be made before I pull the strands of this chapter together and offer some conclusions. It is clear that it is not adequate to make inferences and judgements about teaching on the basis of behavioural observation alone. Teachers' theorising repays close attention, for not only does its study enhance our – and their[7] – understanding of this complex and demanding job, but it may also be, as theory, as sustainable as any which outsiders offer, and certainly far more so than the unfocused rhetoric of informality (or whatever succeeds it). In the present example, concerning grouping, several of these teachers had evolved operationally viable and theoretically coherent strategies for meeting the challenge of providing individual diagnosis and attention in the context of large classes. Yet they conformed neither to the older 'equal attention all the time' imperative nor to the more recent imperative that all groupwork should be 'co-operative'. At the same time, the teachers' anxieties in the face of ideological and other kinds of external expectation made the successful operationalisation of their experientially derived theories more difficult than was necessary.

CONCLUSION

This chapter has raised a large number of issues and it is not sensible to try to summarise every single one of them. Rather, let me highlight five of the main strands.

The first is professional development. I have departed from conventional practice by presenting professional development as a personal journey rather than a formal sequence of pre-service and in-service events and activities. In emphasising the person within the professional I have noted a number of issues, each of which has implications for how we conceive of and structure formal professional development activities: the power, but the randomness, of individual experience; the influence – good, bad and indifferent – of teachers on one another; the inseparability of professional development from personal growth and from individual temperament, intellect, imagination, values and beliefs; and the way, therefore, that it is not just the teacher that changes, but also the job, in so far as increased understanding and expertise in relation to classroom decisions and practices allows that job to be, for and by each teacher, redefined. I showed how this redefinition can take any of a number of forms, but how while for some the job becomes easier and more routine, for others it becomes more complex, challenging and perhaps difficult – though in different ways and at deeper levels from those confronting the younger teacher.

The job of primary teaching, then, is not a preordained, standardised reality but an individual, shifting and therefore (considering how much it is talked about) a surprisingly elusive construct.

Clearly, this has implications for informal agents and agencies of professional development and appraisal – advisers, heads and teacher educators in particular. Proper account needs to be taken of the teacher as a person: in fostering personal growth and autonomy; in encouraging the individual to develop a professional style which exploits rather than opposes their personal characteristics and strengths; in matching initial/in-service experience to where a teacher is, developmentally; and in encouraging, respecting and building upon each teacher's own articulation of the job of teaching as they progress through their career. We need, therefore, to examine carefully the degree of congruence which exists or might exist between professional development as an officially defined and provided procedure, and professional development as an experienced human process. This is not to restate familiar arguments (or slogans) about the 'relevance' or otherwise of pre-service or in-service activities to the 'real world', the 'chalk-face of practice 'as it is'. Such versions of practice as are offered or implied in this kind of context tend to be arbitrary or even stereotypical. More serious, in the light of this discussion, is the way that in presenting the job of teaching as 'out there' they fail to acknowledge either its reflexive, subjective character or the way as reality it changes as the teacher changes.[8]

This would suggest that teaching 'as it is' may have more meaning for, say a student teacher when defined and explicated by a probationer than by a head. I do not argue that students cannot learn from experienced teachers – on the contrary, the thrust of this chapter is that they can and should (and IT/INSET schemes show how – Ashton *et al.* 1982); rather, that they will learn most when the job as conceptualised and enacted for them is not too far removed from their existing perceptions and capacities (which is only to apply a basic learning principle which is familiar enough in the primary classroom). Similarly, the potential benefits of procedures whereby experienced teachers can learn from one another seem to be considerable. Yet these benefits remain largely unexploited. It is true that teachers talk about teaching away from the classroom, but how often are they given opportunities to observe and enter into one another's ideas and practices within it?

The second strand was the societal context of British primary education within which the individual teacher operates and which, too, is also a powerful influence upon the way the teacher defines, enacts and evolves his or her professional role. Here again I emphasised diversity, change and conflict – not to be perverse, but because these are facts of the educational present and past which are too often ignored. I offered a view of primary education today in which ideologies and traditions that have emerged at different times during the past century or so are still very much with us, in an agglomeration of ideas, values and practices which are far from coherent, consistent and harmonious, but that schools and teachers have somehow to reconcile and present as such. Sometimes the juxtaposition (of progressive and developmental ideas, for instance) is a reasonably comfortable one, but elsewhere (for example, in respect of central questions, encapsulated as the Curriculum I/II tension, concerning what children should learn) the dilemmas are constant and perhaps more difficult to resolve.

Again, it seems to me, we help ourselves by viewing diversity and divergence in primary values, ideas and practices not as an inconvenience but as a fact of life. These values are not, as so often in the primary world they are portrayed, extraneous and unreasonable 'demands' and 'pressures', irritants or irrelevancies which frustrate those who simply want to 'get on with the job', but an essential and necessary part of the package: they are the job. This fact, too, has to be confronted by those responsible for organising professional development and training procedures, and it is not an easy matter to deal with. The trainee teacher should certainly be aware of the value divergences and dilemmas embedded in the job, and that the particular curricular and organisational arrangements that they happen to come across are by no means pre-ordained. But they also need security, confidence and a basic framework for classroom action which works and can be justified, otherwise the questioning will undermine the very capacities it is intended to enhance.

I brought together the first two themes – personal/professional development and value plurality – through the idea of 'competing imperatives' as the third main strand of this chapter: the hypothesis that teachers are confronted on a day-to-day basis not only by 'practical' choices and options of a more or less resolvable kind, but by more fundamental dilemmas and tensions which have their roots partly in the diverging and competing values which constitute primary education as a whole, partly in each teacher's particular school and classroom contexts – and partly within teachers themselves, as unique and changing individuals.

The fourth strand, and a pervasive one, was the public language of primary education in general and of informal primary education in particular. This language is so singularly unhelpful to dispassionate professional discourse about the day-to-day detail of classroom practice that, I suggested, we probably have to acknowledge that this is not its main function. In any case, I argued, it is possible that none of our existing ways of talking collectively about primary education – including the academic – yet has the capacity to grasp the full subtlety and complexity of classroom processes; and if this is our objective, which it surely should be, it can be achieved only by taking far more account of everyday teacher theorising than we have hitherto, and that in turn dictates that we penetrate well beyond the 'espoused theory' to which the public primary language tends to restrict itself.

This language, I suggested – notwithstanding the way that the informal Primaryspeak of the 1960s and 1970s is being superseded by the ostensibly tougher and more instrumental vocabulary of the 1980s – is still more about solidarity or power than meaning. To point up these functions I introduced and exploited the 'shibboleth' idea, those key words and phrases which pepper primary professional discourse, which teachers feel obliged to use to demonstrate their professional allegiance and which, in their practice, they have somehow to enact. The language of primary education, then, is the medium through which not a few of the competing imperatives are conveyed, and I showed how the vagueness of the language can cause the teacher serious problems at the point of operationalisation, yet, because the imperatives arrive as officially endorsed orthodoxies backed by hierarchic power, they cannot easily be questioned.

A more sophisticated, precise and neutral language, then, is the minimum precondition for promoting the kind of professional dialogue upon which school and teacher development depend. The chicken-and-egg problem here, of course, is that it is the dialogue which will generate the language – it will have little meaning or validity if evolved away from the classroom. Perhaps there are grounds for optimism here in the apparent shift, encouraged by the enhancement of the curriculum consultancy role, towards more 'collegial' relationships in primary schools (though, since that word is currently one of the most prominent of all the new wave of shibboleths, we must be extremely cautious about assuming any correlation between frequency of use and change of practice).

All of these strands were illustrated by considering the responses of a number of experienced teachers to the four most prominent and recurrent challenges of informal pedagogy as they presented themselves in our data: openness and flexibility, planning, 'intervening' in children's learning, and the central organisational device of grouping. Many other illustrations are possible, but space does not permit them. One cluster, for example, concerns 'balance' in the curriculum as a whole (like grouping, a shibboleth currently in the process of being updated). Another concerns 'community', whether this means children working together, team teaching, or collegial approaches to school policy-making – the latter two, again, coming to the forefront of official and professional consciousness at this moment.[9]

The final strand was my linguistic excursion into the 'jungle' as an alternative metaphor for capturing the tensions, dilemmas, conflicts and paradoxes within primary education at both societal and classroom level, but which also, in a positive way, evokes primary education's richness and diversity. The 'jungle' is offered as a corrective to that pseudo-consensus which has been so salient a feature of primary education since the 1960s and which has proved so frustrating both to meaningful and productive debate about educational purposes and processes and to the personal/professional development of individual teachers in the sense in which it has been defined in this chapter. But the 'jungle' bears on professional development in another, more fundamental way. For professional development, as inseparable from personal maturation, is about coming to terms with the inner as well as the outer world, with resolving the tensions of the psyche as well as the dilemmas of the classroom. The jungle is in each of us. So too is the need and urge to make sense of and impose order upon the outer world in order to achieve inner equilibrium, to turn the jungle into a garden.

In this respect, two final points can be made about the particular collection of ideas and practices connoted by the word 'informal'. One is the empirical observation, that – regardless of semantic connotations or official ideals – 'informal' as successfully operationalised by experienced teachers is highly structured, conceptually and organisationally. The word 'informal', therefore, is singularly inappropriate if it is taken to imply 'without form or order'. The second point is that, as shibboleth, 'informal', and those of its associated terms which suggest an unbounded openness and flexibility, may have placed an unreasonable and in some cases intolerable burden on those teachers for whom among all the competing professional imperatives the overriding one was the personal need to avoid or resolve uncertainty, ambivalence and dissonance, to know and be convinced about what they were doing and why.

The reality of primary education may sometimes be nearer the jungle than the garden, and we do not help ourselves by pretending otherwise, but this does not invalidate the garden as symbol of a basic and necessary human quest.

NOTES

1 If this was a sensitive issue in the mid-1980s, it was not much less so in the mid-1990s, as the outrage which greeted the 1992 DES primary discussion paper's consideration of the use of teachers' specialist expertise (Alexander 1992, paras 139–50) demonstrated. However, by 1995 the subject imperatives of the National Curriculum, especially at Key Stage 2, had begun to erode these loyalties, and not only were teachers more happy to entertain teacher roles other then the traditional class teacher one, but schools were introducing such alternatives – subject, of course, to funding (on which see Chapter 6).

2 The first prediction – of a resurgence of behaviourist and mechanistic models of education, has proved correct. The second, less so: the HMI curriculum framework enjoyed brief celebrity before being ousted by the National Curriculum. On the other hand, HMI's consistent advocacy of a single, coherent curriculum for the whole of compulsory schooling (5–16) paid off. Let that, at least, be their epitaph.

3 When I wrote this in 1987 I contrasted in a footnote the government's version of educational relevance as informed solely by the needs of the economy with those of some urban LEAs who, while accepting this imperative, were also seeking to address problems of inner-city decay, social disadvantage and discrimination against minority groups. Leeds LEA's Primary Needs Programme, which provides the context for the studies of teachers and teaching in this book's third and fourth chapters, is a good example of this kind of initiative. The 1985 HMI curriculum framework, referred to above, also offered a more comprehensive version of relevance, with its list

of 'essential issues' like political awareness, economic understanding, equal opportunities and so on which were to inform whole-curriculum planning. This survived the arrival of the National Curriculum as a set of cross-curricular 'themes', 'skills' and 'dimensions' – though only just, according to the National Curriculum Council's first chairman (Graham 1993): Prime Minister Thatcher liked it not one bit. It did not survive Dearing's 1993–94 slimming-down of the National Curriculum, however. Presumably he was under orders to slim down the ideology as well as the content.

4 Maurice Galton suggested this usage to me.

5 It was not to be, as I noted at 2 above. However, the effort is worth recording. The HMI framework included nine 'areas of learning and experience' (aesthetic and creative, human and social, linguistic and literary, mathematical, moral, physical, scientific, spiritual, technological) interpenetrated by four 'elements of learning' (knowledge, concepts, skills and attitudes) and the various 'essential issues' I have already mentioned. Not a very tidy model, admittedly, but important in that it provided a reasoned alternative to the growing stridency of government statements on educational matters – something HMI, under their then Senior Chief Inspector Eric Bolton, were happy to offer, most notably in their 1981 *A View of the Curriculum* (DES 1981b), a counterblast to the government's *Framework for the School Curriculum* (DES 1981a). Would OFSTED dare, or even be capable of, such a challenge, I wonder?

6 The extent to which this problem is intrinsic (though of course not unique) to the class-teacher system was subsequently underscored in our Leeds PRINDEP research, where the generous enhanced staffing provided by the LEA gave teachers opportunities to work intensively with small groups of children. As we noted (though not in the studies included in the present volume): 'Teachers found that taking smaller numbers of pupils challenged their own expertise in particular areas of the curriculum, since sustained questioning and discussion require a teacher to have a clear framework of the kinds of understanding he/she wishes to promote' (Alexander *et al.* 1989: 236).

7 We monitored the impact on these teachers of their being involved in so intensive a programme of observation, recording, discussion and – above all – self-confrontation. We also brought them together, at their request, to view and discuss one another's videotapes. All strongly endorsed (and in the interview transcripts demonstrated) the considerable potential of such procedures in professional and school development programmes. Naturally, some found such exposure hard to cope with initially – one of the group confessed to hiding her videotapes under the bed for two weeks before she could summon up the courage to view them.

8 This was written some years before the government launched its attack on teacher training institutions as purveyors of irrelevant theory and left-wing ideology and proposed instead an apprentice model which would take place largely in schools and indeed would under certain variants exclude higher education altogether (DFE 1992b, 1993a, 1993b). To argue that trainee and experienced teachers acquire much of the art and skill of teaching in the classroom – which is self-evident – is not the same as arguing that the classroom is the only place where such knowledge and skill can be acquired. For the record, the teachers whose reflections are recorded in this chapter, having no cause to plead for higher education, were convinced of the necessity to maintain the multiple perspectives on classroom practice that partnership between schools and higher education, at best, can offer.

9 Anyone who trained to teach in primary schools after 1989 may find at least three of the dilemma areas – openness, planning and intervention – somewhat

puzzling. Why, they may ask, all this agonising when of course the curriculum must be planned comprehensively in advance and of course the teacher must intervene rather than merely facilitate? Well, yes: the curriculum is now closed and to a large extent pre-planned; and because of this the teacher must intervene to ensure that the programmes of study are in fact being studied and what children are attaining are the attainment targets required by law. When one considers how many thousands of teachers struggled during the post-war period to find professional equilibrium in the dilemma areas illustrated here, the capacity of governments to get to the heart of the matter with one quick burst of legislation is truly remarkable. But have the problems really gone away? Is the only remaining dilemma really that of fitting the National Curriculum into the time available (see Chapter 5)? Are value-questions no longer on the educational agenda?

Chapter 3

Decisions and dilemmas*

The next version of primary education comes from 1988, a year after the government announced its intended legislative programme covering the National Curriculum, assessment, delegated school budgets and 'opting out', but before any of these were implemented. The version of primary education in question is that provided by one LEA as part of an ambitious reform programme whose provisions were very different from those of the 1988 Act. Where the Act saw curriculum, assessment and accountability as the means of raising standards, the LEA concentrated on classroom practice and the physical environment of learning. The study is one of several undertaken as part of the large-scale evaluation of these reforms, and it uses a combination of observation and interviews to portray and probe behind the practice of some sixty primary teachers. The study is continued in Chapter 4.

However wide-ranging, complex and ambitious a programme of educational reform may be – and the Leeds initiative was certainly all of these – its ultimate test must always be the same: its impact on classrooms, teachers and, above all, pupils. It is easy enough and proper to voice such a sentiment, rather more difficult to devise the research procedure which will deliver the evidence required, even assuming that we can agree on the criteria by which the impact of an initiative should be judged.

The study which follows is part of PRINDEP's attempt to explore the kinds of classroom practice associated with the Leeds LEA's Primary Needs Programme (PNP). Our aim was to look at practice in each of sixty (about a quarter) of the city's primary schools. The study was conceived as having three 'levels', each one more concentrated and detailed than the last. Level One (forty classrooms) was to involve a

* This chapter was written jointly by Robin Alexander, Kay Kinder and John Willcocks.

single classroom visit and interview; Level Two (ten more classrooms) a visit, one lesson observation and two interviews; Level Three (a further ten classrooms) an intensive programme of interviews and systematic observation of teachers and children at work over a two-week period. Further details about the methodology of this study and the project as a whole appear in Appendix 2.

The teachers at Levels One and Two were chosen because they had all attended one of the courses on classroom organisation which formed the subject of one of PRINDEP's earlier evaluation studies (Alexander *et al*. 1989: 191–222). These courses, attended over PNP's duration by large numbers of teachers, had a central function in defining and delivering the principles and models of good practice to which the LEA was committed and which it wished to see implemented in its primary schools. All the teachers in the present study were therefore in possession, in some form or other, of these ideas. In addition, while all the schools in the study had received support from the LEA as part of PNP in the form of enhanced staffing, increased capitation and the like (for full details of the programme's expenditure see Alexander 1992, chap. 1), the schools at Level Three had received relatively substantial allocations.

The schools and their teachers might thus be said to have been thoroughly immersed in the culture of primary education prevailing in Leeds from the mid-1980s to the early 1990s. The word 'culture' is deployed here not in its rather loose everyday sense but in its stricter anthropological usage of encompassing ideas, values and norms, social structures and institutions, modes of social control, and physical structures with their attendant material aspects. Naturally, the culture of LEAs during their heyday varied considerably on all these dimensions, partly as a consequence of their dominant political affiliations and the policies these yielded, partly as a reflection of the values and styles of their senior officers, advisers and inspectors, partly for geographical and historical reasons. But serving as a primary teacher in many of the higher-profile LEAs during this period required a conscious response to the culture – whether acquiescence, endorsement, loyalty, resistance, rejection, or strategic compliance.

The chapter is in three parts, encompassing the study's Levels One and Two followed by a commentary. We begin with the survey of the classrooms and accounts of practice from the teachers at Level One. The material here is predominantly factual, but it focuses increasingly on the problems teachers encountered in responding to the LEA's versions of good practice. We then provide five case studies of individual teachers from the ten observed and interviewed at Level Two, and here we look in greater detail at some of the central decisions they faced on a daily basis and how they responded to them. Finally, we explore some of the main issues raised by the data, especially the questions of how teachers can be helped to improve their practice and how, indeed, practice might be defined in the context of professional action and development. The headings in the section which follows may look somewhat arbitrary. In fact, they reflect the emphases of the LEA's series of courses on classroom organisation which all these teachers attended and which were an important part of the LEA's strategy for transforming the city's primary schools.

MESSAGE AND RESPONSE: THE LEVEL ONE SURVEY

The teachers

The proposed sample of forty teachers shrank by two to thirty-eight. In the main the teachers were very experienced: more than three-quarters of them had been teaching for over ten years, and more than half for over fifteen years. A third of them were working mainly or exclusively with 7 to 8-year old children; the rest had pupils of various ages from 5 to 11. Thirty-six of them had classrooms of their own. Two of them shared with other teachers on a long-term, full-time basis, and in all three-quarters had support teachers in their classrooms for part of the time.

The classrooms themselves held as few as seven and as many as fifty-two pupils, although only eight of them housed fewer than twenty, while eight others had more than thirty. Seven of the teachers (about a fifth of the sample) had the use of areas outside the classroom to augment their teaching space and to store bulky equipment.

Influences on practice

The development and spread of new ideas through an LEA occurs in many ways and takes place over a number of years, quite independently of any courses which may subsequently be mounted to advance them. According to the teachers in this sample, the main influence on their practice came from their colleagues at school. Just over two-thirds of them said that this influence was substantial, and they singled out the head and the PNP co-ordinator for the most frequent mention. In only a few cases was the influence negative: one teacher claimed that her colleagues were powerful models of poor practice, making her determined to be as different from them as possible; and half-a-dozen others said that they had been discouraged by lack of support from their colleagues in implementing the kinds of change associated with PNP. Staff meetings were a common way in which colleagues exerted their influence, and were mentioned by two-fifths of the sample. All but one of these references were positive.

Only a third of the teachers in the sample said that they were influenced by what they read, and of these only three spoke of specific books or research reports in the area of primary education. *Child Education* and *Junior Education* were mentioned, and one or two teachers said that they had been helped by *Bright Ideas*, course handouts, documents circulating in the school, and so on.

A little under a third of the sample said that they had been influenced by courses other than those provided by the LEA, about half of them mentioning attendances at outside institutions, sometimes for fairly straightforward and conventional INSET activities, and sometimes for lengthy and formal courses of study leading to higher degrees or diplomas. It is important to note here, however, that teachers' attendance at such courses is dependent not only on their wish to take part but also upon the opportunities they are offered to do so.

A quarter of the sample said that members of the advisory service had been a major influence on their practice. One teacher said that a particular advisory teacher had had more influence on him than anyone or anything else, and another that an adviser's visit had started her thinking positively. Four other teachers spoke in very negative terms of the same service, one claiming that she had been given wrong advice which had affected her career prospects, two saying that they had asked for help but received none, and the fourth expressing the view that visits from advisory staff were more of a threat than a help, and that in any case advisers gave conflicting opinions about the nature of good primary practice.

Perceived influence of the classroom organisation courses

Although the teachers' responses to the courses varied a good deal, most of them fell into six main categories:

- Type A: Eight teachers said that they had already been working along the lines advocated by the courses, and their subsequent account of their practice suggested that this was indeed the case. For some of them the courses had seemed somewhat redundant, while for others they had provided the reassurance of confirming their existing practice.
- Type B: Seven teachers were enthusiastic converts. They had made major changes to the layouts of their classrooms, and adopted the teaching strategies recommended on the courses. In general these teachers praised the courses highly, and several of them said that they had been inspired by them.

- Type C: Five teachers were partial converts. They had been impressed with the course proposals, had made some changes and were contemplating others; but they were experiencing difficulties of organisation and were feeling their way carefully.
- Type D: Nine teachers had made token changes but made it clear that they were in fundamental disagreement with some of the main recommendations of the courses. Seven of the nine felt strongly that each pupil should have his or her own place, with a chair; and of these, two had tried the more informal seating arrangements proposed on the courses, but had quickly reverted to the old familiar system on the grounds that it made the children feel happier and more secure.
- Type E: Three teachers said they could not make the kinds of organisational change recommended on the courses because of cramped and unsuitable conditions in their classrooms.
- Type F: Six teachers had rejected the courses entirely. They reported no changes of any kind: their classrooms, their daily practice and their basic beliefs about classroom organisation were all exactly as before. One reported that the courses had had a short-term effect on her in that they had worried her and made her reappraise her practice; however, she had decided that she was not going to change.

By their own accounts, the courses were to some extent inappropriate for three of these groups of teachers: those who made Type A responses claimed that they were already working along the lines they advocated, while those making Type E responses protested that the courses did not apply to them, and those making Type F responses rejected the messages entirely. Although some members of these three groups said that they had enjoyed the courses, it cannot be claimed that they had played a significant part for any of them in furthering the aspirations and objectives of the LEA's Primary Needs Programme.

The relative sizes of the six groups are shown in Figure 3.1. Just under half of the teachers made responses of Types A, E or F, all indicating that the LEA's courses had been in some way unsuitable for their current needs. The rest can be divided into two groups. Those making Type D responses accounted for a quarter of the sample; they had embarked upon relatively superficial changes, and for them the success of the courses remained a matter of doubt. Finally, there were those who made Type B or C responses, indicating major changes in their organisation and practice as a direct result of their attendance at the courses. Some of these teachers were experiencing difficulties and reservations, but all were convinced that the changes they were making were for the better. There can be little doubt that for this final group, constituting a little under a third of the sample, the LEA's courses had been a considerable success.

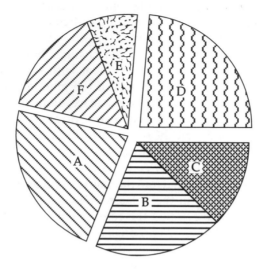

Figure 3.1 Teacher response types

In general, the teachers' accounts of their practice revealed that the LEA's core pedagogic principle of *flexible teaching strategies within a quality environment rich in stimulus and challenge* had found a place in the common parlance of primary education in Leeds, and that other more specific recommendations had been adopted by at least some of the teachers in the sample, often working with unpromising accommodation and equipment. In all, just over half of the sample complained that they were hampered to some extent by the shape, size, age or location of their classrooms.

The classrooms

Architecturally, the rooms in question showed a wide variety of styles, ranging from the solidly Victorian to the uncompromisingly modern. One was a school hall, and three others were huts or prefabricated structures. In about half of them the windows were too high for the children to be able to look out, and in five of them they were so small as to make the room seem dark. In general, the rooms were in a reasonable state of repair, although one had crumbling plaster and another a leaking roof. In ten rooms there were partitions or alcoves, sometimes resulting in substantial areas which were out of the teacher's line of vision from the main part of the room. More than half were fitted with a sink of one kind or another, and three rooms had tiled wet areas.

A model classroom, furnished and laid out in accordance with the advisory service's specifications, was a central feature of the classroom organisation courses. It was therefore not surprising that the courses had exerted their most immediately apparent influence on the class-rooms themselves, and only three of the teachers claimed to have made no changes to their rooms at all as a direct consequence of their attendance.

Display

The most visually striking features of the classrooms were the displays, many of which were clearly influenced by the advisory service's house style, with its preference for draped fabric, double mounting and neutral colours. More than two-thirds of the rooms contained large and elaborate displays: every room had something on show on the walls, and just over half had additional material displayed on tables, shelves or other flat surfaces. Three-dimensional items had been incorporated into the displays in all but five of the rooms, and ten rooms had mobiles hanging from the ceilings.

In every room, examples of children's work formed part of the display. About half of them included items which were there not because they were of a particularly high standard, but because whatever their quality they represented special effort on the part of the children who had produced them. More than four-fifths of the rooms had examples of the teacher's work as well, often of an informative nature, and sometimes as a model of excellence. In about a third of the rooms the displays incorporated commercially produced visual aids.

It is perhaps not surprising that art accounted for a high proportion of the work on display, but mathematics came a close second, with topic work not far behind it. In thirty-one of the rooms the displays bore some obvious and unambiguous relationship to the current work of the children, and in eight rooms they were related to other material on show elsewhere in the school.

About three-quarters of the displays looked fresh and new. In twenty-six of the rooms, at least some of the displays were examples of work in progress, developing and changing with the passage of time. Techniques of presentation varied a good deal, from ambitious set pieces involving hessian, drapes and double mounting, to very basic and straightforward arrangements of sheets of paper on a pinboard.

Equipment

In twenty-seven of the classrooms, items of work equipment were set out in plain view. Again they varied in both age and state of repair, and they were displayed in ways which ranged from the elaborately methodical to the apparently haphazard.

A quarter of the teachers had introduced equipment which had been recommended on the courses, and a fifth had made their classroom equipment more easily and directly available to the children. To this end, seven teachers had changed and expanded their system of labelling. In just over half of the rooms there were specific items of equipment which could not be seen by the observer although their presence was apparent from labels on boxes, doors and so on.

However, in view of the emphasis placed by the advisory service on labelling as an aid to children's independence in the classroom, it was striking that in almost a third of the rooms there were no labels of any kind to indicate the nature or location of equipment.

Furniture

Like the classrooms themselves, the furniture ranged from the outdated to the very modern, and from the somewhat neglected to the carefully maintained. In all, a third of the teachers were experiencing problems with old, heavy, inadequate or immovable furniture; for example, one room was dominated by an enormous old science bench complete with gas taps. However, there were other rooms which had been entirely refitted with brand new furniture of the type recommended by the authority's advisory team and used in the model classroom. Three-quarters of the rooms were at least partially carpeted, though this was not infrequently with carpets brought in by the teachers themselves.

Classroom layout

Fifteen teachers (two-fifths of the sample) said that they had rearranged their furniture as a direct result of suggestions made on the LEA's courses. Even here there were occasional problems. One teacher claimed that she could not make the changes she wanted because the caretaker liked all the furniture to be against the wall. Whether this was a convenient excuse, or an example of the kind of seemingly trivial difficulty that in the real world can completely sabotage genuine human effort, is hard to determine.

A few of the recommendations made on the courses about the deployment of furniture had been fairly generally rejected: in only three of the classrooms had the teacher dispensed with the convention that each pupil should have his or her own place, and moved over to the more fluid arrangement where there might be fewer chairs than children, and where children simply used the most appropriate place for the immediate task in hand.

The possibility of dispensing with the teacher's desk provoked a mixed reaction, although a substantial minority of teachers were giving it a try: a fifth of the sample had no desk or table at all and another fifth were using their desks for display or other purposes not traditionally associated with this item of furniture.

In other ways, however, many of the layouts echoed that of the model classroom, notably in the disposition of the furniture into work bays. These bays were generally, though not invariably, dedicated to specific areas of the curriculum; in some classrooms their function was nothing more than to break up the available space and provide corners in which groups could work without too much distraction.

Four layout types

Three of the classrooms had no work bays at all. For the purposes of the analyses which follow, these have been termed Type 1 classrooms, and a specimen plan (along with examples of three other classroom types) will be found in Figures 3.2–3.5.

Exactly half of the classrooms observed in the Level One survey had only one work bay each, and in every case this was a class library or reading corner. These eighteen classrooms have been allocated to Type 2. Type 3 classrooms, of which there were fourteen in all, each had several work bays, although there was in every case a substantial part of the room not laid out in this way. A single classroom, the sole representative here of Type 4, was very much like the authority's model classroom. It had been entirely set out in work bays of various kinds, and contained seven of them.

Not surprisingly, the teachers who claimed to have accepted the main messages of the LEA's courses tended to have classrooms more like the model classroom than those teachers who said they had not been able to implement the message, either because of their own convictions or because of such external problems as unsuitable furniture. The extent of the relationship between the teachers' reactions to the course (response types A to F, discussed earlier) and the layout of their classrooms (layout types 1 to 4) is shown in Table 3.1. It should be noted that the two support teachers in the sample have been omitted from this table since they were not responsible for the layout of the classrooms in which they worked.

The relationship between the reported impact of the LEA's courses and the physical appearance of the classroom is unambiguous and statistically significant. The importance of this finding lies in its confirmation that, in general, those teachers who said they had been influenced by the ideas developed in the courses did indeed have classrooms which showed the impact of those ideas; while those teachers whose classrooms

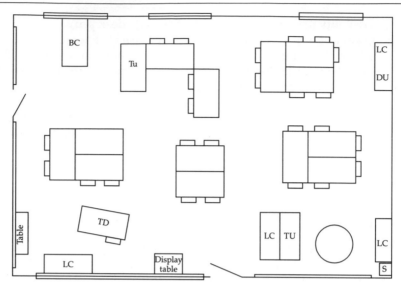

Figure 3.2 Type 1 classroom layout

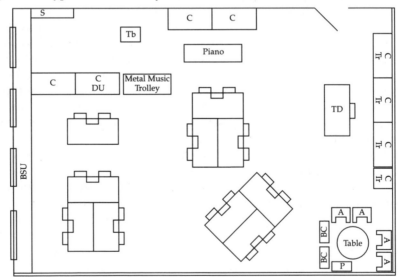

Figure 3.3 Type 2 classroom layout

A	–	Armchair	Msh	–	Maths shelves
AVA	–	Audiovisual aids	MTU	–	Maths tray unit
BC	–	Bookcase	P	–	Plant stand
BSU	–	Built-in-shelf unit	S	–	Sink
C	–	Cupboard	Sh	–	Shelves
Cu	–	Cushion	Tb	–	Tub-like container on castors
DTB	–	Daily task board	TD	–	Teacher's desk
DU	–	Display unit	Tr	–	Trays
LC	–	Low cupboard	Tu	–	Tray units
MET	–	Maths equipment table	⌐⌐	–	Built-in tray units
Ms	–	Movable screen			

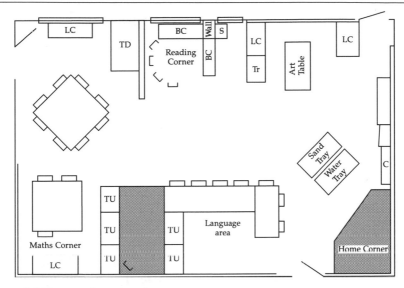

Figure 3.4 Type 3 classroom layout

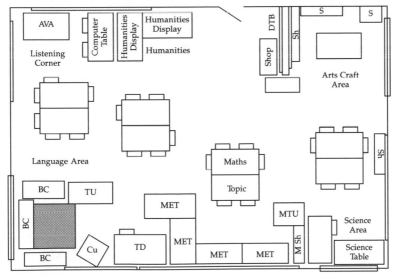

Figure 3.5 Type 4 classroom layout

were closest to the PNP ideal generally acknowledged the influence of the course on their thinking and practice.

There were, however, a few anomalies. Two teachers who made Type B (or *enthusiastic converts*) responses to the course had Type 2 classrooms in which the only concession to the recommended style of layout was a reading corner. Elsewhere, one Type D (or *fundamental disagreement*)

Table 3.1 Classroom layout and response to the LEA's courses on classroom organisation

Classroom type			Teacher response type			
	A	B	C	D	E	F
1	–	–	–	1	1	1
2	–	2	3	7	1	5
3	7	4	1	1	1	–
4	–	–	1	–	–	–

and one Type E (or *unsuitable conditions*) response came from teachers in Type 3 classrooms which had several work bays and a number of other features that were reminiscent of the model classroom. Although infrequent, these anomalous responses illustrate the sizeable and significant gaps which can exist between expressed beliefs and observable behaviour, and confirm the advantage, in an enquiry such as this, of a combination of interview and observation over either on its own.

Classroom layout and the curriculum

Since attending the LEA's courses, ten teachers had allocated or reallocated parts of the classroom to specific curriculum areas, even though the chairs and tables usually had to double as pupils' regular places. These curriculum-specific work areas were often, though by no means always, housed in work bays formed by the physical arrangement of cupboards, bookcases and other items of furniture. The extent to which the classrooms had curriculum-specific work areas (either in or out of work bays) is shown in Table 3.2.

Table 3.2 Curriculum-specific work areas in thirty-six classrooms

Areas per room	Number of rooms	Number of areas
0	3	–
1	9	9
2	5	10
3	6	18
4	8	32
5	2	10
6	2	12
7	1	7
Total	36	98

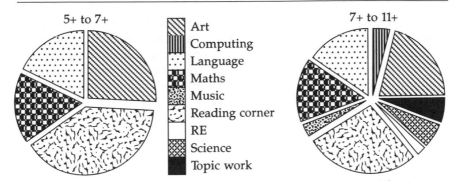

Figure 3.6 Curriculum-specific work areas

It is clear from this table that in spite of the suggestions made on the courses, backed by the example of the model classroom, a third of the teachers (3+9 = 12 out of 36) had either totally rejected the idea of curriculum-specific work areas or had restricted themselves to one such area in the classroom (in every case a reading corner or class library). At the other extreme, a few teachers had organised their classrooms entirely into these areas, forming as many as six or seven of them. Across the sample as a whole, the average number of areas per classroom was 2.7, and this remained fairly stable over the different age ranges, showing only a slight and statistically insignificant increase in the classrooms of older children.

A common arrangement involved four curriculum-specific work areas, and in seven of the eight classrooms where this arrangement occurred the four areas were devoted to reading, art, mathematics and language. The comparative frequency with which the various areas of the curriculum were allocated space of their own is indicated in Figure 3.6, and major discrepancies are immediately apparent.

First, the pattern of allocation was markedly different between younger and older pupils. In the classrooms of children up to 7+ there was not a single example of a curriculum-specific work area devoted to anything other than reading, art, mathematics or language. In contrast, a fifth of those provided for older children were devoted to a range of other curriculum areas: computing, science, topic work, music and RE.

The reasons for this difference are clear enough when one considers the scope and character of the curriculum as conventionally devised for older and younger primary children. Similarly, the pre-eminence of reading corners at all ages is hardly surprising, given the priority it has always had in primary education. In these particular classrooms it was allocated more space than anything else, accounting for no less than one-third of all curriculum-specific work areas.

However, the allocation of space to other aspects of the curriculum is less straightforward, and a comparison of art and science is particularly instructive. In the present enquiry art came second in prominence only to reading, with more space devoted to it than to mathematics or language, accounting for just over a quarter of all curriculum-specific work areas for younger pupils, and a fifth of those for older pupils. In contrast, and in spite of the example set in the authority's model classroom, only four of the ninety-eight curriculum-specific work areas in these classrooms were devoted to science.

There are two main reasons why an aspect of the curriculum acquires space in this way. One is its perceived importance, and the other is the kind of activity it entails (the character, incidence and influence of these generic curriculum activities is discussed in more detail in Chapter 4). In the case of art, the latter reason seems paramount; art can be messy, requiring running water as well as a wide range of special materials and equipment, and the strategy of segregating both the activity and the children doing it therefore seems sensible. However, science too involves practical activity which makes use of apparatus and equipment, even if not on the scale of art and craft, and for this reason one might expect it to feature more prominently in the physical layout of classrooms, particularly given both the recommendations of the Authority and its high profile in national policy.

We suggest that this anomaly captures primary classrooms and the primary curriculum in a state of transition. Though never a 'basic', art has always enjoyed high standing in primary education. In contrast, although science is now a National Curriculum core subject, it is a relative newcomer, and the messages about its primacy in the curriculum are taking some time to become reflected in classroom practice. A similar time lag was noted in the analysis of schools' curriculum development priorities and strategies in one of the earlier PRINDEP evaluation studies (Alexander *et al.* 1989: chap. 4), with science trailing well behind mathematics and language in terms of posts of responsibility, review, development and expenditure. All this is now changing rapidly as a result of the legislation since 1988. Nevertheless, if the physical arrangement of a classroom is indeed – as the Authority has argued – a reflection and embodiment of educational principles and priorities, then it would seem sensible for schools to keep this matter under review, monitoring the relationship between policy, layout and practice, and helping teachers to keep the three in step.

Grouping and group work

Teachers asserted that the major influence of the LEA's classroom organisation courses on their daily practice was the encouragement of groupwork, although individual teachers also mentioned a move towards an integrated day, the introduction of whole-class activities and an experiment in co-operative teaching. Groupwork was now playing a greater part than previously in the classes of a third of the teachers interviewed; and four other teachers, who had not increased the amount of groupwork in their classes, had none the less revised their grouping systems.

In a little over two-thirds of the classes, groups were formed on the basis of the teachers' perceptions of their pupils' ability. Most frequently the aim was to make the groups as homogeneous as possible, and groups formed in this way generally remained relatively stable, moving as a whole from one activity to another. In a very small minority of classes, however, ability groups of this type were formed only for specific activities (generally mathematics) and disbanded for the rest of the day.

An alternative way of grouping by ability was to ensure that there was a relatively wide range of ability in each group. A third of the teachers in the sample made use of this kind of mixed-ability grouping, and again there were a few examples of the formation of such groups for specific activities only.

Six teachers reported that they switched from one of these two grouping strategies to the other as the activities of individuals and groups of pupils changed. Such a policy would clearly have presented an organisational problem to any teachers who were dedicated to the orthodoxy that at any one time each group should be working in a different curriculum area; but by no means all the teachers in the sample subscribed to this view. In addition to these grouping strategies, an eighth of the teachers opted for friendship groups for at least a part of the time, and one teacher grouped her pupils by age.

It should not be supposed that the pupils of these thirty-eight teachers spent the whole of their time working in groups. One teacher had no groups at all but organised her pupils so that they always worked either on their own or as part of a class lesson. For the rest, nearly two-thirds favoured a balance of individual, group and whole-class teaching.

The changing activities of the day and the fluctuating numbers of teachers in many of the classrooms meant that the formation of appropriate working groups could be a complex problem, and teachers tackled it in a wide range of different ways. For example, one teacher of a class of 5- and 6-year-olds reported that her pupils were organised in groups based mainly on friendship, but that a small number of less able children were grouped together for language work. The grouping was flexible, but she usually had two groups doing practical or written work in maths, two groups doing writing or another language task, and two groups doing activities such as Lego or jigsaws. Groupwork usually took place during the mornings, and art and craft, PE, reading, stories and library work took place in the afternoons. The class came together for stories, RE, PE, singing, work with flashcards and a daily conversation session.

Another teacher, whose pupils were a year older, tackled things very differently. In the mornings, all her pupils did mathematics at the same time, and then moved on to English. She organised the children into ability groups for mathematics, but because they had different objectives she expected them to work individually within their groups. English usually involved using a story card to write a story, and when the children had finished their stories, they were expected to read. She liked to ensure that every child did some reading each day. Children who did not finish their mathematics and English tasks in the mornings continued with them during the afternoons, which were officially given over to art, craft and other activities. Topic work was done as a class activity. The teacher said it consisted of looking, talking, drawing and writing.

A third teacher, whose pupils were 7 and 8 years old, rejected the idea of group teaching altogether: 'I don't see the point of wasting time saying the same thing to five or six different groups when I can say it once to one large group'. She asserted that keeping her pupils together as a whole class maximised her time for teaching as opposed to merely monitoring what the children were doing, and she was confident that her pupils learned more when she taught them all the same thing at the same time. She said that she had found the LEA's courses very short of hard evidence that children were learning better under the prescribed methods.

These three examples cannot be fully representative of the others in the sample, and their strategies are outlined here chiefly to give an illustration of the complexity of the task of grouping children for a day's work, and of the very different ways in which the task was tackled.

We might describe the first of these three teachers as 'convinced'. She was attempting to change the essence as well as the trappings of her classroom practice, but she was facing a number of difficulties as she became fully aware of the repercussions of the changes she was implementing. She had opted for friendship groups but found it necessary to preselect a small number of children for a low-ability group, even though this inevitably meant that they had to be deprived of the freedom to choose their own companions. She also ran mathematics and language groups alongside groups working with Lego and jigsaws, thus ensuring that not all the children were engaged in activities which required much of her own attention or intervention. This proved to be a common strategy: it is one which has been observed in other studies, and is a topic to which we shall return in more detail later.

The second teacher can perhaps best be described as 'ostensibly convinced'. She had changed the appearance of her classroom to make it blend in with the new orthodoxy, yet she had made no alterations at all to her long-established ways of working. She used groups simply as a form of seating arrangement, firmly rejecting the notion that different groups should be engaged in different tasks, as well as the proposition that the children within each group should work co-operatively. Her pupils were all engaged on the same curriculum area at the same time, often sitting in groups, and sometimes sitting in ability groups, but always working either individually or as part of a class lesson.

The third teacher could fairly be designated 'totally unconvinced'. She attended the LEA's courses, heard the messages about classroom organisation, and then persisted with a familiar way of working that suited her purposes, justifying her stance on the grounds of the success she was enjoying with her pupils, and asking for a lot more in the way of hard evidence if she was to be expected to make major changes.

Even so, most of the teachers had made some changes, and this being so, it is scarcely surprising that four-fifths of the teachers also reported changes in the children themselves. Almost a third said that their pupils were becoming more independent, and several remarked on the increased quantity and better quality of their work, on the smaller delays between different activities, on the new, quieter atmosphere in the class and on improved social integration. On the other hand, one teacher somewhat ruefully remarked that the course's chief influence on her pupils was that their reading had suffered.

Planning

The teachers' planning varied in three basic ways: in its time scale, in its degree of formality, and in its structure. The time scale ranged from the very short-term to the comparatively long-term: from daily to yearly, with many intermediate steps. The degree of formality ranged from elaborate and schematic written documents to a simple mental rehearsal of what would happen next. The structure also showed considerable variation. Some teachers' planning involved a *comprehensive* awareness of the balance of different lessons and their place in the curriculum as a whole, as well as a very clear concern with progression, continuity, the acquisition of underlying skills and the achievement of goals. Other teachers adopted a more *incremental* approach, planning as they went along.[1] They were much less concerned with the details or wider curricular context of future activities, and much more interested in trying out ideas in practice before moving on to further planning.

To a very large extent, these three basic variables appeared to operate independently of one another; thus it was possible to be a comprehensive yearly or termly planner, drawing up elaborate written schedules, but to plan informally and incrementally on a day-to-day basis; or to plan comprehensively for the day-to-day details but within a fairly vague framework which might or might not be written down.

There were very few teachers in the sample who did not make some written plans in advance. Twelve of the thirty-eight had a powerful incentive to do so, since their headteachers looked at their plans of work regularly, at least once a term; five teachers submitted their work plans to their headteachers every week. One teacher reported that each day she planned her number, reading and written work for the following day. The head usually took the less able children and planned his own activities. In maths and reading this teacher followed published schemes, so that to a large extent the work was already planned for her in those areas. At the end of the week she entered an account of the children's work in a record book. Her headteacher liked his staff to plan as far ahead as possible for topic work. She had had to tell him what her topic for the summer term would be before the previous Christmas, and she had planned this topic in the form of a flow chart. There was also a whole-school topic which was planned at staff meetings. Other teachers prepared written plans of work even though nobody demanded it of them, and several prepared long-, medium- and short-term plans, often in parallel. In all, half of the sample made detailed and comprehensive written plans for each week, and a fifth made daily plans; fifteen teachers planned by the term, and twelve by the half-term.

As described by the teachers, some of the planning was very elaborate. One described how he wrote a fortnightly forecast of his programme of work, and then made a daily plan for each group. He wrote the daily work plans on the blackboard, and also read them out to ensure that even the poor readers would be fully aware of their programmes. All written work was collected in at the end of each session so that he could monitor what the children had done. A profile of each child was kept, together with a record of his or her progress in mathematics and reading. At the end of each fortnight the teacher commented upon his last fortnightly forecast in the class record book. He planned a subject-based programme half-termly, and at the time of his interview with us he was trying to organise more time for discussion with the support teacher about this programme. All his records were given to the headteacher half-termly, and returned with the head's comments.

Discussion and collaboration with colleagues played an important part in the planning of fifteen of the teachers. For example, one teacher had an outside commitment which took her away from the school for one and a half days a week, when her place was taken by a colleague. On one afternoon each week she swapped classes with another colleague so that she could take his class swimming. In addition, the PNP appointee worked with her class for two half-days each week. For this teacher, as for many others, effective planning could not be done in isolation. The long-term planning for her class took place at half-termly year group meetings attended by the PNP appointee (who also discussed the work programme with the class teacher on an informal basis whenever the need arose). The support teacher met the class teacher once a month to discuss the topic work: the support teacher had responsibility for the art and craft side of this work while the class teacher dealt with the language and maths involved. Notes were left on the teacher's desk to pass any urgent messages between them. The children were told at the beginning of each session what they were to do, and on Friday afternoons the class teacher ensured that they had completed the week's work.

In contrast, a few teachers did the whole of their planning in a very informal and entirely incremental way. One said that she knew the children so well that she was aware of their needs and could plan as she went along. Another gave an account which blurred the distinction between planning and record-keeping, saying that in maths and reading she kept formal checklists to give an indication of what the children could do, but that for all other planning she tended to play it by ear, basing her judgements on the children's successes and failures in their topic work.

This partial amalgamation of planning and record-keeping was by no means infrequent. Many of the teachers in the sample used checklists of tasks already accomplished as the starting point of their plans for the following day or days; and from there it was perhaps a natural short cut for some of them to begin to see the record of what had already happened as the plan for what would happen next. Conversely, one teacher claimed that her fortnightly forecasts for the headteacher acted as 'a kind of record' of work done, and although this may indeed have been the case if she was very good at forecasting, it was clearly not necessarily so.

Record-keeping

Only the teacher who had reported that she could plan as she went along claimed that she kept no records of any kind. The records kept by all the rest varied from the elaborately formal and comprehensive, involving a good deal of work, to the admittedly casual and labour-saving. Some were limited to checklists of work completed, while others were equally concerned with the acquisition and improvement of underlying skills.

There was one teacher who kept what she called 'mental notes' throughout the day as she worked with the children in their groups. At the end of the day she sorted through the trays of finished work, and then updated a set of tables which showed the specific work activities completed by each child in each of the main curriculum areas. The published mathematics and language schemes which she used provided ready-made records, although she felt that in mathematics particularly these needed augmenting with other things outside the scheme. She thought that the school as a whole should move towards a system of records based on objectives and skills. She kept a reading record for each child, with details of the books they had read, and a commentary. She was not altogether happy with her system as it stood, and was considering ways to improve it.

Another teacher, while acknowledging the importance of records, had found an easier and far less rigorous solution. She said that by organising the class so that everyone was working on the same subject at the same time she could keep track of what the children had done without spending a lot of time on written records. She thought her pupils (at 7+) were too young to make a record of their own work, so she kept a notebook and once a fortnight she wrote down what the children had been doing and anything else of note. She said that she found it easy to talk about the children because she knew them so well, but that she found it hard to write down what she knew.

Level One: summary

The Level One study gave a clear picture of a complex situation. There was no doubt that the LEA's principal messages on pedagogy had been heard and considered by a high proportion of the teachers interviewed. The classroom organisation courses had played their part in this process, but they were naturally not the only sources of information and ideas. There was also a great deal of both formal and informal consultation among colleagues during which key LEA ideas were handed on, discussed at length and sometimes modified before finding their way into everyday practice; and many of these colleagues had heard their version of the messages from other sources entirely. Wherever it came from, and however they understood it, most of the teachers found the LEA's PNP philosophy congenial, although many had reservations, and a few found it lacking in persuasiveness or substance.

In their own classrooms, the teachers were in settings which were sometimes very unlike the model classroom which they had studied while attending the classroom organisation courses. They were also experiencing varying degrees of freedom to accept or reject the LEA's messages, and varying amounts of support. Any help was almost universally experienced as coming not from the LEA but from within the school itself. However, problems and difficulties, although occasionally stemming from the hostility or scepticism of colleagues, were far more often seen as a matter of inadequate accommodation, furniture or resources.

For the most part, the LEA's guidance documents for primary schools covered a wide range of material, dealing with both broad, abstract ideas and more specific practical matters. The classroom organisation courses also followed this pattern, ranging in their subject matter from fundamental organisational strategies to minute details of equipment and display. The clear advantage of this breadth of content is that it maximises the likelihood that every reader or listener, irrespective of initial attitude or previous experience, will find something relevant to their own situation and needs. However, this advantage is purchased at a cost, as the courses plainly illustrated. They left the maximum leeway for individual teachers to claim, quite truthfully, that they had implemented a good many of the LEA's ideas and recommendations, even though their basic beliefs and practice had sometimes remained relatively untouched. Similarly, there were teachers who said that they had already been doing most of the things recommended by the LEA, but who went on to describe their practice in a way which revealed similarities of peripheral detail yet profound differences between their own organisational preferences and those which were officially espoused. In general, however, there was a clear tendency for the warmest agreement with the LEA's ideas on classroom practice to be expressed by those teachers whose classrooms were set out along the lines being recommended.

The emphasis on grouping was almost unanimously accepted by the teachers interviewed as the obviously right way to organise children's learning experiences, although about two-thirds of them favoured a balance between individual, group and whole-class teaching (a view which was also endorsed by the LEA itself).

However, the arrangement of the classroom into bays dedicated to specific curriculum areas presented a number of anomalies. Although most of the teachers found it an attractive idea, most of them were simultaneously quite unwilling to give up the principle that every child should have a place of their own, or to introduce a system whereby there were fewer chairs than children. The clear implication of curriculum-specific seating areas is that different curricular activities should be going on simultaneously, and this complicated things further for a number of teachers who strongly felt that they could keep a firmer grip on their classroom organisation if everyone in the class pursued the same curriculum area at the same time. Consequently, a common pattern was for teachers to adopt some of the LEA's proposals on such matters while rejecting others, and when this happened there was inevitably a certain amount of muddle as they tried to balance the sometimes conflicting demands of many different activities going on simultaneously, of a wide variety of grouping strategies, and of curriculum-specific work areas together with pupils' 'own places'.

Some teachers were endeavouring to ease the situation by ensuring that at least some of their groups were engaged in activities which rendered them unlikely to need much help or attention; but since help is generally required only when difficulties arise, such a solution necessarily involves the use of very undemanding tasks.[2]

The confusion of partial change also had repercussions in the areas of planning and record-keeping, areas where only a third of the teachers were working under any kind of supervision, although a somewhat higher proportion were collaborating with colleagues. There were teachers in the sample who were grappling with several complex long-term and short-term schedules and forecasts at a time, and others whose only apparent work plan was to set up a succession of *ad hoc* activities with little long-term coherence or progression. At the same time, there were teachers who were keeping no methodical record of what had been going on in their classrooms, as well as others who were devoting quite extraordinary amounts of time and effort to the problem.

The overall picture was of a very mixed group of teachers, stimulated by new ideas and making a genuine effort to bring about quite complex changes in their classroom practice, but often thwarted by mundane practical difficulties, and sometimes floundering as they encountered conflicting demands and pressures. The Level One study also confirmed earlier PRINDEP discussion of the character and fate of LEA messages about educational practice: for example, the problems of ambiguity and misunderstanding; or the tendency for any idea delivered by an authoritative source to be treated as a requirement, even when its status is no more than an option or suggestion (Alexander *et al*. 1989: chaps. 4 and 6). For many recipients of such messages, therefore, the force of an idea resides less in its substance than in the status and power of its purveyor.

DECISIONS AND COMPROMISES: CASES FROM LEVEL TWO

Helping teachers to change their practice is a complex and delicate process. From the inception of the Primary Needs Programme, Leeds LEA demonstrated a long-term commitment to improving its teachers' classroom delivery of the 'broadly-based curriculum', emphasising teaching style as well as curriculum substance. The PNP messages about flexible teaching strategies were reinforced by an in-service programme which annually featured courses on the organisation of children's learning in the classroom. In addition, the work of the primary advisory team in schools encouraged teachers to evaluate their own classroom practice. Finally, the creation of the innovative role of PNP co-ordinator provided each PNP school with a relatively senior teacher whose job description and INSET training carried a strong implication that they exemplified good practice.[3] Together, these various strategies for bringing about change might be expected to form an irresistible combination of imperative, suggestion and example.

However, LEA strategies have to operate in the context of individual schools, where the leadership style and the overall professional climate exert their own pressures on teachers to keep pace with – or to ignore – the LEA's current thinking on curriculum delivery and classroom management.[4] Beyond the school context, it is ultimately classroom teachers themselves who have to decide whether to accept and how to put into operation recommended teaching approaches.

Level Two of the present enquiry involved a study of each of the ten teachers who had attended the classroom organisation courses and were also working in the sample of thirty schools selected at the start of the PRINDEP evaluation project as representative of the city's primary system as a whole (see Appendix 2). Five of these case studies have been selected for discussion here.

The teachers at Level Two were observed in action and asked to talk about their preferred classroom procedures and the reasons behind them. In discussing organisational issues such as grouping, curriculum content and planning, they revealed the very wide variation that exists in teachers' views about what is important in children's learning and what is achievable in the classroom. The observations of their classroom practice showed how such personalised curriculum priorities were usually delivered in the style that seemed most acceptable and comfortable to the individual teacher. The studies also illustrate the teachers' varying degrees of readiness to implement the LEA messages about good practice. Some were faced with an enormous challenge in being asked to change what had always seemed appropriate classroom management, a challenge that could seem invigorating or overwhelming. Others believed they had had their current practice reassuringly reinforced.

Above all, the case studies indicate a fundamental problem for every primary teacher. Teaching is essentially a series of compromises. The primary teacher alone is responsible for delivering the whole curriculum to perhaps thirty children, and usually has to do so in the context of less than perfect classroom resources and facilities. This necessitates selective decision-making in several major and closely connected areas: (1) what the children will learn that day; (2) which children's learning will receive the teacher's attention at any one time; (3) how the working environment can best facilitate that learning. In the case studies which follow, each teacher is, in effect, talking about her solutions to these problems.

The studies are concerned with three major aspects of practice around which, as a reflection of the teachers' most pressing concerns, discussion revolved. First, under the heading *Classroom organisation*, there is an outline of the kinds of decision which the teacher generally made before (and sometimes after) working with her pupils: matters like classroom layout, organisation of children and curriculum, record-keeping and planning. The teacher's views on how – or if – these decisions had been influenced by the LEA's courses are also recorded.

Second, under the heading *Management of learning*, the teacher is described in action in the classroom, and we give a brief outline of a single observed lesson. Here the main focus is upon the kinds of teaching interactions which resulted from the teacher's prior organisational decisions, and also upon the nature of the activities provided for the children. In a third section, *The wider context*, we consider school influences upon the teacher's practice and make reference to the PNP co-ordinator's role as well as the perspective of the headteacher. A discussion of the teacher's particular and unique set of compromises concludes each case study.

It is important to stress that the following portraits of practice cannot validly be used as the basis of general statements about teachers as a whole. They do no more than illustrate something of the variety of teaching behaviours and teacher viewpoints in the authority's primary schools. Equally, the studies should not be seen as definitive portraits of the five teachers involved: their attitudes, intentions and actual classroom practice were considered in a series of two interviews and one observed lesson in the spring term of 1988, and it would devalue the complexity of primary teaching to claim that this had comprehensively captured their repertoire of teaching approaches or was the sum of their professional thinking. Nevertheless, common issues do emerge, and these are presented as general points, or propositions, in the summary which follows the case studies.

Case study 1

Mrs A was a 48-year-old redeployed middle-school teacher, with twenty-four years' teaching experience. She had a class of eighteen 8–9-year-olds in a Phase One school.[5]

Classroom organisation

In terms of the classroom layout types described and illustrated above (Figures 3.2–3.5), Mrs A's classroom was of Type 4. There were clearly defined areas for language, reading, maths, practical maths, topic work, science, and art and craft. The old-fashioned desks had lift-up lids, but they had been pushed together to make groups of tables, and covered with thick pieces of cardboard to create reasonable writing surfaces. In order to provide maximum mobility for her groups, Mrs A did not allow the children to use the desks for storage: books, pencils and equipment were located elsewhere in the room, and all were clearly labelled.

Mrs A explained that her groups had formerly been determined by the children's mathematical ability, but that since attending the LEA's courses she had reorganised her class into four mixed-ability, topic-based groups. She described her way of working as a roundabout system: she wrote on the board the order in which each group should undertake art, language, topic work and maths, and divided the working day into four sessions to accommodate this range of activities. She said that the system was the result of much experimentation, and that she now made sure that all the children had work they could go on to if they finished one task before the designated time to change activities.

She completed the school's mathematics and language records, which were entirely based on the Peak and Ginn schemes, but was also experimenting with her own topic-based checklists. Here, she was attempting to keep a record of the new skills and understanding which children were acquiring instead of simply noting their completion of prescribed activities, but she was finding this a very complex task. While aware of the authority's view that language and mathematics should be integrated into topic work, she acknowledged that much of the children's work in these two areas was dictated by the school's agreed schemes. Nevertheless, she stressed that her preparations for topic work always included activities designed to incorporate some language and mathematics. These preparations were under way many weeks before the children were introduced to the topic.

Her response to the classroom organisation courses was of Type B: she had found it 'absolutely splendid', and had afterwards totally reorganised her classroom layout during the summer vacation. As well as altering her system of grouping children, she had changed from single-area to mixed-curriculum teaching. She acknowledged that there had been difficulties of adjustment, including 'traffic jams' when children from different groups had needed attention simultaneously, but she felt that she was overcoming them and that the children were now able to work more co-operatively and independently. She herself was enjoying greater contact with pupils, in groups and individually, and she felt she was working in a 'more intense way'. She had got into the habit of questioning her practice at all times.

Management of learning

When Mrs A was observed at work in her classroom, she had organised four activities for the children – mathematics worksheets and Peak workbooks, worksheets for topic work and language and a co-operative topic-based craft activity. In one hour of observed teaching, she spent twenty-six minutes working with children undertaking mathematics tasks, fifteen with each of those groups doing topic work and language and four minutes with the craft group. The great majority of these interactions were with individuals and at least half of all work-related interactions were initiated by pupils. Mrs A acknowledged that she worked mostly in this responsive way. The class size assisted this teaching style, and she did not think that the high number of what she termed 'problem' children in the class would be able to cope with the situation if she gave her attention exclusively to single groups for extended periods. However, she was convinced of the appropriateness of teaching several curriculum areas simultaneously: 'It's much better. . . . The children are more motivated and I think teacher time is better used.'[6]

The wider context

Mrs A was described by her head as willing to try new ideas, hard-working and open-minded, and she had made considerable adjustments to her practice after encountering the LEA's ideas about classroom organisation. However, it is possible to identify other school factors which also contributed to her teaching approach.

She herself mentioned the externally appointed co-ordinator, who had operated in a support teaching role and whose expertise she had willingly accepted: 'The PNP co-ordinator has worked with me in the past, and through that and talking with her, I have been greatly influenced in my approach and teaching style.' She also said that her head had given her support, and for his part, the head said that his policy was to praise rather than pressurise his staff to make changes.

With regard to the influence of other staff, Mrs A expressed some sense of isolation in the school because of the location of her classroom and the reservations of a neighbouring colleague about undertaking collaborative teaching with their two classes. Nevertheless, she indicated that colleagues were beginning to discuss classroom organisation, and referred to a staff visit to the LEA's model classroom. She also felt that the size of her class was ideal for experimentation, and that as this was her second year as their teacher, she was in a doubly advantageous position to undertake major organisational changes.

However, the head also indicated that implementing LEA ideas about classroom practice was left in the hands of the individual teacher, and this meant that Mrs A had to devise her own methods for organising her class and training the children to work in a new way. In addition, the head's curriculum management strategy did not include a major commitment to delegated curriculum leadership so that Mrs A received very little support in this area, and had to sort out for herself the complexities of a curriculum delivered through the medium of topic work.

Her isolation was intensified by the PNP co-ordinator's involvement in an unsuccessful collaboration elsewhere in the school. In fact it would seem that in general this school's co-ordinator was never entirely successful in influencing the practice of colleagues (with the exception of Mrs A and one or two others) and she subsequently undertook a new role as a full-time class teacher. In this way, Mrs A effectively lost a potentially valuable consultant on classroom practice.

Against this background, it is not difficult to understand Mrs A's decisions about what her pupils should learn, which children would get the bulk of her attention, and how the classroom itself could best facilitate the children's learning. Although the classroom gave clear evidence of a 'broad' curriculum, with science, CDT and practical mathematics occupying curriculum-specific work areas, the structure and guidance for Mrs A's work came mainly in the 'basics' of mathematics and language, and by and large from publishers' schemes in these areas. Even so, she demonstrated her commitment to an integrated curriculum: teacher-devised, topic-based activities were a prominent feature on the day of observation. She was one of the few teachers in the sample who said she read educational books, as opposed to magazines. She mentioned the work of Joan Tough, and of several authors on the subject of reading extension. These had exerted a noticeable influence on her questioning technique and the worksheets she prepared. The classroom itself illustrated her resourcefulness in creating a working environment which complemented her commitment to curriculum breadth and grouping.

It would seem that the extra teacher time which Mrs A believed mixed-curriculum teaching had created was in fact spent almost exclusively on children engaged in mathematics and language activities, with mathematics receiving substantially more of her attention than any other curriculum area. She had chosen mixed-ability grouping and she had a very favourable teacher–pupil ratio. This combination of factors undoubtedly contributed to the success of the individual and responsive work-interactions that characterised her teaching approach on the day she was observed, as well as encouraging and enabling her to provide intellectually challenging activities for all her pupils. She said she would have to change her approach the following year when she would have a larger class, and referred to the necessity of providing 'occupying' work for children: the implication being that groups of children could not as easily be stretched and challenged if a teacher was any less accessible than she was at that present time.

Case study 2

Mrs B was a 40-year-old primary-trained teacher who had taught children with special educational needs in a previous post. She had a class of thirty-one 7–9-year-olds in a Phase One school.

Classroom organisation

Mrs B's classroom was a Portacabin in the school playground, with a Type 2 layout. It had a carpeted reading or quiet area, a space at the front of the room for watching television, and resource areas for mathematics and art. There was no sink. The desks had lift-up lids, and had been pushed together to make five tables. The arrangement of the room had been worked out with the PNP co-ordinator after Mrs B had attended the LEA's courses.

Mrs B explained that the children were grouped by reading ability and remained permanently at their places because of lack of space. She said they all worked at mathematics, language and 'activities' every day.[7] She now insisted that they did not interrupt her when she was teaching a group, and they had the materials for plenty of extra activities stored in their desks for use when they finished or were stuck. Each day she planned to work with the groups that had the most difficult task or needed most oral work.

She planned topics half-termly, and often linked them to television programmes. There were no completed mathematics or language schemes in the school, although schemes were being developed at staff meetings. At present she was following what she described as 'basic number progression for basic mathematics'. When asked about record-keeping, she said that she recorded the names of the books children had read from the reading scheme, and the results of spelling tests; and that these records helped her plan her language work. She also recorded the activities undertaken by each child in her half-termly topic plan.

Mrs B's response to the LEA's ideas about classroom practice was of Type B. She said it had given her the confidence to make changes in the way she taught. She no longer devoted the afternoons to activities but now devoted the whole day to mixed-curriculum teaching. She was now less anxious about the need for children to record their mathematics work in books, and was consequently undertaking more investigative work in mathematics. She was enthusiastic about the results:

> This way of working has enabled the poorer ones to have a bit more confidence, because I'm not always at their beck and call. ... The brighter ones can do problem-solving; ... they know they're not going to get told off if they talk.

It's a much more enjoyable way to teach, especially when there are two [teachers] in the room. It's how we should teach; it's how we should spend our day. . . and it just looks so nice when you go to schools and see children doing different things in bays.

Management of learning

In the observed lesson, Mrs B carefully introduced each group to its tasks while the rest of the children occupied themselves with their reading books. First she set up some shape games and an activity involving the colouring of number bond patterns for a group who would work later in the session with a support teacher. Then she explained a task of matching words and pictures to a language group. Next she worked with a group on the basic concepts of mapping (a theme that had arisen from a television programme). Finally she worked with an 'activities' group, encouraging discussion of what the children had done in relation to some work on colour and light. In all she spent twenty-eight minutes of the one-hour lesson with this group (in blocks of eight and twenty minutes). She spent fifteen minutes with the mapping group, and ten minutes with the language group, hearing some children read and checking the results of their matching task.

In this way, Mrs B created time for extended and uninterrupted inter-actions with one group at a time. Only about 5 per cent of her interactions were with pupils not in her current group, and they were invariably work interactions initiated by individual pupils themselves.

The wider context

There had been a marked change in Mrs B's practice since she had attended LEA courses on classroom organisation. However, it is impor-tant to note that at this time the school itself was experiencing a veritable perestroika in relation to classroom practice. Under its previous head it had been – in the words of Mrs B – 'formal and insular'. The PNP co-ordinator had been marginalised, classes were streamed and children's desks were in rows. Since the arrival of a new head, shortly after Mrs B attended her courses, several significant changes had taken place. The PNP co-ordinator had been appointed acting deputy head, thus acquiring additional status, and now had a support role that allowed for involvement in the whole curriculum rather than an exclusive concern with special educational needs. The whole culture and discourse of the staffroom had been transformed.

Mrs B singled out the new headteacher, and the staff discussion she had generated, as the major influence on her practice; and for her part the head made it clear that she was working quite deliberately and systematically to exert precisely this kind of influence:

I try to get people to think what their philosophy of education is. I'm trying to focus the staff's attention on the needs of children and how they learn. . . . I've said, 'If you believe children learn when they are motivated and involved, you have to decide what's the best way to organise the physical environment to get them to learn.'

I use certain words when discussing curriculum. I've talked about 'themes' and . . . about 'integrating the curriculum.' I do not talk about 'the integrated day' . . .

I've discussed with staff the differences between teaching a class, a group, [and] an individual. I've talked about the greater response from a group, and [pointed out] that it's possibly harder because you do more teaching. I've probably advocated group teaching in these discussions: I've said [that] in group teaching you're able to monitor the effect you're having, and you are able to alter the strategy in response to this. . . .

I've given everyone a piece of carpet, [and] this has influenced class-room organisation. I've used vocabulary such as 'work bays' and 'reading corners,' [and] I refer to 'your art cupboard.' In other words I drop hints like bricks about what I expect teachers to have in their classrooms. . . .

The school's adviser had been asked by the head to lead a staff meeting on classroom organisation. Thus from a formal in-service course, from the staffroom, and in classroom collaboration too, a consistent set of messages about practice was being delivered to this teacher and her colleagues. In relation to decisions about what children should learn and which children's learning would receive her attention, her organisation now demonstrated a commitment to mixed-curriculum teaching and to teacher-investment in areas of the curriculum other than the 'basics', as the very lengthy interaction with her activity group demonstrated. She spoke positively about the value of investigative mathematics, problem-solving and group discussion, and in doing so she gave clear evidence of the impact of the staff's curriculum development work.

The observed lesson demonstrated a further commitment to creating time for extended interactions with her groups, and this was no doubt facilitated by the presence of another teacher in the room. However, this teaching strategy was achieved only at a price. The children in her mapping group were, in effect, left to decorate their worksheets with felt-tipped pens for almost half the lesson, and Mrs B herself expressed some regret at not being able to hear the language group read. Clearly, desk-bound children and cramped working conditions presented some limitations to the possibilities for independent working. Perhaps the permanent space for television-viewing, which appeared to feature strongly in Mrs B's curriculum planning, also contributed to the children's lack of mobility.

Despite all the positive support and reinforcement she was now receiving, Mrs B herself expressed a slight reservation about her new approach in the classroom: 'I've got so far, and it's difficult to go on. I'm still formally structured, and it's difficult to know how to progress.' In this way, Mrs B indicated how the goal of informality is more than a matter of rearranged furniture, regrouped children or a retimetabled curriculum. In her newly reorganised classroom a teacher faces further major tasks. She must acquire the necessary curricular expertise to set work appropriate to the children's apparent ability, especially if some of her groups are to be left unattended for long periods of time. She must also develop the skills necessary for small-group teaching, and learn how to pace her own input.

Mrs B's observed lesson showed how successfully she had adopted a style of organisation that gave her 'time for actual teaching at group level'. However, it was also clear from her group interactions and the tasks she set, that an equal emphasis on curriculum and pedagogy should accompany discussion of classroom management. Mrs B stated that she did not read educational books. The only reading that had any influence on her practice was handouts provided at LEA courses.

Case study 3

Mrs C was a 36-year-old teacher with a total of seven years' teaching experience. She had a class of twenty-seven 5- to 6-year-olds in a Phase One school.

Classroom organisation

Mrs C's classroom had a Type 2 layout, with labelled storage spaces for mathematics equipment, textbooks, a library and other reading materials. There was an annexe at the back of the room which was used for painting and also served as a cloakroom. It was at the opposite end of the room from the child-level sink.

Mrs C explained that she did single area teaching at all times. The children were grouped by ability for mathematics and language. These two areas of the curriculum were undertaken every morning, and a non-teaching assistant (NTA) sometimes took a group for art at that time. Children who finished their prescribed activity before the end of the session were expected to read. In the afternoon, the children were allowed to sit in friendship groups while they worked as a class for topic work. The mathematics activities were usually taken from the Scottish mathematics scheme, and in language the children generally worked through various comprehension books, phonic workbooks and teacher-made workcards.

Mrs C explained that she kept all records in her head. She was aware of the children's ability and therefore knew what work to provide next. She said that she kept some very basic plans in her record-book, but that planning ahead was difficult because she didn't know how quickly the children would get on.

When she was asked about the impact of the LEA's courses on classroom practice Mrs C said she had already been doing what the LEA advocated. However, her subsequent account of her practice made it clear that this was not really the case. She said that she had returned from the courses feeling uplifted and enthusiastic, and had made workbays in her classroom. Soon after this, she had put her cupboards back against the wall because she didn't work an integrated day, and in any case the new arrangement had taken up too much space in a classroom that was already too small. However, the courses had made her realise that it was better to keep the equipment and resources for each subject area together. All in all, this response to the courses might reasonably be allocated to Type D.

Management of learning

In the observed lesson, the class was grouped by ability and each of the four groups was involved in a language activity. The 'top' group worked through a textbook comprehension exercise, a second group used headphones to listen to a story, and Mrs C spent the majority of her own time teaching phonics to the third group, using an exercise from another workbook. The 'bottom' group worked through workcards with the PNP co-ordinator, who also doubled as the school's special needs support teacher on workcards. Mrs C had no contact of any kind with these children or their teacher.

Some class discussion of phonics had preceded the dividing of children into groups, and, in all, the group activities lasted for three-quarters of an hour. During that time, Mrs C left her phonics group to monitor the two other groups for just under ten minutes. There were only five occasions when children approached her about their work. The children worked quietly, but became distinctly, though discreetly, restless by the end of the session.

The wider context

Mrs C's commitment to single-curriculum focus teaching, and her apparent adherence to teaching the 'basics' primarily through textbook exercises, represented a considerable divergence from the LEA's views of good practice. Given that her school had already had three years within the PNP programme, it is important to identify possible reasons for this incongruity.

In this context it must be significant that, according to Mrs C, there was no discussion about pedagogy in her school. She said that at staff meetings everyone was 'too busy'. She believed that her colleagues all taught differently, but that there was little chance of their influencing one another because of their isolation. In addition, the PNP co-ordinator, who had been internally appointed, had a self-chosen and very substantial role in the area of special educational needs, and was hence unlikely to exert much influence upon her colleagues' mainstream practice. Indeed, she herself referred to her colleagues as a stable and experienced staff, not in need of much advice, but also added: 'I feel we are all in a comfortable rut. . . . We don't really want to make too much effort or change anything, [and] this is why it's so difficult to get anything off the ground.' Similarly, the school's head said that she believed in adopting a very low profile when it came to influencing her colleagues' practice:

> I have no influence on the grouping of children, or on teaching style.
> I do not interfere. I don't try to interfere in my teachers' planning
> style either. If it is working and I can see the results, I think it is best
> to leave my staff to it and let them have the freedom to work as they
> see fit. Classroom layout is also up to them... [although] I sometimes
> suggest they change the pictures if they are getting tatty.

Thus, two possible sources of direction or guidance in the adaptation of classroom practice were not available to Mrs C.

As it was, Mrs C expressed clear reasons for the tightly controlled and structured organisation which characterised her decisions about how and what her pupils should learn. First, she described the children in the part of the city in which she was teaching as 'difficult' and 'different', and said that all her colleagues shared this view. She thought that such children needed stability, and that the way she structured their work session by session provided this. Second, she expressed the opinion that single-curriculum focus teaching also provided security because if more than one activity was occurring in the classroom, the children would become confused. She herself also liked to know what everyone was doing. Third, she thought it best that children of this age should do maths and language in the morning while they were still fresh.[8]

In this way, Mrs C justified her own curricular and classroom manage-ment priorities as coinciding with the needs of her pupils. Her commitment to control and structure, and the very high priority she gave to the 'basics' in her timetabling and classroom layout, seem markedly different from the LEA's messages on breadth, integration and flexibility. Yet she was relieved of the need to confront the disparity by finding sufficient in the authority's version of good practice – for example, grouping and the organisation of resources – to justify and reinforce her own. Another factor was identified by the head:

> The course Mrs C attended was useful . . . in that it provided new ideas and emphasised group work and classroom discussion. I can't say what she got out of it. Each person takes out what is useful to them. Mrs C's classroom is certainly better organised [and] her teaching seems a bit livelier. She had a bad class last year, and was jaded and lacking in confidence.

If Mrs C had been experiencing problems of classroom control in the recent past, her position in relation to LEA's messages on good practice becomes much easier to understand. Her initial willingness to implement some of the ideas she encountered, as evidenced by her reorganisation of the classroom, needed careful nurturing and guidance, but nobody was at hand to provide this. She also commented that she could not recall reading anything at all which had influenced her practice. It is not surprising that she reverted to her original views on pedagogy. With little sense of either imperative or reward, changing her practice must have seemed simply too daunting, difficult or dangerous.

Case study 4

Mrs D was a 35-year-old teacher with six years' primary teaching experience. She had a vertically grouped class of twenty-six 5–7-year-olds in a Phase Two infant school.

Classroom organisation

Mrs D's classroom had a Type 3 layout, with areas set aside for language and activities, a mathematics area which included a post-office shop, a reading corner and a home corner. A further two tables were described as being for overflow work from other areas and table-top work. Play activity materials such as sand and wood were located outside the classroom.

Mrs D's pupils were allocated by age to three groups: reception, middle infants and top infants. They were then often subdivided by ability for mathematics and language. In each of three daily working sessions, the groups worked at mathematics, language or activities. The order in which each group undertook its work in the three areas rarely varied; for example, the middle infants always started with activities and moved on to mathematics, while the top infants undertook activities in the afternoons. On each day, a different aspect of language and mathematics was covered: number on Mondays, time on Tuesdays, money on Wednesdays and so on. Free-writing, comprehension, phonics and handwriting were regular weekly components of the children's language work. She kept detailed maths and language records for every child.

Mrs D said that she tried to work with one group at a time, but that children from other groups inevitably approached her, and the reception group needed her attention at least at the beginning of every activity she set them.

For topic work there was a whole-school theme: members of staff pooled their ideas, and then each teacher prepared her own termly flow chart. Mrs D also explained that when curriculum areas were reviewed, the staff discussed appropriate classroom organisation and teaching strategies.

Mrs D felt she was already doing much of what the LEA suggested with regard to classroom organisation. However, her response would more properly be allocated to Type B than Type A, since she said she had found the LEA courses 'inspiring', and had reorganised her room to create subject area bays.

Management of learning

In the observed lesson, Mrs D began with a comparatively lengthy whole-class discussion, undertaking incidental teaching about the mathematics involved in registration and dinner numbers, and the phonics and spelling generated by various objects the children had brought in for the phonics table. She also encouraged responses to the style and substance of stories written by some of the children the previous day. The immediate work programme for each group was then explained to all the children. Mrs D spent nearly all of the remainder of the session – some thirty-five minutes – sitting with her reception group where the children were all doing the same exercise from their mathematics workbooks to consolidate practical work undertaken previously. Her teaching role was, therefore, essentially responsive. She monitored these children's work by allowing them to show her their workbooks after each question, and constantly repeated the vocabulary of length as she did so. During this time she also took part in more than thirty pupil-initiated interactions with children from the top infant group who were writing stories and who wanted to know how to spell particular words. An observational drawing exercise was the task for the middle-infant group, followed by free-choice play when they had finished. Each child was directed to this orally after they showed their completed pictures. In all Mrs D spent no more than five minutes with these children once their work was under way.

The wider context

The PNP programme had provided the school with extra staffing, and this made it possible for the deputy head to take on the role of support teacher and PNP co-ordinator. She commented that working alongside colleagues enabled her to give practical help and advice, as well as making them more accountable: 'They have to plan and prepare more thoroughly when they know a senior member of staff is coming in.' In this co-ordinator, Mrs D had an outstanding colleague working along-side her for a day and a half every week, teaching language to both the reception and top infant groups, and mathematics to a group of less able older children. However, Mrs D did not mention this collaboration as a particular influence on her practice.

She said she did not generally have time for educational reading, but sometimes got 'the odd idea' from *Child Education*.

The school itself was considered a model of good practice within the LEA, and had a consistent policy of grouping and cross-curricular approaches, reinforced by the headteacher's emphasis on whole staff discussion:

> There is a common thread running through the school on organisation and learning. All the teachers have an integrated day and work in groups; . . . if they did not I would tell them [to do so].

> For our whole-school cross curriculum theme, all staff discuss and decide together. We all put in suggestions, but each teacher plans her own class's work. I see plans and record books and I'm in and out of classrooms, [but] I don't give specific instructions as long as the organisation and learning are flexible and reflect the needs of the children.

> My staff are professionals. They think about their jobs, [and] it would be wrong of me to be dogmatic and tell them how to do things. . . . I see myself as the team leader, not a head. I encourage and praise and say things like 'I liked . . .' and 'I'd like to see more of . . .'

Perhaps Mrs D usefully illustrates that, however supportive the profes-sional climate of a school may be, change is more likely to take place in response to a powerful external stimulus.[9] Even so, Mrs D, rather like Mrs B, did not concern herself with the curricular and pedagogical issues implicit in some of the LEA's suggestions on classroom management.

For example, although she had begun to encourage her pupils to select their own paper and materials for art activities, it was obviously difficult to find teaching time to discuss the options and outcomes of such aesthetic decision-making with them. Indeed, it became increasingly obvious during the classroom observations as a whole that art was sometimes used as an organisational device to allow the teacher to devote her time to other activities elsewhere in the classroom – generally the 'basics' of the primary curriculum. Mrs D's practice was certainly an example of this.

The observed lesson also illustrated the enormous pressure faced by teachers of young children. Mrs D's management of learning necessitated two kinds of compromise, one child-related and the other a curriculum issue.

She felt that vertical grouping was a definite advantage in her attempts to create extended periods of time to work systematically with a group. At the same time, she acknowledged that when she was working alone, any such time tended to be given to the children in her reception group, unless they were involved in 'activities'. In other words, the older children were likely to receive less of her attention while they were working, and this perhaps explains the compensatory attention given by the support teacher.

With regard to the curriculum, Mrs D's thorough and carefully structured weekly learning programme involved three subject areas: mathematics, language and art and craft. This meant that 'subjects such as science are fitted in; they can be part of the writing side of language or be linked to practical maths'. It is plain that within this kind of organisation, important and topical curriculum issues such as children's scientific understanding, or the kinds of learning mediated by play and 'activities', may have to occur without close monitoring by the teacher, or may not even be considered at all.

Case study 5

Mrs E was a 37-year-old teacher with seven years' teaching experience, some of it in secondary schools. She had a class of twenty-four 10- and 11-year-olds in a Phase 2 school.

Classroom organisation

The class was housed in a very large old hall, in which Mrs E had created a Type 2 layout with what she called bays. One of these was fitted with a carpet and was intended for quiet reading, while equipment for mathematics and art was displayed in another. Mrs E explained that these bays were not used as working areas because of the large size of the room;

there had been proper work bays in her previous classroom, but she had been moved from that room because it was structurally unsafe.

The children were organised by mathematical ability, based on the stage they had reached in the school's adopted mathematics scheme. Mrs E said that in previous years the children appeared to have worked through the scheme's workbooks individually, but that this year she had tried to create groups. These groupings were flexible and therefore did not have names. She also had language-ability groupings based on the stages children had reached in the two published language schemes she used. She explained that the rest of her language work was 'integrated into the curriculum,' and that for this the groups were generally of mixed ability, as they were for topic work. She said that she liked to make topic work include language and practical mathematics, and that she tried 'to make it as cross curricular as possible . . . [and to] make it reflect the school's aims of first hand experience'.

She thought mixed-curriculum teaching was less demanding than single-area teaching, and she usually had mathematics, language, and 'activities' under way simultaneously.

Every morning she discussed the day's work programme with her class, and the five tasks involved were also listed on a board so that the children could read them. Her rule was that the two or three high-priority tasks at the top of the list must be done first, and that the rest could then be selected in any order. She acknowledged that meticulous planning was needed to succeed in this kind of organisation, but also stated that the children were not bored; they were well behaved because they were in control of their own learning, and there were no queues. She spoke of other staff in the school, who commented on the good behaviour of her class, but she added, 'They don't seem to connect class-room organisation with the way children behave in it.'

In mathematics and language the published schemes themselves formed the basis of her records of children's work, while for topic work she maintained a checklist of activities completed. She said the whole staff was unhappy about the current school records.

Mrs E believed that the LEA's classroom organisation courses had confirmed all that she was doing, although she singled out only one of their effects for special mention: 'Perhaps after the courses I have felt more justified in having non-intensive activities like painting and drawing.' Her classic Type B response to the LEA's ideas about good practice was that 'whatever the circumstances and age of children, it's possible to make it work if you want to'.

This teacher was one of the very few in the sample who mentioned advisers and advisory teachers as a supportive influence on her practice. She added that her classroom was shown to advisory staff whenever they visited the school.

Management of learning

Mrs E said that her intention was to be 'free-ranging' during the session in which she was observed at work in the classroom, since she had spent her time with two maths groups during the previous session before play. However, she also said that she had organised things so she could concentrate on maths. Some of the children were finishing off a particular section in the published mathematics scheme, and were then moving on to other activities, including topic-related painting and clay work.

During the hour-long session, Mrs E moved around the room quite rapidly from one table to another, and children approached her continuously. Usually from one to three children were beside her waiting for attention. In all she devoted half of the hour to individual children working at their mathematics. Much of this time was spent monitoring or marking, although it still involved some discussion of the task. Just over three-quarters of the mathematics interactions were initiated by pupils, and there was a very small number of extended interactions when particular children had problems. She gave her attention to the group undertaking art activities for nineteen minutes in all, and again most interactions occurred when pupils approached her. She did address this group about the procedures for mixing paint and the appropriate use of brushes, but made no teaching points to other groups.

The children collected equipment and stored completed work without reference to the teacher.

The wider context

When asked about the main influences on her practice, Mrs E mentioned two colleagues: a teacher who 'structured the day round a child's interest' and a newly qualified teacher with whom she had had many useful conversations. She did not specifically mention the PNP co-ordinator, who was working full-time as a class teacher and year-group leader in another part of the school, after a period of support-teaching which staff in the school generally agreed had not worked successfully. Since then, the year group of two large classes had been made into three smaller ones, and the co-ordinator was teaching one of them. Mrs E and the co-ordinator were both described by the head as setting standards and giving a good example to rest of the staff, even though Mrs E's classroom was on a separate site from most of the school.

Mrs E was generally unenthusiastic about school support in relation to either curriculum or record-keeping, and felt that some of her colleagues were tokenistic in their attitudes to change: 'At staff meetings, they say what it's expected to [say] . . . and then go off and do their own thing.' In effect, Mrs E felt obliged to bypass her school's professional culture, and independently seek out LEA material to provide guidance and reaffirmation for her practice, although she did also mention reading a number of books on topic-based approaches to learning.

In the observed lesson, she successfully translated her intention into practice. She monitored the children (or as she – and LEA's advisers – expressed it, 'free-ranged') in a classroom atmosphere of quiet industriousness. As the teacher in the sample of fifty in the Level One and Two studies who was perhaps most attentive to the LEA's views on pedagogy, she offered a clear rationale for her practice, adopting the vocabulary of progressivism in general and the Primary Needs Programme in particular. Yet it was hard to avoid the conclusion that her assertions, when put against observed practice, did not accurately capture the way she worked.[10]

The successful management of her teaching seemed to depend on a number of factors. First, she felt comfortable with the idea of art as a low teacher-investment activity. Second, in spite of what she said about the absence of queues, she effectively encouraged them by relying on children to approach her so that she could identify their learning difficulties. Third, although she explained that 'teaching at group level means I can work through new things with children at their own level, and then leave them to work on their own on reinforcement', her concentration on the mathematics group during the observed session indicated that her extended periods of teaching did not and could not replace the minute-by-minute diagnostic attention that her pupils, like all primary children, often required. Finally, Mrs E's session (and her grouping) was a clear example of how the basics are given overrriding priority, even by teachers who have a genuine commitment to curriculum breadth and balance.

To pinpoint these discrepancies is not to undermine the commitment and talent of Mrs E herself. It rather implies that the official versions of good practice were neither subtle nor precise enough to help her represent – to others and even to herself – what was actually happening in her classroom.

Level Two: interim issues

Changing a teacher's practice

In each of the ten schools in this part of the study the interviews and observation dealt in some detail with the ways in which teachers were influenced to develop or modify their teaching. All the heads in the sample expressed their unwillingness to intervene too forcefully in their teachers' practice. At the same time, most of the PNP co-ordinators felt themselves incapable of affecting colleagues' teaching in the long term, while most of the teachers themselves reported that no adviser had made any direct impact on the way they worked.

This combination of responses in respect of the three main groups with formal responsibility for teacher development – as defined by Leeds LEA at this time – seems to imply a no-go area surrounding classroom practice, and one, moreover, which is tacitly accepted as such by all concerned. It therefore raises the vital but troublesome question: how are teachers effectively helped to accept and implement change in pedagogy?

The general strategy seemed to be one of concentrating not so much on the *substance* as the *context* of teaching. Thus, even the most interventive of heads in the sample attempted to bring about a desired pattern of teaching interactions in classrooms by focusing not on the interactions themselves but on classroom layout and appearance. In this he echoed an underlying assumption of the whole PNP philosophy: namely, that changes in the physical character of the room would of themselves generate changes in organisation, and hence in interaction and eventually the quality of pupil learning.

In general, therefore, the main evidential basis for appraising teachers' practice – whether by heads or advisers – appeared to be visual clues, and these usually in relation to the classroom as a whole rather than specific pupils or events. These can undoubtedly tell knowledgeable and experienced observers a great deal, yet successful teaching depends on communications between teacher and pupil which such an approach may barely hint at. Thus, for example, although it is clear that having groups of children simultaneously undertaking different activities discourages one form of communication – that of whole-class teaching – it does not of itself ensure the quality of the desired alternative – that of interaction with groups and individuals. Nor does the visual evidence of variegated group activities, attractive though they may seem, say much about the quality and effectiveness of the communications in which the success of such arrangements is claimed to reside. Nor, of course, are there firm grounds for supposing that a shift to such an arrangement will of itself transform the teacher's curriculum expertise and pedagogical skills, let alone his or her educational beliefs.

Planning

Of all the aspects of the primary curriculum, mathematics was the one where teachers in the sample found the clearest structure and sense of progression. In this they were obviously aided by school guidelines and commercial schemes, which, before the arrival of the National Curriculum, shaped this area of the curriculum more thoroughly than any other. Such material not only provided much of the content for children's learning but also tended to determine teachers' views of their pupils' levels of progress and dominated the way they allocated time and attention in the classroom. That being so, the quality of the guidelines and schemes used becomes a significant factor in the quality of practice overall, for such material can constrain or distort as well as structure and liberate.

In contrast, these teachers did not always find it easy to describe their own curriculum planning. Written plans were frequently produced for the head, and for the teachers themselves as a sort of visual map or prompt. Translating intentions into a readily communicated set of principles and procedures was less familiar, and this may account for some of the problems experienced by teachers teaching together.[11]

Managing learning

Grouping children was an organisational device as much as a teaching approach, a way of maximising the opportunities for productive teacher–child interactions as well as a means of encouraging flexibility in curriculum and co-operation among the children. It raises important questions, therefore, about two kinds of activities: those allocated to children with whom the teacher expects to spend time, and those given to the others. The latter tends to be a neglected issue. If a child is to receive little teacher attention while on task, what kinds of work can that child be asked and expected to do?

We have noted how frequently art and craft activities were defined and employed as needing little investment of teacher time and attention, once they had been planned and set up, thus inviting the question of whether they require less teacher–child interaction by their nature, or whether they were being made to serve as a device to free teachers to concentrate their attention elsewhere. Art was not the only aspect of the curriculum to feature in this context, and the whole issue of children not under direct or constant teacher supervision generated major differences of opinion among the respondents.

Those teachers who favoured single-curriculum area teaching (and there were several others besides Mrs C) consistently voiced the opinion that their pupils would be at grave risk of underachieving if the activities in the classroom were so varied that the teacher could not monitor them all effectively. In contrast, those teachers who advocated mixed-curriculum teaching saw it as a device for securing greater manoeuvrability and flexibility. They tended to respond to the risk that some children might be underachieving in curriculum activities in which little teacher attention was invested by arguing that working for relatively long periods unsupervised enabled other educational and social goals, like independence, co-operation and free expression, to be achieved.

The multiple dilemma which this analysis exposes can be expressed as follows. The more accessible teachers seek to make themselves to all their pupils as individuals, the less time they have for direct, extended and challenging interaction with any of them; but the more time they give to such extended interaction with some children, the less demanding on them as teachers must be the activities they give to the rest; and the less demanding of their time and attention as teachers, the more the likelihood that the activity in question will demand very little of the child.

Teachers responded to this dilemma in different ways, but almost invariably they resolved it by making the *curriculum* the safety valve for releasing the pressure which the dilemma created. They first established which curriculum areas mattered most and accorded them protected status, and then devised low-demand/low-investment tasks in the curriculum areas they deemed less important. Or, as one teacher honestly and succinctly put it: 'If a child leaves my class and can't paint, that's a pity; if he leaves and can't read, that's a problem.'

This dilemma is compounded by another, equally pressing. The teacher has to decide which children need close attention and which can be left to get on by themselves. In the face of the manifest requirement that the teacher concentrate a great deal of time and thought on certain children in their class, they have to be able to assume that other children are able to make do with less. The most able, the oldest, the best-behaved, girls – they may all, at different times, be seen as the 'undemanding ones' who can be left to their own devices, and the fact that they do just that, without drawing attention to themselves, is taken as evidence that this is both a reasonable expectation and a sensible strategy. However, the price that some of these children may pay for demanding little of the teacher may be that they are given work which demands little of them.

In the end, classroom practice, or educational beliefs in action, should perhaps be judged not only by the actions of the teacher and those children with whom he or she is working, but also by what the teacher believes it is appropriate to give the rest of the class to do.

IMPROVING CLASSROOM PRACTICE

So far, we have discussed material from the first two of the three levels of the PRINDEP study of practice in sixty primary classrooms. The data presented and discussed in the present chapter come from interviews and observations in nearly fifty schools. The common thread is the access which all of them had to a single set of ideas about classroom practice conveyed by representatives of their LEA. We now consider four ways in which this material can be used.

First, it can be read as a record of some of the many variations in classroom practice in this one LEA and can thus serve as discussion material in a variety of professional contexts. So, for example, a comparison of the typical classroom layouts will prompt questions about their purposes, advantages and disadvantages. Or readers can use the general findings about furniture, display, equipment, labelling and so on to focus their own thinking about these and other aspects of the physical organisation of classrooms which make both for smooth running and an attractive learning environment. Or the various approaches to planning – written/unwritten, comprehensive/incremental, yearly/termly/weekly/daily – can each be explored and compared in order to address basic questions about the most appropriate and useful ways to plan for teaching and learning. Or, again, the material can be used to address the matter of grouping: the familiar alternatives of ability, mixed-ability and friendship grouping, and the associated questions concerning the proper nature of activities undertaken in groups and of the balance of whole-class, group and individual teaching. And so on: each aspect of practice discussed here can be opened up in this way.

Second, because all the teachers concerned were in various ways influenced by a particular series of courses conveying the central PNP messages about classroom practice, the foregoing can be read as a commentary on those courses and the ideas they conveyed.[12] For example, readers can consider the implications of the six very different kinds of teacher response to the LEA's suggestions and recommendations, ranging as these did from enthusiastic acceptance to outright rejection, with varying degrees of partial, reluctant or tokenistic adoption in between. They can explore the divergences between the classroom layout commended by the LEA and the arrangements actually encountered, and exemplified here. They can look again at the issue of planning and its relationship to record-keeping, noting and questioning the tendency for the latter to focus more on tasks undertaken than learning achieved (the two are of course not synonymous). They can consider the question of the efficacy of curriculum-specific bays, areas or groups. Are they really the best arrangement? How far may the drawbacks – for both children and teachers – outweigh the gains? These are just a few examples.

Digging deeper, however, we come to the third and fourth uses of this material. The third is to treat it as a springboard for considering not so much the one in-service strategy adopted by the one LEA as the basic conception of teacher development which it illustrates. For such an exercise, the starting points might be the discrepancies between what some teachers said they were doing and what they were actually doing; and the way the LEA's strategy seemed to allow such discrepancies, focusing as it did on material minutiae as much as on deeper principles, so that the former could be implemented while the latter remained untouched – even though teachers could truthfully claim that the LEA had had a powerful impact on their teaching. Or we might look at some of the tensions presented when teachers sought to implement different parts of the 'good practice' package presented to them: the combination of curriculum-specific bays and varied grouping arrangements discussed in the first part of this chapter is a good example, one of several.

This third kind of analysis, therefore, will provoke consideration of fundamentally important questions about the goals and means of improving classroom practice which are at the heart of an initiative like the Primary Needs Programme. What, in short, are the most effective strategies for bringing about change in the ways that teachers work with children? How is the professional development of teachers best conceived? As a generalised set of multi-purpose messages for all teachers or as strategies more sharply focused on individuals within their unique working contexts? As ideas disseminated downwards from the LEA (or central government and its agencies)[13] or generated with and by the teachers themselves? As training or as self-development?

Finally, and in similar vein, we can use the material, and perhaps especially the case studies, to begin to probe beneath the visible surface of practice and to move beyond the cosy platitudes which all too often constitute the main medium through which such practice is discussed. Rhetoric is inevitable in any job as complex and exposed as teaching. It is a necessary device for preserving professional solidarity and morale.[14] Ideals, too, are an essential part of the educational endeavour, for without them teaching becomes aimless and habitual, lapsing before long into time-serving cynicism. But beyond the words, what are the realities?

In this final section we do not propose to say any more in relation to the first two of these four applications of the findings and issues we have presented. The factual material is clear and self-explanatory. The third and fourth applications – strategies for improving classroom practice and alternative ways of looking at the latter – do require further comment, however.

Strategies for improving practice

The Primary Needs Programme was an initiative which sought to facilitate and enhance what is seen as good practice where it exists, and to promote it where it does not, whether that practice concerns teaching and learning, school management or relations between school, home and community. This purpose was reflected in the various complementary strands of the programme (see Appendix 2): policies of positive discrimination in favour of primary schools in general, and of inner-city primary schools in particular, enhanced staffing, a raised advisory profile, increased and refocused INSET, the refurbishment of school buildings, increased capitation and so on. Putting together all these components – the strategies, the messages and their impact – in the context of the present chapter, what can we conclude?

First, and most important, it is clear that what ought to have been an irresistible combination – progressive policies, substantial resources, specially appointed people geared up to making the initiative work – had in the event a somewhat uneven impact on classroom practice. The facts reported here and in several of PRINDEP's other studies speak for themselves. Though overall the picture is one of livelier classrooms and more open and forward-looking professional communities, the extremes on the continuum are a long way apart, with a substantial minority of class teachers and heads apparently affected very little by the ideas central to the LEA's policy.

Second, the present study confirms and strengthens our earlier findings about the formidable influence, both positive and negative, of each school's professional culture in relation to what individual teachers do in their classrooms. On the one hand we find heads, co-ordinators and class teachers working together to promote and consolidate what they believe to be good practice, and generating a climate of excitement and commitment which develops its own momentum and makes each new initiative more likely to succeed. On the other, we have class teachers lacking support from head, co-ordinator or both; co-ordinators confronting inertia, complacency, anxiety or hostility; heads unable or unwilling to generate the climate of openness and collective discussion and commitment upon which progress seems to depend.

Third, this study reinforces and extends our earlier concern with the substance and manner of the messages being conveyed. Their frequent diffuseness and ambiguity make possible a wide range of interpretations and allow teachers and heads to assert, not untruthfully, that they are implementing the LEA's policies and principles. They can do this partly because many of the messages are generalised enough to allow virtually any interpretation – hence the oft-repeated claim 'we do this already'[15] – and partly because the messages combine minute practical detail with very broad general principle. This, as we saw in the present study, allows teachers to change the surface appearance of their practice without altering its substance.

We can now add two more comments on the matter of strategies for promoting change in the classroom.

The need for linkage

The first harks back to the reference above to the 'irresistible combination' which PNP embodied. Taken separately, each element in the strategy –

INSET, advisory support, enhanced staffing, co-ordinators and so on – does indeed have great potential. Too often, however, there is little or no *linkage* between them. Thus, class teachers go on a course about classroom practice of whose contents their heads and/or colleagues may be unaware. Or they may be aware but not geared up to helping the teacher put the course's ideas into operation. In this context the label 'co-ordinator' can sometimes seem almost ironical when the person concerned is unable to liaise regularly either with advisory staff or with colleagues over the policies and principles of classroom practice which he or she should presumably be co-ordinating.

The fragmentation of effort, the lack of linkage between the key agents in the change process, can affect people at all levels. Thus, here, the work-load of many advisory staff made it very difficult for them always to follow through into classrooms, and nurture there, over time, the ideas they had promoted. Some heads felt so overwhelmed by the tide of new developments – first PNP, then the deluge of documents and requirements associated with the Education Reform Act – that they too could do little more than register that someone has been on a course about something to do with classroom practice. Co-ordinators had job-specifications so extensive and diverse that their best intentions could be subverted. And this is to presume that the various parties wished to pull in the same direction if they were able. In fact, of course, the lack of structural linkage could be greatly exacerbated by conflicts of value and belief about both strategy and substance.

At the end of the line, as we have said, is the class teacher. Unless he or she has encountered the messages about practice directly and in person, the chances are that these messages will have been through a series of filters (or gatekeepers) before the class teacher receives them: head, co-ordinator, colleagues, summaries of documents rather than originals, and so on, perhaps slightly but significantly changing their meaning at each stage as in the manner of a children's game – the 'cascade' model at its worst. Usually, indeed, the class teacher is defined as the recipient of ideas about practice; more rarely as a contributor, let alone a generator. Yet the practice in question touches the class teacher much more directly than it touches any of the other people in the chain – it is, after all, the teacher's own. So not only is there sometimes a lack of linkage between formally designated change agents like co-ordinators, advisers and heads, but the class teacher as the most vital link in the chain may be missing altogether in such liaison as does take place.

The inviolability of the classroom

We noted above how in this study the day-to-day and minute-to-minute aspects of a teacher's classroom practice emerged not infrequently as something of a no-go area. For one reason or another, the plethora of messages about good practice from advisers, heads, co-ordinators and others seemed to stop just short of the classroom door. From that point on, many of those concerned might be rather less happy to intervene in what the teacher did even though all would probably endorse the statement at the beginning of this chapter about its critical importance to the child.

Coupled with this reluctance to engage with the detail of a teacher's practice – and indeed a logical consequence of it – was the tendency for judgements about practice to be based on evidence from observation rather than interaction. Similarly, practice was talked about less in terms of operational detail than in terms of broad sentiments and commitments; less in terms of learning processes than in terms of what is called 'the environment of learning': a kind of conceptual skirting round of the very act which is at the heart of education.

Apart from denying class teachers access to vital support in respect of the task of developing and improving their practice, this tendency increased further the isolation and vulnerability that some of them felt. These in turn lead to the erection of defensive shields in the face of scrutiny, advice and new ideas.

The paradox here is that to explore a class teacher's practice is to make him or her vulnerable. But not to do so is to compound that vulnerability, particularly at a time, such as the present, when teachers are under extreme pressure to change the ways they work.

To sum up so far: among the many factors in the success of policies and strategies aimed at improving classroom practice, three seem, in combination, to have a particularly powerful influence. Thus, taking the evidence of this and other PRINDEP studies, change at a more than surface level seems to require:

- messages about the practices commended which are clear and unambiguous not just in their substance but also as to their status – whether as requirement, recommendation, suggestion or option;
- consistency and close linkage between the various change agents having a role in the improvement of practice (advisory staff, head, co-ordinator etc), not excluding class teachers themselves;
- direct engagement by some at least of these change agents in the deeper levels of the day-to-day classroom practice of the teachers concerned.

Conversely, our evidence indicates that change of a token or surface kind, or no change at all, or even practice directly contrary to that sought, are associated with:

- messages whose substance and/or status is vague or ambiguous;

- lack of consistency and linkage between the change agents;
- exclusion of the class teacher from the process of defining good classroom practice;
- avoidance of direct engagement by the change agents in the actual classroom practice of the teachers concerned, other than at the surface level.

Observation and interaction

The references above to 'surface' and 'deeper' levels of practice beg definitions. In one sense, what we mean by these different levels will be readily apparent to anyone familiar with the job of teaching. 'Surface' is just that – what we see and hear on entering somebody else's classroom: the way the room is arranged; the equipment and display; the way children are grouped and the kinds of work they are undertaking; their apparent involvement, interest and enthusiasm; the way they and the teacher relate to each other.

Much can be inferred from such cues, particularly by someone combining professional experience and personal sensitivity, and they will always and necessarily provide an important springboard for those responsible for supporting teacher development or assessing classroom practice. Equally, the visible cues may be reduced to the superficialities of 'display' and 'business' – a distortion of classroom life which accords far higher priority to the judgmental imperatives of the head, adviser, inspector or teacher trainer offering such slick asessments than to the true complexities of teaching and learning.

In this sense, what is meant by the 'deeper' levels of practice will be as readily recognised. They are what are encountered when, after watching and listening, one begins to interact with the participants. Thus, discussion with the teacher will reveal the intentions underlying what has been observed, and will also of course show the extent to which what the teacher does has been properly thought through. Discussion with the children will enable one to begin to judge the kinds of understanding they are gaining from the tasks the teacher has set, and the degree to which those tasks are appropriate to their abilities. It will also enable one to penetrate the strategies many children employ to seek the teacher's attention or, conversely, to look busy and avoid it.

Our evidence suggests that, although observation of teachers at work was common enough, it was less common for the observer to interact with the teacher and the children, despite the fact that such interaction is a necessary part of any attempt to discover and judge the direction and quality of the children's learning. So when we refer to 'direct engagement' with a teacher's practice at the end of the previous section we mean, as a minimum, one-to-one interaction with the children and their teacher.

Moreover, the nature of the job undertaken by heads, advisers and inspectors means that they see but a tiny proportion of the class teacher's practice. Their visits are inevitably short and relatively infrequent. Practice is sampled, and a great deal can hang on the quality and typicality of what at the time of the visit happens to be going on. It is this which provokes among teachers such frustration: 'But she's only seen me teach once.' 'He has never even seen me in action.' 'She came in and looked round then went out without even saying anything.' 'How can they possibly claim such-and-such about my practice on that basis?'

One reality that is quite frequently missing from an outsider's observation, then, is that of teaching over a period of time: the way the various individual sessions observed come together to form a whole which is far more than the sum of its parts. If the function of the outsider's visit to a classroom is merely to gain an impression, then the one-off is sufficient. But if the context is that of professional development, with the aim of enhancing and improving the teacher's practice, then a more extended engagement is called for.

There are many more ways of defining what is going on in primary classrooms and schools. In the remainder of this section we propose to concentrate on three alternative realities, all of them prominent in the PRINDEP data, and all of direct relevance to the central concern of the Leeds initiative with the improvement of classroom practice.

Teaching strategies: for the children or for the teacher?

The question why, as teachers, we employ a particular teaching strategy can always be answered in two ways. One is that it is best for the children, and the other is that it is best for the teacher. Naturally, we presume that the two are related, and that the more comfortable we feel with a particular way of working the more likely it is that we are being effective in helping children to learn.

However, the Level One and Two data remind us that the connection is not an inevitable one, and indeed that it is possible to provide child-centred justifications for almost anything one does.

The most familiar instances of strategies employed to serve the teacher's rather than the child's interests are the 'time-fillers', those activities children are given when the main task is completed 'to keep them quiet until playtime.' However, beyond these is the possibility that more substantial activities may serve, in part at least, a similar function. The data, for instance, provoke questions about the real function of some art, craft and topic work. Is it offered in pursuit of exclusively educational goals or does it serve in addition (or even instead) to create time for the teacher to concentrate his or her attention elsewhere? Do art and craft activities, by their nature, require less teacher–child interaction than mathematics and language, or do they get less teacher–child interaction because they are deemed less important? And is the quite substantial amount of time they are sometimes allocated less a reflection of their value than of their strategic usefulness to the busy teacher of a large class?

In short, is one of the functions of some educational activities to create time and space for the teacher to concentrate on others? If so, how far is this function an appropriate one?

The reality of the broadly based curriculum

Questions about the balance of an activity's strategic and educational functions take us on to the issue of the curriculum as a whole. The 'broadly based curriculum' was a cornerstone of the Primary Needs Programme (and the phrase also appears, though used somewhat differently, in the first chapter of the 1988 Education Reform Act). How far is the principle reflected in practice?

In one of the earlier PRINDEP studies (Alexander *et al.* 1989: chap. 4), we charted systematically five main aspects of the management of curriculum and curriculum development in Leeds primary schools during this period. These were: (1) the ways in which curriculum posts of responsibility were allocated; (2) the main strategies for school-based curriculum development; (3) the range and priorities of curriculum areas under review; (4) schools' use of INSET to support curriculum development; (5) schools' use of the increased provided under PNP. There we showed how the traditional 'basics' of mathematics and language, and especially mathematics, dominated the league tables of posts of responsibility, development initiatives, INSET, resourcing and so on, and how these tendencies were subtly buttressed by staff gender and status to convey messages to both staff and children about what aspects of the curriculum really matter. The study acknowledged that our educational system places different areas of the curriculum in a clear pecking order, and, this being so, that it makes sense to resource fairly generously the areas accorded highest priority.

However, the discrepancies in terms of curriculum management and development were sometimes so marked as to raise the question of whether there might be a minimum level of attention, initiative and resourcing below which one might as well provide nothing as a little. Commenting on the principles of depth, balance, relevance, differentiation, progression and continuity with which curriculum breadth is conventionally linked, we suggested (Alexander *et al.* 1989: 160):

> If a curriculum can meet all the latter criteria it will certainly in the best sense be broad. But equally, a curriculum will have no chance

at all of meeting such criteria unless each of its constituent parts (not just those one or two parts deemed the most important) is supported by an adequate level of curriculum development.

The classroom data of the present study allow us to take this argument further. For the discrepancies in curriculum management in the school seem to be matched by discrepancies in curriculum delivery in the classroom. We stress that the issue is not one of mere time. Different parts of the curriculum are allocated different amounts of time in accordance with both their perceived importance and their nature, and although there may be arguments about the educational priorities such allocations reflect, the principle seems eminently sensible.

The issue, then, concerns not time but treatment. The Level One and Two classroom material raises important questions about the seriousness of professional intentions in respect of certain 'non-basic' curriculum areas; about provision for them on a day-to-day basis in terms of layout and resources; about the extent to which children are being adequately challenged and stimulated in these areas; and about the degree to which their learning is being properly monitored and assessed.

The Level Three data (presented in the next chapter), including as it does the systematic recording of activities and interactions over time, will allow us to pursue further this idea of the reality of curriculum breadth and balance, for, in the final analysis, the version of the curriculum which matters most is not the one prescribed by governments or LEAs, but that experienced by the child.

Practice as inherently problematic

So far, we have outlined two alternative 'realities' which need to be acknowledged and explored by those seeking to understand and improve classroom practice. The first was what might emerge from an attempt honestly to address the question whether some purportedly educational activities may occasionally be undertaken as much for the teacher's benefit as for the children's. The second came from the need to look beyond the rhetoric of the broadly based curriculum to the consequences for children, in terms of the curriculum they actually experience, of particular strategies for curriculum management and delivery. The third such 'reality' is even more fundamental. It concerns how we conceive of and discuss 'practice' itself.

In undertaking this study we believed that to understand classroom practice one must engage with the way teachers think about their work as well as with what they can be seen to do, and that the latter cannot be properly understood without reference to the former. PRINDEP's study of classroom practice at each of the three levels sought to apply this principle.

What emerged was a sense of day-to-day decisions being made in a context of pressures and constraints, some of them intrinsic to the job of teaching, some of them particular to a school, and some of them resulting from LEA policies and expectations. Frequently, these were compounded by the isolation which some teachers felt and/or the barriers to outside influence which they erected.

We explored some of the critical decisions teachers had to make and reconcile: concerning what the children should learn on each occasion, which children should receive the teacher's attention at any one time, and how the classroom and the children should be organised to facilitate each of these. We illustrated the way different teachers responded to these requirements, and the compromises they found themselves having to make as a result.

We also showed how consciousness of others' views of 'good practice' was an additional and sometimes powerful influence on teachers' decision-making. Sometimes these views could be accommodated without difficulty and were helpful and productive, but on other occasions they caused problems. For example, some teachers found that the external messages conflicted with their own views; or with their particular classroom circumstances; or even that different messages seemed to conflict with one another, or at any rate proved quite difficult to reconcile.

One of the most critical of these areas concerned the vital question of how a teacher responsible for teaching the whole curriculum to a large number of children so organises both the curriculum and the children's learning that he or she can give all the children the attention they need. It is a challenge to which no single solution seems wholly satisfactory, and teachers devised various compromises, most of them variations on two linked themes: reducing the level of challenge of activities in lower-status curriculum areas so that children could work for long periods relatively unsupervised and allow the teacher to invest attention in what were seen as the more important activities; and/or defining certain children as 'undemanding' and giving them, too, less attention.

This version of practice, then, is one in which dilemmas and compromises play a prominent part. It contrasts sharply with the versions of practice which many primary teachers are given or feel obliged to claim: the one where a teacher operates, or claims to operate, in accordance with a predetermined set of 'principles of good primary practice' which are rarely defined, let alone argued through and justified; the one expressed in language of such unclouded certainty that few care to express doubts or propose alternatives; the one where there are only two kinds of problem – those which one cannot admit to because they stem from lack of competence, and those which one can admit to because they are somebody else's fault.[16]

Our alternative version of practice reflects rather different assumptions. First, that teaching is a difficult and complex job and therefore the basic condition for professional development must be one in which the open discussion of the difficulties and complexities is encouraged rather than avoided. Such discussion is then seen as a mark of professional maturity rather than of professional weakness.

Second, that while some of the problems teachers daily experience do of course relate to professional expertise and/or the particular circumstances in they work – the children, the school, colleagues, resources, time and so on – others are intrinsic to the job itself. Teaching, then, has at its core the making of decisions which by their nature create dilemmas and require compromises. The fact that these dilemmas exist is a reflection not on the individual teacher, therefore, but on the job itself.

Third, that classroom practice improves by progress being made in parallel on three fronts. First, by sharpening, refining and extending teachers' professional knowledge, understanding and skills. Next, by identifying the dilemmas which lie at the heart of primary teaching, confronting them, analysing why they exist, and considering how best they can be resolved. Finally, by ensuring that the professional knowledge, skills and understanding one aims to develop relate to teaching as it really is, problems, dilemmas and compromises included, rather than to a tidied-up version of the job from which such inconveniences are removed.

CONCLUSION

This chapter has had two main themes: the character of classroom practice in one LEA's primary schools and the LEA's strategies for improving it. The first part (Level One) surveyed the physical arrangements in the classrooms of nearly forty teachers, reported their accounts of how they dealt with day-to-day matters like grouping, curriculum delivery, planning, record-keeping and so on, and recorded their responses to some of the LEA's ideas about how their classrooms and teaching might be organised. The second part (Level Two) presented five of the case studies of a further ten teachers at work, showing how they tackled some of the basic decisions of which teaching is constituted, and identifying some of the critical points at which dilemmas were confronted and compromises were required.The third part explored the use which might be made of this material. One, relatively straightforward, was concerned with the particulars of the data – the variations in organisation and practice as recorded, and the role of the LEA's ideas about good practice. The other was more complex and wide-ranging. It raised fundamental questions not only about the most appropriate strategies for improving classroom practice, but also about the very way in which such practice is defined and discussed. Some of the central points in this latter analysis were as follows.

First, the present study consolidates the findings of previous PRINDEP reports about some of the main factors facilitating or frustrating change in classroom practice in Leeds primary schools during the mid-late 1980s. Second, the study confirms the considerable potential of each of the separate elements and roles in the LEA's reform strategy, but suggests that this potential would be enhanced if there were more effective linkage between them. Third, the class teacher is shown to be very much at the end of a line: receiving messages about practice which he or she has had little or no part in constructing and which may be ambiguous and imprecise; undertaking complex and demanding tasks with which some of those outside the classroom fail to engage except at a relatively superficial level; and therefore sometimes forced into a defensive or rationalising posture in the face of new ideas. Fourth, it is probable, therefore, that both classroom practice and the confidence of the practitioner would gain if these trends could be reversed. Fifth, the modification of strategy alone, however, is not enough. There also needs to be a shift in the way that practice itself is defined and conceived, and in the aspects of classroom life upon which strategies for improving practice focus and operate.

In this context it is worth recalling the present report's suggestion that notwithstanding the undoubted importance of classroom layout and organisation, they are but the framework within which the acts and interactions central to teaching and learning take place, and it is the latter which should brought to the fore in definitions of 'practice' and strategies for improving it. Moreover, this view is supported by earlier PRINDEP data as well as that gathered for the present study. In our seventh report, for example (Alexander *et al.* 1989: 25–86), we argued that insufficient attention appeared to be given to the day-to-day procedures whereby teachers diagnose the learning needs of individual children and assess their progress.

Diagnosis and assessment are skills which are fundamental to teaching, yet – standardised tests apart – are peculiarly difficult to define in a form which provides guidance for effective action. It is not surprising, therefore, that their relative neglect in the professional development of experienced teachers is matched by comparable neglect in initial training. It is now widely recognised that this must change, not least because of the requirements of the National Curriculum.

Finally, the complexity and elusiveness of classroom diagnosis and assessment serve to underline the importance of the main shift argued for in the latter part of this chapter, namely, towards a more open acknowledgement of the problematic in teaching: the everyday decisions which have to be made; the difficulty of reconciling ideals and practice; the dilemmas and compromises; the possibility of conflict between the teacher's and the child's interests in decisions about curriculum content, group activities, and the monitoring of learning; and the inevitably imperfect solutions.

Though vision in education is essential, it needs to be combined with realism, honesty and a preparedness always to ask questions about the impact on children of what one does. Without the latter, ideals and practice will always remain a long way apart.

NOTES

1 For an elaboration of 'comprehensive' and 'incremental' planning, see Calderhead (1984). His typology is also used in this book's second chapter.

2 This aspect of primary pedagogy has acquired considerable prominence in recent years. Our PRINDEP study followed hard on the heels of the findings of Mortimore's team that a 'limited focus within sessions' could be deemed one of the twelve key factors in primary school effectiveness (Mortimore *et al.* 1988), which chimes with the findings of other studies (notably Galton *et al.* 1980a and 1980b and Bennett *et al.* 1984) that the organisational complexity of primary classrooms introduced to reflect principles like 'flexibility' or the 'integrated day' could in some circumstances prove counter-productive in terms of pupil concentration and time on task and on the teacher's capacity properly to diagnose, interact, monitor and assess. Following the DES primary discussion paper's emphasis on this issue (Alexander *et al.* 1992: chap. 6), OFSTED, too, have turned 'a manageable number of teaching groups and learning activities, usually four or fewer', into a principle of effective practice (OFSTED 1993a, 1993b, 1994a).

3 The PNP co-ordinator's role was pivotal. He or she was an experienced teacher charged with the responsibility of encouraging and engineering change in the school along the lines set out in the various LEA policy statements and through the in-service programme. For a detailed discussion of how these teachers were used, the different roles they fulfilled, the successes they achieved and the problems they encountered, and for a general assessment of the Leeds co-ordinator model as a change strategy, see Alexander (1992: 29–32 and 102–8).

4 The power of the head in this and other matters is discussed in the project's final report (Alexander 1992: 112–15).

5 The Leeds Primary Needs Programme was introduced in three phases. The seventy-one Phase One schools deemed (on the basis of reading scores and the proportion of children qualifying for free meals) as demonstrating the greatest educational and social need were given the largest share of the programme's £14 million budget, starting in September 1985. The fifty-six Phase Two and 103 Phase Three schools joined the programme, weighed against the same criteria, in January 1987 and September 1988 respectively. For full details of PNP phasing and expenditure, see Alexander (1992: 3–10). In the five case studies reported here (selected from the ten undertaken

at Level Two of this part of the evaluation project) the first three are from PNP Phase One, the others from Phase Two. Mrs A's school was thus, in comparison with many primary schools in Britain at this time, well resourced.

6 Which belief, of course, runs counter to the research findings at note 2 above. Mrs A was not necessarily wrong: teaching being in such large measure a function of the kind of person a teacher is, classroom methodology cannot be reduced to simple prescriptions like 'No more than four activities simultaneously'.

7 Those brought up in the era of the National Curriculum may need to know that this tripartite arrangement (see also case studies 4 and 5) was very much a legacy of the primary philosophy of the West Riding in the 1960s and early 1970s – a philosophy which had much more than local influence (see Chapter 6) and in the present case acquired prominence in Leeds once many West Riding schools were absorbed into the city following the 1974 local government reorganisation and the diaspora of the old county's most dedicated LEA advisers. Sometimes the third area (as, indeed for the teacher Joyce in Chapter 2) was designated 'choosing'. Either way, it effectively split the curriculum – and the time allocated – three ways between Language, Mathematics and the rest.

8 Perhaps we should point out that Mrs C was hardly unique in believing this. It is one of the hoariest adages in the primary book, and almost certainly goes back to those nineteenth-century elementary schools whose inspectors closely monitored the relationship between concentration, time of day, posture and the availability of fresh air.

9 Which, writ large, was the view of this LEA in 1985 and the British government in 1987.

10 See Chapter 2 for further examples and discussion of this discrepancy.

11 Collaborative teaching was another important part of the LEA's strategy for improving primary schools' performance, and the policy of enhanced staffing made this possible. Because of its perceived importance, PRINDEP undertook an evaluation study specifically of the practices associated with what we (and subsequently the LEA) termed 'teachers teaching together' (TTT) – an acronym chosen to avoid the prescriptive connotations of 'team teaching' and allow for a variety of forms of classroom collaboration, some of them unique to Leeds. The evaluation of TTT is reported in Alexander et al. (1989: 223–38) and in Alexander (1992: 82–5).

12 The first stage of the evaluation of the LEA's classroom organisation courses was reported in Alexander et al. (1989: 91–222). On the LEA's in-service and professional support strategies in general, see Alexander (1992: 119–35).

13 The question is even more pressing now than when this was written, though by neutering the LEAs the government would have us believe otherwise. Since 1988, successive Secretaries of State for Education have taken to themselves unprecedented powers of intervention in the work of schools, many of which they have delegated to unelected and non-accountable quangoes like the School Curriculum and Assessment Authority (SCAA) and the Teacher Training Agency (TTA) as well as to OFSTED. Whatever else can be said about the uses and abuses of LEA power in the light of the PRINDEP studies, LEAs were, and remain, elected bodies.

14 A central theme of this book's second chapter.

15 Again, nothing unique here. This was a widespread claim, nation-wide, in the early days of the National Curriculum. It was even made, proactively, by advisers, inspectors and heads running National Curriculum training

courses but anxious to allay teachers' incipient panic in the face of the deluge of documention, which hit primary teachers much harder than secondary (nine ring binders to the secondary subject specialist's one): 'Don't worry about these statements of attainment – you do all this already.'

16 It is instructive to examine the OFSTED school inspection framework (OFSTED 1994b) with considerations such as these in mind.

Chapter 4

Task, time and talk*

In this study, a sequel to the one described in the previous chapter, we come even closer to the core of primary education – children and teachers at work. The study is grounded in systematic classroom observation, backed by extensive transcript material of teacher–pupil discourse, and uses a mixture of quantitative and qualitative methods to explore how lessons are structured and sequenced, the learning tasks pupils are given, how they respond to them, how teachers and pupils spend their time, and the character of that all-important feature of classroom life, talk. It raises questions not just about the fine detail of what is observed, but also about the versions of good practice which teachers such as these seek to emulate, especially in respect of notions like curriculum balance, groupwork and 'exploratory' learning.

This chapter takes us into Level Three of the PRINDEP study of practice in sixty primary classrooms. The study was undertaken by a team from Leeds University as part of the evaluation of Leeds LEA's Primary Needs Programme and constituted an intensive analysis of children and teachers at work in ten classrooms over a period of two weeks in each case. The study as a whole sought to describe and examine the kinds of classroom practice associated with Leeds LEA's ambitious attempt to reform its primary schools and secure for them appropriate levels of financial and professional support within a policy of positive discrimination in favour of those children and schools demonstrating the greatest social and educational need.

All the teachers in the study had attended the special courses on classroom organisation mounted by the advisory service. These courses (described in detail in Alexander *et al.* 1989: 191–222) delivered messages whose impact we assessed in Chapter 3, though we were clear that a

---

* **This chapter was written jointly by Robin Alexander and John Willcocks.**

simple causal relationship between such in-service activity, however high its profile, and the ways teachers work in the relative privacy of their class-rooms, could never be presumed. Nevertheless, through courses like these, and through LEA policy statements, guidelines, advisory visits and the system of appointment and promotion then obtaining in the LEA, a powerful set of pedagogical norms emerged, a unique variant on the prevailing educational values of the time, and all set within the more complex culture of English primary education which all the studies in this book, in different ways, are attempting to capture and understand.

The three levels of our study represent levels of both methodological penetration and professional action. Methodologically, that is to say, at Level One we undertook a single observational session and an interview with the teacher concerned; at Level Two we observed a session and interviewed the class-teacher both before and after the observed session, combining this with other interview data from the school involving the head, deputy, co-ordinator and other staff; but at Level Three we stayed in each school for two weeks to undertake a sustained programme of interviews and observation, focusing systematically on both teachers and pupils, and using two observers per school and the technology of radio microphones in order to combine schedules and field notes completed on the spot with tape recordings of all the interviews and observed teaching sessions for later transcription and analysis (see Appendix 2 for a more detailed account).

Similarly, in terms of professional action, while at Level One we were chiefly concerned with the direct or indirect influence of the LEA's ideas about good classroom practice, at Level Two we sought to probe the day-to-day decisions teachers had to make and the dilemmas those posed, as a consequence not just of LEA policy but also of more imme-diate imperatives to do with the culture of the school and its particular physical and social circumstances, as all of these were mediated by the unique personality and biography of the teachers themselves. At Level Three we sought to open up some of the finer detail of classroom life, and of pedagogy in particular. Using a combination of quantitative and qualitative analysis, derived respectively from the observation schedules and the lesson transcripts, we examined the following:

In the quantitative analysis:

- the learning tasks teachers set;
- children's behavioural responses to these tasks;
- the organisational settings within which the tasks were undertaken, including matters like adult–pupil ratio and group size;
- the structure and sequence of individual teaching sessions;
- the main kinds of teacher–pupil interaction and the balance of these in different settings;

- the influence of factors like pupil gender and perceived ability;
- time spent on different aspects of the curriculum as defined by the teachers;
- time spent on the constituent generic activities of the curriculum;
- the relationship between curriculum thus defined and pupil task-related behaviour.

In the qualitative analysis:

- the general features of teacher and pupil talk;
- the character and impact of teachers' questions;
- verbal devices for achieving balance between pre-existing pupil skill and learning challenge;
- the teacher's approach to providing motivation and choice;
- the use of praise;
- pupil responses and how teachers handled them;
- dealing with interruptions;
- barriers to communication;
- the sharing and imparting of knowledge.

The schools participated on the understanding that they would not be identified in any published account of the enquiry, and they have all been given pseudonyms. Children and teachers are referred to by letters having no connection with their names. A brief account of the schools and classes follows. In each of them, the classrooms have been allocated to one of four layout types according to the extent to which the available space was broken up into separate work bays. Type 1 classrooms had no work bays at all; type 2 had one (generally a library or reading corner); type 3 had several, and type 4 were entirely given over to separate work bays. These layout types are described in Chapter 3 and illustrated in Figures 3.2–3.5. The phasing of the Primary Needs Programme (PNP), which was an element in the sampling, is described there also.

Applegarth Junior was a Phase One school built in the late 1970s. It served a mining community on the outskirts of the city, and there were 124 children on roll. The PNP staff consisted of one Scale 2 PNP co-ordinator and one Scale 1 teacher. Observation took place in a class of twenty-eight 10- to 11-year-olds in a type 3 classroom where collaborative teaching had been a particular organisational feature since the advent of PNP.

Blakemore Primary was a Phase Two school in the inner city, built in the middle 1970s. It had a high reputation in the area of special educational needs and computerised record-keeping. There were 148 children on roll, and a twenty-six-place nursery. The school's PNP staff consisted of one Scale 2 PNP co-ordinator and one Scale 1 teacher. Observation took place in a class of thirty-eight 5- to 6-year-olds in a type 3 classroom where a team of two nursery nurses and one part-time teacher worked under the leadership of the class-teacher.

Claybourn Infant was a Phase Two school on the outskirts of the city, built in the early 1970s. It had 132 children on roll and a thirty-nine-place nursery. Its PNP staff consisted of one Scale 1 teacher. The school had a reputation for good practice in the areas of creative play and staff collaboration. Observation took place in a reception class of twenty-two children, taught by two teachers who worked with two quite distinct and separate groups in different areas of a type 4 classroom.

Deacondale Primary was a Phase One school built in the middle 1970s and serving a predominantly Afro-Caribbean community in the inner city. There were 261 children on roll and a thirty-nine-place nursery. The school's PNP staff consisted of one Scale 3 co-ordinator for multicultural education, one Scale 2 PNP co-ordinator, four full-time and one part-time Scale 1 teachers, two nursery nurses and three home–school liaison officers. Observation took place in a registration group of thirty-three 5- to 6-year-olds, part of a year group of sixty-six children who for most of the time were divided into five work groups under the supervision of six adults. There were no separate classrooms in this school, but in terms of the layout categories employed here the overall teaching area could most appropriately be allocated to type 4.

Easterbrook Primary was a Phase One school in the inner city, with 229 children on roll and a thirty-nine-place nursery. The buildings dated from the early 1930s, but they had been very extensively refurbished as part of the Primary Needs Programme. The PNP staff consisted of one Scale 3 PNP co-ordinator and four Scale 1 teachers. Observation took place in a class of twenty-four 7- to 8-year-olds in a type 1 classroom where the teacher had expressed a particular commitment to parental involvement. A senior member of staff was undertaking the role of support teacher, dividing the week between this and a parallel class.

Freshwater Primary was a Phase One school in the inner city, with 248 children on roll and a thirty-nine-place nursery. The buildings dated from the late 1960s, but the infant block had been refurbished as part of the Primary Needs Programme. The PNP staff consisted of one Scale 3 PNP co-ordinator, three Scale 1 teachers and one nursery nurse. Observation took place in a class of twenty-two 6- to 7-year-olds in a type 3 classroom. The year group of forty-four children shared two classrooms and three teachers. One teacher was the designated leader of this team, and her role explicitly included the professional development of her two colleagues.

Greystock St George's Church of England Junior and Infant was a Phase Two school built in the late 1960s and situated in an affluent market town close to the city. There were 139 children on roll and a twenty-six-place nursery. The school's PNP staff consisted of one Scale 2 PNP co-ordinator. Observation took place in a class of twenty-one 10- to 11-year-olds in a type 1 classroom. There was an advanced degree of collaboration between the teachers of this and a parallel class, using the help of a support teacher in the area of CDT.

Hartfield Primary was a Phase One school with 127 children on roll and a thirty-nine-place nursery. The building dated from the middle 1920s, but had been refurbished as part of the Primary Needs Programme. The PNP staff consisted of one Scale 2 PNP co-ordinator, and two Scale 1 teachers. Observation took place in a class of twenty-one 8- to 9-year-olds in a type 2 classroom. The class was shared by two teachers who were each with it for half of the time. They divided the curriculum between them and both favoured single curriculum area teaching.

Illingworth Primary was a newly built Phase One school in the inner city, with 268 children on roll and a thirty-nine-place nursery. Its PNP staff consisted of a multicultural co-ordinator and a special educational needs co-ordinator, both on Scale 3, four Scale 1 teachers, two nursery nurses and two home–school liaison officers. The school had a high reputation for its home–school links with the predominantly Asian community in which it was located. Observation took place in a class of thirty-six 7- to 8-year-olds in a type 2 classroom. The two classes in this year group of seventy-four children shared one full-time support teacher.

Jeffcote Primary was a very large Phase One inner-city primary school built in the late 1870s. It had 449 children on roll and a twenty-six-place nursery. Its PNP staff consisted of one Scale 3 PNP co-ordinator, one Scale 3 multi-cultural co-ordinator, one Scale 2 and four Scale 1 teachers, one nursery nurse and two home–school liaison officers. The school served a very mixed community in terms of both social class and ethnic origin. Observation took place in a class of twenty-nine 8- to 9-year-olds in a small and hence crowded type 3 classroom. The teacher was particularly committed to equal opportunities. Because of staff absences no support teacher was available to work in the class during the fortnight in which the observation took place.

Six pupils were selected from each of these ten classes for detailed observation during ten one-hour stints over a period of a fortnight. The identity of the target pupils was unknown to both the pupils and their teachers. During each one-hour stint of observation the target pupils were observed one at a time for ten minutes each. The order in which they were observed was decided in advance and changed for each separate stint of observation. Alongside the pupil observations, a second observer monitored the activity of the teacher (or, if there were several teachers present, of one of them). The target teacher wore a radio microphone so that all her interactions with children during the observation stint could be clearly heard by the observer and also recorded for detailed analysis later.

The actions of the pupils and the target teacher were coded in accordance with specially devised systematic observation schedules, and subsequently subjected to computer analysis. This procedure offers two main advantages over non-systematic observation on its own. Instead of general impressions, it gives precise details of the balance of different kinds of behaviour. In addition, though it is selective in the items the researchers choose to include or exclude, in operation it is relatively impartial: the decision about what will be observed is made in advance, and the observer's attention is not constantly diverted towards events and situations which might in other circumstances prove irresistibly interesting. The resulting account includes the unremarkable and the unexceptional as well as the dramatic incidents of the day, and reflects quite accurately the full range of what has gone on in the classroom.

The drawback of this kind of systematic observation is that in coding and systematising behaviour we necessarily oversimplify it. We may record, for example, that a child is on task, or that a particular interaction of a teacher is disciplinary, but if we do this and nothing more we lose the human detail that enables us – and other people – to visualise, reconstruct and make full sense of the event we are describing. It is for this reason that in the present enquiry the systematic observation of behaviour was supported not only by the tape recordings of teacher–pupil interactions mentioned above, but also by interviews and detailed impressionistic accounts, so that basic facts and figures could be illuminated by more extended descriptions of specific classroom situations.

For clarity in the analyses which follow, some terms have been given a more restricted and precisely defined meaning than they might carry in other contexts. In particular, 'tasks', 'task-related behaviour', 'activities' and 'curriculum designation' are terms which are clearly differentiated and not used interchangeably. As each of them is introduced into the text, its use will be explained and illustrated.

The structure of the chapter is as follows. In the first part we present the outcomes of a computerised analysis of the systematic observation data, supplemented where appropriate from the interview material. In the second part we provide a qualitative analysis of some of the main characteristics of teacher–pupil interaction, based on the many hours of tape recordings and transcripts from each classroom, again supplemented from the interviews. Finally, we summarise the main findings of the previous sections and identify major issues and implications.

TASK-RELATED BEHAVIOUR

Tasks

In all ten classrooms the day was structured by a series of very specific exercises or pieces of work set by the class-teacher, as in these examples from the field notes:

> The children worked in pairs. One drew a picture and then described it over a telephone to the other, who attempted to reproduce it from the description. . . .

The teacher demonstrated halves and quarters by folding paper and also by cutting potatoes into pieces. The pupils had to demonstrate their understanding of the concept of halves and quarters by choosing and naming pieces of potato. They then attempted exercises from a work card which involved drawing and colouring squares to show halves and quarters. . . .

The children described to the teacher a tie-and-dye activity which they had previously done with another teacher. Afterwards they were required to give a written account of this.

In this account such pieces of work are termed 'tasks', and a major purpose of the analysis was to examine the ways in which pupils related to them: how hard they worked, how much time they spent doing other things, and so on.

Behaviour

However well-organised a class may be, there are times when pupils are not getting on with the work which has been set. This does not necessarily mean that they are chattering or daydreaming; individual pupils might, for example, be sharpening a pencil, or hunting for a missing piece of apparatus, or tidying up after completing a messy piece of work. Alternatively, they might be waiting for the teacher's attention, either standing in a queue or sitting in their places with their hands up. In the present study, all these possibilities were treated as different kinds of task-related behaviour and allocated to five categories as follows:

- *Working.* If a pupil was carrying out the task which had been set, even if it was undemanding and not very clearly related to any particular area of the curriculum, that pupil's behaviour was coded as WORKING.

- *Routine.* If the pupil was not carrying out the set task but was performing some necessary ancillary activity (such as sharpening a pencil or fetching a pair of scissors), the behaviour was coded as ROUTINE.

- *Awaiting attention.* If the pupil was waiting for help or feedback from a teacher or other adult, the behaviour was coded as AWAITING ATTENTION.

- *Distracted.* If the pupil was doing anything else, the implication was that he or she was distracted from the task in hand, and the behaviour was coded as DISTRACTED.

- *Not observed*. On the few occasions when a target pupil moved out of the observer's range of vision (behind other children for example) the behaviour was coded as NOT OBSERVED.

It should be noted that routine activities could also be tasks in their own right. If, for example, the task was to mix paint in preparation for a painting session later, then a child who was mixing paint would be WORKING. If, however, the task was to paint a picture of a hedgerow in autumn, then a child who was mixing paint would be carrying out a ROUTINE activity.

During the period of the study, the pupils spent, on average:

- 59 per cent of their time working on the tasks which had been set,
- 11 per cent on task-related routine activities,
- 8 per cent waiting for attention,
- 21 per cent of their time distracted from their tasks.[1]

A decade earlier, in the ORACLE project, Galton *et al.* (1980a) made a systematic study of a wide range of primary classrooms in several local authorities, and found a similar balance of task-related activites (although a complete item-by-item comparison is not possible because of differences between the ORACLE and PRINDEP observation schedules). However, it is worth noting that the pupils in the ORACLE sample were spending 58.1 per cent of their time 'co-operating on task' and 11.9 per cent 'co-operating on routine', proportions which are remarkably close to those in the WORKING and ROUTINE categories of the present study; but that the proportion of time spent 'waiting for teacher' by the ORACLE pupils was, at 4.3 per cent, only about half as much as that spent by pupils in the PRINDEP sample. It seems likely that the generally complex organisation of the Leeds classes played a part in this apparent increase, although it must be stressed that the two sets of figures come from studies in which there are extreme differences of sampling, scope and methodology, and that while it is interesting to observe general similarities in the findings it would be unsafe to read too much into the detailed differences between them.

It should also be noted that the figures quoted above refer only to the average incidence of the different kinds of task-related behaviour among all the pupils in relation to all their tasks. Although averages of this kind are informative, they mask the variation between the responses of different groups of pupils to individual situations.

Children's task-related behaviour is influenced by a variety of factors, some of them unique to particular circumstances and individuals, others common to a wide range of situations. Four kinds of factor are especially influential: the settings and organisational structures in which the children are taught; the kinds of interaction which take place between the children and their teachers; the children themselves; and the various tasks they are asked to perform.

FACTORS AFFECTING TASK-RELATED BEHAVIOUR

1 Settings and structures

Some of the variation in children's task-related behaviour arises from basic differences in the ways in which they are organised and supervised by their teachers. Schools differ greatly in the number of children per class and the number of teachers and other adults who are available to help them. This variation in the ratio of pupils to teachers means that the children in a particular class may have only one adult to turn to, or a choice of three or four, while the adults may each find themselves in charge of few children or many. Partly as a consequence of this, the children may be set to work individually or in groups or as part of a whole-class lesson.

Teacher–pupil ratios

In large-scale surveys, teacher–pupil ratios are often used and are easily calculated: the total number of children in a school or LEA is divided by the total number of teachers on the payroll, part-timers counting as fractions of a teacher. For a minute-by-minute study of events in a small number of individual classrooms, however, such an approach can lead to problems of three quite different kinds.

First, the special characteristics of a particular teacher or class of children can exert an influence which is strong enough to outweigh a favourable or unfavourable teacher–pupil ratio. A teacher on her own with a very large class may manage to select tasks and devise strategies which keep her pupils busily involved in their work for a very high proportion of the time. A different class teacher with fewer pupils and several support teachers may find herself embroiled in some of the conflicts about status, role, purpose, organisation or collaborative style which can beset teachers teaching together and which we have discussed at length in an earlier study (Alexander *et al.* 1989: chap. 7). If this happens, the result may be confusion and distraction in spite of a very favourable teacher–pupil ratio. In a large-scale study such anomalous teachers may be expected to cancel one another out; the picture which emerges may not be true of this or that particular classroom but it has a general validity and relates to trends rather than individual cases. In a small-scale study, however, anomalous teachers simply lead to anomalous results.

Second, the presence of nursery nurses, home–school liaison officers, parent helpers and so on (whose function, strictly speaking, is not to teach, but whose activities are sometimes indistinguishable from those of teachers) makes it difficult to decide who should be included and who left out of a teacher–pupil ratio if it is to give a reasonable reflection of the extent of children's access to help and support with their learning tasks. There may be no very satisfactory solution to this second problem but it can be at least acknowledged by the calculation of adult–pupil rather than teacher–pupil ratios.

The third difficulty relates to fluctuating numbers. The adult–pupil ratio of a class is calculated from two specific numerical values, yet the number of pupils varies, not only from day to day through absence from school, but also from hour to hour and minute to minute as children start and finish other activities elsewhere in the building. The same is true of the adults, some of whom in any case may have only a part-time involvement with the pupils which does not necessarily coincide with observation sessions; while others may have no formal responsibility for the class at all, but may nevertherless be waylaid and momentarily drawn into its activities as they pass through its territory.

The detailed monitoring of these constant fluctuations and of any systematic differences between the behaviour of participants of differing status would be possible in principle but would demand a separate study with greater resources than were available to the present enquiry. However, since the alternative was to bypass adult–pupil ratios altogether, a basic analysis has been undertaken in spite of the problems outlined here. The formula for adult–pupil ratios has been computed on the basis of the total number of children on roll in each class (irrespective of temporary absences) and the number of adults most usually observed working with them (irrespective of fluctuations from day to day, and of the official status of the involvement). It will be appreciated that such an analysis can give only a very broad picture of the constantly changing situation in these ten classrooms.

Table 4.1 lists the classes in order of adult–pupil ratio and summarises the task-related behaviour of the children. Each class is labelled with the initial letter of its school's pseudonym: class A is from Applegarth Junior, class B from Blakemore Primary and so on. The table reveals wide differences in the balance of task-related behaviour from class to class: the proportion of time spent working varied from 52 to 70 per cent, and the time awaiting attention from 3 to 15 per cent. In some schools children were distracted for twice as much of the time as in others. However, the table offers no evidence of a systematic relationship between task-related behaviour and formal adult–pupil ratio even though the smallest number of pupils per adult was only nine and the largest was more than three times as great. It is clear that the differences which exist cannot

Table 4.1   Percentage of time spent on task-related behaviour in ten classes
with different adult–pupil ratios

Class	Minutes observed	A–P ratio	Working	Routine	Awaiting attention	Distracted	Not observed
A	604	1:9	59	16	4	19	2
B	528	1:10	70	9	7	14	<1
C	590	1:11	52	13	12	24	0
D	453	1:11	52	8	15	26	0
E	598	1:12	67	12	7	13	1
F	510	1:15	60	9	6	26	0
G	301	1:16	63	10	6	20	1
H	510	1:21	61	10	8	20	1
I	547	1:25	55	11	9	24	1
J	527	1:29	54	15	3	28	0
All	5,168	1:14	59	11	8	21	1

be explained in terms of adult–pupil ratio alone, but that they arise at least in part from the individuality of the teachers and pupils concerned and the organisational structures within which they worked.

For example, the highest proportion of working time was found in Blakemore Primary School, in a class where the adult–pupil ratio was certainly favourable although not markedly different from the ratio in two other classes where the proportion of time spent working was very low. The outstanding feature of the class at Blakemore was a combination of meticulous planning and genuine teamwork which owed a great deal to the exceptional managerial and organisational skills of the class-teacher. This teacher held regular detailed planning meetings with her support team, whose members were actively encouraged to contribute ideas, and whose contributions were often accepted, developed through discussion into detailed schemes of work, and implemented as soon as the necessary preparations had been made. The importance of this kind of discussion seems self-evident in principle, but in any case, as we noted in an earlier study (Alexander *et al.* 1989: 235), the experience of teachers attempting to teach successfully together in the Primary Needs Programme

> has clearly demonstrated that agreement . . . about curriculum content and teaching methods cannot be assumed or taken for granted. . . . Ultimately the sharing of ideas can only be meaningful and productive where there is an underlying consensus. In other words, TTT can operate, somehow, with limited resources and cramped conditions, but without unity of purpose and consistency of practice between the participants its benefits are likely to be limited.

At Blakemore, the quest for this kind of underlying consensus clearly led to high team morale, which in turn meant that ideas tended to be successfully carried through into action. The class-teacher kept a large book in which were listed the tasks to be performed by each child in the class, so that as soon as one piece of work had been completed its author could be given another without delay. Because of the very tight scheduling operated by the teaching team, slow workers in a particular work bay might have delayed or obstructed new groups wanting to take over the space to begin their own tasks, but this potential difficulty had been removed by the institution of a spacious 'finishing-off' table to which children could move if they were holding up the flow of events.

At Deacondale Primary School the organisation was very different. The formal adult–pupil ratio of the observed class was almost the same as that of the class at Blakemore, but the children spent far more of their time either distracted or waiting for attention, and were joint bottom of the league table for time spent working. It cannot be claimed that the physical circumstances at Deacondale were the sole cause of this situation, but they must have aggravated it. Large open spaces without partitions, screens or tall items of furniture, and a consequent lack of acoustically absorbent surfaces, caused or encouraged major visual and auditory distraction. The organisation of the year group into two register groups and five work groups simultaneously, may have added to the problem. In the pursuit of their tasks children often roamed all over the work space and soon lost touch with their supervising adults. If they needed help they tended to turn to the nearest adult, who did not necessarily know much about the task in hand, or to join in some other task which had just attracted their attention and which seemed more appealing than their own. Interestingly enough, the superimposition of a larger number of working groups upon a smaller number of register groups was also a feature of the organisational structure at Freshwater Primary School where, in spite of very tightly structured tasks, the proportion of distracted time was as high as at Deacondale, even though the Freshwater pupils spent a greater proportion of their time working and a smaller proportion waiting for attention.

The rate of distraction at Deacondale and Freshwater was exceeded only at Jeffcote Primary School, where the organisational structure was again very different. Here the adult–pupil ratio was the least favourable of all the ten classes observed. Each day the teacher was expecting to be joined by support staff, and planned her work accordingly; and each day she learned at the last minute that because of staff absence elsewhere in the school, or some other factor beyond her control, she would have to work on her own. The children's tasks were tightly planned and the classroom was buzzing with activity, but because of the wide range of simultaneous tasks, there was simply too much for one teacher to supervise properly. When they encountered difficulties the children spent very little time waiting for attention, presumably because they knew they would be in for a very long wait; instead they turned to other activities which were by no means always frivolous and some of which would have been quite acceptable to the teacher if she had known about them. However, in terms of the observation schedule, they were not the tasks which had been set and hence they constituted distraction.

The children in this class were extremely self-reliant and undertook many routine activities on their own initiative. This was in sharp contrast to the situation in Class D at Deacondale where the children were younger, and where there was a lower incidence of routine activity than anywhere else: the tendency there was for the adults rather than the children to put out the equipment at the beginning of a task, and for children not to clear up or put things away when they had finished. Routine activities then became tasks in their own right for adults or other children to carry out later.

The powerful influence of individual organisational structures is apparent in these examples, and it will be important to bear this in mind as we turn to an examination of the overall impact of the extra staffing which was such a prominent feature of the Leeds Primary Needs Programme.

Access to adults

Table 4.2 summarises a minute-by-minute analysis of the number of adults to whom the target children had access. This analysis is free from the problems involved in the use of global adult–pupil ratios since it takes account of the fact that pupils' access to the adults in the classroom did not remain constant but depended on the varying location and activities of both pupils and adults.

The picture which emerges from this analysis is much clearer than that from the analysis of adult–pupil ratios. Irrespective of the number

Table 4.2 Percentage of time spent on task-related behaviour by pupils having access to different numbers of adults

	Minutes observed	Working	Routine	Awaiting attention	Distracted	Not observed
No adults	40	50	3	3	45	0
One adult	4,651	59	12	8	22	<1
Two adults	203	67	6	9	15	2
3 or more adults	243	61	12	8	19	0
Average	5,137	59	11	8	21	1

of teachers and helpers in the room, for about 90 per cent of the time (4,651 minutes out of 5,137) the pupils in this enquiry had access to a single adult; that is to say, only one adult was supervising their task or group. Even when pupils were temporarily without supervision of any kind, they spent half of their time working at their tasks. With one adult to turn to, they worked for considerably more of the time, and with access to two adults there was a further sharp increase. However, when they had the choice of three or more adults the amount of time they spent working dropped back almost to the level of the children who were supervised by only one adult, and this raises the possibility that beyond a certain point the availability of more and more adults for consultation does not in itself lead children to spend more of their time working.

Supervision by one adult produced the same proportion of routine behaviour as supervision by three or more adults. However, when they were supervised by two adults, children spent only half as much time on routine behaviour, largely because their actions were more closely monitored: it was not so much that fewer pencils were sharpened but rather that less time was spent in sharpening them. When children had access to no adults at all the amount of routine behaviour was very small; in this situation such activities as pencil-sharpening quickly turned into lengthy bouts of conversational distraction.

The overall pattern in relation to distraction from work also suggests that there may come a point where access to more and more adults either makes no difference or even begins to be counterproductive: unsupervised children were distracted for 45 per cent of the time; access to one adult reduced the amount by half, and access to a second adult brought about a further reduction. Beyond that point, however, there was a slight increase in the amount of pupil distraction, and this was largely because, with more and more adults in the room, pupils were surrounded by more and more distracting tasks and activities.

It might have been expected that the availability of additional adults would greatly reduce the amount of time spent waiting for attention, but this was not the case. Children who were set to work without supervision at all tended not to wait for attention: the figures suggest that they became distracted instead. They also seem to indicate that so long as at least one adult was available, the number of adults made no difference to the amount of time spent waiting for attention: one adult managed as well as two, three or more.

Group size

The sizes of the groups in which the children worked also appears to have exerted an influence on the pattern of their task-related behaviour,

Table 4.3   Percentage of time spent on task-related behaviour in working groups of different sizes

Group size	Minutes observed	Working	Routine	Awaiting attention	Distracted	Not observed
1 to 3	1,161	62	12	6	20	<1
4 to 5	1,045	60	11	6	23	<1
6 to 20	1,523	55	12	8	24	1
21+	1,265	62	10	10	17	1
All	4,994	59	11	8	21	1

and Table 4.3 summarises all the observation data from sessions where the group size was known and recorded. The data have been grouped to produce four categories derived from as nearly as possible equal amounts of observation.

As the size of the working groups increased from one to twenty, children spent slightly less time working and slightly more time distracted or awaiting attention. In groups of more than twenty children, however, the picture was different. As much time was spent working as in the very smallest groups; there was comparatively little distraction, but children spent unusually large amounts of time waiting for attention. The explanation for this finding is quite straightforward: groups of more than twenty were whole classes, and when they were engaged in whole-class teaching the teachers adopted a different style from that used with groups.

The structure of teaching sessions

A final aspect of organisational structure, and a very powerful one in terms of its impact on task-related behaviour, was the range of ways in which individual teaching sessions were planned and carried out. To illustrate something of this range, the structure of one observed session from each school is summarised here. Except in a very broad sense it cannot be claimed that the individual sessions selected for this treatment were typical of the teachers who conducted them, since some of the teachers varied their organisational strategies in different sessions. The sole aim in making the selection has been to convey as many as possible of both the similarities and differences between sessions in the sample as a whole. The letter or letters in parentheses at the end of each section of each session indicate that the teacher's main inter-actions during that section were with the whole class (C), a group (G), several groups (GG), an individual child (I) or a sequence of individual children (II).

Applegarth Junior (session beginning at 10.51 a.m.)

3 minutes: teacher settles the class down after playtime (C)
7 minutes: introduces the task (C)
19 minutes: listens with the children to a story on tape (G)
12 minutes: discusses story so far (G)
6 minutes: listens with the children to next part of story (G)
4 minutes: discusses story (G)
3 minutes: listens with the children to next part of story (G)
2 minutes: discusses story (G)
4 minutes: plays the rest of the story but talks to the group and to individuals returning from other groups at the same time (G+II)
1 minute: comments on story; describes next task; sends children off for their dinner (G+II)

Blakemore Primary (session beginning at 10.50 a.m.)

2 minutes: teacher settles the class down after playtime (C)
2 minutes: allocates tasks (C)
2 minutes: works with language group (G)
1 minute: gives a task to an unsupervised number group and asks the nursery nurse who should be with them how long she will be (G)
16 minutes: returns to work with language group (G)
2 minutes: monitors jigsaw group (G)
1 minute: gives new task to computer group whose supervising nursery nurse has given them a task which is too difficult (G)
5 minutes: works with writing group whose teacher has been called away (G)
5 minutes: supervises change over of free-choice activities and then monitors maths group and two language groups (GG)
3 minutes: supervises tidying up (GG)
3 minutes: children sit and sing in the book corner (C)
9 minutes: teacher tells a story (C)
5 minutes: informal activities (e.g. clapping a rhythm) (C)

Claybourn Infant (session beginning at 10.59 a.m.)

1 minute: teacher allocates tasks (C)
5 minutes: monitors a child's maths; small-talk with the same child; fleetingly monitors some children's work in language (II)
3 minutes: school nurse arrives; teacher sorts out which children will see her (C)
37 minutes: teacher monitors the work of various individuals and groups, allocates new tasks, engages in small-talk, sorts out complaints, etc. (II+GG)
7 minutes: supervises tidying up (GG)
2 minutes: children sit on the carpet, waiting for dinner (C)

Deacondale Primary (session beginning at 11.15 a.m.)

14 minutes: teacher allocates tasks (C)
12 minutes: works with language group: tells story and then writes a scrambled sentence for the children to unscramble (G)

12 minutes: enters into long public conversation with unexpected visitors (a former classroom helper accompanied by her cousins from overseas) (teacher interacts mainly with the visitors, but in a way which is intended to involve the group)

 7 minutes: resumes work with language group, although the tasks are now different. Children begin to arrive back from other groups. Teacher monitors the work of the language group and also talks to the children arriving back (G+II)

 2 minutes: monitors tidying up (G)

 4 minutes: settles children on carpet (C)

 7 minutes: reads a story until dinner time (C)

Easterbrook Primary (session beginning at 10.52 a.m.)

 4 minutes: teacher settles the class down after playtime (C)

10 minutes: works with language group (G)

46 minutes: monitors the work of all groups (GG+II)

Freshwater Primary (session beginning at 9.16 a.m.)

51 minutes: teacher works with maths group, briefly dealing with a number of interruptions by children from other groups and quickly returning to the task in hand (G+II)

 3 minutes: works with a child doing a jigsaw (I)

 4 minutes: talks with a child about his absence (I)

 2 minutes: monitors work of a group using building blocks (G)

 4 minutes: supervises tidying up (GG)

Greystock St George's Junior and Infant (session beginning at 9.00 a.m.)

 3 minutes: register and other administrative matters (C)

 3 minutes: teacher previews future baking task (C)

 4 minutes: allocates tasks (C+GG)

 1 minute: small talk (I)

13 minutes: hears children read and discusses what they are reading, for part of the time simultaneously opening money envelopes and counting contents (II)

 5 minutes: sets up and works with maths group (G)

12 minutes: works with language group, discussing pictures and setting a writing task (G)

17 minutes: monitors the work of all groups and deals with individuals seeking help (GG+II)

Hartfield Primary (session beginning at 9.34 a.m.)

11 minutes: teacher allocates and explains two different science tasks (C)

23 minutes: works with first group (G)

 2 minutes: monitors work of second group (G)

 2 minutes: monitors work of first group (G)

 6 minutes: monitors work of second group (G)

 8 minutes: monitors work of first group (G)

 3 minutes: monitors work of second group (G)

 5 minutes: monitors work of first group (G)

Illingworth Primary (session beginning at 1.06 p.m.)

8 minutes: teacher takes register and then describes and allocates tasks (C)

14 minutes: monitors the work of all groups and deals with individuals who seek his help (GG+II)

7 minutes: works with language group (G)

8 minutes: works with science group (G)

2 minutes: monitors work of language and maths groups (GG+II)

7 minutes: gives new task to maths group (G)

11 minutes: works with science group and deals with individuals seeking help (GG+II)

Jeffcote Primary (session beginning at 11.02 a.m.)

3 minutes: teacher talks with class about a Victorian penny brought in by a child, and about penny-farthing bicycles (C)

7 minutes: sorts out group choices for the afternoon session (C)

11 minutes: allocates tasks for current session

11 minutes: works with, and then monitors work of, maths group (G)

16 minutes: monitors the work of all groups and deals with individuals seeking help (GG+II)

7 minutes: supervises tidying up (C)

In these ten specimen sessions one particular style of organisation predominates, although within it there are wide variations of practice. In the main the teachers settled the children down, explained the task or tasks, allocated children to groups, worked with one or more of the groups and then, if the work was not to run on into the next session, supervised a brief tidying up operation. Those who finished early generally led the children in a gentle and undemanding whole-class task as a time filler until the end of the session.

Nobody gave a class lesson, even though one teacher came close to it: Ms A, at Applegarth, who had two support staff, organised a single task for the whole class and then split the class into three groups which went to separate places to carry out the same task: the children were to listen to a tape-recorded story and then discuss it with their teacher. In her interview with the PRINDEP observer Ms A explained that she had chosen this particular task 'to balance the curriculum': the children had had a good deal of practice at expressing themselves in speech, but very little at listening attentively to others.

In every other teaching session, different tasks were tackled simultaneously, even where this presented the teacher with severe organisational problems. For example, Ms H at Hartfield, working on her own with twenty children, had set up two parallel tasks in science: the members of one group were to finish picture strips for use in a zoetrope, while the other group was about to embark on some work with light-sensitive paper, making images by placing various objects upon it. Both tasks needed lengthy initial explanations, which were given to the whole class even though each explanation was relevant to only half of it. Thus at this stage in the session all the children found themselves spending several minutes listening to instructions which they were not to follow. Once the activities were under way, misunderstandings came to light and were dealt with by the teacher, as in the following extract from the observation transcripts.

EXTRACT 1

Note: For ease of reference, each contribution to the conversation in this and all subsequent extracts is numbered: for example, 1:3 signifies the third utterance in Extract 1.

[1:1] *Child:*   Can they be the same colour?
[1:2] *Ms H:*   Can what be the same colour?
[1:3] *Child:*   The men.
[1:4] *Ms H:*   Do you mean can the men be all coloured in the same colour, or can each of the pictures be the same?
[1:5] *Child:*   Can each of the pictures be the same.
[1:6] *Ms H:*   Each of the pictures has *got* to be the same. I keep saying that. Come and look over here . . . Each of these pictures is identical except for that arm that's moving. They are coloured in the same, the same number of pockets, the same number of buttons, feet are in the same position, the stick's at the same angle. You see it's quite difficult, Tina, it's quite complicated. . . .

The task was certainly difficult for this child, who had missed the point completely after nearly three-quarters of an hour of the current session and the whole of an earlier one. If Ms H had given herself only one complicated task to explain and supervise she might have had a greater chance of success. This particular possibility had occurred to Ms J at Jeffcote, who said in her interview that she was finding whole-class teaching a useful technique on occasions and was making increasing use of it, not for whole sessions but for parts of them:

[It] varies. I do have some days when I sit quite a long time with one group in which case I try to position myself physically so I can see the rest of the room. I find myself doing more whole-class input . . . than I used to because if you go over the same ground with each group each time they come to it, it seems like a waste of teacher input. Even though that does mean there are perhaps four or five who don't pick it up, but I hope to mop them up when they're actually doing the activity. I'm still experimenting with that, quite honestly.

Ms H, however, expressed herself satisfied with the way her double-activity science session had gone:

> I thought it worked well. It was done deliberately because I knew that [the work with the photographic paper] would be very time-consuming for me. ... When I started [the zoetrope exercise] on Tuesday I knew they'd have something they could be getting on with. I think you've got to do that or you spend so much time telling everybody what to do you never get anything done. ...

Here Ms H highlighted one of the major differences between the ten sessions. The amount of time spent settling children, introducing and allocating tasks and tidying up afterwards varied greatly, from only four minutes in Easterbrook and Freshwater to twenty-five (out of fifty-five) at Jeffcote. This finding is consistent with research evidence from other studies (Bennett 1978 and 1982) that one of the most important determinants of pupils' achievement in any topic is simply the amount of time they spend actively engaged in it; and in a class where almost half of the time is spent on organisational matters, the time left over for active engagement in learning tasks is dramatically curtailed.

There are several explanations for the differences between sessions in this respect. Some sessions begin where previous ones have ended and need no setting up at all. Some tasks are more complex than others and need more introductory explanation. Children of different ages demand different kinds and degrees of support and supervision. A teacher may be concerned with only one group while support staff deal with the rest, or she may (like Ms J at Jeffcote) be working on her own with a large class split into several groups all tackling different activities. Beyond that, teachers, like other people, vary in their ability to explain things succinctly, as well as in their willingness to plan in advance, a topic considered in the previous chapter.

Some of these differences are illustrated in the following sequence of five extracts from observation transcripts. In each of them the teacher is allocating work. Class teachers are indicated by the letters A to J (corresponding with the initial letters of the schools from which they came), children by the letters K to W (and then if necessary KK, LL and so on), and support staff by X, Y and Z.

EXTRACT 2

[2:1] *Ms A*: Right, shall we go straight into groups, and then we can talk about it when we've got started. [*She gets off her desk and looks around to think of groupings.*]

[*To Ms X*] Shall we just do them by tables?

[2:2] *Ms X*: It's up to you.

[2:3] *Ms A*: That's the easiest isn't it?

[2:4] *Ms X*: There'll be about ten in each group won't there?

[2:5] *Ms A*: Yes. If Ms Y has that table, plus K, L and M, right? With Ms Y. And I will have N, O, P, Q, R, S and you and you. And you'll be with Ms X.

[2:6] *Ms X*: And I shall be in the music room. [*To Ms Y, quietly:*] Everything will be all mixed up.

Ms A had told the observer on an earlier occasion that there were no permanent groups in her class; they were set up afresh as the need arose. It therefore came as no surprise that she had not thought in advance about how she would allocate her pupils to groups on this occasion. Because she was purposeful and gave pupils no choice in the matter (2:5), the whole procedure was over in a few seconds. The remainder of the *sotto voce* conversation between the two support teachers (2:6) was not picked up by Ms A's radio microphone and thus cannot be quoted verbatim, but the observer noted that they were complaining to each other about Ms A's unilateral breaking of traditional groupings. Their exchange illustrates one of the hazards of collaborative teaching discussed in one of the project's other studies (Alexander *et al.* 1989: chap. 7).

EXTRACT 3

[3:1] *Ms B*: OK, if you were with Ms X before playtime, would you go back please. And because only K and L out of your group are here today, would you go with Ms Y. And on the other table it's M, N, O – no, no! – and P . . .

[3:2] *Pupil*: Please Ms B, can I choose . . .?

[3:3] *Ms B*: No, I'm telling you where you are going today because we had a few silly people this morning throwing sand. So whoever it was, we know who it was. We're having no more of that. OK, so I want five people in the [Wendy] house. Put your hand up if you would like to play in the house. One, two, three, four, five – off you go. Just a minute, K, be careful. Three people can play in the sand. Put your hand up if you would like to play in the sand. Q, R and S.

Four people with the water: T, U, V and W.

K, you stay here . . .

Ms B had all her groupings worked out in advance, and knew exactly how she wanted to regroup her pupils after playtime. She changed her original plan for the session in two ways: because of the absence of several children she amalgamated two groups (3:1); and she supervised the selection of activities by the 'choosing' group in response to some unruly behaviour before playtime when the equivalent group had had a completely free hand in the matter (3:3). Some choice still remained to the children in that they could bid for the activities they wanted; but there was no dialogue in the allocation procedure, and hence no discussion or argument. Both of Ms B's changes of plan were incorporated very smoothly into her instructions, so that the groups were formed and the work started with the minimum of delay.

EXTRACT 4

[4:1] *Ms C*:   Now; do you remember? We looked at K's lovely shells in her bucket this morning. K, go and find out who else have got their buckets up there. They look absolutely super. Now, is yours up? Well you go and point to yours, L, because it looks very smart; and you go and point to yours, M.

[4:2] *Pupil*:   M hasn't done one yet.

[4:3] *Ms C*:   M, just listen; then you'll know. Right! Come back! Thank you. Don't they look lovely? Now, N, you have nearly finished, but you haven't written your sentence so I would like you to come first please. Now, what's N got to do? Please look this way, O, because I can't stay at this table all afternoon, and you are going to have to listen now. All right. When you have cut your shells out and you have stuck them on to the white bucket, you have then got to write your sentence. Now, I have helped you today because I can't stay here all afternoon; I need to be all round the room helping everybody. I have put a Breakthrough sentence here with some of you this morning. OK? So will you help me read it?

[4:4] *Pupils*:   I ... have ...

[4:5] *Ms C*:   And then a big space, and I will explain about that space in a moment. Oh! N is going to fill the space in for me. Just a minute. He is thinking this afternoon, isn't he? Ready?

[4:6] *Pupils*:   I ... have ... four ... shells ... in ... my ... bucket!

[4:7] *Ms C*:   Very good! Does that make sense?

[4:8] *Pupils*:   Yes.

[4:9] *Ms C*:   It does. Now, let's see if he's right. Go on, N; you hold your lovely bucket of shells up. Now, shall we count together? You point to them, N, and we will count.

[4:10] *All*:   One, two, three, four!

[4:11] *Ms C*:   And don't they look lovely? All we need to make that really super for our wall, N, is your sentence. Now, you did stick your top shell a little bit high. Can you try like K did – and whose is this? P's – to keep your shells at the bottom, nearer the bottom, just to give yourself room to write that sentence at the top. OK. So P has to come and do her sentence, and N. No, just a minute, L, you are interrupting. N, sit there, please, and Q. Oh, don't they look beautiful? She has cut them out carefully! You really have. Beautiful are those, Q.

[4:12] *Pupil*:   We'll have to leave that one out of the way.

[4:13] *Ms C*:   Just put it in the middle, then. So; I think we'll let you three do the writing before we get any sticking done, on that table. All right? So that's you three. If you are called to go on to that table, cut your shells out and stick them on the bucket, please. Sit down please, Q!

[4:14] *L*:   Am I going in the home corner?

[4:15] *Ms C*:   No, because you are interrupting me, and I haven't finished speaking yet, L. Yes, you are going to have to be first, and be quick, then. All right. O, come and write, please; and R and L. S! I do like your picture on your new book, S: lovely!

[4:16] *L*:   There's no chair.

[4:17] *Ms C*:   Well, L, we have lots of chairs in our room. What do you think you should do? And P! You've done your picture, P; you've got your Breakthrough out, love; you've just not finished off, have you?
                  Right, let's see who have got their number to do. T, K, U, V. Put it in the middle of the table, because somebody else might need it, T. I'm glad you don't need it to do your numbers round the right way, but someone might.

[4:18] *V*:   This time you haven't!

[4:19] *Ms C*:   I've put Book Seven out this time, V.

[4:20] *V*:   I don't need one of these.

[4:21] *Ms C*:   Well just wait there. Have you looked inside the money page? Ssshh!

[4:22] *V*:   I've done my numbers.

[4:23] *Ms C*:   And N! As soon as you've finished your shells, love, you have your number to do. Now, M, you are chatty this afternoon! All right love? Number people! Could you just quieten down a little, please? Right! Who would like to go and play the house game? We haven't played it for a few days. W would! Well, M, I would like you to go and play it with W, please.

[4:24] *M*:   I don't know how to play it.
[4:25] *Ms C*:   M, I'll come and I'll explain it, but you do know; you
                 know because you have played it before. Would you go
                 and help S? I'd be really pleased if you would. I think
                 they need somebody sensible like you; and what about
                 KK? Would you go and have a go with the boys first of
                 all? [*KK looks very miserable at the prospect.*] Don't you want
                 to play the house game?
[4:26] *Pupil*: What about LL?
[4:27] *Ms C*:   Go and sort those. I'll move you round, LL; I won't leave
                 you there all afternoon. Are you all right on here? What
                 did I say about those thick pencils? They are really for
                 people who haven't been at school for as long as you and
                 who need a very thick pencil. Could you show me two
                 hands please? Everyone! M, show me two empty hands.
                 Now, please. There is far too much noise. MM, there is
                 no need to shout; you know I'll come to your number
                 table in just a minute, so if you have a problem, be looking
                 at the last page you did. I'll be there. If you put your
                 hand up, I'll be there even quicker. Now, KK; you're
                 going to be lonely!
[4:28] *KK*:   I want to go in the home corner.
[4:29] *Ms C*:   Do you? Do you want to start on your own? I'll send a
                 friend in a moment . . .

Ms C's approach to the allocation of work was very different from those
of Ms A and Ms B in that she combined her instructions with lengthy
discussion of the work already in progress, and comments on individual
children's efforts. This procedure necessarily extended the time required
for the allocation of work, although it presented no major problems
because the children were already in their separate work groups before
she began, and she dealt with one group at a time. In principle, this
meant that no child had to listen to irrelevant instructions; groups could
be getting on with something until the teacher came round to allocate
fresh work. In practice the children who were waiting for instructions
became a little restless (4:11; 4:13), and Ms C became increasingly
concerned about the noise level (4:21; 4:23; 4:27), and finally told one
child that there was no need to shout (4:27).

EXTRACT 5

[5:1] *Ms D*:   Let's see what we're going to do now. Can you remember
                 what I said this morning? What sort of work are we doing
                 today? Let me see how many children know and put their

hands up. Goodness! Only two children know what we're doing today? [*More hands go up.*] That's better; you should all have your hands up. K, you just came to us at Easter didn't you? Can you tell us what we're doing today? Making . . .? [*No response*] Making pictures. For the . . .? [*No response*] For what?

[5:2] *Pupils*: Carnival! Carnival!

[5:3] *Ms D*: When is the carnival?

[5:4] *Pupils*: Friday! Friday! Next Friday! Next week!

[5:5] *Ms D*: Somebody shouted out. When is the carnival? No, I want a hand up. When is the carnival? [*Some hands are raised.*] L, when is the carnival?

[5:6] *L*: Friday.

[5:7] *Ms D*: It's on Friday. Good boy. But it isn't tomorrow; it's the . . . ?

[5:8] *L*: Other Friday.

[5:9] *Ms D*: Don't call it the other Friday; it's next . . . ?

[5:10] *L*: Next Friday.

[5:11] *Ms D*: Next Friday, that's right: next week. And what are we making costumes about? [*Children call out.*] What are our costumes? You shouted out. I can't hear you if you shout out. [*More calling out*] Put your hands up. M, good girl!

[5:12] *M*: Seaside costumes.

[5:13] *Ms D*: Seaside costumes. So if you're in the orange group some of you will be doing a seaside costume. K, if you're in the blue group you have a very, very special job. If you noticed, we've taken down our yellow submarine. It's gone. And we're going to make . . . ?

[5:14] *Pupils*: Seaside!

[5:15] *Ms D*: A seaside café for next week.

[5:16] *Pupils*: Yeah!

[5:17] *Ms D*: But there are things in there that perhaps aren't as tidy as they should be, OK? So will you make sure you go through all the cupboards and make sure there aren't any knives and forks in the fridge [*Laughter*] or any dirty clothes in the oven [*Laughter*] and that all our dresses and shirts for dressing up are folded neatly; and table cloths do not need to be on a coat hanger. [*Laughter*] Well, when the blue group go in they might see quite a lot that needs tidying up. Ms X in the number corner is doing some special work. What's she doing? [*Hands are raised.*] Oh, it's your hand again. Let's see if somebody else can tell me. N?

[5:18] *N*: Number.

[5:19] *Ms D*: She's doing number. Is she doing it in your books?

[5:20] *Pupils*: No.

[5:21] *Ms D*: No. Where is she doing it, O?

[5:22] *O*: Folders.

[5:23] *Ms D*: Folders, that's right. What are these folders for? P? You don't know? Sh! Sh! Q, perhaps you could tell me what the folders are for? What are the folders for that you're doing your number work and your writing work in today? Who are they for? R?

[5:24] *R*: Teachers.

[5:25] *Ms D*: It's for your next teacher to see how nicely you work, isn't it? And you have to try very, very hard, don't you S? That's right. So I think now the blue group could go and make a start in the home bay. Would you like to?

[5:26] *Pupils*: Yes! [*They run out.*]

[5:27] *Ms D*: When you've tidied it ... [*But by now they have gone.*] They went out sensibly didn't they? Nobody fidgeted. Right!

[5:28] *Pupils*: Orange! Orange!

[5:29] *Ms D*: Do you think the orange group should go next?

[5:30] *Pupils*: Yes! No!

[5:31] *Ms D*: No, no S. Not if you're going to call out. Yellow group, where are you going to be? Look at the wheel [*The wheel is an adjustable chart on which a cardboard circle divided into coloured segments can be revolved on a rectangular surround marked with different locations.*]

[5:32] *Pupil*: Stay in here.

[5:33] *Ms D*: Good boy. Yellow group are staying here. Would the green group, if you have a sentence maker, please get it and go to the writing table. If you haven't, come and see Ms Y, and she's got some work for you to do at the other tables. You're in the red group, T. Where do you think you're going, T? [*She indicates the wheel.*] Look, where are you going? Red! Where are you going? [*T does not reply.*] Are you in the red group, U?

[5:34] *U*: Yes.

[5:35] *Ms D*: Good boy. Just say excuse me and then walk through. Orange group, are you going to be a seaweed queen?

[5:36] *Pupils*: Yes.

[5:37] *Ms D*: Off you go ...

Ms D wanted the children in her class to work in their usual groups. The allocation of tasks had been planned in advance, and the 'wheel'

(5:31) had been turned to show where each group should be. It would therefore have been possible in principle for the children to be settled in their work bases within a few seconds of the beginning of the session, and for each group's task to be fully explained *in situ* by one of the adults in the room. However, Ms D, like Ms C in Extract 4, chose to take a long time over the allocation of groups, making it an opportunity for lengthy dialogue with the whole class, not only about the tasks to be performed but also about other associated matters. This approach brought Ms D some problems of rapport and control, and she acknowledged these in her interview after the session:

> It proved difficult to remain calm today. I usually give praise but today I found that harder and I had to stop and take command. But I feel that the majority of our children receive a negative approach at home and that some of them have contempt for positive reinforcement. . . . The whole week has been like this. It's the rain and inside playtimes plus the excitement about our carnival. There's a lot of freedom in the air; but once the children are in their work groups they are working.

Although aware of problems, she did not, at least in the interview, associate them with the approach she had adopted for allocating work. In her comments she used a device described by King (1978), whereby poor progress or unsatisfactory behaviour are attributed to home or family circumstances, factors which cannot be blamed on the children or the teacher. Ms D went so far as to express the view 'that the majority of our children receive a negative approach at home', and for good measure she added unfavourable weather conditions and natural excitement about an unusual forthcoming event to her explanation. King (1978: 94–5) asserts that this kind of laying of the blame elsewhere enables teachers to preserve

> two important ideological elements: . . . Firstly the innocence of the children. They could not be blamed for their lack of progress or poor behaviour, which were due to their backgrounds. . . . Secondly, the 'theory' meant that the children's lack of progress and poor behaviour were not the fault of the teachers, which meant that their methods and practices were not questioned nor were the child-centred ideologies underlying them.

Ms D's tendency to prolong the allocation of tasks and delay the formation of groups greatly reduced the amount of time available for groupwork, and her belief that her pupils worked once they were in their groups was not supported by the observation evidence. Over the observation sessions as a whole, there was no class in which the children worked for a smaller proportion of the time.

EXTRACT 6

[6:1] *Mr I*:   First thing: people in the green group, if you remembered to bring your library book back, go to your drawer and get it now, and go to the library with Ms X. Everybody else sit very quietly. [*Waits for the children with library books to leave.*]

K, come and sit near L.

Now, people who are left, sit up nicely and look at me.

I'm going to let another group this afternoon try some of the collage pictures of the birds this afternoon. The yellow group did some really nice pictures this morning; if they're not quite finished you'll be able to finish them tomorrow.

The first group who are going to try the collage this afternoon is the blue group.

Yellow group this afternoon are going to start with some tens and units sums.

The red group are going to finish off those cards we were doing this morning, and then we're going to do some more writing about the different kinds of clothes that we're wearing . . . that we can wear.

If you're working in the wet area, the blue group, you've to be sensible. You've to be careful with the glue and the scissors. Don't stick one big piece of material for the whole shape of the bird: cut the material into small pieces, and put different material to make up a pattern for the body of the bird. That way it looks much better when it's finished.

I want to see the yellow table working each one on your own to begin with this afternoon, not doing the sum with your friend or the person sitting next to you, but doing it on your own, to see what answer you're going to get.

Red group: when you've finished the card that you were doing from this morning, then you draw the picture that's on the white sheet and leave enough space to put the words that go with the different pieces of clothing, and I will come and read them to you.

So; if the blue group go quietly outside there are some pieces of paper with the shape of a bird already on them, and there are some blank pieces.

[*To a hovering home–school liaison officer*] Do you want to sit here, Mr Y? [*Mr Y's response is not audible on the tape.*] Do you need this chair?

[6:2] *Mr Y:*   No . . .

[6:3] *Mr I:*   Oh, maybe if you sit. . . . Are you all right there?

[6:4] *Mr Y:*   I shall be moving in a moment.

[6:5] *Mr I:*   You don't want the desk, though?

[6:6] *Mr Y:*   No, that's all right.

[6:7] *Mr I:*   Do you want to sit there, then?

Red table go and sit down.

M, the green table went to the library.

[6:8] *M:*   I forgot my book.

[6:9] *Mr I:*   You forgot your book? You look at a book in the book corner while your group comes back. You look at a book in the book corner while your group comes back. Yellow group come and sit down . . .

Mr I's allocation of tasks to groups was very unlike that of Ms C or Ms D. It involved tight control and an insistence on attention. The presentation was slow, direct and methodical: he knew in advance what he wanted to say, and after briefly telling each group what it would be doing, he gave each in turn enough detailed instruction for it to make a start. He did not engage the children in dialogue or attempt to teach and organise simultaneously, and while he was talking nobody ventured to interrupt him (although he interrupted himself three times, once to tell a pupil where to sit, once to make sure that a home–school liaison officer was comfortably settled, and once to prevent someone from being unoccupied while waiting for the return of his group).

In these five extracts from the transcripts, the allocation of work is seen to be a delicate matter involving important decisions on at least two levels. First, teachers must choose between planning it in advance, negotiating it with their pupils on the spot or simply making it up as they go along. At the same time, they must decide whether to make it an opportunity for extended dialogue, an activity which they may value highly in its own right, or whether to deal with it as succinctly as possible so that they can maximise the amount of time available for the main tasks of the day.

In every other stage of the ten sessions summarised above, a range of similarities and differences of treatment was clearly apparent, although a detailed treatment of each stage is not practicable in a report of this length. For the purposes of the present study, the most significant part of each session was the period when the children were working at their tasks under the supervision of their teachers. It was here that the nature and quality of the teachers' interactions with their pupils revealed themselves most clearly as another powerful influence on task-related behaviour.

2 Teacher–pupil interactions

The analysis of teacher–pupil interactions presents a number of problems, the first of which is the formulation of a satisfactory definition of an interaction. One might, for example, be hard pressed to decide how many interactions take place in the following extract:

EXTRACT 7

[7:1]	Ms C:	Now then, K, what are you going to do now?
[7:2]	K:	Play in the water.
[7:3]	Ms C:	Well, can you? [*i.e. is there a space at the water tray?*]
[7:4]	L:	Can I tell you my colours?
[7:5]	Ms C:	Just a minute darling.
[7:6]	K:	I think they've had a long go.
[7:7]	Ms C:	You think they've had a long go? Do you think it's fair then if we say one of them come out? [*K nods.*] You think that's fair then? Why don't you speak to M, because he's been there a long time. M! I think you've been in a long time . . .
[7:8]	M:	I haven't, Miss.
[7:9]	Ms C:	I think you have. You come out now and let K have a little turn. [*To L:*] What are you going to go and get me? A book to tell me your colours? Go and get a book and you can point at them.
[7:10]	M:	Can I do one of them pictures?
[7:11]	Ms C:	Yes, M. Which one do you want to do? Which would you like to draw? [*M points to a picture.*] The boats? How many boats have you to draw? Draw . . . ?
[7:12]	M:	One.
[7:13]	Ms C:	One. Are you going to do it in that window there? There's the nice thin crayons. [*To O:*] Just a minute young man! What's that on the floor? Have you left it? Did you leave it for P? [*O nods.*] That's all right then. [*To L, who has returned with a book:*] Are you going to point at them and tell me them then? Go on then.
[7:14]	L:	Yellow . . . pink . . . red . . . yellow . . .

In formal discourse analysis, a technique developed by Sinclair and Coulthard (1975) for their study of teaching and learning in secondary classrooms, the basic 'exchange structure' consists of an initiation, generally by the teacher, to which someone makes a response, which in turn provokes from the teacher an evaluative comment or feedback. This 'initiation-response-feedback' (or I-R-F) structure occurs over and over again in Extract 7 (for example, 7:1, 7:2, 7:3). At first glance it seems like a suitable starting point for a definition of an interaction. However, it raises at least three tantalising questions.

First, a feedback comment frequently has the function of a new initiation: it provokes a new response which in turn provokes new feedback; but is that a new interaction or a continuation of the old one?

Second, a teacher's conversation with a child is often interrupted by an exchange with another child, and sometimes a lengthy conversation is 'interleaved' with several others, as was the main conversation in Extract 7, involving Ms C and K. When the teacher returns to the original conversation after an interruption, is she beginning a new interaction or continuing an old one?

Third, a response is sometimes unspoken, as when N pointed at a picture of a boat (7:11), or is understood from behavioural cues which are imperceptible to an outside observer, as in O's reaction – if indeed there was one – to Ms C's first two questions about the equipment on the floor (7:13). At what point does an imperceptible response become no response at all; and if no response is made, can an interaction be said to have taken place?

It can of course be argued that it does not matter how an interaction is defined so long as the criteria are unambiguously set out and consistently applied; yet if the resulting analysis is to be of any practical interest or value, the formal definition must broadly match our everyday understanding of the term, and unfortunately everyday understanding tends to seem self-evident yet be imprecise and full of ambiguities.

A neat way of avoiding the problem would be to adopt a time-sampling technique like that used in the ORACLE and ILEA projects (Galton et al. 1980a; Mortimore et al. 1988). In those studies, each observer wore an earpiece with an electronic bleeper, inaudible to everyone else in the room, which made a signal at regular intervals of twenty-five seconds. No attempt was made to monitor interactions continuously or to record their verbal content, but at each bleep the observer ticked relevant boxes in a grid to make a meticulous record of the nature of any teacher–pupil interaction taking place at that instant, assigning it to various categories (task, routine or disciplinary; pupil-initiated or teacher-initiated; open question or closed question, and so on). After many thousands of bleeps in a large number of classrooms over a period of several years, the data were analysed to show not the number of interactions but simply the proportion of the total time devoted to each category of interaction. Time sampling has the advantage that observers need not concern themselves with the question of when the interactions began, when they will end, or whether they are still the same interactions as they were earlier: the question to be answered is not about the number of interactions, nor about their average length, but simply about the teacher's allocation of time among different types of interaction.

In a large-scale study, a quantitative approach of this general kind is the most appropriate way to deal with the amount of data involved; it would simply not be a practical proposition to answer the questions posed by the ORACLE and ILEA teams from a detailed textual analysis of hundreds of transcripts. The major limitation of the approach, however, is that the quest for features by which interactions can be grouped for analysis necessarily leads to an emphasis on their general type at the expense of their specific content; yet for all practical purposes the important thing about an interaction is not its category but its unique meaning: the knowledge that someone has just asked us a closed question rather than an open one will not help us to answer the question unless we also know what it was about. In systematic observation schedules, the specific content and the idiosyncratic formal features of individual interactions are not recorded and hence cannot inform or illuminate subsequent analysis. It is in studies in depth of small numbers of classrooms that some kind of qualitative approach becomes a promising and manageable alternative.

However, qualitative analysis brings problems of its own, not the least of which is the controversy among social scientists about its credibility. It is reputed to lack both rigour and objectivity, and it is undeniably the case that, with nothing but their convictions to support their conclusions, different analysts acting in good faith can interpret the same data quite differently. The supporters of qualitative analysis might answer these charges by pointing to the immaculately methodical work of such practitioners as Edwards and Mercer (1987), by insisting that even the most aseptic systematic observation schedule starts from somebody's entirely subjective views about what aspects of behaviour are worth observing, and by questioning the quantitative researchers' own conviction that the fixed and bounded categories on their schedules bear any valid relationship to the informal and fluid human actions they are intended to represent.

Rather than taking sides in the matter, we have undertaken both quantitative and qualitative analyses of our observation data.

A quantitative analysis of the interaction data

For the purposes of the quantitative analysis which follows, a teacher–pupil interaction is a complete 'stanza' of conversation between the teacher and an individual, group or whole class of children. It may consist of a single I-R-F structure or a sequence of linked I-R-F structures where each feedback acts as an initiation to the next response. The frequency of interruptions is a particularly intrusive problem in the analysis of this kind of interaction: the ruling here is that if, after an interruption, a conversation continues where it left off, the continuation is counted as part of the original interaction. However, if the conversation after the interruption enters a new phase or embarks upon a new topic, that marks the beginning of a fresh interaction. The interruption counts as an interaction (or part of an interaction) in its own right. By these criteria Extract 7 contains seven interactions: one each involving pupils K, M, N and O, and three involving L.

The types of interaction included in the analysis are broadly parallel to the categories of task-related behaviour outlined on pages 109 and 110, and are listed below with an example of each. For reasons of space the examples are brief, although it must be emphasised that, as defined here, interactions can be very lengthy:

Work   If a teacher–pupil interaction dealt with the content of the current task it was coded as WORK.

> *Teacher*:   OK. First thing of all, you take little lumps of soil in your fingers and put it in the tray. [*The children pick up soil.*] But while you're doing it, press it down lightly with your fingers.

Monitoring   If the interaction was concerned with the progression of the task or the correctness or acceptability of an answer or finished piece of work, but did not deal with the content of the task it was coded as MONITORING.

> *Teacher*:   Have you copied that right? [*Child looks at his work with a blank expression.*] You have a look at my board. [*Teacher moves to another pupil.*]

Routine   If the interaction dealt with activities associated with the task but not themselves part of the task it was coded as ROUTINE.

> *Teacher*:   Throw this rubbish away, K. [*K starts to pick up offcuts from a cutting-out task.*] Do you want some glue?
> *K*:   In a minute.
> *Teacher*:   There's some on L's table.

Disciplinary   If the interaction had no task content but was concerned solely with a pupil's conduct, or the maintenance of control in the classroom, it was coded as DISCIPLINARY.

> *Teacher*:   Look at me please, K. Right! Can you tell me one of our rules in this school? We do not . . . ? What do we not do? [*K remains silent.*] You tell him what we don't do, L, because you don't do it.
> *L*:   We don't thump, Miss.
> *Teacher*:   We don't thump, K. Now you look at M and apologise . . .

Other If the interaction was about anything else it was coded as OTHER.

Teacher: What's the matter with you, K?
K: Banged my head.
Teacher: You banged your head? How did you do that?
K: Don't know.
Teacher: Were you being silly?
K: No . . .

The absolute and relative frequencies of different types of teacher–pupil interaction monitored during the systematic observation of teachers are given in Table 4.4. Well over a third of all interactions were about the content of the tasks which had been set, and a further fifth were concerned with checking, marking or otherwise monitoring progress. Routine matters accounted for just over a quarter, and discipline and control for one in ten. Only 6 per cent of teacher–pupil interactions fell outside these four categories.

Table 4.4 Type and frequency (*f*) of teacher–pupil interaction based on systematic observation of teachers

	f	%
Work interactions	4,564	37
Monitoring interactions	2,452	20
Routine interactions	3,322	27
Disciplinary interactions	1,260	10
Other interactions	729	6
Total interactions	12,327	100

It must be stressed that we are dealing here with the numbers of interactions which took place, and not with the proportion of time they filled. Many work interactions were lengthy, for example, and many monitoring interactions extremely brief. As a rough and ready rule of thumb it can be said that, across the classes as a whole, for every four work interactions between teachers and pupils there were three routine, two monitoring and one disciplinary interaction.

The low incidence of interactions concerned with discipline and control may seem surprising in view of the complex organisational structures outlined in the previous section, and the LEA's emphasis on classroom organisation as one of the keys to maximising pupils' opportunities to learn (see Chapter 3). In this kind of context, as Bennett (1987: 51) has pointed out, 'the teacher [is] seen as the manager of the attention and time of pupils in relation to the educational ends of the classroom. In other words, the teacher is conceived as the manager of the scarce resources of attention and time.'

This being so, it might have been expected that teachers would engage in far more disciplinary interactions (which, after all, were not necessarily severe dressings down, but were simply concerned with conduct and control rather than tasks). An examination of the transcripts, however, reveals what the quantitative analysis on its own cannot: namely, that control was often exerted by means of work and monitoring interactions; teachers frequently drew a distracted or misbehaving child's attention back to the task by referring not to the unacceptable behaviour but to the task itself. It was a variation on the oblique form of control observed by King (1978: 50) in his study of infant classrooms:

> the teachers' . . . methods of control were typically oblique, particularly with younger children. Their preference was to make requests rather than to give orders, to reward good behaviour rather than punish the bad. These actions were consonant with the idea of the children being innocent. They were capable of being naughty but did not have naughty intentions.

One might add that such an approach also avoids confrontation, an understandable move by a teacher who wants to maintain an air of friendly co-operation, and a particularly wise one by a teacher who is not sure of her ability to come off best in a battle of wills.

The balance of different types of interaction in the ten classrooms is summarised in Table 4.5, which is based on the teacher observations. Since the time spent in each classroom was not identical the figures have been made comparable by calculating for each class the mean number of interactions per hour.

Table 4.5   Rate of each type of teacher–pupil interaction in each school, based on systematic observation of the teachers

	Work	Monitoring	Routine	Disciplinary	Other	Total	
Applegarth	67	56	88	26	8	245	
Blakemore	44	31	40	19	11	145	
Claybourn	54	35	131	22	15	257	
Deacondale	52	26	52	47	14	191	
Easterbrook	68	87	34	4	17	210	
Freshwater	47	62	55	17	14	195	
Greystock	48	15	41	23	4	131	
Hartfield	59	40	28	19	4	150	
Illingworth	61	31	45	7	4	148	
Jeffcote	79	43	62	31	13	228	
Mean rate	58	43	58	22	10	191	(190)

Note: Rate = mean number of interactions per hour

The wide differences between classes in the overall number of teacher–pupil interactions are shown in the final column. In the class with the lowest rate, at Greystock, there were almost exactly half as many interactions per hour as there were in the class with the highest rate, at Claybourn. It should not be supposed, however, that people sat around at Greystock not communicating with one another; the implication of a 'low score' in this context is not that little was said, but rather that the interactions tended to be longer. The figures for the different types of interaction show that, in the two classes mentioned, there was very little difference in the rate of work or disciplinary interactions. At Claybourn, however, there was a high rate of 'other' interactions (mainly small talk), an exceptionally high rate of very brief routine interactions, and more than twice as many monitoring interactions as at Greystock.

The rate of work interactions also varied widely from class to class, ranging from seventy-nine per hour at Jeffcote to forty-four per hour at Blakemore. Comparison with Table 4.1 indicates a slight inverse relationship between the number of teacher–pupil work interactions and the percentage of time the pupils spent working: for example, the lowest rate of work interactions was at Blakemore, in the class where children spent the highest proportion of time working; and the highest rate was at Jeffcote, in a class which came very near the bottom of the league table for the time spent by pupils working. The implication of this seems clear: a high rate of teacher–pupil work interactions in a class is not in itself enough to make pupils spend a high proportion of the time working; if anything, a high work rate is more likely in a class where the overall number of work interactions is lower, and where there is consequently more time for individual interactions to be extended and developed.

There was also a wide range of routine and monitoring interactions illustrating marked differences in the patterns of teacher–pupil interaction from one class to another. The foregoing analyses, however, were both based on observation of teachers. Although, in the main, the teachers in the sample were involved in a very large number of interactions with their pupils, this should not be taken to imply that individual pupils were involved in a large number of interactions with their teachers. Indeed, a marked imbalance in this matter was noted by Galton et al. (1980a: 60), although they were concerned with the amount of time spent interacting, rather than with the number of interactions:

> One striking feature of the junior school classroom ... emerges very clearly from analysis of our data. This is the 'asymmetry' of teacher–pupil interaction; the fact that, while the 'typical' teacher spends most of the lesson time interacting with pupils (either individually, as a member of a group, or of the class), each individual pupil, by contrast,

interacts with the teacher for only a small proportion of his time. And most of that interaction is experienced by the pupil when the teacher is addressing the whole class.

Because of this reported imbalance, a further analysis of teacher–pupil interactions was carried out, this time using data from pupil rather than teacher observation. It will be recalled that here the focus of the observers' attention was a sequence of six children per class. Since the identity of these children had to remain unknown to the teacher and the pupils until all the observations were complete, they could not be given radio microphones to wear; and since they were not wearing radio microphones, some of their interactions were not audible to the observers. It was therefore necessary to add an extra category to the list of types of interaction:

Unknown   If the interaction was inaudible it was coded as UNKNOWN.

Table 4.6   Rate of each type of teacher–pupil interaction in each school, based on systematic observation of the sample pupils

	Work	Monitoring	Routine	Disciplinary	Other	Unknown	Total
Applegarth	2	2	2	<1	1	<1	7
Blakemore	6	3	3	1	1	<1	14
Claybourn	4	1	5	1	1	1	13
Deacondale	4	2	2	2	1	<1	11
Easterbrook	8	2	2	1	2	1	16
Freshwater	11	0	2	2	2	1	18
Greystock	2	1	1	1	1	0	6
Hartfield	3	2	2	1	1	0	9
Illingworth	5	1	2	1	<1	<1	9
Jeffcote	4	1	2	2	1	1	11
Mean rate	5	2	2	1	1	<1	11

Note: Rate = mean number of interactions per hour

In spite of the different unit of measurement, the ORACLE finding is confirmed by the analysis summarised in Table 4.6. On the whole individual children were involved in very few interactions with their teachers. The rate was lowest in the class at Greystock, where individual children were involved, on average, in only one work interaction every half-hour, and only one interaction of any kind every ten minutes, while the teacher was involved in more than twenty times as many teacher–pupil interactions as the pupils, a rate which exceeded one every half-minute. At the other end of the scale, the rate was highest in the class at Freshwater, where almost two-thirds of the interactions were about work; here the children were involved in three times as many teacher–pupil interactions (and more than five times as many work interactions) as those at Greystock; but at the same time the teacher was involved in well over ten times as many teacher–pupil interactions as the pupils, or one every eight and a half seconds.

However, the point has already been made that the crucial thing about an interaction is its content; and a detailed qualitative analysis of the discourse between this sample of teachers and their pupils will be found in the second part of this chapter.

3 The children themselves

Some of the variation in task-related behaviour arises from differences between the children themselves, and the present enquiry included separate analyses of the data from children of differing gender and age, as well as from children whose ability level was rated on a three-point scale (from above average to below average) by their teachers. The breakdown of task-related behaviour by pupil gender is summarised in Table 4.7.

In the past, investigations of gender differences in classroom behaviour (for example, Galton *et al.* 1980; Mortimore *et al.* 1988; Tizard *et al.* 1988) have tended to concentrate on differences in achievement and teacher–pupil interaction. Table 4.7 summarises the differences between the task-related behaviour of boys and girls in the present study. These differences were not great, but they were all in the direction that earlier studies would lead us to expect: the girls spent more of their time than the boys working and doing routine jobs like preparing materials and tidying up, while the boys spent more of their time than the girls distracted from their work or waiting for the teacher's attention.

Table 4.7 Percentage of time spent on task-related behaviour by girls and boys

	Minutes observed	Working	Routine	Awaiting attention	Distracted	Not observed
Girls	2,555	60	13	7	19	<1
Boys	2,613	58	10	8	23	<1
All pupils	5,168	59	11	8	21	1

The analysis of task-related behaviour in relation to age is summarised in Table 4.8. The two older groups spent less time than the youngest group waiting for attention from their teachers, presumably because they had developed the habit of moving on from one stage of their work to another without constantly seeking guidance or approval. The older children also tended to be less distracted and to spend more time working and carrying out routine activites.

Table 4.8 Percentage of time spent on task-related behaviour by pupils of differing ages

	Minutes observed	Working	Routine	Awaiting attention	Distracted	Not observed
5+ and 6+	2,081	58	10	10	22	<1
7+ and 8+	1,672	59	12	6	21	1
9+ and 10+	1,415	60	13	6	20	1
All pupils	5,168	59	11	8	21	1

In relation to the task-related behaviour of children of differing levels of ability, a major problem is the lack of any manageable and convincing objective measure of ability. For the purposes of the present enquiry, the sole criterion used was that which informs the vast majority of educational judgements – namely the class-teacher's assessment – and where teachers felt unable or unwilling to make such an assessment the matter was not pressed. It is acknowledged that any relationship demonstrated between perceived ability and task-related behaviour is as likely to illuminate the kinds of behaviour which lead a teacher to perceive a child as bright as to reveal any real differences between the behaviour of children of genuinely different levels of ability.

The findings from this particular analysis, which are summarised in Table 4.9, can therefore be construed in two quite different ways.

Table 4.9 Percentage of time spent on task-related behaviour by pupils of different ability, as perceived by their teachers

	Minutes observed	Working	Routine	Awaiting attention	Distracted	Not observed
Above average	1,401	63	10	7	19	<1
Average	1,365	59	9	9	22	<1
Below average	1,109	64	13	8	15	<1
All pupils	3,875	59	11	8	21	1

One interpretation is that children of average ability spent less time working and doing routine activities, and more time distracted or waiting for attention, than either the most or the least able children. This interpretation would lead us to suppose that the latter groups get more than their fair share of the teacher's attention, while the unexceptional pupils in the middle get less, a finding which would certainly be in line with the results of earlier studies.

The alternative reading is that children whose work is closely monitored and who consequently do not spend so much of their time distracted from what they are supposed to be doing are seen by the teacher as coming nearer the extremes of the ability range than their less obtrusive companions who, for want of any other evidence, are then rated 'average'. In this way, the assessment of ability is often carried out very informally, on the basis of social rather than intellectual characteristics. There is an impressive body of evidence that where this happens, children's subsequent levels of achievement will tend to match their teachers' estimates of their ability, even though these estimates may have been based largely on social behaviour (Brophy 1983).

Intriguing as they are, the differences between the task-related behaviour of the groups in Tables 4.7, 4.8 and 4.9 are less marked than those which are revealed by the study of the pupils' behaviour in relation to specific tasks, and the most striking of these will be discussed in detail later.

4 The nature of the task

For the purposes of the present analysis, tasks have been coded in two different ways. They have been grouped according to the curriculum areas to which they were allocated by the teachers themselves, and they have also been broken down into their component generic activities (writing, listening and so on). Although neither treatment does full justice to the tasks on its own, in conjunction they capture their detail and their essential nature reasonably well.

Curriculum designation

As a first step the tasks have been grouped by curriculum area, although it must be stressed that occasions when everyone in a classroom was working in the same curriculum area were rare. In line with the organisational style described earlier, the most common arrangement involved several tasks in different curriculum areas taking place at the same time. Pupils (including target pupils) might be involved in any one of them, and might move from one to another during a single stint of observation. Teachers (including the target teacher) were free to devote their attention to different groups or individuals as the need arose, for as long or as short a time as they wanted. In view of this complexity of classroom organisation it is appropriate, in presenting a breakdown of the proportion of time devoted to each curriculum area, to compile separate lists for teachers and pupils, and to stress that they refer to the teachers and pupils who were observed rather than the whole class.

It should also be added that quite similar tasks were allocated to different areas of the curriculum by different teachers, a situation which parallels that found by Mortimore *et al.* (1988: 78–9) in their study of junior classrooms:

> The teachers in the sample detailed the areas in which they worked with their children ... Variation was very largely the result of the degree to which individual teachers chose to replace smaller subject divisions by broader areas such as project work or environmental studies. Some teachers chose to maintain the traditional boundaries, keeping each subject area separate, whereas at the opposite extreme, a few teachers attempted to organise almost the entire curriculum around a particular project theme.

Further ambiguities arose in relation to tasks which seemed to straddle two or more curriculum areas at the same time – where, for example, children might be engaged in an interactive number task with a computer, and where the teacher might refer to them either as the maths group or the computer group. It was clear that in their curriculum designations teachers were using the notion of curriculum in two rather different ways, some referring to the kinds of learning they were seeking to promote, and some to the kinds of task and activity through which they were hoping to bring it about. Consequently there was sometimes an element of arbitrariness in the curricular designation chosen by the teachers for the various tasks observed.[2]

In Table 4.10 and elsewhere in this chapter, the term 'Admin' refers to the supervision of routine chores and the giving of information and instructions about forthcoming activities. The term 'Free ranging' is borrowed from the LEA's classroom organisation course, and refers to movement around a classroom during which teachers oversee the activities of a substantial number of their pupils in quick succession, rather in the style of the individual monitors of the ORACLE study (Galton *et al.* 1980a). It is acknowledged that these two headings do not refer to areas of the curriculum in quite the same way as the other headings listed; their use is justified on the grounds that between them they account for a substantial proportion of the teachers' and pupils' time in the classroom, and that this time is given over almost entirely to transactions about the more conventional curriculum areas.

Table 4.10 underlines a point which has already been made: the aim of the present study was to look at the behaviour and interactions of a small number of teachers and pupils in considerable detail rather than to conduct a wide-ranging survey of classroom practice. Although the most popular areas of the curriculum were observed at some length (language alone accounting for well over fifty hours, for example) there were other areas in which teachers or pupils were observed for only a

Table 4.10   Time spent in different curriculum areas (teachers' own definitions) by target teachers and pupils

| | Teachers | | Pupils | |
	Minutes	Percentage	Minutes	Percentage
Admin	391	9.2	331	6.4
Art	298	7.0	314	6.1
CDT	60	1.4	203	3.9
Choosing	–	–	105	2.0
Computer	90	2.1	43	0.8
Cooking	72	1.7	20	0.4
Env. studies	83	1.9	90	1.7
Free ranging	153	3.6	–	–
Language	1,478	34.7	1,625	31.5
Maths	895	21.0	1,042	20.2
Music	57	1.3	97	1.9
PE	74	1.7	277	5.4
Play	134	3.1	224	4.3
Science	317	7.4	440	8.5
Sewing	–	–	49	0.9
Table games	9	0.2	48	0.9
Television	–	–	19	0.4
Topic	150	3.5	231	4.5
All areas	4,261	100.0	5,158	100.0

few minutes. From those brief observations it would be quite inappropriate to generalise, and some of what follows will necessarily report what this particular group of teachers and pupils did, without making any claims about the more general applicability of the findings.

With that reservation firmly in mind it may be asserted that Table 4.10 gives a clear indication of the very large amounts of time which are still spent by both teachers and pupils on language and maths. There is of course nothing new in this finding: in an HMI survey (DES 1989b), conducted since the introduction of the National Curriculum, English and maths accounted for 33 and 23 per cent respectively of average class time in primary schools. In a slightly earlier, pre-National Curriculum survey of junior classes (DES 1988), the comparable figures were 27 and 22 per cent. At the time of the ORACLE project a decade earlier, when traditional curricular boundaries were still largely intact, language and maths were even more prominent, taking up 36 and 29 per cent respectively of pupil time, and 38 and 33 per cent of teacher time.[3]

The apparently insignificant status of science in Table 4.10 is also worthy of note, echoing as it does the findings of the Level One study reported in Chapter 3. The present study took place shortly before the introduction of the National Curriculum, at a time when the coming emphasis on science in primary schools was a matter of public aware-ness, yet the teachers and pupils in the sample were spending well under a tenth of their time (7.4 and 8.5 per cent respectively) on tasks which were defined as science. The apparent arbitrariness of curricular labelling was certainly a factor here, for there were many tasks which might have been termed science but which were in fact given some other curricular label by the teacher, as in the following examples from the field notes:

> The teacher had brought in several different things to use as dyes: tea, onion skins, beetroot etc. The children were encouraged to touch, taste and smell them. They discussed the best way to use them as dyes, and predicted the colours they would produce. . . .
>
> [Teacher's designation: topic]

> The children carried out tests to see whether a load was easier to drag on the floorboards or on rollers. They were then asked to write about what they had been doing. . . .
>
> [Teacher's designation: CDT]

> The teacher and the children closely observed several different flowers. They talked about and named the various parts, and discussed the way in which the pollen is collected by bees. . . .
>
> [Teacher's designation: language]

> The pupils used worksheets containing pictures of vehicles, people and animals. They had to consider each picture in turn and decide where it moved, how it moved, what supported its weight, which part made it move, and what fuel it ran on. . . .
>
> [Teacher's designation: maths]

> After making tunnels using different materials, and devising tests of their strength, the children had to find a simple method of recording their findings. . . .
>
> [Teacher's designation: CDT]

> The children were asked to design a watertight model of a canal small enough to fit into a tidy tray, and to devise tests for water evaporation and leakage. . . .
>
> [Teacher's designation: topic]

It is not suggested that these examples of teachers' curriculum desig-nations were in some way wrong or perverse. At the very least they were comprehensible alternatives to science, and some of them reflected entirely orthodox current thinking about the labelling of the curriculum (the tunnel-testing and canal-designing tasks were, in this sense, quint-essentially technology as it is now defined). Nevertheless, they illustrate a lingering yet diminishing tendency in the field of primary education before the introduction of the National Curriculum to think of scientific enquiry and the use of scientific methods as something other than science. In the HMI survey of junior classes (DES 1988) the proportion of 'average class time' devoted to science was, at 6.4 per cent, somewhat less than in the present enquiry; and in the ORACLE study, conducted in the late seventies, science did not feature as a separate curriculum area at all. However, the later HMI survey of 1989, conducted after the introduction of the National Curriculum and specifically concerned with its implementation, shows a dramatic increase in the proportion of time spent on activities designated as science and reports a national average figure of 14 per cent (DES 1989b).

Table 4.10 also throws additional light on an issue discussed in the previous chapter. The Level One survey and Level Two case studies revealed classrooms where some children were occupied with relatively undemanding activities, apparently as a way of releasing the teacher to give her full attention to other children and other areas of the curriculum. On the whole this arrangement was seen by the teachers concerned as a matter of the relative importance of different curriculum areas; thus, one teacher quoted in Chapter 3 reported that 'she also ran maths and language groups alongside groups working with Lego and jigsaws, thus ensuring that not all the children were engaged in activities which required much of her own attention or intervention'.

Although most of the differences between the two sets of values are small, Table 4.10 suggests that in general the teachers in the present study, like those quoted in Chapter 3, and indeed those in the ORACLE study, were devoting more of their time than their pupils to both language and maths, and less to what ORACLE called general studies – in this case CDT, music, PE, play activities, science, sewing, table games, television and topic work. This offers clear support for the proposition that some areas of the curriculum are seen as more worthy of the teachers' attention than others.

However, the need for caution here is highlighted by the seemingly anomalous position of art, which accounted for 7 per cent of the teachers' time and only 6.1 per cent of the children's time, even though, to the observer who conducted the case studies of a different sample of teachers at Level Two 'it became increasingly obvious . . . that art was sometimes used as an organizational device to allow the teacher to devote her time to other activities elsewhere in the classroom'.

The evidence from Table 4.10 does not in itself suggest that the teachers in the present sample were using art in this way. As a curriculum area, it accounted for well under a tenth of the time of both pupils and teachers, and, although the difference was very slight, these particular teachers spent a higher proportion of their time on it than the pupils. However, it will be recalled that, unlike the much larger group of teachers who were interviewed and observed for the Level One survey and the Level Two case studies, those in the Level Three study were deliberately chosen because they were in charge of classrooms which in some sense reflected the characteristics and ideals of the LEA's primary initiative. This being so, their apparent tendency not to treat art as a mere time-filler for the children need come as no surprise, and the problem therefore remains one which demands attention in many schools.

An additional factor relates to the matter of curriculum designation. When a maths or language task includes (as it often does) a requirement to draw pictures or to colour things in, the task is conveniently spun out in an undemanding way, and consequently the children are highly unlikely to need the teacher's attention. However, while they are doing the drawing or the colouring they are still in the maths or language group and still nominally working in the area of maths or language, although at this stage their task and its curricular label are totally mismatched.

Curriculum designation and task-related behaviour

We have seen that, on average, pupils spent about three-fifths of their time working, one-fifth distracted from their work, and the remaining fifth either waiting for attention or performing routine activities. When we look at tasks from different curriculum areas separately, however, we find wide differences in task-related behaviour, and these are summarised in Table 4.11.

The proportion of time spent WORKING ranged from 51 per cent in PE and computer sessions to 70 per cent in play sessions. It will be recalled that the term 'working' in this context implies only that the child was engaged in the task which had been set. It follows that if a particular task was both congenial and undemanding, and if a child sat over it for a long time, a high rate of working would be scored, even though the word 'working' might seem a somewhat extravagant term to apply to what the child was doing. For example, on her teacher's instructions, one child spent the whole of a ten-minute observation stint during a topic session drawing 'things you can put in a fridge'; another child had a language worksheet which included an instruction to colour in a printed picture, and he spent the whole of an observation stint doing so.

In five curriculum areas (admin, art, language, maths and science) there was a very substantial amount of pupil observation, ranging from five to twenty-seven hours. In science, where tasks often had high novelty value and hence tended to be especially interesting, pupils spent a higher proportion of the time working and a lower proportion

Table 4.11   Percentage of time spent by pupils on task-related behaviour in different areas of the curriculum, as defined by their teachers

	Minutes observed	Working	Routine	Awaiting attention	Distracted	Not observed
Language	1,625	55	11	7	26	<1
Maths	1,042	59	10	9	23	<1
Science	440	64	8	5	20	2
Admin	331	64	5	11	18	1
Art	314	65	16	3	16	0
PE	277	51	21	18	10	0
Topic	231	55	21	6	16	3
Play	224	70	10	2	18	0
CDT	203	69	5	4	22	0
Choosing	105	63	16	7	14	0
Music	97	67	8	9	13	2
Env. studies	90	63	6	6	26	0
Sewing	49	57	20	14	8	0
Table games	48	69	13	6	13	0
Computer	43	51	19	26	5	0
Cooking	20	55	15	0	30	0
Television	19	58	0	32	11	0
All areas	5,158	59	11	8	21	1

distracted or awaiting attention than they did in language or maths, where the tasks were generally tougher. The same applied in art, where tasks were nearly always pleasant and undemanding: children spent more than 80 per cent of the time either working or carrying out routine activities. The time spent awaiting attention was exceptionally low since for the most part they simply did not need any attention. The amount of distraction was also lower than in any of the other major curriculum areas, partly because in this particular area children could work and discuss irrelevant matters at the same time, and so long as they continued working they were not, in the terms of the observation schedule, distracted.

Fewer observation data were gathered in the other curriculum areas, but although comparisons among them must be made with caution they throw some interesting sidelights upon classroom practice and behaviour. For example, in PE and computer sessions the proportion of time spent working was equally low. However, an examination of what went on during the half of the time when the children were not working reveals a marked difference between the two areas. In both, a comparatively high proportion (about a fifth) of the time was spent on routine activities, but when they were set to work with the computer the children spent considerably more time waiting for the teacher's attention, and correspondingly less time distracted from their work than in PE. It is relevant to note that PE always occupied the whole of a teacher's attention in the sense that she was never required to take a PE session and monitor other groups at the same time. Children working at the computer, however, were left to get on with what they were doing, and had to compete for the teacher's attention when they got stuck. This being so, the comparatively large amount of time spent waiting for the teacher's attention is easy to understand. The settings in which the two kinds of session took place were undoubtedly an additional factor: there are simply more tempting distractions during a PE session in a hall full of hoops, footballs and the like than during a computer session in a screened corner with a single VDU.

In spite of this difference, the proportion of time during which pupils were distracted from their work in each of these two curriculum areas was only a fraction of that in some others. Cooking was the area in which pupils were most distracted, although it is fair to say that only two were observed cooking, each of them for a single ten-minute stint. This particular form of cookery was a straightforward balance of work and routine activities in which neither child spent a single moment waiting for the teacher's attention, but in which they were distracted from the task in hand for almost a third of the time. Perhaps in its very nature cooking involves periods of inaction which distract the cook's attention: a watched pot never boils, and to cope with this, the real-life cook doesn't watch the pot but simply gets on with some other task until the pot is ready. The two boys who were observed cooking in the present study certainly behaved in this way, doing other tasks while they waited for things to cook, and gathering a good many distracted codings as they did so.

We might also want to ask whether the gender of the two pupils in question was a factor in their tendency towards distraction, although of course there is nothing in the data to help us towards an answer in relation to cooking. In some other curriculum areas, however, there is a considerable quantity of relevant data: Language alone accounted for more than twenty-seven hours of pupil observation as well as an almost equal amount of teacher observation, and from such a body of information it is valid to draw general conclusions.

Table 4.12 offers a complete summary of gender differences in work-related behaviour in the present study. In maths there was a striking similarity between the work-related behaviour of girls and boys: indeed, the proportion of time spent distracted from work in this area was identical, and the proportion of time spent working, nearly so. In language, science, admin and art, girls worked for more of the time than boys, while boys were distracted for more of the time than girls. The differences were particularly marked in art and science, areas which on

Table 4.12   Task-related behaviour of boys and girls in each curriculum area, as defined by their teachers

	Minutes observed		Working		Routine		Awaiting attention		Distracted		Not observed	
	G	B	G	B	G	B	G	B	G	B	G	B
Language	791	834	57	53	12	10	6	8	25	28	<1	<1
Maths	531	511	58	59	11	9	8	10	23	23	<1	<1
Science	240	200	72	54	6	10	2	9	17	25	2	2
Admin	144	187	65	64	4	6	15	8	15	21	2	0
Art	170	144	71	58	14	19	4	1	11	21	0	0
PE	132	145	42	59	27	16	23	13	8	12	0	0
Topic	128	103	51	59	23	17	5	6	18	15	2	3
Play	98	126	65	73	12	9	2	2	20	17	0	0
CDT	60	143	75	67	8	3	8	2	8	27	0	0
Choosing	53	52	60	65	23	10	0	13	17	11	0	0
Music	45	52	73	62	13	4	11	8	2	23	0	4
Env. studies	50	40	66	60	8	2	4	7	22	30	0	0
Sewing	32	17	44	82	28	6	22	0	6	12	0	0
Table games	38	10	61	100	16	0	8	0	16	0	0	0
Computer	23	20	70	30	17	20	4	50	9	0	0	0
Cooking	–	20	–	55	–	15	–	0	–	30	–	0
Television	10	9	60	56	0	0	40	22	0	22	0	0
All areas	2,515	2,613	60	58	13	10	7	8	19	23	1	1

Note: Values in each category are percentages of total time spent in each curriculum area

the basis of this evidence were more attractive to the girls than to the boys. In science boys spent a comparatively large amount (though still only about a tenth) of the time waiting for the teacher's attention, and this was sometimes a transparent ruse to avoid continuing with an uncongenial task. The girls did not do this, presumably because they found the tasks more to their liking. In admin the position was reversed: the girls spent a good deal of time passively waiting while the teachers sorted out problems involving the boys.

Differences between the task-related behaviour of children thought by their teachers to be above average, average or below average in ability are summarised in Table 4.13.

Again, there are two completely different ways of interpreting this table. If we assume that the teachers were right in their assessments, we must conclude (among other things) that in maths and science children of above-average ability spend more time working and less time distracted than other children; that children whose ability is below average are particularly hardworking in language, PE, CDT, environmental studies and play but unusually distractable in maths and science; and that children of average ability stick at their work in art but

Table 4.13 Task-related behaviour in each curriculum area of children of different abilities, as rated by their teachers

	Minutes observed			Working			Routine			Awaiting attention			Distracted			Not observed		
	AA	A	BA	AA	A	BA	AA	A	BA	AA	A	BA	AA	A	BA	AA	A	BA
Language	420	130	259	59	50	73	14	11	16	4	9	7	23	29	4	<1	<1	0
Maths	321	190	247	66	65	57	10	7	8	8	13	8	16	15	26	<1	0	0
Science	170	130	130	73	62	54	8	8	8	3	6	8	15	20	28	2	4	2
Admin	132	100	36	66	66	67	7	1	6	0	12	14	17	21	14	2	0	0
Art	50	120	100	56	73	61	12	8	24	2	2	2	30	16	13	0	0	0
PE	38	55	30	34	36	67	16	22	13	34	25	10	16	16	10	0	0	0
Topic	22	48	36	73	69	56	18	19	14	5	0	17	5	12	14	0	0	0
Play	65	44	66	68	73	76	8	5	17	2	7	2	23	20	5	0	0	0
CDT	70	60	50	60	65	74	9	2	6	4	7	2	27	27	18	0	0	0
Choosing	30	25	50	70	64	58	10	20	18	10	0	8	10	16	16	0	0	0
Music	20	20	45	85	80	60	0	0	11	0	10	11	10	10	16	5	0	2
Env. studies	41	20	30	51	70	73	10	0	7	5	5	7	34	25	14	0	0	0
Sewing	0	10	0	–	30	–	–	20	–	–	50	–	–	0	–	–	–	–
Table games	0	28	20	–	61	80	–	11	15	–	11	0	–	18	5	–	0	0
Computer	13	30	0	15	67	–	8	23	–	77	3	–	0	7	–	0	0	–
Cooking	0	0	0	–	–	–	–	–	–	–	–	–	–	–	–	–	–	–
Television	9	0	10	56	–	60	0	–	0	22	–	40	22	–	0	0	–	0
All areas	1,401	1,365	1,109	63	59	64	10	9	13	7	9	8	19	22	15	1	1	<1

Notes: Values in each category are percentages of total time spent in each curriculum area
(AA=Above average ability; A=Average ability; BA=Below average ability)

are easily distracted in language sessions where they are more likely than other children to be kept waiting for attention, as they are in maths also.

However, since it is likely that the teachers' assessments were made at least partly on the basis of pupils' task-related behaviour, the table can also be used to give an indication of the patterns of pupil behaviour which seem to teachers to go along with different levels of ability. By this token, sticking at maths and science tasks without becoming distracted would be the mark of above average-ability, while a preference for language, PE, CDT, environmental studies and play would suggest the opposite. It might even be the case that children who are prepared to wait for a long time for attention are seen as somewhat passive and hence average: the assumption here would be that children of above average-ability would puzzle it out for themselves or turn to an alternative activity, while those of low ability would simply become distracted.

Differences between the task-related behaviour of children of different ages are summarised in Table 4.14.

In those curriculum areas where the largest amount of observation data was collected at all ages, and where it is reasonable to compare percentage values from the three age groups, some age-related trends are apparent. In language, maths and art there were systematic relationships between age on the one hand and both working and distraction on the other: older children spent more of their time than younger children working at their language and maths, and less of their time distracted in those curriculum areas. In art the relationship was different: children in the youngest group were much more diligent and much less distractable than those in the other two groups, whose patterns of behaviour in this respect resembled each other closely.

There was also a general tendency for the children in the youngest group to spend less time than those in the other two groups performing routine activities, and more time waiting for attention.

A fuller understanding of the significance of the differences between children as they tackle various areas of the curriculum would depend on a knowledge of the pupils' activities while they were engaged in the tasks which had been set. The tables in this section have listed areas of the curriculum and indicated the extent to which children were working in each, but they give no information at all about the precise nature of their work. To complete the picture of what children were actually doing while they worked, it is necessary to examine their tasks in a different way.

Curriculum as generic activities

Whatever their curriculum labels, all the tasks commonly set by teachers are made up of a rather small number of relatively simple basic activities,

Table 4.14 Task-related behaviour in each curriculum area of children of different ages

	Minutes observed			Working			Routine			Awaiting attention			Distracted			Not observed		
	5+	7+	9+	5+	7+	9+	5+	7+	9+	5+	7-	9+	5+	7+	9+	5+	7+	9+
Language	595	650	380	51	54	63	11	12	11	9	6	6	29	28	19	0	1	<1
Maths	382	276	384	54	59	63	7	12	12	10	7	8	28	22	17	0	<1	<1
Science	20	140	280	60	66	63	10	9	7	10	6	5	20	16	23	0	3	2
Admin	196	129	6	62	71	0	5	6	17	17	2	17	16	21	50	1	0	17
Art	134	110	70	72	58	61	13	22	14	5	0	3	10	20	21	0	0	0
PE	163	50	64	52	44	55	12	36	31	23	16	5	12	4	9	0	0	0
Topic	6	86	139	0	71	47	17	20	22	83	1	5	0	8	22	0	0	4
Play	224	–	–	70	–	–	10	–	–	2	–	–	18	–	–	0	–	–
CDT	73	130	–	60	75	–	3	6	–	0	6	–	37	13	–	0	–	–
Choosing	105	–	–	63	–	–	16	–	–	7	–	–	14	–	–	0	–	–
Music	55	30	12	75	63	42	0	17	25	9	7	17	16	7	17	0	7	0
Env. studies	10	20	60	60	50	68	10	5	5	10	10	3	20	35	23	0	0	0
Sewing	39	10	–	64	30	–	21	20	–	5	50	–	10	0	–	0	0	–
Table games	30	18	–	87	39	–	10	17	–	0	17	–	3	28	–	0	0	–
Computer	20	23	–	55	48	–	35	4	–	5	43	–	5	4	–	0	0	–
Cooking	–	–	20	–	–	55	–	–	15	–	–	0	–	–	30	–	–	0
Television	19	–	–	58	–	–	0	–	–	32	–	–	10	–	–	0	–	–
Unclassified	10	–	–	0	–	–	0	–	–	0	–	–	100	–	–	0	–	–
All areas	2,081	1,672	1,415	58	59	60	10	12	13	10	6	6	22	21	20	<1	<1	1

Note: Values in each category are percentages of total time spent in each curriculum area

one or more of which are necessarily involved in the successful completion of each task. A detailed analysis of the individual tasks set by all teachers in the present study yielded a list of ten of these essential component activities:

- *Writing*
- *Using task-specific apparatus*, which might range from computers and chronometers to needles and thread, but does not include such general-purpose equipment like pens and paper.
- *Reading*, either silently or aloud, including the use of work cards, etc.
- *Listening/looking*, usually to/at the teacher, but also involving other children, the television, radio, tape-recorder or class audio-visual material.
- *Drawing and/or painting.*
- *Collaboration* with another child or children.
- *Movement* from one place to another (not simply movement of,say, the hands).
- *Talking to the teacher.*
- *Construction*, including model-making, craft, technological construction, building with Lego, etc.
- *Talking to the class.*

Table 4.15 shows the prevalence of each of these ten generic activities in the tasks set by the teachers, and also clarifies the relationship between the activities and the curriculum areas to which teachers allocated the various tasks. Thus, to take one very straightforward example, the whole of the time spent on the tasks which were defined by the teacher as table games involved the use of task-specific apparatus, and nearly two-thirds (in fact 63 per cent) of the time involved collaboration between pupils (while the remaining third of the time was given over to games for single players). None of the tasks in this curriculum area involved any of the other eight activities.

It should perhaps be stressed that this does not mean that no child spoke to the teacher (or moved about, wrote, drew a picture or read something) while he or she was supposed to be playing a table game; the status of the ten activities is not that children happened to perform them but rather that their performance was an integral and essential part of the completion of the task and, as such, was required by the teacher. Of course, a child who was not attending to the task which had been set might have been involved in any or even none of them.

The two rows of values at the bottom of Table 4.15 show the overall allocation of time to the ten listed activities. The percentage values in the table are derived from all ten classes, and there was sometimes a wide range between the highest and lowest individual class scores from which they were computed. However, the general emphasis in these ten

Table 4.15 Percentage of time spent by pupils on ten generic activities in the different areas of the curriculum, as defined by their teachers

	Write	Apparatus	Read	Listen/Look	Draw/Paint	Collaborate	Move about	Talk to teacher	Construct	Talk to class
Language	56	4	35	24	17	9	5	9	0	1
Maths	55	37	42	7	21	14	4	2	0	0
Science	16	39	5	27	25	20	5	18	11	2
Admin	0	2	5	82	0	9	29	30	0	0
Art	0	57	3	3	55	7	4	0	6	0
PE	0	18	0	18	0	27	100	0	0	0
Topic	41	0	19	12	47	15	3	8	0	4
Play	0	87	2	0	0	42	47	4	21	0
CDT	5	84	5	0	0	56	0	0	95	0
Choosing	10	49	19	19	29	44	28	0	0	0
Music	0	12	10	21	0	88	12	0	0	0
Env. studies	44	0	0	44	33	0	0	22	0	0
Sewing	0	100	0	0	0	0	0	0	0	0
Table games	0	100	0	0	0	63	0	0	0	0
Computer	53	47	53	23	0	30	0	23	0	0
Cooking	0	100	0	0	0	0	100	0	0	0
Television	0	0	0	100	0	0	0	0	0	0
All areas (%)	33	28	24	20	19	18	14	8	6	1
All areas (mins)	1,727	1,422	1,238	1,055	956	916	698	394	309	30

Note: The values in this table are percentages of the total time spent in each curriculum area. The rows generally sum to considerably more than 100 because the listed activities are not mutually exclusive.

PNP classrooms on reading and writing rather than oral work is very clear, as is the limited amount of time devoted to tasks which required children to collaborate with one another. Table 4.15 also offers a number of insights into key areas of the curriculum.

Language
In spite of the importance currently attached to the spoken word in primary education, language was dominated by reading and writing. Children were offered few opportunities to talk in a structured way, and most of the relatively small amount of oral work which took place involved talking by the teacher and listening by the pupils. Drawing and painting accounted for almost twice as much time as talking to the teacher.

Mathematics
Mathematics also involved a substantial amount of reading and writing, as well as drawing, painting and the use of apparatus. Contact with the teacher was slight: pupils were required to listen to their teachers for only 7 per cent of the time, and talk to them for only one minute in every fifty. In terms of their component activities (though not, of course, in their subject matter) language and mathematics were very similar: they involved virtually identical amounts of reading, writing, movement and so on. The major differences between the two areas lay in the extent to which special apparatus was used, and the amounts of time spent interacting with the teacher and with fellow-pupils: the language tasks demanded more listening and talking to the teacher, while the mathematics tasks required more collaboration between pupils.

Science
Science was far more interactive than either language or maths, involving more collaboration between pupils and much more conversation with the teacher. It was an area in which drawing, painting and the use of apparatus were much in evidence, but in which very little reading or writing were required.

Art
The tasks set in art were characterised by an almost total absence of reading, writing or conversation. Very little collaboration between pupils was required, and although pupils worked alongside each other, the prevailing picture was of individual children setting about their separate tasks and completing them on their own.

It is clear from Table 4.15 that by no means all the drawing or painting demanded of children was categorised as art and, conversely, that by no means all art tasks involved drawing and painting. Throughout the period of observation, the target pupils were required to draw or paint during 55 per cent of the time devoted to art; but since there were few formal art sessions, this accounted for only 3.4 per cent of total observation time. In the performance of tasks generally, however, they were required to draw or paint for no less than 19 per cent of total observation time – for virtually half of the time spent on topics, a third of that spent on environmental studies, a quarter of that spent on science, a fifth of that spent on maths, and so on.

Generic activities and task-related behaviour

Before leaving the matter of time spent on various generic activities and curriculum areas, it is appropriate to look at the relationship between such activities and pupils' task-related behaviour: to consider what the pupils actually did as well as what they were supposed to do.

To know simply that a fifth of their time was given over to mathematics, and that a fifth of their tasks in this curriculum area involved drawing, for example, is to know a good deal about the teachers' intentions but not very much about the pupils' behaviour. To put it at its simplest, we also need to ask whether the pupils attended to their tasks and performed the activities required of them.

The relationship between generic activities and task-related behaviour is set out in Table 4.16. The activities are listed in descending order of popularity, from writing, which was involved in more than twenty-eight hours of the pupil observation, down to talking to the class, which accounted for only half an hour.

Table 4.16 Pupils' task-related behaviour in different generic activities

	Minutes observed	Working	Routine	Awaiting attention	Distracted	Not observed
			(Percentage of pupil time)			
Writing	1,727	52	13	8	28	<1
Apparatus	1,422	65	12	6	17	<1
Reading	1,238	57	12	6	24	<1
Listen/look	1,055	68	6	10	15	1
Drawing/painting	956	55	14	5	25	1
Collaboration	916	67	11	6	15	<1
Movement	698	54	15	14	17	<1
Talking to teacher	394	71	11	6	10	2
Construction	309	70	7	3	20	0
Talking to class	30	100	0	0	0	0
All activities	8,745	59	11	8	21	1

Pupils spent a very high proportion of the time working when they were engaged in tasks which involved talking to the class, talking to the teacher, construction, listening or collaboration. Their work levels were at their lowest in writing, drawing or tasks which involved movement from one part of the room to another, and all three of these activities generated very high levels of routine behaviour. For the most part, high levels of distraction were found where work levels were low, and the highest levels of all were in tasks involving writing, drawing and reading.

In general, the most work and the least distraction occurred in the rarest activities. An attractively simple explanation for this is that familiarity breeds contempt and that the novelty value of comparatively infrequent activities is in itself enough to keep children involved in their work. However, the table contains enough exceptions to make such an explanation less than entirely convincing: for example, one of the highest levels of work was in listening activities which were quite common, and one of the lowest was in movement activities which were much rarer.

The striking feature of the activities at which children worked for a high proportion of the time was involvement with other people. With the single exception of construction, all of them required pupils to talk, listen or in some way collaborate with others; and construction was very different from the other activities in that a high work level was combined with a relatively high level of distraction.

Conversely, all but one of the activities at which children worked for the lowest proportion of the time – writing, movement, drawing and reading – involved no other people and could have been carried out most effectively in isolation; movement was different from the other activities in that it involved exceptionally large amounts of routine behaviour and time spent waiting for attention, which automatically reduced the time left for working.

This pattern of relationships suggests the possibility that some of the commonest classroom tasks may actively discourage pupil involvement simply because they are more appropriate for individuals in isolation than for a busy classroom setting where everyone can see what everyone else is doing. Tasks involving interaction and collaboration appear to be far more suitable for such a setting, and the evidence offered here is that they may also encourage high levels of work and low levels of distraction.

TEACHER–PUPIL INTERACTION: A QUALITATIVE ANALYSIS

The last two decades have seen a number of different approaches to the analysis of classroom interactions, and the substantial literature which has grown out of them is reviewed by Edwards and Mercer (1987). It is not our intention either to emulate their review or to replicate any of the major studies of the last few years, but rather to focus on some of the detail of the interactions which took place in the ten classrooms of the present study and look for ways in which they may have influenced the task-related behaviour of the pupils. As Edwards and Mercer suggest, 'it is essentially in the discourse between teacher and pupils that education is done, or fails to be done', a view consistent with prevailing models of learning which highlight the role of language and social interaction.

We have chosen to make one extended extract the starting point of the qualitative analysis, and to illustrate and amplify the various points it raises by the use of further quotations from the total range of transcripts.

EXTRACT 8

[8:1] *Ms X:* Yesterday I think you did discuss – last thing yesterday afternoon – which three stories we were going to read and listen to and perhaps do some work about afterwards; and you were told the names of the three authors who wrote these stories, am I right? [*No response*] Because we thought it was important for you to find out when these stories were written, because that really makes a big difference to your attitude to the stories. And I think I saw some members of Class Ten diligently looking inside *Encyclopedia Britannica* yesterday and finding out some information about the three authors. Put your hands up if you were the people who looked up about them. [*Some hands go up.*] Right, can you tell us which one you found out about then, K?

[8:2] *K:* Journ . . .

[8:3] *Ms X:* Shall we put the names on the board, and then we'll get to know them, won't we? [*She moves to the blackboard.*]

[8:4] *K:* *Journey to the Centre of the Earth.*

[8:5] *Ms X:* And who was that by?

[8:6] *K:* Jules Verne. [*Ms X writes: Jules Verne.*]

[8:7] *Ms X:* Jules Verne you found out about. So did you find out about when he lived?

[8:8] *K:* No.

[8:9] *Ms X:* Well that was the vital thing wasn't it?

[8:10] *Ms A:* Some of you did.

[8:11] *Ms X:* Anybody find out about Jules Verne? When he was born and died?

[8:12] *L:* Born 1828; died 1905. [*Ms X writes this on the blackboard.*]

[8:13] *Ms X:*   So this story's not going to be a story about – well, it's not a story about the world at his time anyway. But the ideas that he's got in his story, we've got to remember that when he wrote it – which is the last century isn't it? Probably about a hundred years ago since he wrote the story. So when we're reading his story we've got to bear that in mind, haven't we; and if we think some of his ideas are a bit funny or old-fashioned, we know why, don't we? When he was around they were probably very modern ideas, weren't they? Right, who found out about one of the other two authors? M, did you do one? [*M does not answer.*] N, who did you find out about?

[8:14] *N:*   I did Sir Arthur Conan Doyle.

[8:15] *Ms X:*   Sir . . . Arthur . . . Conan . . . Doyle. [*Ms X writes: Sir Arthur Connan Doyle.*] I hope I'm spelling these right.

[8:16] *Ms A:*   I think you are, Ms X.

[8:17] *Ms X:*   Tell me if I'm not, won't you? [*To N:*] Did you find his dates then?

[8:18] *N:*   Yes. I've got them in my tray.

[8:19] *Ms X:*   Go and find them. [*To the class:*] And who's the other?

[8:20] *Ms A:*   Come on.

[8:21] *O:*   Jules Verne.

[8:22] *Ms X:*   Again? So that the same man wrote two of these stories, and he [*pointing at Sir Arthur Conan Doyle's name on the blackboard*] wrote the other one. What was the other one he [*pointing at Jules Verne's name*] wrote?

[8:23] *O:*   *Around the World in Eighty Days.*

[8:24] *Ms X:*   *Around the World in Eighty Days.* And which was the one he [*pointing at Sir Arthur Conan Doyle's name again*] wrote?

[8:25] *L:*   *Lost World.*

[8:26] *Ms X:*   Now there's going to be something very similar. We've deliberately picked these three stories out because we think there are certain similarities which we hope you'll spot when you've heard them.

[8:27] *P:*   They're all to do with the earth.

[8:28] *Ms X:*   They're all something to do . . . something peculiar to do with it, aren't they?

[8:29] *Q:*   When he wrote these stories he didn't know they'd come true, but most of his facts have come true.

[8:30] *Ms X:*   What do we call – what do we call that kind of fiction now, that's about strange things that might be going to happen in the future, and some of them have already happened? Q?

[8:31] *Q:*   Science fiction.

[8:32] *Ms X:* It's what we call science fiction, isn't it? Only this is an old kind of science fiction that was written before things happened like men going to the moon, which now – it's true, isn't it? We're doing finding out work about that now, aren't we? And they were writing about it as if it would never happen, as if it was fantasy. So we've got to bear that in mind when we're reading these stories. So we're going to split into three big groups and we're going to listen to the whole of the story through first. There might be bits that you don't understand. Your teacher might decide to keep stopping the tape if anyone's stuck with the story, or they might decide just to keep listening; and then we'll talk about it after you've listened to the whole thing. We'll see how you're taking it – how hard it is for you when you start. [*N returns with Sir Arthur Conan Doyle's dates.*]

[8:33] *N:* He lived 1859 to 1930. [*Ms X writes the dates on the blackboard.*]

[8:34] *Ms X:* So he's a little bit later, isn't he? But still sort of from one century to another. Isn't he? [*No response*]

[8:35] *Ms A:* What was the word you found out, R? [*R does not answer.*] About Jules Verne? [*No response*] Can you remember? [*No response*] The first person in relation to science fiction . . . ?

[8:36] *R:* Pioneer.

[8:37] *Ms A:* Yes, pioneer. Of . . . ?

[8:38] *Ms X:* He started it all, did he?

[8:39] *Ms A:* . . . this type of writing.

[8:40] *Ms X:* How many of you like science fiction? [*No response*] Or read some from the library? [*A few hands go up.*] How many of you don't like it? [*No response*] Put your hands up if you don't like it. [*No response*] If you don't pick science fiction. [*Many hands go up.*] I don't usually, so I'll be interested to see whether I enjoy it or not.

The prevalence of questions

Throughout the extract, and indeed throughout the entire teaching session, much of Ms X's talk was in the form of questions. Sometimes they demanded answers (for example, 8:11). Often, however, they were no more than a conversational device, as in the isn't it, haven't we, don't we, weren't they sequence [8:13] where she neither waited for nor presumably wanted any response. Occasionally the pupils seemed unclear about the purpose of a question and did not attempt to answer it unless it was repeated or reformulated (such as 8:34, 8:40).

In view of the finding of the ORACLE team (Galton *et al.* 1980a) that among their sample of teachers whole-class teaching was associated with a high incidence of teacher questions, it might be supposed that Ms X's questioning approach in Extract 8 was determined by the fact that she was working with the whole class, rather than with an individual or a small group. However, this explanation does not bear close examination. In the first place, the questions which differentiated the 'class enquirers' from the other teachers in the ORACLE study were characterised by an emphasis on problem-solving and ideas, and took the form of 'higher level cognitive interactions'. They certainly bore little resemblance to the token questions in Extract 8. Second, Ms X asked just as many questions when working with groups or individuals as she did when working with the whole class, and she was by no means unusual in this respect. Although there were exceptions, most of the teachers in the sample framed the bulk of their discourse in the form of questions. For example, instead of saying, 'Today we're going to make pictures for the carnival on Friday week', Ms D in Extract 5 initiated a section of dialogue involving thirteen questions (some of them repetitions or reformulations of earlier questions) covering five different aspects of the matter: she began by asking whether the children could remember what she had said they would be doing on that day (5:1); she asked them what they would be making (5:1); she wanted them to tell her why they would be painting pictures (5:1); she asked when the carnival would be taking place (5:3–5:6), and ended with questions to make sure they knew which Friday they were talking about (5:7–5:11). Throughout the sample as a whole, an almost automatic questioning mode was the norm, and there are two obvious reasons why this should be so.

First, whatever else it is, classroom interaction is also an example of people talking to one another, and consequently it shares many of the ordinary conversational conventions of our culture. In everyday life it is by no means unusual for commands and instructions to be expressed in the form of questions (such as, 'Could you make a little less noise?' or 'Would you care to stack those boxes over there?'). It is a verbal formula which might confuse and even seem devious or hypocritical to a member of a different culture or to a child who has not yet learned the conventions of his or her own, but within its context it is accepted quite unselfconsciously as the way certain kinds of transaction are carried out. It appears in classrooms just as it appears anywhere else.

Second, one of most stable features of post-Plowden primary education has been an antipathy towards didactic modes of teaching: it would have been a bold and eccentric primary teacher who, at any time during the last twenty years, had tried to secure a teaching post by stating at interview that their principal teaching strategy was to sit the children in rows and tell them things. Ideas of first-hand experience, learning through discovery, self-directed activity and so on, made it seem that classrooms are places where questions are raised rather than places where information is handed on, and a consequence of this could be that teachers might substitute some kind of exploratory dialogue with their pupils for even the most straightforward transmission of facts or instructions.

However, although the transcripts are full of questions of all kinds, there are relatively few that show unmistakable signs of leading to what Edwards and Mercer (1987) call 'joint understanding arising out of joint activity and discourse'. The virtually impossible task of the teacher is to pitch his or her questions at such a level that they form an appropriate challenge for all the pupils simultaneously, since pupils invariably and inevitably have widely differing skills and abilities.

Balancing skills and challenges

The notion that a balance between skills and challenges is a prerequisite of successful learning has a familiar ring. Well over half a century ago, as the zone of proximal development, it played a key role in Vygotsky's long suppressed but subsequently influential developmental psychology (Vygotsky 1978). More recently it was characterised by Csikszentmihalyi (1975) as one of the two main features of the state which he termed 'flow', in which people become able to 'concentrate their attention on a limited stimulus field, forget personal problems, lose their sense of time and of themselves, feel competent and in control, and have a sense of harmony and union with their surroundings'. Under the pseudonym of 'match', it was relaunched by HMI in the late seventies (DES 1978) and has remained part of the vocabulary of primary education ever since.

It is clear that in any work undertaken with a large number of children at once, the achievement of a lasting communal or group balance between skills and challenges is virtually impossible; there will always be some who are bored because they are marking time and others who are anxious or alienated because they are struggling to keep up. For as long as the teacher is simply holding forth or making statements in the form of token questions which require no answers, this state of affairs can remain conveniently hidden. Occasional genuine questions, drawing answers from those children who can give them, advance the cognitive content of the session and maintain the illusion that 'the class' is involved in a learning process. However, genuine dialogue involving all the children and consisting of questions requiring genuine answers would quickly bring the session to a halt as the widespread lack of balance between skills and challenges among the participating children became apparent and inescapable.

With smaller groups the situation is slightly easier. Here, token questions are still an option, although a more common device is the pitching of genuine questions at a very low level, and the acceptance of responses which are barely adequate or relevant, as in the following extract from the transcripts where the teacher was working with a small group.

EXTRACT 9

[9:1]   *Ms E:*   Right! I'm going to write up here the title: A Day at the Fair. A . . . and when you're writing a title or a sentence . . . What is very special about the first letter of a sentence?

[9:2]   *K:*   It's a capital letter.

[9:3]   *Ms E:*   Good, K. [*To L, a child from another group*] Can't you get it out?

[9:4]   *M:*   Something else what you remember; . . .

[9:5]   *Ms E:*   [*To L*] There we are.

[9:6]   *M:*   . . . it's about leaving a finger space.

[9:7]   *Ms E:*   [*To L:*] Can you manage?

[9:8]   *M:*   Miss . . .

[9:9]   *Ms E:*   [*To M, whose contribution she heard even though she was dealing with L:*] A finger space after each word.

[9:10]   *N:*   Yeh; and a full stop at the end.

[9:11]   *Ms E:*   And a full stop at the end. A Day . . . [*Several children read aloud the words as she writes them:*] A Day . . . at . . . the . . . Fair. Now . . . Now . . . Now, I'm going to read the little bit that I've – I've started the story off for you, and then you're going to finish it, but we're going to talk about how we might finish it before you start writing. And the sheet's divided into two, so you've got – what does it say on the top? Can anybody tell me?

[9:12]   *M:*   Draw your picture.

[9:13]   *Ms E:*   Draw your picture. And what does it say? . . . A Day at the Fair. [*She reads:*] We were all very excited as the bus stopped at the bus stop. In our bags were our packed lunches and . . . And then that's where I stop; and that's where you're going to think about what we're going to write about next.

[9:14]   *K:*   And sandwiches.

[9:15]   *Ms E:*   Packed lunches and sandwiches?

[9:16]   *M:*   And pop.

[9:17]   *Ms E:*   [*To a child in another group*] Er, O! Is there a problem? [*The response is unintelligible.*] Thank you. [*To her current group:*] What else might you have in your . . .

[9:18]   *M:*   Pop.

[9:19] *N*:   Comic.
[9:20] *K*:   Crisps.
[9:21] *Ms E*:   Comic. You might have had a comic with you.
[9:22] *M*:   Pop.
[9:23] *Ms E*:   Pop, yes. Why would you have pop with you?
[9:24] *M*:   In case you get thirsty.
[9:25] *Ms E*:   In case you get thirsty. What else might you have in your
                 bag?
[9:26] *K*:   Cake.
[9:27] *P*:   You could have – er, er, – buns.
[9:28] *Ms E*:   Buns.
[9:29] *M*:   Apples.
[9:30] *Ms E*:   Apples.
[9:31] *M*:   Money.
[9:32] *Ms E*:   Money. Why might you want money?
[9:33] *M*:   To buy someth . . .
[9:34] *Ms E*:   To buy . . . what sort of stuff might you want to buy? . . .
[9:35] *M*:   Teddy.
[9:36] *Ms E*:   Teddy.
[9:37] *K*:   Sweets.
[9:38] *Ms E*:   Sweets.
[9:39] *N*:   A present.
[9:40] *Ms E*:   A present. Who would you buy a present for, N?
[9:41] *N*:   My mam.
[9:42] *Ms E*:   Your mam. That would be lovely, wouldn't it? . . .

At the outset, Ms E adopted the common strategy of delivering an instruction which turned into a question (9:1). Because she was working with only a small number of children, she could afford to ask real questions which were likely to elicit real answers. However, two of the three answers she was given (9:6 and 9:10) in response to her first question were totally irrelevant: though perfectly good statements about the way things were done in that particular class, they simply did not relate to the question she had asked (9:1). Thus, within seconds the point had been reached where the lesson as planned would have been seriously disrupted if Ms E had entered into a genuine dialogue with her pupils about the points they were making – points, incidentally, which they would never have made if she had not turned her first instruction into a question.

She dealt with the matter by repeating their answers without comment (9:9 and 9:11) and moving on, telling the children (9:11) that she had written the first part of a story about a day at a fair, and that they would be required to finish it, and adding, 'but we're going to talk about how we might finish it before you start writing'. This marks a point in the session where a genuine dialogue might have provided the pupils with enough background information to give the task some meaning and offer them some prospect of success. However, there would also have been a risk that such a dialogue might reveal the task as basically unsuitable for a group of children who were really rather unlikely ever to have spent an entire day at a fair and who in any case would have found considerable difficulty in summing up the experiences of a whole day in writing even if we assume that they had something they wanted to express.

In the event, the dialogue did not take place; Ms E avoided the risk it would have involved by engaging her pupils instead (9:13 onwards) in a series of questions about what they might carry in their bags along with their packed lunches. The very first answer she was offered (9:14) was almost startling in its incongruity, yet she accepted it, just as she accepted a number of others which bore little relevance to a day's outing to a fairground. Sometimes she added follow-up questions such as 'Why would you have pop with you?' (9:23) and 'Why might you want money?' (9:32) which were pitched at such a low level that even someone who had no idea what the conversation was about could have furnished answers as good as those offered to, and accepted by, Ms E (it was suggested to her, for example, that children might want to take money to a fair to buy a teddy (9:35), sweets (9:37) and a present (9:39), but none of the children showed any sign of realising that they would need money to pay for rides and other fairground amusements, nor did Ms E point this out to them). In striving to avoid the frustration or anxiety which might have arisen from too hard a challenge, she ran a heavy risk of provoking the kind of boredom which generally accompanies tasks in which there is no challenge at all. It should be stressed that the purpose of this analysis is not to be critical of Ms E or to suggest that she was somehow failing in her duties. Faced with a formidable set of conflicting demands she opted for what she could manage and for what would allow her teaching session to progress in a way she could predict and control. In the setting in which she found herself, the attempt to balance skills and challenges accurately was just too formidable a task.

She was also facing another challenge which was no less daunting.

Motivation and choice

It is clear that, however accomplished Ms E might have been at balancing skills and challenges, she could not hope for much success with the members of her group unless they were also adequately motivated. In the wider world of informal learning, the motivation to overcome a particular challenge or acquire a new skill is not generally imposed by a third party. We learn something because we want to; as the American runner Roger Eischens puts it, 'the doors of learning are opened from the inside' (Eischens *et al.* 1977). It would be convenient if classrooms could operate on the same principle, but an entirely free choice of activities was not, and never could be, an option for the teacher or the pupils in Ms E's or any other class. There are strict conventions about the kinds of activity which are permissible in schools, as is illustrated by a comment made by Ms C in one of her interviews:

> We try and say no running, because of the shoes [lying on the floor at the entrance to the wet area]; I mean they'll break their necks on some of the shoes. We normally say don't bring the pram right out here and that's really sort of getting on with your class because if somebody's doing number they don't particularly want the pram going over their shoes – over their clothes and things. Just safety things like that: no running; no climbing; no sort of climbing in the cupboard and locking somebody in it; but apart from that, at this particular moment we're not restricting at all.

Even in very informal classrooms, many activities which might be assumed to appeal to children are for various reasons explicitly (or more often tacitly) forbidden. There are also strict limits on the resources available to facilitate those activities which are approved. Consequently, for most of the time in the present study, pupils had no say in the tasks they were given, and where the allocation of tasks involved questions like 'Will you help me read it?' (4:3) or 'Would you like to?' (5:25) this was simply the conversational device described earlier, and not an indication that the pupil had a choice. Indeed, on the few occasions when children who had not yet grasped the convention of expressing orders as questions took such questions literally and offered a negative answer, the teacher simply substituted a more direct instruction.

Where some degree of choice was in operation it took one of three forms. Sometimes the teacher called out the names of group activities one by one, and the pupils had to raise their hands to indicate which group they wanted to join (10:1). This constituted choice only in a very restricted sense, for in the first place there might have been children in the class who, given a wider choice, would never have chosen any of the group activities on offer, and in the second place, as the procedure continued, those pupils who were not selected for the group of their first choice faced a dwindling number of alternatives which they had already implicitly rejected, a situation which sometimes caused such difficulties that the teacher simply cancelled the exercise altogether:

EXTRACT 10

[10:1] *Ms J*: Be quiet while I sort out the other people. Of the rest of you, who'd like to go to Ms X to do PE? [*All the children*

> *raise their hands.*] Oh, oh! You can't all do that! Let's do it
> the other way round. Put your hands down. Who'd
> specially like to go to Ms Y to do some music? [*No response*]
> Oh, you enjoy doing music with Ms Y! [*No response*]
> Nobody? Right. Mr Z? [*K raises her hand*] K, you've just
> said you're going to computers! You can't do both. Can't
> be in two places at once. [*K lowers her hand*] Anybody else
> like to go to Mr Z today? [*No response*] Right, I'll just have
> to share out the other three groups then, and I'll do that
> later on so we won't take any more time now. Lots of
> people like doing PE, don't they? . . .

In the second form of choice, one of the group activities of the session was itself called 'choosing' (a label and form of curricular organisation which we discuss in the context of the case studies in the previous chapter), and some children were allocated to it. The 'choosing' group's options were generally limited to a small range of low-status activities requiring minimal supervision. The existence of the group enabled the teacher to spend virtually all her time with pupils engaged in activities of higher status in other groups elsewhere. From the pupils' point of view, allocation to the 'choosing' group offered similar drawbacks to those of the first form of choice. The sand tray, water tray and home corner do not necessarily appeal to all children, especially when there are adults around to call a halt to the more adventurous and innovative things that can be done in them. Apart from that, the element of choice between these activities was in practice negligible. Each could accommodate only a limited number of children (a fact which was emphasised at Blakemore by notices specifying the maximum number permitted on each piece of equipment) and the children who were slowest off the mark were obliged to fit in wherever they could. Furthermore, as in the allocation of groups itself, the teachers could quite arbitrarily rescind the element of choice to whatever degree they chose (3:2–3:3).

The third form of choice involved individual children who had finished a piece of work, or who were otherwise at a loose end, and who asked if they could engage in some particular activity. Sometimes they were lucky; they wanted to do something that was permitted, and the relevant apparatus or space was available (4:28–4:29). Occasionally their good fortune came at the expense of somebody else who was taken away from a congenial task to make room for the newcomer (7:1–7:9). More often they were unlucky, although the teacher would sometimes contrive to maintain an illusion of choice even while refusing it, as in the following exchange:

EXTRACT 11

[11:1] *K*:   Can I get the cars out?
[11:2] *Ms B*: No, just the jigsaws this morning. You can try all of those
              jigsaws.

Here K expressed a wish to play with toy cars and was told to do a
jigsaw instead. However, the imposition of the alternative task was
softened by the suggestion that he could try all of the available jigsaws.
On the face of it he was still being offered a choice: he could sample
the total range of jigsaws (rather as one might try on shoes or taste a
few cheeses) before deciding which one suited him best. The essential
emptiness of this offer becomes apparent if we pause to consider how
and in what sense K could possibly try a series of jigsaws before deciding
which one he would do. In effect he was being told to tackle a jigsaw
and change it for an easier one if it proved too hard. The element of
choice was almost entirely illusory, as it was in another situation,
described by Ms C:

> I notice, yesterday and again today, K has chosen to go on [the water
> tray]. Now tomorrow, if he immediately says can I go on the water,
> I'll direct him somewhere else and let ... it seems a shame, but I'll
> let somebody else have a go so that by the end ... again it would be
> fortnightly; I would say by the end of a fortnight everyone would
> have moved throughout the choice areas. Because otherwise you get
> the same children, you know, they do have, they do. .... I know they
> feel familiar and happy with it ... but they tend to, you know, have
> a favourite and go back and back again and they're not extending,
> or having a breadth of experience if they do that.

In reality, then, the pupils had very little say in the allocation of work,
and this being so, an important task for the teachers was to make the
activities which they imposed on their pupils seem as attractive as
possible. Offering the illusion of choice was simply one of the ways in
which they sought to achieve this; it was another respect in which classroom interaction echoed the everyday transactions of the outside world.

Part of the difficulty was the presence of more than one learner: both
the matching of challenges to skills, and the task of motivating pupils
become less and less practicable as the size of the group increases. Even
when there is only one learner, however, the likelihood of success in
these two matters is not great if the task and the ground rules are determined by somebody else. Extract 12 is taken from a session between a
teacher and a single pupil. The pupil was allowed to choose the book
from which he would read, but of course the task of reading to the
teacher was imposed upon him.

EXTRACT 12

[12:1] *Ms G:*   K, come and read to me please.

[12:2] *K:*   This is on canals.

[12:3] *Ms G:*   Oh, lovely. That's a good one to find; well done. Shall we read that to everybody later on? That's smashing. Are you going to read it to me now? And there's another one of those pictures with a castle in it.

[12:4] *K:*   Yes.

[12:5] *Ms G:*   Well spotted!

[*K begins to read. He hesitates over 'towpath'.*]

Towpath.

[*K continues reading, but is having difficulty.*]

What's it start with?

[*K continues haltingly. Ms G takes over and reads a few sentences for him:*] 'No-one hears the pebble ring of iron shoe now.' What do you think pebble ring of iron shoe means? [*No response*] What wears an iron shoe?

[12:6] *K:*   The horse.

[12:7] *Ms G:*   That's right; it's talking about the old days now.

[*She reads aloud to the end of the section.*]

Go on.

[*He begins to read again, haltingly.*]

Good!

[12:8] *K:*   the . . . long . . . steamed . . .

[12:9] *Ms G:*   That's a hard one: 'the long-stemmed, velvet candled sedge, where voles in a fur float silently and hide . . . ' What do you think the long-stemmed, velvet candled sedge is? Any idea? [*No response*] Is it on the boat or beside the canal?

[12:10] *K:*   Beside the canal.

[12:11] *Ms G:*   Yes! It's the reeds. It's those long grasses that grow, and sometimes you get the bulrushes. Have you ever seen a bulrush? [*No response*] They have a long brown top to them and sometimes they feel very furry. In fact they feel rather like a mole. Moles have very, very soft fur. That's a bulrush. So bulrushes grow very tall and have a black-brown head on the top, and that's what it means. They are rather like a candle; it looks like a candle; they're rather like a candle. 'Where voles . . . ' Voles are little water creatures . . . 'Float silently and hide.' That's very nice, isn't it?

[*K doesn't answer the question, but begins reading again and reads a few sentences.*] Right! Would you like to go and get yourself a story book to read as well?

[12:12] K: Yes.
[12:13] Ms G: OK. Thank you very much, K. L! Can I hear you read, please? . . .

In selecting the book K had misjudged its level of difficulty, and it proved too hard for him. There was no balance between outer challenge and inner skills, and K's behaviour in reading to the teacher was motivated by external pressures rather than by the enjoyment of reading. There was no real prospect of a successful outcome unless either the book or the task was changed: Ms G could have insisted upon an easier book, or discussed the level of difficulty with K and asked him if he would like to make a different choice. Instead, she did most of the work herself, reading a substantial part of the text for him (12:5; 12:7), and giving a commentary which, in spite of its questions, proved scarcely more than a monologue. Because she was working with a single child she was released from the need to relate to several different levels of skill at the same time, and had the option of tailoring her questions to K's particular interests and ability level. It was an option which she seemed about to take up in her questions about the pebble ring of iron shoe (12:5) and the long-stemmed, velvet candled sedge (12:9), but her treatment of K's answer to the latter question (12:10; 12:11) marks her final retreat from the challenge. K's response (12:10) to the final version of the question gives no reason to suppose that he had any idea at all what the long-stemmed, velvet candled sedge was (any more than he had shown any sign of understanding what 'the pebble ring of iron shoe' meant), and it is clear that Ms G was chiefly concerned to reformulate her questions in such a way that K would have the experience of answering them successfully even though he had not understood what he was reading. She must have realised that he was sinking under the burden of a task which was too difficult, and that a genuine discussion of the text would inevitably bring his failure and the basic unsuitability of the task into the open. Her solution was to protect the illusion that he was successfully engaged in a self-chosen enjoyable activity by reducing the challenge of her questions until he could not fail them, in much the same way as Ms E had done in the fairground discussion in Extract 9.

This reduction of demand to a very low level was a common strategy, and it is easy to see why. When tasks have to be imposed rather than chosen, and when it is impossible to balance outer challenges with inner skills, the imposition of a very small quantity of extremely easy work is a convenient option, maximising the number of children who can proceed without assistance, and offering at least the illusion of motivation through enjoyment. It explains the widespread use of undemanding play activities, as well as interactions like the following:

EXTRACT 13

[Forty-four minutes into the session, K brings her maths to be marked.]

[13:1] *Ms F:*   It's a lot better, a lot better colouring in. [*She begins to mark the work.*] Four take away three leaves one. Four take away two leaves two; well done! Three and two make five; oh, that's an easy one! Have you tried a harder one? [*No response*] Two and three make five. Do you want to try another card?

[13:2] *K:*   No.

[13:3] *Ms F:*   No? Why not? How many sums have you done this morning?

[13:4] *L:*   [*from another group:*] Can I try this?

[13:5] *K:*   Four.

[13:6] *Ms F:*   Four sums. Right, then that will do then. Have a rest. You can do some more later.

[13:7] *L:*   Miss, miss!
    [*Ms F turns her attention to L.*]

We cannot know what proportion of the eleven minutes per sum was spent by K on 'colouring in'. It is an activity which may not be entirely without value for young childen but which in the context of a maths session is an obvious time-filler with no bearing on the number skills being practised. We do know, however, that in the time left over from colouring in, K did four sums correctly, and there is a strong implication in Ms F's comments (13:1) that she found the work easy. Under closer supervision, and without the redundant colouring activity, she might well have been able to complete the work in a tenth of the time it took her, yet with a quarter of an hour still to go until the end of the session Ms F invited her to have a rest. The only unusual thing about this episode was the openness of the teacher's invitation; it was more usual for children to be invited to finish off some other work and for the progress of the other work not to be monitored subsequently.

Praise and power

A further feature of the conversation between K and Ms G, similar in its tone though not perhaps in its significance to Ms G's acceptance of incomplete answers as correct, was her somewhat exaggerated use of praise (12:3 and 12:5). Although by no means all the teachers in the sample used this interaction strategy, Ms G was not alone in her liking for it, and indeed made less use of it than Ms C, whose lavish and almost mechanical repertoire of praise was a prominent feature of an earlier extract (4:1, 4:3, 4:9, 4:11, and so on). Like instructions disguised as questions and imposition disguised as choice, praise is a common feature not only of classroom interaction but also of everyday conversation, where some of us make far more use of it than others, and where too much of it can be as disconcerting as too little until the person at whom it is aimed has realised that it is not to be taken at face value.

These three interaction strategies, together with the non-reciprocal use of first names which is also a normal feature of classroom life, are all peculiar to hierarchical situations, and have in common their covert assertion of power. Teachers can choose what they will call their pupils, and generally use their first names, but are in a position to specify how they will be addressed in return. They can and do ask questions which must be treated as instructions and obeyed, but are in a position to decide how, if at all, they will respond to such questions as the pupils themselves may ask. They can and do from time to time tell their pupils that they may choose what they will do, but are in a position to overrule any choices they make or to cancel the arrangement at any time. Teachers can and do both praise and criticise pupils' diligence, competence, neatness and conduct to whatever extent they choose, while their own diligence, competence, neatness and conduct are usually exempt from classroom comment or discussion.

It is not suggested that this power relationship is in any sense unreasonable, and certainly an institutionalised educational system could not function without hierarchies of some kind. This particular version is informal and unobtrusive, yet so pervasive and effective that when pupils break its unwritten rules they are quickly put in their place; and if teachers attempt to step outside it, even temporarily, they are likely to experience resistance from pupils as well as colleagues. For example, during a class discussion of three novels, Ms X at Applegarth correctly suspected that she might have misspelt an author's name on the blackboard [8:15] and asked Ms A and the class to correct her if she had made a mistake [8:17]. Several pupils had spent time the previous day seeking basic information about the author in an encyclopaedia [8:1]. It is inconceivable that neither of Ms A's two colleagues, who had both helped to select the author [8:26] and who were both in the room at the time, and none of the pupils who had been making notes about him, knew the correct spelling of his name. However, the pupils remained silent and Ms A went so far as to legitimise the incorrect spelling by publicly saying that she thought it was right. In this way the power structure remained intact, in spite of Ms X's very human willingness to admit to poor spelling and lack of preparation in front of the pupils she was teaching.

Nor was this an isolated incident, although the idea of the teacher's infallibility was more often encouraged by the teacher herself than by the other people present. In Extract 4, for example, Ms C told M to go and point to his collage of a bucket of shells (4:1), an impossible task since he had not made one. When this was pointed out to Ms C (4:2), she dealt with the matter by treating M as if the mistake was his, saying, 'M, just listen; then you'll know. Right! Come back! Thank you' (4:3).

It is through the experience of such incidents that pupils learn how the classroom works and what behaviours are appropriate within it. It is clear, for example, that if praise becomes a mere mannerism, either in ordinary conversation or in classroom interaction, it loses any reinforcement value it would otherwise have, and when this happens a pupil who wants to understand what is happening must attempt to work out the unwritten rules which govern the allocation of praise and blame in that particular classroom, and the unspoken messages they imply. This is by no means always an easy task. Occasionally, teachers in the sample appeared to be giving high praise to work which they were simultaneously finding unsatisfactory, so that a child who was genuinely trying to make sense of the situation might well have been confused:

EXTRACT 14

[14:1] *Ms C*:   Now that's beautiful! I knew you could do it. You see! I can't make out what that says over there. I'm not even going to tick that writing. I'll tick the picture because the picture's lovely, but that writing [*pointing at some earlier work*] is a lot better than that [*pointing at the current work*]. Put it in the 'finished' basket.

Until the final sentence, Extract 14 makes perfectly good sense: the child had produced a picture which Ms C described as both beautiful and lovely, and some writing which was so poor that it did not even merit a tick. However, Ms C went on to accept the work, telling the child to put it in the 'finished' basket; and this raises puzzling questions about what constituted acceptable work in Ms C's class, and what the supposed function of a tick might have been.

Teachers' treatment of pupils' responses

A central feature of the power structure of the classroom is the teacher's freedom to accept, reject or ignore the utterances of the pupils. Skilfully used, it is a way of ensuring that seemingly unstructured and open-ended dialogue leads in the direction teachers want their teaching sessions to go. Sometimes they may block off an avenue of discussion by ignoring a response altogether (9:20) or by simply repeating it and moving on (9:29–30; 9:35–36). If they want further responses they may repeat or paraphrase the original question without commenting on the answers they have already received (18:1–18:9). This procedure seems to arise, in part, from a understandable reluctance to discourage children by pronouncing their answers wrong; indeed, sometimes in the sample classrooms this reluctance led teachers to react positively to an answer before setting it aside:

EXTRACT 15

[Ms B is reading an illustrated book with a small group]

[15:1] *Ms B:* What's happening on this page? [*No response*] K?
[15:2] *K:* Don't know.
[15:3] *Ms B:* Well have a look.
[15:4] *K:* Wrestling.
[15:5] *Ms B:* Yes! There's a man with a hairy chest! I think he's weight lifting. It doesn't look as if he's wrestling . . .

Here, K's answer was unequivocally wrong, since the picture was of a circus strong man; yet at first Ms B implied that it was right, and even made explicit the grounds upon which she assumed K had reached it (the man in the picture had a hairy chest) before saying that she thought the man was doing something else (15:5). In this respect, her behaviour was rather like that of Ms C who, in Extract 14, appeared to be praising work and finding it unacceptable simultaneously. On another occasion, Ms C went even further:

EXTRACT 16

[Ms C is introducing a visiting nurse to the class. The nurse is not in uniform]

[16:1] *Ms C:* This is Nurse Z. What do nurses usually wear? [*No response*] What do they have on? [*No response*] You remember our picture of a nurse.
[16:2] *K:* Hats and coats.
[16:3] *Ms C:* Well, they wear special hats but they don't usually wear coats I don't think. What do they wear?
[16:4] *L:* A nurse suit.
[16:5] *Ms C:* A nurse suit; that's a good answer. Well, I'm afraid Nurse Z hasn't got her uniform on . . .

Here, Ms C failed to elicit the word she was looking for ('uniform') and was given a substitute ('nurse suit') instead. Her reaction was to praise L publicly for 'a good answer' and then to use the word 'uniform' in a comment about the nurse without explaining that this was the word she had been seeking. Such a technique is undoubtedly gentle and even generous towards a pupil who has given the wrong answer. Its weakness lies in its inefficiency: in Extract 16, for example, any pupils who already knew the word 'uniform' were reminded of it (16:5), but were also led to believe that 'nurse suit' was a perfectly acceptable alternative, while pupils who had never heard the word before were given no indication of its meaning when Ms C eventually used it. It is unlikely that anyone learned anything new about what nurses usually wear.

This kind of consequence was not confined to situations where the teacher was reluctant to tell children that an answer was incorrect:

EXTRACT 17

[In this extract it has been necessary to drop the convention of using letters of the alphabet in place of children's names because names and initials are the subject of the conversation. The names used here are substitutes for the originals.]

[17:1] *Ms B*: Let's see who's going to go and wash their hands first! If your name begins with 'M', go and wash your hands.
[17:2] *Darren*: Can I go?
[17:3] *Ms B*: No. What does your name begin with?
[17:4] *Darren*: D.
[17:5] *Ms B*: D. Well go and sit down then. [*To the class:*] M for Michael; M for Mark . . .
[17:6] *Lynne*: M for Rodney.
[17:7] *Ms B*: No! What does Rodney's name begin with?
[17:8] *Pupils*: R! R!
[17:9] *John*: M for Matthew?
[17:10] *Ms B*: M for Matthew; has he gone? [*To Paul:*] Put your glasses on. [*To the class:*] If your name begins with R, you can go to the toilet first. Don't forget to wash your hands. R for Rodney; R for Robert . . .

Extract 17 concerns an entirely informal activity at the end of a teaching session, and there is no reason to suppose that anyone involved expected much learning to take place. Nevertheless, it took the form of a classroom task, and it illustrates how easily situations can arise where most of the participants either know something already (and learn nothing new) or don't know it already (and hence cannot fully understand the nature of the task). It is clear from Ms B's promptings (17:5 and 17:10) that there were a number of children in the class who either did not know the first letter of their own name or had not grasped what Ms B was asking them to do. Darren (17:2) was in the second category; when questioned by Ms B (17:3) he was able to give his initial without hesitation. However, we cannot know whether he understood the task which had been set because Ms B did not engage him in any dialogue which would have illuminated the matter. Lynne (17:6) might conceivably have known her own initial but obviously lacked the phonic expertise to make sensible suggestions about initials in general. Ms B was quite brisk and forthright with both Lynne and Darren, but so far as we can tell, neither child learned anything about the task or its underlying purpose; nor did the children (17:8) who were able to call out the right answers so readily, for the task was well within (or even below) their level of competence. Perhaps John (17:9) learned something: his suggestion was tentative as if he was almost but not quite sure that he was right, and Ms B's validation of his response might have aided or confirmed his understanding of the principle involved.

Initial praise of an inappropriate answer was not always a prelude to its dismissal. Occasionally, when a wrong answer promised to lead the session in a direction approved by the teacher it was accepted as correct; conversely, correct answers which were tangential to the teacher's train of thought were sometimes accorded the token praise normally given to incorrect answers, and then dismissed. An example of both occurrences appeared in Extract 8, and is worth repeating here:

[8:26] *Ms X:* Now there's going to be something very similar. We've deliberately picked these three stories out because we think there are certain similarities which we hope you'll spot when you've heard them.

[8:27] *P:* They're all to do with the earth.

[8:28] *Ms X:* They're all something to do . . . something peculiar to do with it, aren't they?

[8:29] *Q:* When he wrote these stories he didn't know they'd come true, but most of his facts have come true.

[8:30] *Ms X:* What do we call – what do we call that kind of fiction now, that's about strange things that might be going to happen in the future, and some of them have already happened? Q?

[8.31] *Q:* Science fiction.

[8:32] *Ms X:* It's what we call science fiction, isn't it? Only this is an old kind of science fiction that was written before things happened like men going to the moon, which now – it's true, isn't it?

P's answer (8:27) took Ms X by surprise, and she completely missed its point – namely, that all three books under discussion were about the earth, that is, the world: *The Lost World, Journey to the Centre of the Earth, Around the World in Eighty Days.* It was a thoughtful answer coming from a child who at that point knew the books only by their titles, and it could have led to useful discussion both before and after the three stories had been told. However, Ms X had something else in mind and was not prepared to be deflected for long enough to find out what P was trying to convey. When Q made her response (8:29) Ms X accepted it without reservation and used it as the starting point of her account of science fiction; it was just what she wanted. However, it was also wrong: even if we ignore the fact that it refers to two separate authors as if they were one and that it calls fantasies facts, it also claims that most of the fictional events in the three novels have since come true, and this is simply not so: to seek no further than the titles for example, the lost world has not been discovered, and there has been no journey to the centre of the earth.

In many of the sessions observed, as in those reported by researchers over many years (for example, Barnes *et al.* 1969; Edwards and Mercer 1987), the factor which determined a teacher's treatment of a pupil's response was not its accuracy or the thought that had gone into it, but rather its accordance with the teacher's own train of thought and the extent to which it enabled her to say the things she wanted to say during that session. There is a close parallel here with the matter of choice: in reality, it is simply not possible for children to choose what they will do in school, but for as long as they are prepared to choose the things they are going to have to do anyway, there can be an illusion of choice. Similarly, it is not strictly possible for the teacher to engage a class of children in genuine open dialogue and at the same time follow a detailed lesson plan, but for as long as there are some children whose responses fit in with the plan, there can be an illusion of open dialogue.

Interruptions

We have already seen that interruptions are a prominent feature of classroom life, and teachers deal with them in a wide range of different ways. It might be argued that an event becomes an interruption only if it is perceived as one, although it quickly became apparent to the PRINDEP observers that their own perceptions in this matter by no means always matched those of the teachers in whose classrooms they were working. However, in the nature of things it was the teacher who decided whether an interruption was taking place. Sometimes occurrences which were extremely distracting to the children were ignored by the teacher and hence, in a sense, were not interruptions at all:

EXTRACT 18

[Ms D has been telling her group about a fictional Mrs Muddle who has problems with the correct use of the terms 'yesterday', 'today' and 'tomorrow'.]

[18:1] *Ms D*:   What day was it yesterday?
[18:2] *K*:   Tuesday.
[18:3] *Ms D*:   Was it?
[18:4] *L*:   Thursday.
[18:5] *Ms D*:   What day is it today?
[18:6] *L*:   Wednesday.
[18:7] *Ms D*:   Today is ... What day is it today?
[18:8] *K*:   Wednesday.
[18:9] *Ms D*:   What have we just had this morning? [*No response*] What
            did we have this morning when we came to school?
[18:10] *Pupils*: Wednesday! Thursday!
[18:11] *Ms D*:   What did we do this morning when we came to school?
            My children are Muddles! [*A girl holding a milk bottle is
            chased into the area by a boy. They dodge among the children
            and then run out again.*]
            What did you do at nine o'clock? [*No response*] What did
            you do at nine o'clock?
[18:12] *K*:   Came to school.
[18:13] *Ms D*:   What did you do when you got here? ...

By the time the incident with the girl, the boy and the milk bottle took place (18:11), Ms D had already made the strategical error of assuming that she could best illustrate the use of the terms in question by linking them to the actual day of the discussion (18:1). Unfortunately, none of her pupils knew what day it was, and her attempt to prompt them by referring to school activities which took place only on specific days (18:9) merely confused them further. The milk-bottle episode certainly did nothing to help matters, but Ms D decided to persist with her attempt to establish what day it was, rather than risk losing the children's attention by halting the discussion and dealing with the interlopers. In other words, she chose not to be interrupted.

Other teachers, while not completely ignoring potential interruptions, nevertheless refused them, acknowledging them only to the extent of making it clear that they did not propose to be deflected from their current activities (for example, 4:11; 4:15); or they deferred dealing with them until they had finished what they were doing (for instance, 7:4 to 7:9; 9:4 to 9:9); or they dealt with them so speedily and efficiently that the disruption they caused was minimal (such as 4:16–4:17; and Extract 19).

EXTRACT 19

[Ms F is working with a number group.]

[19:1] *Ms F*:   Is the number three there?
[19:2] *Pupils*: No.

[19:3] *Ms F*:   No? What's the next number then?

[19:4] *Pupils*:   Number four.

> [K, *from another group, brings her work book and, without saying anything, shows it to Ms F.*]
>
> [*To K:*] Colour it in.
>
> [*To the number group:*] Number four. Is there a number four? Count them please . . .

[19:5] *Pupils*:   One . . . Two . . . Three . . . Four . . .

Thus in various ways, teachers sought to minimise the impact of the many distractions which presented themselves. At other times, however, they did precisely the opposite, choosing to draw attention to situations or incidents which might otherwise have passed unnoticed; we have already seen how Mr I did this three times in Extract 6, but there were many other examples:

EXTRACT 20

[20:1] *Ms J*:   Now, the choices will be between going down to the computer place with Mrs X, going to . . . Put your hands down and listen.

> [K *belches*.]
>
> [*To K:*] What do you say?

[20:2] *K*:   Pardon.

[20:3] *Ms J*:   That's better. [*To the class:*] And then the people who stay in school, it'll be between Mrs Y and some PE, Mr Z . . . I'm not quite sure what he's doing today but it will probably be some kind of story drama just as a one-off thing . . .

In Extract 20 Ms J chose to elevate K's belch to the status of an interruption, taking the opportunity to draw attention to behaviour which she found distasteful and imposing a form of etiquette which she considered appropriate. This particular strategy was very common: throughout the observation period no teacher devoted a teaching session to socially acceptable behaviour, but several deliberately interrupted sessions on other matters to focus their full attention on behaviour they did not like: examples included sitting 'like a little pixie' with the feet up on a chair in front, not being willing to share a bean bag with two other children, taking a second bottle of milk, chewing a hair band, and saying belly (instead of tummy).

Occasionally an interruption received such detailed treatment that it became an important part of the session in its own right. The most dramatic example of this was an incident in the Deacondale session which is summarised on page 118, where the arrival of a former classroom helper and her young American cousins prompted the teacher to jettison the language task she was doing with her group and engage the visitors in a public conversation which lasted twelve minutes, and which the group appeared to find at least as interesting as the work which had been interrupted. When the visitors finally left, the thread of the language work had been so completely broken that the teacher simply began a new set of tasks with the children.

In the light of these reactions to the many distractions of the teaching day, it will be seen that there is an almost paradoxical element in the very concept of a classroom interruption. Irritating as they may find an irrelevant or distracting occurrence, teachers can choose to ignore it, refuse it, postpone it or deal with it without turning aside from what they are doing; and in any of those events it really does not interrupt in any significant way. Alternatively they can seize upon it, make much of it, incorporate it into what they are doing or even cast aside their prearranged programme in its favour; and in any of those events they are using it as they would any other educational resource, so that it is less an interruption than an extension to the planned curriculum.

Very often teachers were the source of their own interruptions, generally because they were trying to do two or more things at once (for example, 7:13) or because they did not have a very clear idea of what they were trying to say (for instance 8:32; 9:11). Since the first of these two states of affairs tended to produce the second, it was not unusual for them to coincide:

EXTRACT 21

[21:1] *Ms J:* Would you put the toys back on the table, boys? That's it. K! K, would you put that back on the table please? [*To the class:*] Come on, you're wasting a lot of time. Settle down. [*Claps.*] I have asked you to settle down! And I don't like having to get cross before it happens; it's a waste of my time and your time. Now, we've got something special happening in our classroom tomorrow at playtime, which you all know about: our bun time, right? [*'Our bun time' involved the sale of buns for charity.*]

We need some more posters to put round the school. [*The majority of the children volunteer by putting their hands up.*] Right! If you're in the middle ... Right, now: L and M, you've only done part of your writing because you were out at recorders. [*To the class:*] If you were doing recorders this morning, keep your hands down. If you were doing maths earlier on this morning and you'd like to do me a poster next, you can. K, you can do me one too. You've finished your writing, haven't you? N, you can do one. O; yes, you can. Yes, all right, we do need lots; that's all right. [*To P, who has her hand up:*] Um ... You were going to do your writing for me next, weren't you? Oh, no; you weren't here for it, were you? I'm sorry. [*To the class:*] Ssshh! Ssshh! Ssshh! Right, I would like ... Q, I'd like you just to finish off that bit of writing you were doing, all right? And then I'd like the children who were doing the Book Three maths with me on Monday to come to the maths table next. One or two of you have just got a couple of things to finish off. R, you need to finish your sentence that you were working on as well, and then you can come and do that with me too. Who else was doing the Book Three maths with me on Monday? S, Q ... We've got people away, haven't we? T and U aren't here. V; right, you can all come to the maths table next. W! You should be over here, not fussing about the glue! I put the glue stick in the water because I needed it. Just sit down. Who's still working on the wheels at the moment? ...

In Extract 21 the confusion arose from the unanticipated absence of Ms J's support staff, and although some of her pupils became impatient and a little unruly, she managed to improvise a temporary programme of work without too much delay or difficulty. It has to be said, however, that confusion in a teacher's discourse was not invariably the result of circumstances beyond her control. Extract 8 (the session on Jules Verne and Sir Arthur Conan Doyle) provides a striking example of a teacher whose difficulty was brought about by obvious lack of preparation, and whose vagueness about what she was trying to convey was a direct consequence of her ignorance of the subject matter of the session: she emphasised that she and her colleagues had deliberately chosen three particular stories because of 'certain similarities' between them, yet it is quite clear that she did not even know what the stories were when she started talking, and that when she found out, she did not know enough about any of them to be able to talk sensibly about them. She thought they were by three different authors (8:1; 8:19) although they were not; she thought that they were all examples of science fiction (8:32; 8:40), although one of them was a straightforward adventure story; and she thought that they were all set in the future (8:28 to 8:32) although none of them was. She even spelt the name of one of the two authors wrongly (8:15), and told the children that the authors of what she called 'an old kind of science fiction' wrote about the future 'as if it would never happen' (8:32) although it is difficult to guess what she can have meant by this. It seems worth making the point that it is simply not reasonable to expect pupils to make more sense of a teacher's discourse than the teacher herself has done.

Sharing knowledge

For most of the time, the teachers in the sample had a very clear idea of what they wanted to teach and of how they wanted to teach it. Because of the problems outlined above, however, this clarity of purpose made their task all the more difficult; and this section ends with an extended account of a single teaching session and of the difficulties which faced the teacher as he attempted to teach a general principle.

The session in question was at Illingworth, and its overall structure is included among the ten individual summaries in an earlier section (page 120). The class of thirty-six children, aged 7 and 8, was divided into four groups working in the areas of science, language, maths and art. The art group worked in the wet area with Ms X, a support teacher, while Mr I, the class teacher, dealt with the other three groups in the main teaching area. The tasks of the language, maths and art groups (red, yellow and blue groups respectively) are summarised in Mr I's own words in Extract 6.

Mr I had planned to devote the bulk of his time to science with the fourth group (green table), and in fact spent twenty-two minutes there as against twelve minutes each with the language and maths groups. It is Mr I's work with the science group that will be examined in the following account.

At the beginning of the session the children from this group went to the library with Ms X to change their books. When they returned they sat at their table to await instructions while Ms X began work with the art group:

EXTRACT 22

[Duration: 5 minutes 42 seconds]

The pupils in the science group are sitting round a table on which there are magnifying glasses and pieces of cloth. Mr I is working with K, a child from the maths group. He looks over towards the science group.]

[22:1] *Mr I*:   Green table, I want to see you sitting, and not touching. L, come and sit down. [*He turns back to K.*]
[22:2] *K*:   Forty-nine.
[22:3] *Mr I*:   Yes, but it's not forty, is it?
[22:4] *K*:   Thirty.
[22:5] *Mr I*:   No. Three and two?

[22:6] M: [*From the science group, holding one of the magnifying glasses:*]
                 Which way do you look through, Mr I?

[22:7] Mr I: [*To N from the language group, who has come up to show him a
                 piece of work:*] You'll have to be careful with your words
                 now, N, because you've drawn him so small. You need to
                 get all those seven words in. You'll have to be very careful.

                 [*To the science group:*] Green table, put the magnifying
                 glasses down for a minute and fold your arms.

                 I'm waiting, M.

                 I'm still waiting.

                 We're going to look very carefully at these pieces of
                 cloth.

[22:8] K: [*who has now worked out the correct answer:*] Sir, I need a
                 rubber.

[22:9] Mr I: [*To K:*] I think there's one on that table. Look underneath
                 the Dienes blocks.

                 [*To the science group:*] We're going to see if with magni-
                 fying glasses you can see any patterns in the cloth . . .

                 [*To K:*] There's one on the red table.

                 [*To the science group:*] . . . and see if you can see anything
                 with the magnifying glass that you can't see without it.
                 Then in a few minutes I'm going to ask you to move the
                 pieces round so that you can have a look at another piece
                 of cloth.

[22:10] M: Do we have to look at both sides?

[22:11] Mr I: That's right; look at the other side as well. See if it's
                 different on the different side.

[22:12] M: There are blue ones . . .

[22:13] Mr I: They're blue, are they? They look black.

                 [*Moves over to the maths group, and looks at a child's work:*]
                 Good girl.

                 [*To the maths group as a whole:*] When you've finished
                 those two sums, you're going to look at page three in this
                 purple book. I'm going to tell you what to do. Next to
                 the lines of sums there are some letters . . .

                 [*To the science group:*] Right, green table: pass the cloth
                 round so that you've got a different piece of cloth.

                 [*To the maths group:*] Right, yellow table: can you see
                 next to the lines of sums, on the book, there are letters.
                 Don't do the line with an A next to it; do the line with a
                 B next to it. This line: the line with a B next to it. Do it
                 very carefully, and use the Dienes blocks.

                 [*To a child from the language group, who has come up to show
                 him a piece of work:*] Very good! Draw the picture on there.

[*To M:*] Where is your different piece of cloth?

[22:14] *M:*   There.

[22:15] *O:*   Sir you can see your eye in that [*i.e. the magnifying glass*].

[22:16] *Mr I:*   You can if you look through it at somebody's eye. You can see her eye, not your eye ...

Perhaps the most striking feature of Extract 22 is its disjointed nature. Mr I's explanation of the science task was disrupted by his interactions with children from the other two groups, even though his unusually tight control of his class (22:1; 22:7 and so on) enabled him to reduce interruptions and disciplinary interactions to a minimum. It must be assumed that this fragmentation of the teacher's attention was at least as distracting to the pupils in the group as it is to the reader of a transcript.

In spite of the difficulty of supervising three groups at once, Mr I managed to explain the task in simple terms; as far as the children were concerned, they were going to look for patterns in the pieces of cloth, and find out whether they could see anything through the magnifying glass that they could not see without it (22:9). In an interview after the session, Mr I talked about the purpose of the science exercise: 'The main aim was to get the children to observe; this is on the checklist of science skills. But also I wanted them to understand about woven and knitted fabrics.' In his explanation to the children he made his main aim explicit: the session was unequivocally about looking at things closely. At this stage, however, he did no more than hint at the secondary aim: the children were to look for 'patterns in the cloth' but without any particular reference to the cloth's structure or construction.

After explaining the task he left the children in the science group to work on their own while he turned his attention to the other two groups. Some minutes later he called across to them, 'Green table, pass the cloth round again and get a different piece, so that you've looked at three pieces.' Once more he concerned himself with the other groups for several minutes before going across to the science group to introduce the next phase of the task.

To make it easier to follow the science thread in the extracts which follow, all extraneous interactions of the kind which were so prominent in Extract 22 have been omitted. However, since their presence must have had a damaging impact on the teacher's effectiveness with the science group, their deletion is signalled in each case with a marker indicating how long they lasted; for example:

Let's look at this picture.

🕐 16 seconds

This picture has got ... Well, you tell me what it's got on it.

It must be stressed that these markers are not indications of natural pauses or of silence, but signify that the teacher's attention was fully distracted from the science task while he dealt with some other matter.

EXTRACT 23

[Duration: 3 minutes 20 seconds]

[23:1] *P*:   Sir, this part is like silver.

[23:2] *Mr I*:   Silver?

[23:3] *O*:   Sir, if you see in this glass you can see your own eye.

[23:4] *Mr I*:   It's not your eye, it's the . . . There are two lenses in there, and it's the circle from the other lens. This magnifying glass has one lens, but this special one has . . . ?

[23:5] *O*:   Two.

[23:6] *Mr I*:   Two lenses; and the circle you can see is the lens of the other magnifying glass. [*To the group:*] Can you put your magnifying glasses down now? Try not to bang them on the table; put them down very quietly. Now, I hope you've been looking very carefully at these pieces of cloth and material, and I'm going to ask each person in turn to tell me something about what you've seen . . . if you've discovered anything. P, would you like to tell me something about what you've been seeing?

[23:7] *P*:   There's like circles and all round them there's little . . . er . . .

[23:8] *Mr I*:   Little what round them?

[23:9] *P*:   Bumps. Spots.

[23:10] *Mr I*:   Little spots round the circles, yes; and what colour are the circles?

[23:11] *P*:   White.

[23:12] *Mr I*:   Do you mean the . . . you don't mean the circles you can see; you mean right inside the cloth there's like little white lumps. That's right. Good. What have you been seeing, Q?

[23:13] *Q*:   It looks like it's moving.

[23:14] *Mr I*:   It looks like it's moving?

[23:15] *Q*:   Yes, 'cause it's got little dots in the middle.

[23:16] *Mr I*:   Little dots in the middle. Very good. What about you, R?

[23:17] *R*:   Squiggly lines.

[23:18] *Mr I*:   Squiggly lines. What about the other side, because that material is very much different on the other side.

[23:19] *R*:   It's got . . . er . . . dots . . . er . . .

[23:20] *Mr I*:   Dots. Have another look through the magnifying glass.

🕐 21 seconds

[23:21] *R*:   It's got lines.
[23:22] *Mr I*:   Lines; and are the lines joined together?
[23:23] *R*:   A little bit.
[23:24] *Mr I*:   A little bit. Are they tied together, do you think?
[23:25] *R*:   Er . . . yes . . .

Extract 23 is a record of the opening minutes of an extended period with the group. By this stage two children, O and P were showing considerable interest in the magnifying glasses themselves (22:15; 23:1; 23:3). This was not part of the intended subject matter of the session, and Mr I dealt with their curiosity briefly and informatively. He then began to elicit from the children their comments on what they had seen through their magnifying glasses. In the light of his stated aims for the session, it is reasonable to assume that he was hoping for responses upon which he could build a dialogue leading to an awareness in the children of the nature of weaving. The first responses from P (23:7; 23:9; 23:11) were curiously ambiguous. On the face of it the 'circles' could have been the spaces between the woven threads, and Mr I's comment (23:12) is difficult to interpret because we cannot know what P had seen through the glass. However, the fact that he confidently told her what she did and did not mean is interesting, carrying as it does a suggestion that he was beginning to steer the conversation in the direction he wanted it to go. This process certainly continued in his responses to Q and R (23:14 and 23:18). Q thought the cloth looked as though it was moving (23:13), a slightly strange suggestion which might have merited more attention, while R had seen squiggly lines (23:17). However, neither of these contributions was likely to carry a discussion in the direction of weaving, and both were politely dismissed using the face-saving techniques described earlier. However, R was invited to look again through the magnifying glass (23:20) and, while Mr I was dealing with another child, he did so. As a result he was able to offer a more useful suggestion (23:21). The lines which he reported might have been the threads from which the cloth was woven, and Mr I asked two further questions (23:22 and 23:24) designed to set him thinking about the relationship of the lines to each other.

It would be illuminating but impracticable to follow the entire subsequent discussion, sentence by sentence. The next breakthrough did not come immediately. One by one the children reported what they had seen, mentioning squares, patterns and little holes, but not offering any suggestions about the construction of the cloth. Then the conversation began to move in the wrong direction altogether, towards the shininess of the cloth and the relative sizes of the patterned spots upon it. At this point Mr I adopted a more directive approach, bringing the discussion back to 'lines' and attempting to force a recognition that the cloth was made up of interwoven threads:

EXTRACT 24

[Duration: 2 minutes 36 seconds]

[24:1] *Mr I:* Look at the cloth. Can you see some lines on the cloth?
[24:2] *S:* Yes sir.
[24:3] *Mr I:* Are the lines all going the same way?
[24:4] *S:* Sir, some are going like that.
[24:5] *Mr I:* Some are going up, and where are the other ones? Some are going up and some are going across. Well now, T, what about your piece of cloth?
[24:6] *T:* It's got like stripes . . .
[24:7] *Mr I:* It's got like stripes in, like little lines; yes. Are the lines all going the same way?
[24:8] *Q:* This has got triangles.
[24:9] *Mr I:* [*To the group:*] Some up and some across. So that's . . . this has got lines going up and across. So has the black cloth. So has the white cloth.
[24:10] *Q:* Sir, this has got triangles.
[24:11] *Mr I:* Triangles?
[24:12] *Q:* Yes.

 15 seconds

[24:13] *P:* Sir, it's got circles.
[24:14] *Mr I:* Little holes where it's joined together.
[24:15] *O:* Sir, if you look at your hand it looks . . . like . . . bigger.
[24:16] *Mr I:* The magnifying glass makes everything look bigger, yes. [*To the group:*] Now, I'm going to give you some . . .
[24:17] *P:* Mr I, what are they made of?
[24:18] *Mr I:* Glass and plastic. Some are made out of plastic and some are made out of glass; and it's bent in a special way, and that makes the things look bigger than they really are, so you can look at them more carefully. It's called a lens: this clear bit is a lens; and these little ones have got two lenses in.
[24:19] *O:* Two lenses?
[24:20] *Mr I:* They're very good at looking at things very closely. You can see the squares. I'm going to give you a piece of paper and you're going to draw very carefully . . .

 8 seconds

... what you can see through your magnifying glass on
your piece of cloth. What you can see; not what the person
next to you can. What you can see, very carefully ... very
carefully ...

Mr I's exchange with S (24:1 to 24:5) took the form of question and
answer, but in effect Mr I gave all the answers as well as asking all the
questions. At this point he had at least nominally established that some
of the 'lines' in the cloth were at right angles to others. However, the
very next contribution, from T (24:6), seemed to ignore the point, referring simply to stripes and saying nothing about their direction. Mr I
countered by changing 'stripes' to 'lines' and again asking whether they
were 'all going the same way' (24:7).

Then Q intervened to say that she could see triangles (24:8). An exploration of what she meant by this would have jeopardised the progress
Mr I had made so far, and he ignored her contribution, telling the group
instead that the pattern of lines he had been talking about was common
to several pieces of cloth: he was establishing a general principle (24:9).
Q would not be denied, however, and repeated her assertion that her
cloth contained triangles (24:10). Mr I refused to be sidetracked, and he
used one of the techniques described earlier to dismiss her suggestion
without actually saying that it was wrong (24:11).

After an interruption, he again rephrased an answer to make it more
useful to the emerging general principle: P said that the cloth had circles
(24:13), and Mr I unobtrusively changed this to 'little holes where
it's joined together' (24:14). Meanwhile, O and P were still finding the
magnifying glasses more interesting than the task itself, and they
engaged Mr I in further conversation about their function and construction (24:15–24:20). There was a marked contrast between his manner of
dealing with these questions and his way of organising the discussion
about weaving. Released from his feeling that he must encourage a
dialogue of discovery, and faced with two children genuinely eager to
know something, he simply told them what they wanted to know and
moved on.

The children's next task was to draw what they could see through
the magnifying glasses (24:20). Mr I gave detailed instructions (not
reproduced here) about the drawing itself, telling the children to draw
a circle to represent the glass, and to make it as large as possible on
their pieces of paper. He also suggested that they should choose the
cloth with the best pattern; and when they were settled he turned his
attention to the other groups.

Some minutes later he spotted one child who had somehow missed
the whole point of the exercise:

EXTRACT 25

[Duration: 1 minute 50 seconds]

[25:1] *Mr I:* I think you can stop drawing, M, and try looking again properly through the magnifying glass at what you can see, because I don't think you can see that through the magnifying glass. You must look through the magnifying glass while you're drawing. Don't put your cloth away because you won't be able to see what you are drawing. You must look at the cloth and then draw what you can see: you're drawing what you can see with the magnifying glass.

 18 seconds

[25:2] *Q:* The dots are blue.

[25:3] *Mr I:* The dots are blue, yes.
L, use the black cloth.
[*To the group:*] Do this drawing very carefully, as carefully ... That's all right, S ... as carefully as you can.
Now look; apart from the dots, what can you see, P? What can you see?

[25:4] *P:* Squares.

[25:5] *Mr I:* Now; so don't forget to put the little squares in as well: what you can see through the magnifying glass.
[*To R:*] Now, I bet you can see squares as well, can't you? [*No response*] Can you see squares as well?

[25:6] *R:* No.

[25:7] *Mr I:* Well, you'd better look more carefully, because I can.

Extract 25 lends powerful support to the earlier suggestion that balancing challenges with skills is particularly difficult in a group. M had spent a considerable amount of time with other children looking at pieces of cloth through a magnifying glass and discussing what they saw. Afterwards he failed to grasp that he should draw on paper what he had seen through the magnifying glass, and Mr I repeated the instructions at length specifically for him (25:1) rather than leaving him to draw aimlessly. While monitoring the work of the group at this stage of the session, he also had a revealing exchange with R (25:5 to 25:7). He had already stressed that children should draw what they had seen (24:20; 25:1) and not allow themselves to be influenced by others (24:20). Faced with their attempts to follow his instructions, however, he began to demand changes, putting them in a somewhat paradoxical situation.

During this stint of monitoring he also noticed that Q's drawing was too small, and he gave her a detailed set of instructions (not reproduced here) repeating what he had said earlier about the size of drawing he wanted. He then dealt with the other two groups, and it was some time later when M, who had missed the point of the exercise earlier, drew attention to himself again:

EXTRACT 26

[Duration: 46 seconds]

[26:1] *M*:   Sir, shall I draw a big cloth?

[26:2] *Mr I*: I want you to draw what you can see through the magnifying glass. You cannot see that through the magnifying glass! When you look at this piece of cloth through the magnifying glass, you don't see that, M. You've looked through the magnifying glass, put it down and drawn something completely different. You're not imagining what you can see; you're drawing what you actually can see through the magnifying glass . . . what you can really see when you look.

M was certainly not ready for this particular task.

After further work with the other two groups, Mr I returned to the science group for the last time. This was the point when the general principle of weaving would have to be elicited and understood if it was not to be deferred until another day.

EXTRACT 27

[Duration: 9 minutes 26 seconds]

[27:1] *Mr I*: Now, the people on this table just stop and let me see how far we've got. We're going to each have a look at our pictures and see what we could see through our magnifying glasses.

      🕐 25 seconds

Let's put all the cloth into the middle of the table. Can you pass that cloth, please, R?

      🕐 24 seconds

And magnifying glasses to the middle of the table.

      🕐 1 minute 1 second

Let's look at this picture.

      🕐 16 seconds

This picture has got ... Well, you tell me what it's got on it, P.

[27:2] *P:* Squares and ... er ... circles.

[27:3] *Mr I:* Squares and circles. I wonder which piece of cloth this one was. [*He takes a piece of cloth from the middle of the table.*] This piece of cloth has got dots on.

🕐 9 seconds

Now, I can't see the squares. Could you see squares when you looked at this through the magnifying glass? I can see the dots but I can't see the squares. Can you see the squares with the magnifying glass? Can you?

[27:4] *P:* Yes sir. That ...

🕐 19 seconds

[27:5] *Mr I:* Now, the squares are ... They're not little squares all on their own. They're made by something. Pass me a piece of white paper. They're made by the ...

[27:6] *R:* Sheep's wool!

🕐 9 seconds

Sir, sheep's wool.

[27:7] *Mr I:* Could be sheep's wool, yes, or cotton.

🕐 16 seconds

[*While he is talking he draws a grid of interwoven lines on the piece of paper.*] I'm making this much bigger than it really is ... P ... and those are the ... We call them threads, threads running through the cloth. There's some threads that are coming loose, and then, going along with them ...

🕐 15 seconds

... are some more threads going the other way. [*He shows his diagram to the group.*] They're much closer together than that; that's just a picture to show you ... Now, there are some pictures made like this in Ms X's wet area, where there's one line going under and then over, under and then over, under and then over. Does anybody know what we call that? [*No response*] Anybody here made a picture like that, where you've had a line going down, made out of cloth or paper, and then some more cloth or paper going under and over, under and over, under and over? [*A few hands go up.*] And what was it called? Can you remember?

🕐 24 seconds

It's called weaving. The threads go in and out; and Ms X's class did it with paper as well, going in and out.

[27:8] L: [*Pointing at the pictures in Ms X's wet area.*] Sir, there they are.

[27:9] Mr I: If we get up quietly we can go and have a look at Ms X's . . .

🕐 1 minute 33 seconds

[*In the wet area:*] Now, can you see? The . . . One line is going under and then over, under then over, under then over, under then over, under then over, under then over, under then over. It's woven together, it's . . . That's how you do weaving, and most of those pieces of cloth that we've been looking at, that's how they're made. The pieces of thread are much, much thinner than this, but that's how they're made. There's one line of threads going along, and the other line of thread's going in and out, in and out across the top, and that's how they're made.

[27:10] R: Sir, can we do those as well?

[27:11] Mr I: We're going to have a go at some weaving. Not today, but another day. My shirt is made like that; if you look through this with a magnifying glass . . .

[27:12] R: Sir, sir, lines and zigzags.

[27:13] Mr I: That's right. You can see where the lines . . . some going down and some going across. Very good.

In this final extract Mr I's undoubted gift for gentle but firm organisation and control is very much in evidence. He was constantly distracted by other things, yet he held the group together without any apparent effort.

His task now was to find something in the drawings that would illustrate or suggest the principle of woven material. The first suggestion came from P (27:2), and, although it was not very promising, Mr I followed it up attempting to lead the children into an awareness that the squares were nothing more than the shapes formed by a grid of interwoven threads: 'They're made by something . . . They're made by the . . . ' (27:5). The difficulty of this undertaking is thrown into high relief by R's confident reply: 'Sheep's wool!' (27:6). It was a perfectly sensible suggestion, and R was proud enough of it to repeat it when he feared that Mr I had not heard it. Unfortunately it was not what Mr I was looking for, and he had to fall back once again on a conventional formula for dealing with useless contributions: he repeated it, added a variation, and moved on.

His subsequent demonstration and long explanation (27:7 and 27:9) represent both his final success and his final capitulation in the face of overwhelming odds. There can be no doubt that by the time he had finished many of the pupils understood the principle of weaving. However, when the principle was finally explicated it bore only a slight relationship to the work which had preceded it, and was delivered as a piece of knowledge from the teacher rather than as something which had emerged naturally from an exploratory dialogue. Furthermore, at least some of the pupils must have known about the principle from the outset since they had made pictures with woven paper before (27:7), yet they had shown no sign of realising what Mr I was trying to elicit from them during the session. His approach was in no way unusual in the context of the sixty classrooms in which the present study took place. It was, however, only one of several ways in which the principle of weaving could be taught, and its strengths and shortcomings deserve equal scrutiny.

Barriers to communication

Before leaving the matter of teacher–pupil interactions, it is worth looking at a brief extract where an informal conversation was motivated purely by a teacher's genuine interest in a particular child, and where there was no task content at all. It is interesting to see how confused the child was by the teacher's questions, and how difficult it was for the teacher to be sure that she was both understanding the child and being understood in turn. Such genuine barriers to communication in a spontaneous and task-free dialogue give a sobering insight into the extreme difficulty of the primary teacher's task.

EXTRACT 28

[Two girls are playing a clapping game.]

[28:1] *Ms F*: Is that the game you were telling me about earlier?
[28:2] *K*:   Yes
[28:3] *Ms F*: Why have you been away?
[28:4] *K*:   'Cause I slit my leg open and I nearly went to the hospital to get it better.
[28:5] *Ms F*: What do you mean: nearly went?
[28:6] *K*:   'Cause I'm – 'cause I slit my leg open.
[28:7] *Ms F*: Let's have a look. [*K shows Ms F her leg.*] Well it's not too bad. Not too bad, is it? How did you know you might have needed one of those butterfly clips? Was it bleeding a lot?

[28:8] *K:* Yeh.

[28:9] *Ms F:* How did it happen?

[28:10] *K:* I fell off a wall. Somebody pushed me.

[28:11] *Ms F:* Somebody pushed you? How high was this wall?

[28:12] *K:* About that big.

[28:13] *Ms F:* Where from? From the ground?

[28:14] *K:* Yeh.

[28:15] *Ms F:* So if you went down . . . Go down. Bend your knees. Bend your knees. So it was about that tall from the ground?

[28:16] *K:* Yeh.

[28:17] *Ms F:* So just there from the ground. What were you doing on this wall?

[28:18] *K:* I were playing on it.

[28:19] *Ms F:* When did this happen? [*K replies unintelligibly.*] When? [*No response*] Can you remember?

[28:20] *K:* When it were . . .

[28:21] *Ms F:* Which day?

[28:22] *K:* Teachers' training day.

[28:23] *Ms F:* So that happened on teachers' training day, on Friday? Well why were you off on Wednesday and Thursday then?

[28:24] *K:* 'Cause somebody said I needed to go to the hospital for some stitches.

[28:25] *Ms F:* For what? [*No response*] For what?

[28:26] *K:* For my leg.

[28:27] *Ms F:* You hadn't done that till Friday. You just told me. Why have you been away?

[28:28] *K:* I went to my Auntie Doreen's.

[28:29] *Ms F:* Why didn't you tell me straight away, instead of all these stories? Did you enjoy yourself? [*No response*] Where's Auntie Doreen live? [*K replies unintelligibly.*] Pardon? [*K replies unintelligibly again.*] On [*a nearby council estate*], is that what you're saying?

[28:30] *K:* We went to the circus.

[28:31] *Ms F:* Did you enjoy yourself?

[28:32] *K:* You know when I went to the circus, . . .

[28:33] *Ms F:* Did you enjoy yourself?

[28:34] *L:* M won't share with me.

[28:35] *Ms F:* Oh, you've got to share. [*She goes off to deal with L and M.*]

There is no reason to suppose that K was trying to mislead Ms F with her account of the cut leg; she was presumably just confused about the sequence of events during the previous week. For her part Ms F worked very hard to draw K into a conversation and elicit sensible answers, and then at the very point where K began to show signs of willingness to talk (28:32), the conversation was interrupted by a child from another group (28:34), and Ms F felt obliged to leave K and deal with a pressing problem elsewhere in the room. The conversation with K was never completed.

SOME ISSUES AND IMPLICATIONS

We begin now the process of pulling together the main threads of this study so far. We remind readers that it deals with the third and most detailed part of a larger study undertaken at three levels and entailing an analysis of practice, and of the thinking behind practice, in some sixty classrooms. The outcomes of the work in the fifty Level One and Level Two classrooms were discussed in Chapter 3, and to gain a sense of the study as a whole readers should therefore take the two chapters together.

TASK-RELATED BEHAVIOUR

The first part of this chapter presented a mainly quantitative analysis of the data arising from the systematic observation of pupils and teachers in ten of the sixty classrooms. It discussed first the central notion of learning tasks, gave figures for the time spent by children on such tasks, and analysed the data dealing with four of the main factors which influence children's task-related behaviour: settings and organisational structures; teacher–pupil interaction; the children themselves; and the actual tasks they are asked to undertake.

Time on task

The analysis of the data on the sixty target pupils – six in each of the ten classrooms – showed that over the two-week observation period they spent on average 59 per cent of their time working on the tasks that had been set, 21 per cent distracted from those tasks, 11 per cent on routine activities, and 8 per cent waiting for attention. However, the variation between classrooms, as Table 4.1 shows, was considerable, with the time which children spent working varying from 52 to 70 per cent.

These figures were broadly consistent with those from other research studies, though we noted a somewhat higher proportion of time spent by the Leeds children waiting for their teachers' attention. We suggested that this might have something to do with the relatively complex organisational patterns in most of these classrooms, but it should also be noted that one might have expected this to have been offset by the presence of extra staff allocated under the LEA's Primary Needs Programme. As we noted in Chapter 3, the gains of enhanced staffing are by no means inevitable: extra staff introduce additional challenges and can increase as well as reduce the organisational complexity of the classroom in which they are placed. Since enhanced staffing has been far and away the largest item of expenditure under the Primary Needs Programme, this question is of obvious importance.

Teacher–pupil ratios

Because some of the adults in these classrooms were not teachers, yet might be undertaking activities identical to some of those which teachers performed, we preferred the more accurate formula of adult–pupil ratios.

We found that the considerable variation between classrooms in respect of the time spent by children on task-related behaviour could not be explained simply in terms of the number of adults present. This factor was clearly outweighed by others, of which, if we take particular cases, meticulous planning, careful organisation and genuine collaboration between the adults involved seemed paramount.

Conversely, where the benefits of enhanced staffing were not apparent in the ways children worked, it was clear that this was because of organisational and interpersonal factors.

It is one thing to spot ways in which organisation is questionable or teachers are having difficulty in collaborating, and previous reports have discussed some of these. But the very detailed work at Level Three, which involved daily interviews with teachers as well as observation, suggests that in some cases the organisational strategies they adopted might be not so much inadequate as over-ambitious for their capacities and circumstances. The teachers in question were seeking, or felt obliged, to put into operation practices with which they were insufficiently comfortable to ensure success. This confirms findings from the Level One and Two material.

Access to adults

A refinement of the analysis of adult–pupil ratios was an examination of the number of adults to which each of the target children had access while engaged in the various kinds of task-related behaviour. Again, we find further confirmation of the fact that enhanced staffing is not an unmixed blessing: access to three or more adults produced the same patterns of behaviour as access to only one. Where time spent waiting for attention was concerned – a notable problem in any busy classroom – one adult managed as well as two, three or four.

Group size

Grouping of some kind is almost universal in primary education, and it certainly was here. Generally, the smaller the group, the more time its members spent working; the larger the group, the more time its members spent distracted or awaiting attention. The question of optimum group size is thus an important one.

The organisation of individual teaching sessions

Most of the sessions which we observed followed a similar general sequence: an introduction, the allocation of tasks, groupwork, finishing off and tidying up. However, there was wide variation in how long each stage took and how teachers chose to undertake it. Thus, for example, introductions could take from four minutes to twenty-five; but in some cases introductions were just that while in others they were essentially the whole-class teaching element in an arrangement otherwise dominated by groupwork.

At the same time, and as Extracts 2 to 6 clearly demonstrate, some teachers were considerably more focused and purposeful than others in the way they presented and organised each session's tasks and activities. In our analysis of these we showed how teachers had to resolve two kinds of decision: first, whether to plan in advance and then instruct children on what they should do, or to enter a process of negotiation, or even to improvise; second, whether to confine the introductory stage of a session to task allocation or to combine this with more wide-ranging discussion. The benefits of the latter, in terms of helping children to make sense of where in their learning they were coming from and going to, are clear; the disadvantage is that the activity can be prolonged to the point where it becomes doubly counterproductive, by making excessive demands on children's concentration span and leaving insufficient time for children to work independently or in groups.

It should be noted, of course, that the age of the children is an important factor in the way a teacher introduces, allocates and monitors learning tasks. Teachers of younger children may spend longer on the kinds of instructions, explanations and routines which teachers of older children can take for granted. Where such routines have been fully internalised by older children therefore, this may well be due only in part to their current teachers: developing children's capacities to work in particular ways is a cumulative process in which the groundwork established in the early years is of critical importance.

Regardless of the considerable variation in the balance of time among the many sessions observed, the overwhelming majority were dominated by a pattern of organisation in which different groups tackled different tasks simultaneously. In some cases, this presented teachers with problems of supervision and control which ranged from the slight to the severe; it was also evident that without adequate supervision and control, and a clear observance by all parties of certain basic routines, much time could be wasted. Moreover, the amount of time spent on the central group-based tasks of a session was only one indicator of the quality of the learning being undertaken, as is demonstrated by both the quantitative and the qualitative data.

The argument for the arrangement whereby a number of different curriculum areas and tasks are pursued at the same time is not often rehearsed, for like many of the principles of modern primary practice it is held to be self-evident. Yet the arrangement is clearly not always an easy one to implement successfully, and in the present study the complexity of some teachers' classroom organisation appeared greatly to increase time spent by children distracted, awaiting attention or working intermittently. The arrangement could also be associated with somewhat low-level activities of the kind that kept children engaged but did not challenge them.

The quantitative analysis of classroom interaction

We started by setting out the pros and cons of quantitative and qualitative analysis of teacher–pupil interaction, together with our conclusion that the rather different benefits of each indicate the need for us to undertake both.

In the quantitative analysis we distinguished between work, monitoring, routine, disciplinary and other interactions, and in Table 4.4 showed the overall proportions of each from all sessions observed in all the classrooms. The combined figure of 84 per cent for work, monitoring and routine interactions may seem satisfyingly high, particularly in relation to the mere 10 per cent of disciplinary interactions. However, we suggested that the higher figure included many disciplinary inter-actions of an oblique kind, and the monitoring and routine figures should be looked at in this light. As with other figures, however, the variation between the classrooms was considerable. First, there was variation on a continuum ranging from frequent short interactions to infrequent longer ones. Second, the actual proportions of work, monitoring, routine and disciplinary interactions varied substantially.

These figures raised many important questions. It is a reasonable assumption that in teaching we should seek to maximise the number of interactions between ourselves and our pupils which are directly related to the content of the learning tasks we have set, and to minimise those of a routine and disciplinary nature. But the quality of our work-related interactions is not necessarily defined by their number, and our evidence suggested that it is equally important for the teacher to ensure that work-related interactions should be as sustained as the task requires: frequent but brief monitorings of a child's learning may achieve rather less than longer though less frequent interactions.

In any event, the asymmetry of classroom interaction noted by Galton *et al.* (1980a) in the ORACLE project was a pronounced feature. Putting the pupil and teacher observation data together reveals how while teachers can be interacting virtually every moment of a teaching session, the child's experience is somewhat different. For example, Table 4.6 shows our sixty target children having an average of just five work-related interactions an hour, with some having as few as two and none having more than eleven.

However, as we have stressed, this is only part of the story: the quality of the interactions is best judged from the transcripts which we illustrated and discussed in the second part of this chapter and to which we refer below.

The children as factors in their task-related behaviour

Of the many different factors relating to children that it is possible to identify, we initially chose in this study to concentrate on four that were particularly prominent in the primary policies of Leeds LEA at this time: ability, age, ethnicity and gender. The nature of our sub-sample – sixty children in ten classrooms – meant that the third of these yielded numbers too small to be valid in this kind of analysis, so we concentrated on the other three.

The gender differences to which we have referred elsewhere (Alexander *et al.* 1989: chaps. 2 and 4) were confirmed and were in line with the findings of other studies: girls in the sample spent more of their time on task-related activities than did boys; boys spent more time distracted or awaiting the teacher's attention than did girls. The age-related differences were also noticeable, with older children spending less time than younger ones distracted or awaiting attention, and more time working. The difficulty of measuring ability objectively meant that, like some other projects, we worked from teachers' own judgements of whether a target child was of average, above-average or below-average ability. Children perceived as average by their teachers spent less time on task-related activities and more time distracted or awaiting attention than either of the other two groups.

We suggested that there are two clear interpretations of this finding: either that children of average ability do indeed get less of their teachers' time and attention than more able or less able children; or that some children happen for various reasons to receive more time and attention than others and as a result are defined as coming nearer the extremes of the notional ability range. The second interpretation is in line with other research which shows teachers making judgements about children's ability on the basis of their social behaviour. In other words, by this analysis, a child who fails to draw attention to itself tends to be labelled 'average'. Given that there is also ample evidence that predictive labels tend to stick, and indeed to become self-fulfilling, this matter has profound implications, not least in the context of the National Curriculum assessment requirements.

The nature of the tasks being undertaken

Naming the various parts of the primary curriculum seemed to present difficulties. There was general agreement about what is denoted by 'mathematics' or 'language', but the area which includes science, environmental studies, topic work, history, geography, humanities and so on gave rise to a certain amount of confusion, with teachers and others adopting different labels for the same activities.

In this enquiry we defined what children were doing at any moment in two ways: by reference to the label given to the task in question by the child's teacher; and by reference to the activity or activities of which the task was constituted. It became clear that regardless of the label, the curriculum as experienced by children consists of a number of generic activities which appear in various curriculum guises and which may well be at least as significant for children's learning as the labels they bear.

Curriculum designation

Table 4.10 shows the league table of named curriculum areas, with language and mathematics dominating the curriculum in these classrooms in the same way that they have been shown by other studies to dominate English primary education generally. This differential between the so-called 'basics' (to which, since the 1988 Education Reform Act, science has now been added) and the rest of the curriculum was further increased by the fact that the Level Three teachers concentrated even more of their time on the basics than did their pupils, thus reducing still further the amount of task-related interaction in the non-basic areas their pupils received.

The proportion of time the sixty target children spent on the various kinds of task-related behaviour – working, routine, awaiting attention, distracted – varied widely between curriculum areas. The findings here are particularly important in relation to the observation we have just made about the dominance of the basics. Although the children spent a great deal of time on language and mathematics tasks, they spent rather less of that time working and rather more of it distracted than when they were undertaking tasks in certain curriculum areas to which less time had been allocated. This deserves thinking about wherever it is believed that the way to achieve curriculum priorities is simply to give the areas of high priority as much time as possible.

The data were analysed further in respect of the three main pupil factors discussed above: gender, age and perceived ability. Here again, some striking differences emerged. Boys and girls worked for similar proportions of time in mathematics, but in language, science and art boys were more commonly distracted. Older children spent more of their time working at their language and mathematics, and less of their time distracted, while with art the situation was reversed, and the younger children appeared more diligent than their older peers. In mathematics and science children defined as of above-average ability spent more time working and less time distracted than other children; while those defined as of below-average ability seemed particularly distractable in those same areas.

Again, however, we must draw attention to the proviso about the complex relationship between a child's behaviour and the way in which their abilities are perceived by the teacher. Since mathematics is widely regarded as a curriculum activity of the highest importance, the child who works hard in mathematics may sometimes come to be perceived as having above-average ability, not just in mathematics, but also in everything else. Indeed, it is not uncommon for teachers to use perceived ability in mathematics as a basis for grouping in other areas of the curriculum.

The evidence that children's perceived ability may have much to do with how they behave has already been referred to; this appears to be compounded by a further possibility – that their performance in certain curriculum areas is taken as an indicator of their overall ability. Clearly, defining children's abilities and achievements is an essential yet hazardous enterprise, and the insistence of the School Examinations and Assessment Council, at an early stage in the implementation of the National Curriculum, that classroom assessments be firmly grounded in proper evidence, can only be welcomed.

Curriculum labels and generic activities

As we have said, the curriculum can be defined in terms of both subject or other stipulative curriculum labels reflecting teachers' intentions and the generic activities which children were actually undertaking, regardless of the label used. Detailed analysis of the tasks our target children undertook under the curriculum headings adopted by their teachers showed a recurrence of ten of the latter.

The league table for these generic activities is shown in Table 4.16. Children's time in the classroom was overwhelmingly dominated by writing, with the use of task-specific apparatus, reading, and listening (usually to the teacher) also paramount, though some way behind. The list then tails off through drawing and painting, collaborative activities with other children and movement, to talking with the teacher and talking to the class as activities on which children are engaged for a very small proportion of the time.

That the classroom is a place where children spend considerably more time on writing than anything else, and well over half their time on reading and writing together, bears careful thought, as does the general balance (or imbalance) of the ten generic activities which our analysis reveals. Though these figures arise from just ten classrooms, our material from Levels One and Two suggests that they are fairly typical.

Equally suggestive is the breakdown of the figures for each curriculum area undertaken in Table 4.15. Language, for instance, was dominated in these classrooms by reading and writing; oracy received much less attention, and in any event was more about children's listening than their talking. This point is powerfully reinforced by analysis of the tape-recorded interaction material.

The picture for other curriculum areas, once their constituent activities are analysed, is not quite so dramatic, though it deserves equally careful consideration. Mathematics was also dominated by reading and writing, though it involved more collaboration than did language; science was considerably more interactive than either, while as a marked contrast, art emerged as a non-collaborative activity with a virtually total absence of opportunities for any kinds of language work. This too seems serious: art is, or should be, a cognitively demanding activity in which the exploration of ideas is as important as the exploration of media and in which it is surely essential for children to have the opportunity to articulate and discuss what they seek to express, represent or create.

Activities and task-related behaviour

Finally, before we turn to the transcript data, the main findings from Table 4.16 should be noted. The target children worked hardest, and were least distracted, when undertaking those activities for which there was least opportunity, and most often distracted when undertaking those activities like writing and reading on which they spent most time. In this regard the 'on task' potential of collaborative activities should be noted, the more so as at a national level it is increasingly being accepted that groupwork in primary classrooms is a seriously under-exploited arena for effective learning.

THE QUALITY OF TEACHER–PUPIL INTERACTION

We tape-recorded nearly all the teaching sessions observed in each of the schools and subjected the recordings and transcripts to qualitative analysis. This not only provided an essential counterbalance to the mainly quantitative analysis of task-related pupil behaviour and teacher–pupil interaction contained in the first part of this chapter, but also enabled us to gain access to some of the most subtle and influential aspects of the teaching process.

The second part of the chapter identified and discussed a number of characteristics of the pupil–teacher discourse in these classrooms. They were not mere minority tendencies or isolated incidents; to have concentrated on these might have been interesting but would have had limited value in an evaluation project seeking to identify trends and issues of importance across the entire spectrum of an LEA's primary schools. Thus, although in a technical sense we can make no claim to the generalisability of the interaction findings, we have been careful to focus only on those phenomena which we know from our other data were occurring elsewhere in the city, bearing in mind that we undertook fieldwork in ninety of these schools and had annual survey returns over a four-year period from all 230 of them.

The prevalence of questions

One of the most striking features of teachers' discourse was the way much of it was in the form of questions. We suggested two reasons for this. One was that classroom discourse, though in certain critical respects quite unlike ordinary everyday conversation, shares with it a tendency to couch certain kinds of utterance in an interrogative form, often when no real question is intended: a question, then, is frequently no more than a conversational device.

The other explanation, increasingly confirmed as we worked through more and more transcripts, is that the teachers were reflecting the antipathy towards didactic modes of teaching which has been such a prominent part of post-Plowden primary thinking. The message they had internalised was that children should find things out for themselves rather than be told, and that the teacher's task was to ask the kinds of questions which would prompt them to do so.

From a distance, this questioning stance may look as impressive in practice as it seems commendable in theory. Indeed it is one of the features of primary classrooms which many visitors find particularly attractive. However, when we looked closely at the form of such questions, and the kinds of responses they evoked (an examination which for many of the more intimate one-to-one exchanges is possible only with the aid of radio microphones) we found that examples of the kinds of carefully focused open questions which encourage children to work through an idea or problem or to build on their previous learning were relatively uncommon. Instead, some questions were rhetorical or pseudo-questions to which no answer of any substance was expected. Others were essentially closed questions requiring simple one- or two-word recall answers, although their apparently open form might have suggested otherwise. Others were inappropriately pitched – too high or, more commonly, too low. And, although questions were indeed prevalent, it was nearly always the teacher who asked them.

We suggested that among the other reasons for this state of affairs, the organisational and temporal pressures of the primary classroom must be significant. For a teacher to interact meaningfully with individual children he or she requires the time and opportunity to do so. It is often asserted that this is an insoluble problem. Evidence from this and other studies, however, suggests that this is not necessarily so.

Balancing skills and challenges

We developed this particular line of analysis in the context of consideration of how the teacher achieves the right balance of outer challenges and inner skills – or 'match' – when interacting with a class or group of children. We noted, however, that teachers whose questions are predominantly token or closed may prevent themselves from recognising the extent of imbalance or mismatch which may exist. The situation seemed likely to be more promising when teachers worked with small groups, yet here the opportunity for more accurately judged dialogue was sometimes missed as teachers sought to shift things along the intended path: low-level questions gained quick but equally low-level answers while divergent answers with real learning potential were not always followed up.

Motivation and choice

Like the commitment to an enquiring mode of discourse, the belief in choice within the classroom is fundamental to recent primary thinking and practice. It was exemplified in a number of ways in this study, but the analysis of pupil–teacher exchanges showed that the choice could sometimes be rather more apparent than real, whether at the beginning of a session, in the middle when children might even be operating under the explicit but to some extent misplaced heading of 'choosing', or when finishing off. This process was complicated by the fact that where choice was genuinely available it might cut across other teaching objectives, particularly that of achieving a balance between skills and challenges. In Extract 12 we showed how a teacher sought to preserve the motivational impact of choice, even when that choice had generated an inappropriate activity. The commonest way of avoiding such difficulties was to reduce the level of demand of a piece of work.

Praise and power

Since Philip Jackson's seminal (1968) study of classroom life we have become aware of some of the many ways in which the power differential between teacher and taught is reflected on a day-to-day basis yet is also as far as possible muted so as to preserve the impression of an open and reciprocal relationship. In the Level Three classrooms there were three common manifestations of this: instructions disguised as questions, imposition disguised as choice, and the extensive use of praise.

However, like questions, praise may not be what it seems. For one thing, it becomes devalued if it is used too often and without discrimination; for another the use of overt praise may be at variance with other messages about children's work which a teacher is conveying and which children readily pick up.

Teachers' treatment of pupils' responses

Praise was one of the commonest kinds of overt feedback given to children in the classrooms, and in some cases, as we have suggested, it may have been used to excess. Relatedly, there was an apparent reluctance to pronounce a child's answer wrong, and several teachers, for wholly understandable reasons, used a number of verbal devices to retain the climate of support and encouragement essential to well-motivated learning. However, there is probably a line to be drawn between this stance and the conveying of inappropriate or confusing messages about what the teacher really thinks of what a child has said or done. In several cases, as we showed, incorrect answers might be praised, especially if they enabled a teacher to keep her discussion on target; or they might be first praised and then dismissed. Conversely, an answer which was correct or interesting, but which if pursued might cause the discussion to deviate, could receive praise of a manifestly token kind or could even be treated as wrong.

Thus, the fate of children's contributions might sometimes have less to do with their quality than with their ability to sustain the teacher's intentions.

Interruptions

A similar tendency was noted where interruptions were concerned. It became clear that however an event might look to an observer, it was the teacher who determined whether it was an interruption and if so whether it was severe or trifling. Thus we found examples of events which by any standards constituted major interruptions and which were ignored; trivial occurrences which were blown up into major incidents, with serious consequences for the flow of a session and the equanimity of both children and teachers; teachers whose pattern of discourse was s..ch that they constantly interrupted themselves; and interruptions turned into teaching points with such a consummate degree of skill that they might almost have been stage-managed.

Interruptions are a commonplace in primary teaching, and many of them are avoidable, yet it is also clear that the teacher's power to define and shape events in the classroom may extend even to matters such as these which might seem as extraneous or beyond control.

Sharing knowledge

We have identified a number of separate but related characteristics of the teacher–pupil discourse in these classrooms. We ended by undertaking a sustained analysis of a twenty-two minute sequence from a session in which one of a class's four groups of children undertook a science activity.

The session displayed many of the characteristics summarised above: the acute pressure on the teacher's management skills resulting from having four groups simultaneously working in different curriculum areas and all requiring not just supervision but also the teacher's productive intervention; the frequency of distractions and interruptions; the prevalence of questions, nearly all of them (in an activity which was ostensibly investigative) posed by the teacher rather than the children; the praising of answers which though poor kept discussion on course while good but divergent answers were marginalised; the use of the device of repeating or rephrasing a question until the required answer emerged.

However, the most significant point in that particular sequence was that the teacher's commitment to a 'discovery' mode of teaching failed to deliver the principle which he wished the children to arrive at, and in the end he felt obliged to tell them what he had wanted them to find out for themselves through observation and discussion. The principle in question was a straightforward one which these children would have grasped without difficulty. The whole sequence, which had its parallels elsewhere, raises important issues not just about the nature and problems of interaction as such, but also about the rhetoric and reality of 'discovery', the ways children most effectively come to an understanding of ideas and principles, and, most importantly, the various ways in which the teacher can bring about such understanding.

FINAL OBSERVATIONS

Beyond the very specific issues which are flagged in the main text there are a number of larger themes, all of considerable importance, and it is with these that we conclude.

The content of the curriculum

In our previous studies (Alexander, Willcocks and Kinder 1989: chap. 4, and Chapter 3 of the present book), we have raised questions about the extent to which the broadly based curriculum espoused by the LEA in its various policy statements on primary education has been reflected in practice. This chapter extends the analysis by going beneath the surface of the familiar curriculum labels to identify the kinds of tasks teachers were setting and the activities of which such tasks were constituted. The principle of curriculum breadth and balance can now be looked at in two ways.

One is the familiar one of judging the range and weighting of the various subjects, and from this analysis comes both confirmation of the dominance of language and mathematics and anxiety about the place and treatment of some other subjects: a theme which is now so familiar that we are in danger of ignoring the fact that the problems of breadth and balance in these terms are still unsolved, and indeed are greatly exacerbated by the National Curriculum.

The other approach is to start with our proposition that behind the labels are a number of generic activities (reading, writing, collaborative work and so on), and to note that the analysis we offer of these makes the breadth/balance problem if anything even more acute. There are two basic questions to ask here about every child's curriculum. Is the overall balance of activities (as opposed to subjects) an educationally appropriate one? And is the range and balance of activities within each curriculum area as it should be?

In our view, the focus for discussion here should be on the very large amount of time spent by children in reading and writing compared with that spent in talking and collaborative work. The fostering of children's capacities to talk and listen emerges as a particular problem from both the quantitative and qualitative data. Our findings here support those of HMI: 'Where the work is less effective than it should be, it is the development of oracy that is often impoverished and given too little time' (DES 1990a: 33).

However, HMI provided little detail about the forms that such oral impoverishment may take, and, this reservation apart, they seemed, in this report at least, to be fairly satisfied with the national picture. In comparison, the PRINDEP data offer the kind of detail needed for the more precise analysis of the strengths and weaknesses of oracy in primary classrooms. Moreover, the data and our analysis indicate that there is little room for complacency, especially when one compares some of the figures and sequences reported here with the statements of attainment and programmes of study required for English Attainment Target One (Speaking and Listening) in the National Curriculum.[4]

The scope of these, and for that matter of some of the interactive Statements of Attainment specified in the (pre-Dearing) statutory orders for science, mathematics and technology, extends a long way beyond the relatively limited talking and listening activities recorded here. Our analysis indicates that this issue deserves attention. In this context it should be noted that there are two related but distinct aspects of the problem needing to be tackled: one is the actual form and content of the verbal exchanges in which children are involved (see below); the other is the patterns of classroom organisation which are needed for the number of such exchanges to be increased and for their quality to be maximised.

It should be added that the schools in the Level Three enquiry were not atypical of the sixty involved in the study as a whole.

Teacher–pupil and pupil–pupil interaction

Children's speaking and listening are part of the larger issue of teacher–pupil and pupil–pupil interaction. Our data here raise important questions about the educational productiveness of particular kinds of interaction, their incidence, and the maximisation of their most productive forms. Because it is clear that each child's access to teacher–pupil interaction is limited (and we have quantified this precisely), the challenge is to make best use of the limited time available.

It is necessary, therefore, to ask fairly searching questions about the modes of interaction exemplified and discussed in this chapter, and particularly in its second part. Is the balance of questions and other kinds of utterance right? What can be done to shift from pseudo-questions to those which genuinely invite an answer; and from closed questions to those which encourage the child to think and solve problems rather than recall low-level information? Shouldn't children themselves be asking more of the questions? What are the contexts in which it is most appropriate to adopt a questioning stance? When is it appropriate to tell rather than ask? How can we strike the right balance between steering discussion down a prescribed path and recognising that apparently divergent responses may contain considerable learning potential? How can we learn to listen to children as well as get them to listen to us? How can we encourage them to talk and listen to one another? How can we ensure that we balance praise and encouragement with clear and useful feedback? How, in short, can we use classroom dialogue as a means of promoting genuine learning and understanding?

Managing teaching and learning

Classroom management has been a recurrent theme in PRINDEP. Prior to this study we concentrated on following through Leeds LEA's commitment to securing what it defined as the most appropriate environment for learning. In doing so we showed (for example, in Chapter 3) how teachers were responding in various ways to what they took to be the LEA's preferences and policies, and how they dealt with the challenges and dilemmas which these posed. The present study penetrates to a deeper level of classroom management. Here we have charted in some detail how children and teachers spent their time on various tasks and activities. We have shown the very different ways that teachers operated within the framework they had in common. This framework comprised a fairly standard sequence for each teaching session (although the proportions of time devoted to each stage and its mode of management varied) and a pattern of organisation in which at any one time different groups of children were undertaking different tasks.

Both aspects of the framework invite questions. What is the best way to introduce and allocate tasks? How can the time and opportunities for children to engage in these tasks be maximised? What kinds of classroom environment will most support children's task engagement? How should interruptions be dealt with? What size and composition of groups are most conducive to learning? What kinds of tasks and activities is it most appropriate for groups to undertake?

More fundamentally, are there some patterns of organisation which are over-ambitious, or in other ways inappropriate, for particular teachers? Instead of identifying preferred patterns for general use, should there be a more serious attempt to help individual teachers establish the ways of organising teaching and learning which are best for them? Equally, how should teachers respond to the growing body of evidence which highlights the problems of securing effective learning in classrooms adopting complex organisational arrangements such as that in which at any one time different groups undertake work in different curriculum areas?

Managing learning and managing time

One of the most significant outcomes of the present study is the challenge it poses to conventional thinking about the management of time in the primary classroom. Everyone concedes that time is a critical ingredient in teaching, and Bennett's (1987) characterisation of the teacher as 'manager of the scarce resources of attention and time', which we quoted earlier, is one which most teachers would accept and which is strongly and sometimes dramatically confirmed in this study.

The two 'resources' are, of course, linked: children need to spend time on their curriculum tasks; they need to give these tasks as far as possible their undivided attention; and the quality of the attention which children give to their learning tasks, and which the teacher gives to the children, is in part a function of how the child's and the teacher's time is allocated and used.

The conventional wisdom about the resource of time is simply that there is not enough of it for teachers to fit in everything which they wish or are obliged to do. The National Curriculum, it is added, has made the situation even worse, particularly in respect of the extensive requirements in subjects like science and mathematics, and the pressures of both ongoing teacher assessment and standard assessment tasks at the ends of Key Stages 1 and 2.

That the curriculum and the school day are finite is not in question. Nor is there much doubt that some educationally essential aspects of the curriculum have been squeezed almost to the point where they might as well not be there at all. This larger aspect of the problem of timetabled time, though pressing and serious, is not our main concern here. Instead, we wish to point up certain aspects to do with the teacher's management of time on a day-to-day basis, where there does seem to be room for manoeuvre.

There are two starting points for the kinds of time-management analysis which our data suggest that teachers might usefully undertake or have someone undertake for them: the children's use of time, and their own. The simplest measure, and one employed in this study, is time spent by children engaged in the learning tasks set by the teacher. Since this was directly related to time spent distracted or awaiting attention, the immediate issue for the teacher is how to increase the first by reducing the second. The solutions would seem to lie partly in the nature of the tasks themselves, some of which required more teacher supervision or intervention than others, and partly in patterns of organisation, some of which made it difficult to give children the degree of attention they needed.

However, it was also noted, both here and in Chapter 3, that a common response to this problem is to give certain groups tasks which would keep them 'busy' by virtue of their undemanding nature. This is a pragmatic solution, but not an educational one.

It was also noted that the proportion of the time spent on task varied from one curriculum area to another: children worked hardest and were least distracted when undertaking those activities for which there was least opportunity; and they were most often distracted during those activities like reading and writing on which they spent most time. This suggests that simply to give a high-priority activity or curriculum area more and more time will not necessarily deliver the learning outcomes sought, and indeed beyond a certain point may become counter-productive. Instead, ways should be sought of encouraging children to use their time more effectively; indeed, a courageous experiment would be to combine this with an actual reduction in time allocated to particular tasks. In any event, there is something paradoxical in complaining about the lack of time to deliver the full range of curriculum experiences while simultaneously deploying time-fillers to keep children occupied.[5]

In fact, of course, time-fillers are used for two purposes: one is to occupy until the end of a session those children who have finished early; the other is to overcome the managerial problem of attending to a large number of children simultaneously. The solution here is partly curricular and partly organisational.

It has been established that teacher–pupil interaction is a centrally important aspect of teaching. Learning, it is now accepted, has a strong social and interactive component, and the teacher's ability to engage children in challenging and stimulating dialogue is a powerful means of advancing their understanding. Similarly, where assessment is concerned the teacher can infer much from such tangible products of learning as written work; but there are certain kinds of learning which can be assessed only while the child is working. Moreover, while written work can indicate whether a child has understood something, it cannot tell the teacher much about the nature and causes of any problems the child has in relation to the concepts, skills or principles in question: these, again, require observation and interaction with the teacher.

However, we then face the undeniable evidence that each child interacts with the teacher for a very small proportion of his or her time. There seem to be two ways of beginning to tackle this problem. One is to look for patterns of classroom organisation which increase the incidence of teacher–pupil interaction. The other is to strive to increase the efficiency of any interaction which does take place.

It is clear from the data that careful planning, sensible and efficient organisation, a shared understanding of classroom routines and so on will increase a teacher's opportunities for interaction with their pupils. Equally, this setting is also likely to ensure that the interaction can be concentrated more on work, and less on routine and disciplinary matters.

However, even the most efficient organisation cannot guarantee the quality of interactions, and here the second part of this study may provide some clues. It will be noted that in some of the transcripts the teacher seems to spend an excessive time getting across ideas of a straightforward kind. This is sometimes to do with the fragmented nature of the sequence, with interruptions or excursions to other parts of the classroom constantly intervening – a tendency which ought to be remediable. Sometimes it may be due to the teacher's own imperfect grasp of the ideas being taught, and this can lead to an excessively roundabout and unfocused kind of discourse. This, too, is remediable, although for some teachers and some areas of the curriculum the deficit in curriculum understanding may be considerable. Equally, however, the time may be wasted simply because a teacher adopts an inappropriate or inefficient mode of interaction. For example, points which could appropriately and rapidly be dealt with as statements may be translated into an interminable guessing game of pseudo-questions. The teacher's use of praise may be either so indiscriminate that children ignore it, or so wayward that it reinforces undesirable and desirable behaviours alike. Or children may simply not be given the opportunities to say what they really know, and the teacher is therefore unable quickly to re-assess and adjust the pace and direction of the learning tasks on which they are working.

This leads us to an important point about assessment. It has been noted that assessment and diagnosis require evidence based on the processes as well as the products of learning. However, a study of the transcripts will show that some kinds of teacher–pupil dialogue are much more effective at eliciting information about children's experience and grasp of processes than others. Token questions produce nothing; closed questions yield evidence of a yes/no or information-recall variety; open questions alone give the teacher access to the thought processes themselves. Even then there are dangers, since questions which are open to the point of vagueness invite vague replies, and the skill lies in combining openness with a clear message about the focus of concern. Similarly, feedback from the teacher which accepts everything, including inappropriate answers, may be unhelpful and confusing to children, just as excessively critical feedback can damage their self-esteem.

Thus, when considering the quality of teacher–pupil interaction, whether in the form of transcript material or in school, there is a quite specific further test to be applied to each particular mode of interaction: is it efficient as a tool for diagnosis, teaching or assessment? If not, ways may need to be sought to ensure that the scarce time for teacher–pupil interaction is better used.

It must also be stressed that even when time for interaction is maximised and the interaction itself is both efficient and genuinely interactive, it will still constitute a relatively small proportion of the child's time – albeit an extremely significant one. Because of this, the potential of other kinds of interaction to promote learning, most notably that of collaborative groupwork, merits detailed exploration. The interactive context of the classroom should be looked at as a whole so that the opportunities for both teacher–pupil and pupil–pupil interaction can be mapped out comprehensively – not least in relation to the demands of the National Curriculum.

However, the general point remains: the 'problem of time' in primary classrooms is not solely due to external pressures. It may in part be a function of the teacher's own practices, and in such cases an analysis of how that teacher uses time, from the broad organisational strategies right down to the minutiae of their moment-to-moment interactions with the children, could be immensely helpful both in creating more time and in making for a more effective and efficient context for learning.

Groupwork: a missed opportunity?

The ORACLE study (Galton *et al.* 1980a, 1980b; Galton and Williamson 1992) reported that children were working everywhere in groups but rarely as groups. Although, since then, many teachers have sought to structure tasks of a genuinely collaborative kind into their groupwork, this study's league table of the activities undertaken under various curriculum headings (Table 4.16) shows the Level Three children still spending only about half as much time on collaborative activities as on writing. The finding is all the more striking because in every one of these classrooms, as in the majority of the many classrooms visited during the project, children were working in groups. This being so, we have to ask whether more should be done to diversify the range of activities undertaken in groups and, in particular, to introduce more collaborative activity. The answer depends on the kinds of justification which can be provided for such a change: to advocate collaboration for no apparent reason is not sufficient. Three main arguments can be advanced, and all are backed by PRINDEP data as well as by other studies.

The first, and most familiar, is that collaborative activity is educationally valuable in itself in that it promotes certain basic social skills which are necessary in everyday life. This argument is widely accepted; we do not need to comment on it further.

The second argument has to do with the management of learning. In some classrooms children are spending a great deal of time waiting for their teachers' attention, and while doing so some of them may be wasting other children's time as well as their own. They are waiting for attention because they have been given tasks which require frequent teacher monitoring and feedback. Some teachers, however, have found that activities which incorporate an element of self-monitoring, especially of the kind that can be undertaken in a group context, can reduce the incidence of waiting and distraction. This view is supported by the findings of the Leverhulme Primary Project (Wragg and Bennett 1990; Dunne and Bennett 1990): where children worked co-operatively, they tended to use the group rather than the teacher as the main reference point, and the ratio of work to routine interactions between pupils and teachers noticeably improved.

The third argument concerns the quality of classroom interaction. We have shown that the amount of productive interaction with the teacher which each child receives can be very small, yet such interaction is an important ingredient in learning. We have noted that even in generously staffed classrooms this is to some degree inevitable, although we have also shown that much can be done to improve the quality of those interactions which do take place. However, if it is accepted that inter-action as such can be a powerful tool in learning, then we should acknowledge that the potential of pupil–pupil as well as teacher–pupil interaction needs to be fully exploited.

We find support for this proposition elsewhere. The Leverhulme team compared groups in which children were working individually with those where they were working collaboratively. In both kinds of group children talked to one another, but the conversation in the collaborative groups was more likely to be task-related. Moreover, collaborative activities appeared to generate greater task involvement than individu-alised activities.

These confirmatory findings underline our sense that while the quality of teacher–pupil interaction reflects aspects of each teacher's knowledge and skill which are quite independent of his or her mode of classroom organisation, the interaction and the organisation are also to some extent bound up with each other. Irrespective of their individual interactive skills, there appears to be much that teachers can do organisationally to increase the opportunities for productive talk within the classroom, not only between themselves and their pupils, but also between one pupil and another. Even so, organisational changes can achieve only so much, and the teacher needs to attend at the same time to the kinds of questions about the substance and style of interaction which we listed in the section on teacher–pupil interaction above.

Collaborative learning tasks, therefore, can promote self-monitoring, reduce the proportion of time spent by the teacher on other than task-related matters, and encourage the kinds of interaction in which effective learning is grounded. They are not necessarily easy to devise, particularly for teachers who have little experience of working this way, and they dictate changes in professional attitude as well as in organisation.

Teachers teaching together: a cautionary note

This report adds important evidence to that provided in this project's earlier studies (notably Alexander *et al.* 1989: chaps, 5 and 7) about the important aspect of the PNP initiative which we termed teachers teaching together, or TTT. Essentially it is to the effect that the relationship between enhanced staffing and improved pupil–teacher ratios, on the one hand, and more effective teaching, on the other, is by no means an inevitable one. TTT was not necessarily associated with children spending more time working, nor with their interacting more frequently or productively with their teachers. The gains visible in some classrooms were offset – in this and the Level One and Level Two studies (Chapter 3) – by the greater organisational complexity, lack of shared purposes and confusing messages which were apparent in others.

Evidence about children

An increased emphasis on assessment dictates greater attention to the quality of the evidence about children on which diagnoses and assessments are made. On a day-to-day basis this is important enough; in the context of National Curriculum Assessment it is vital. This study has shown some significant differences in the task-related behaviour of different groups of children: older and younger children, girls and boys, and those perceived by their teachers to be of average, above-average and below-average ability. These differences concerned the amount of time children spent on the various kinds of task-related behaviour – working, routine, awaiting attention, distracted – both as a whole and in relation to each area of the curriculum.

Though the differences were in line with the findings of other studies, this does not mean that they should occasion no comment or action. Indeed, to accept such findings as a mere fact of life is to ensure that nothing will change. We now know that judgements about children's abilities and attainments can be based on inappropriate evidence. We also know – and have evidence from earlier PRINDEP studies (see Alexander *et al*. 1989: chap. 2) – that some teachers may hold expectations and preconceptions about individual children on the basis of their assumptions about the group to which they seem to belong – whether age, ability, gender or race. We know too that such expectations and preconceptions can be extremely persistent, even in the face of contrary evidence, to the extent that they become self-fulfilling.

The relationship of all this to our present discussion is clear. Accurate diagnosis and assessment, free from preconceptions, is every child's right. But it is heavily dependent on the teacher's access to two kinds of knowledge: knowledge of the child, and knowledge of the aspect of the curriculum in which evidence of the child's capacities and progress is sought. Curriculum knowledge, in the sense of mastery of the subject matter to be taught, has sometimes tended to be underrated in the primary professional culture, and is also particularly problematic given the way the class-teacher system places such a heavy burden of curriculum understanding on the teacher. However, though this is important, our focus of concern here is more on the other kind of knowledge the teacher needs, about the child.

This in turn depends for its quality and comprehensiveness on the opportunities available to the teacher for interacting with the child and with the products and processes of the child's learning. All the earlier points about the management of time, resources and events in the class-room, and about the quality and efficiency of teacher–pupil interaction, apply as much to diagnosis and assessment as they do to teaching. Indeed, the three are in reality so closely linked as to be inseparable: we teach on the basis of what we know about the child; what we come to know about the child depends on the opportunities we give ourselves to acquire this knowledge; and what the child demonstrates by way of progress is in part a reflection of the appropriateness of the learning tasks we have provided; our judgements of the child are therefore to some extent judgements on ourselves.[6]

It is for these reasons that we need to generate patterns of organisa-tion and modes of interaction which maximise our opportunities for genuine engagement with the child's learning.

Surface and substance

In Chapter 3 we provided evidence that the central processes in teaching and learning may not have been addressed as closely or as compre-hensively in the Primary Needs Programme as was necessary. We referred to the 'inviolability of the classroom', an apparent reluctance to engage directly with the interactive processes on which successful learning so heavily depends, and the tendency to concentrate too much on 'surface' aspects of classroom practice.

This chapter has tried to offer material for progressing to that deeper level of engagement with teaching. The fact that the PRINDEP study of classroom practice had three levels, of which this is the third, reflects this intention. It also hints at the possibility of going even deeper. Level Four, if we had time and resources, would open up even more issues and insights: teaching is infinitely complex and, fortunately, infinitely improvable.

NOTES

1 The remaining 1 per cent, of course, constitutes behaviour which could not be classified in this way. This table, repeated in the project's final report (Alexander 1991: para 4.28) was the one most eagerly seized on by the press in their extensive and somewhat hysterical coverage during the summer and autumn of 1991. The *Daily Telegraph* of 19 September, for example, ignored the status of the table as relating to a small sub-sample of teachers in one LEA and offered the banner headline 'A generation of wasted time', claiming that our data showed that children, nation-wide, were wasting 40 per cent of the school day ('the education of millions of primary school children . . . blighted in the name of an anarchic ideology, says a new study'). Their claim was then picked up by other newspapers and commentators, including some senior figures within the education service. Thus are myths created.

2 Such 'arbitrariness' no longer obtains, to the same extent at any rate. Readers trained since the government defined the primary curriculum as a canon of nine subjects will find the long list of curriculum areas in Table 4.10, and the five tables which follow, intriguing. They may even dispute the notion that 'administration' or 'free ranging' or 'television' can be defined as part of the curriculum at all. In terms of the National Curriculum they cannot; but for most of the post-war period teachers have exercised considerable freedom in the matter of curricular designation, tacitly adopting the notion that the curriculum comprises all those experiences provided by the school to promote learning. Thus, our teachers would assert – and did – that 'administrative' activities like dealing with the register or dinner money are curricular in the sense that they are a vehicle for the acquisition of social, interactive and for that matter mathematical abilities. In this study we are neutral on the question of the validity of the various curriculum labels. Our task was to observe and understand what was happening in these classrooms, and to do so we needed to respect the terms of reference of the teachers themselves where central questions like curriculum were concerned. These were their labels, therefore, not ours. On the other hand, it is worth noting the finding of Campbell and his team (see below) that since the inception of the National Curriculum teachers report that time spent on administrative activities, many of them falling outside even the most liberal definition of curriculum, has spiralled almost out of control.

3 The most recent and comprehensive analysis of time and the curriculum is provided by Campbell and his colleagues in a major study undertaken since the introduction of the National Curriculum (Campbell *et al.* 1994a, 1994b, 1994c). He also compares his findings with earlier ones undertaken by Bassey, Bennett, Galton, Tizard, Meyer and ourselves, and demonstrates (1994b: 212) a remarkable consistency in the balance of the 'basics' and the rest of the curriculum in the post-war period, confirming a suggestion I made a decade earlier (Alexander 1984: chap. 3). This effectively demolishes right-wing criticisms that primary teachers have pursued progressive ideals at the expense of the basics. Curriculum balance – or imbalance – has in fact been constant: the issue is one of *pedagogy* rather than content, as this chapter demonstrates. The idea of fundamental historical continuities underlying apparent revolutions in primary education is also central to the present book's second and sixth chapters.

4 As originally specified, English Attainment Target One was rather more extensive than it ended up after Dearing's review. Even so, the final version of this attainment target (SCAA 1994) listed among the purposes which speaking and listening in the primary school should serve: (at Key Stage 1) telling stories, both real and imagined; imaginative play and drama; reading and listening to nursery rhymes and poetry; reading aloud; exploring, developing and clarifying ideas; predicting outcomes and discussing possibilities; describing events, observations and experiences; making simple, clear explanations of choices; giving reasons for opinions and actions; (and at Key Stage 2) exploring, developing and explaining ideas; planning, predicting and investigating; sharing ideas, insights and opinions; reading aloud, telling and enacting stories and poems; reporting and describing events and observations; presenting to audiences, live or on tape. The gulf between such requirements and some of the more unfocused, random and low-level interactions in these transcript extracts (which we can verify as being representative of the study as a whole) is a substantial one and may take more than government fiat to remedy.

5 All this was written, of course, before the issue of curriculum manageability at Key Stages 1 and 2 finally exploded in the faces of those (at NCC and in government) who had written it off between 1989 and 1993 as mere 'teething problems'. The outcome was Dearing's review and the 1995 remodelled National Curriculum, presented as the version to survive, unchanged, until the year 2000 at least. The studies of Jim Campbell and his colleagues provided some of the most powerful ammunition for those who insisted that NCC and the government were ignoring, or covering up, a problem of considerable gravity and urgency, and we are aware that in this study we may seem to underplay the problem of time as they so lucidly and convincingly presented it. This is not the case: the problem was substantial and undeniable. What we are saying here is that if time is used least efficiently on subjects which are conventionally allocated most, then the calculations in bodies like SCAA about how much time each subject needs may well be seriously inaccurate, and in any event will do little to solve the other problem of time as we have identified it here – namely, as the economy or diseconomy of the pedagogic practices through which the curriculum as specified on paper is translated into pupil learning experiences. When you add to the equation the questions about teacher talk which arise from this study's qualitative analysis of the transcript material, then the problem of time in primary classrooms becomes far more complex than Dearing's simple arithmetic can ever encompass.

6 One of the most extensive and illuminating studies of the way observation and interaction provide the basis for classroom assessment is that of Drummond (1993), published some time after we undertook the PRINDEP study.

Chapter 5

Change and continuity*

By now the version of primary education in question is that required by law: a National Curriculum of nine subjects. This study starts by exploring how teachers nationally are responding to the statutory requirements before returning to the theme of teacher–pupil talk. This time, instead of the combination of quantitative and qualitative methods used in Chapter 4, we experiment with a computerised system of discourse analysis. The study brings together the teachers from Chapter 2 (1986), Chapters 3 and 4 (1988) and Chapter 5 (1992) in an attempt to discover what, in this most fundamental aspect of teaching, has changed as a result of primary teachers working to a version of curriculum required by law rather than one devised by themselves, and how, more generally, the earlier dilemmas of the primary classroom are being replaced by other concerns.

The National Curriculum had its earliest and possibly its most far-reaching impact in primary schools. It represented a view of curriculum which was strongly at variance with the dominant professional ideology (Kelly 1990), and it exposed and tested three central aspects of primary teachers' expertise: their subject knowledge, especially where relatively new areas like science and technology were concerned; their ability to diagnose and assess in the explicit and systematic way required by the statutory orders; and their capacity to modify classroom practice in order to deliver the content, outcomes and assessments required.

Given that the rhetoric surrounding the introduction of the National Curriculum was chiefly concerned with the raising of standards, it was important to explore the extent to which the government's programme for achieving this goal was in fact doing so. The policy hinged on prescribed content, testing at the end of each Key Stage, and the

* This chapter was written jointly by Robin Alexander, John Willcocks and Nick Nelson.

increased accountability signalled by procedures for reporting to governors, parents and the LEA, and the associated device of league tables.
However, the National Curriculum did not involve prescription over
pedagogy, and though government intervened in the debate about
primary teaching methods in 1991–92, it held to its original promise to
leave decisions about such matters to teachers themselves.[1]

Thus, a significant contrast was built in from the start between the
assumptions about what was needed in order to improve standards
made by government and those suggested by research. For government,
the key was a fairly draconian combination of prescribed content, testing
and accountability, well-captured in the list of items schools were now
obliged to report on annually to governors and parents, as summarised
in the Parent's Charter (DFE 1994a). Here the emphasis was on
conformity to National Curriculum subject requirements, test results,
employment statistics, expenditure, and the continuing governmental
pressure to encourage schools to 'opt out'.

The picture emerging from research was, inevitably, rather more
complex. There was indeed growing consensus about the importance of
subject matter – with or without the National Curriculum – and hence of
teachers' subject knowledge (Shulman 1986, 1987; Bennett and Carré 1993;
OFSTED 1994a) – an aspect of professional expertise historically under-
played and indeed frequently rejected in primary ideology (Alexander
1984). Researchers also highlighted assessment, while avoiding the government tendency to equate it with testing and arguing for a proper balance
of the summative and formative and the need, in particular, to refine the
diagnostic process (Bennett et al. 1984; Gipps 1988; Drummond 1993).

At the same time, research evidence suggested a necessary concern,
of at least equal seriousness, with matters like the following: the existing
knowledge and capacities of the learner, captured in Ausubel's maxim
that 'the single most important factor influencing learning is what the
pupil already knows: ascertain this and teach accordingly' (Ausubel
1968; Bennett 1992); the capacity of the teacher to provide learning tasks
which provide a bridge between this learner knowledge and the understandings to which teaching is directed (Vygotsky 1962, 1978; Bruner
and Haste 1987); the teacher's ability to use time as economically
and efficiently as possible in order to maximise opportunities for
those interactions with pupils which are such an important element in
diagnosis, task design, assessment and learning (Bennett et al. 1984;
Mortimore et al. 1988; Galton 1989; Alexander 1992; Bennett 1995); the
understanding and skill needed in order to make these interactions of
the highest quality possible (Galton et al. 1980a, 1980b; Edwards and
Mercer 1987; Willcocks and Alexander in this volume, Chapter 4); the
teacher's possession of a broad repertoire of organisational strategies
and his or her ability to deploy these flexibly and appropriately (Galton

1989; Gipps 1992; Alexander 1992); the need to rethink and refocus the established strategies of whole-class teaching, individual attention and groupwork, paying particular attention to the collaborative potential of the latter (Bennett and Dunne 1992; Galton and Williamson 1992); the adoption of patterns of classroom organisation which, while flexible, are not over-complex and allow events to be managed rather than merely crisis-managed (Bennett et al. 1984; Mortimore et al.1988; OFSTED 1993a, 1993b, 1994a); the underpinning of these by a range of generic skills like observation, questioning, explaining, instructing, providing both evaluative and critical feedback, managing space and resources, and handling behaviour (Brown and McIntyre 1993; Wragg 1989, 1992).

The alternative focus, then, was firmly on *learning* and *pedagogy* as much as content and assessment, and the emphasis on pedagogic flexibility and diversity and what the 1992 DES primary discussion paper called 'fitness for purpose' (Alexander et al. 1992: para 101) contrasted strongly with the advocacy by the government and right-wing pressure groups of one-dimensional pedagogical formulae like whole-class teaching, subject teaching and an almost exclusive concentration on the so-called 'basics'.[2]

At the same time, researchers and professional groups also pointed up certain critically-important contextual factors: the way in which staff were deployed in primary schools (House of Commons 1986, 1994a); the expertise required for the increasingly diverse roles primary teachers were being expected to undertake (Campbell et al. 1990, 1991; Bennett and Carré 1993; OFSTED 1993c, 1994a); the increasingly acute problem of time in primary schools as teachers struggled to accommodate more and more tasks, many of them outside the classroom altogether, within a finite working week (Campbell and Neill 1992, 1994a, 1994b, 1994c); the need to adopt funding policies which would allow more flexible deployment patterns than the class-teacher system alone, would reduce classes to a level which would permit the amount and quality of inter-action needed, and would allow teachers properly to undertake the tasks now required of them (House of Commons 1994a); and, finally, the National Curriculum itself, eventually acknowledged by government and its agencies to be not only unmanageable but also to have had unmanageability structured into it from the outset by virtue of the planning strategy adopted by the National Curriculum Council (OFSTED 1993d; NCC 1993; Dearing 1993a, 1993b).

ASSESSING THE IMPACT OF THE NATIONAL CURRICULUM

The scenario of major and rapid change, and the incongruence between official and professional views of the factors critical to the raising of educational standards (always supposing that 'standards' could be defined and measured) made it essential that the impact of the National Curriculum be carefully assessed.

The monitoring programmes instituted by the National Curriculum Council and the School Examination and Assessment Council (which merged in 1993 to form the School Curriculum and Assessment Authority), and by HMI/OFSTED, tended – perhaps inevitably – to define 'impact' mainly in terms of the government's agenda. For them the principal question to be addressed was how far the requirements of the 1988 Education Reform Act, and the claims by which it was justified, were being put into practice. Independent research teams were able to approach the notion of 'impact' more openly. Thus while the official implementation studies concentrated on those aspects of teaching which related in obvious ways to the content/assessment ambience of the National Curriculum – planning, schemes and guidelines, subject expertise, the use of time, school management, initial and in-service training in subject content and statutory assessment (for example, NCC 1991; DES 1991a, 1991b) – independent studies sought to pursue the question of how the task of the primary teacher, and indeed the nature of primary education itself, was changing.

Thus, the succession of studies from Campbell *et al.* (1990, 1991, 1992) showed the dramatic and damaging consequences for the teacher and the curriculum – in terms of professional stress and the marginalisation of the non-core subjects – of the changed and increased time demands. The Bristol PACE study showed significant shifts in the balance of whole-class, group and individual teaching, the erosion of 'real teaching time', and a significant decline in professional autonomy and morale. It also pinpointed major tensions between the a priori view of knowledge espoused by government and the received/reflexive paradigm preferred by many primary teachers, and it identified as critical loci for change school management, teacher autonomy, and the subject framing of the teacher's work (Pollard *et al.* 1994). The Exeter Leverhulme studies pinpointed the consequences of a shortfall between subject requirements and subject expertise and began the essential task of mapping out the knowledge bases for teaching dictated by the statutory requirements (Bennett and Carré 1993). Webb's work, like that of several others, showed how the National Curriculum had brought both benefits and problems: professional co-operation on the one hand, professional stress on the other; entitlement to a broad curriculum, but at the same time the increasing vulnerability of the non-core foundation subjects (Webb 1993, 1994) – not that the balance between 'basics' and the rest of the curriculum had been anything other than problematic before 1989.

Looking at these various implementation studies now, over six years after the 1988 Act, we can begin to perceive the seeds of three basic propositions. First, that the National Curriculum has made a considerable impact on *teachers*. Second, that the impact of the National Curriculum on those who were supposed to be its chief beneficiaries, the *pupils*, is rather less clear. Third, that the most significant ingredient in this emerging discrepancy is the very aspect of professional practice on which the government chose not to legislate, namely *pedagogy*. Put another way, legislation reduced teacher autonomy in respect of content and assessment, but left it pretty well intact in respect of the means by which content is translated into managed learning tasks and events. These are the propositions on which this chapter, and the project on which it is based, provide a commentary.

THE CICADA STUDY

Our project – Changes in Curriculum-Associated Discourse and Pedagogy in the Primary School (CICADA) – was one of the implementation studies referred to above. However, it was different from others in that its base line for examining the impact of the National Curriculum was not the 1988 Act but data gathered earlier. It also focused firmly upon pedagogy. It did so because it arose from a study, and a particular tradition in primary education research, which had demonstrated both the power and the problematic nature of pedagogy in the primary school.

The earlier study, PRINDEP (part of whose classroom data forms the subject of Chapters 3 and 4 of this book), had examined the impact of a major LEA development initiative on a complete local system of primary education, from town hall to school and classroom, from policy to management, curriculum and classroom practice. Probably its most significant findings – certainly those which were most eagerly exploited by government and the press – concerned the politics and practice of pedagogy – that is to say, the way views of 'good practice' are defined, transmitted and indeed enforced within an LEA and its schools; and the way such versions of 'good practice' are responded to and enacted by teachers in classrooms. The project, then, uncovered a *power* dimension of pedagogy to place alongside the more familiar research preoccupation with *process*.

In respect of the latter, however, Chapters 3 and 4 show how PRINDEP's findings were broadly in line with those of earlier studies from Galton, Bennett, Mortimore, Tizard and their colleagues, highlighting matters such as organisational economy, breadth and flexibility of pedagogical repertoire, the management of time, and the quality of interaction. It also pinpointed the problematic nature of certain pedagogic 'recipes' which by the 1980s had gained strong currency in English primary schools: for example, multiple curriculum focus teaching, groupwork, the 'enquiry' mode of teacher–pupil interaction, and the emphasis on facilitation rather than intervention in the teacher role.

CICADA chose to continue just one of PRINDEP's many strands of enquiry: that of pupil–teacher discourse. It did so partly for opportunistic reasons: PRINDEP, and *its* predecessor (a small-scale project on primary teachers' professional knowledge in action – the subject of this book's second chapter) had yielded valuable classroom transcript data which deserved re-analysis and could provide a basis for a longitudinal study of change in primary classrooms. However, the main justification for the focus on discourse was its centrality in teaching and learning. Several other projects referred to earlier, including the PRINDEP study, had highlighted the powerful role played by focused and challenging talk – both teacher–pupil and pupil–pupil – in the promotion of learning. Moreover, this conclusion, much of it derived empirically from process-product data, chimed with the emerging consensus – to which we have also alluded – concerning the essentially interactive nature of children's learning. Thus it is discourse which translates educational legislation into a living curriculum; it is discourse which animates pedagogy; and, powerfully though of course not uniquely, it is discourse which engages and advances pupil thinking and learning. Classroom discourse, then, represented a necessary and critical focus for the effort to chart and understand the impact of the National Curriculum.

CICADA's principal objective was to conduct a further programme of interviews and classroom observation with a group of primary teachers from whom an extensive body of data had been gathered as part of PRINDEP, and to chart changes in the style and substance of their discourse and classroom organisation over the period of the introduction of the National Curriculum. A further objective was to set the observation study in the context of a national survey of teachers' attitudes to the National Curriculum and its impact on their work.

In relation to the first objective, a major problem was encountered during the first year of the project when the LEA in which the PRINDEP research had been carried out withdrew access to its schools following the publication of the project's final evaluation report (Alexander 1991) and the attendant press coverage and political exploitation, but before any new data had been gathered for the present project. This necessitated a radical revision of CICADA's research design since the use of classroom observation data gathered in 1992 from the same ten teachers who had provided data in 1988 was a pivotal part of the original plan.

After negotiation with CICADA's sponsors, the Economic and Social Research Council, a modified research design was approved involving the analysis of pedagogical discourse recorded during classroom observation sessions with primary teachers in 1986 and 1988, and the isolation of those features which were relatively independent of time or location but sensitive to major curriculum changes. Data gathered in two different LEAs in 1992 would then be analysed using the techniques already developed, in order to identify any significantly different features of pedagogical discourse which had appeared since the introduction of the National Curriculum.

METHODS

The principal research technique was classroom observation involving the use of radio microphones and tape-recorders to record classroom interaction between teachers and their pupils. A variety of different coding systems contributed to the analysis of this material. Classroom observation was augmented by interviews with teachers, and these intensive but localised studies were set in a wider context through a questionnnaire survey of a national sample of primary school teachers. A detailed account of these methods now follows.

Teacher interviews and survey questionnaire

The national survey was undertaken to explore the attitudes of primary teachers to the demands of the National Curriculum and the changes it brought in its wake. The questionnaire items were all derived from responses given by practising primary teachers during the extended interviews which formed part of the project fieldwork in two local authorities in the summer of 1992.

Rather than simply presenting a series of questions reflecting the research team's preconceptions in the matter, these interviews were designed to give teachers the maximum opportunity to voice their own individual National Curriculum preoccupations. At the same time they had to be structured enough to yield comparable material irrespective of interviewer or interviewee, partly to aid analysis, and partly because there would inevitably be issues which individual teachers might not happen to raise spontaneously but upon which they would have plenty to say if asked.

With these requirements in mind, a strategy of hierarchical focusing (Tomlinson 1989) was adopted in the design and conduct of the interviews, and a hierarchically focused interview schedule was devised which, after extensive piloting, covered the impact of the National Curriculum on seven aspects of practice: classroom management, the curriculum, school organisation, assessment, record-keeping, contact with the local education authority, and general morale. Each of these areas was divided into sub-categories, many of which were then divided further.

The initial questions in each interview were of a very general nature (for example, *Has the National Curriculum actually had much of an impact on your life as a teacher?*), and the interviewer then followed the respondent's lead, ticking off items on the schedule as they were covered, and leading the interview on to a new topic or new aspects of an old topic only when the respondent became unduly repetitive or ran out of things to say.

The interviews were tape-recorded and transcribed in full. The transcripts, amounting to some 40,000 words, were closely studied by members of the research team who independently selected enough individual statements to reflect the range of frequently expressed views, together with a few idiosyncratic and seemingly provocative statements to leaven the mix with a touch of the unexpected. After much discussion, thirty-one of the statements were selected as raw material for questionnaire items. Some of them were usable as they stood; others needed modifying in the interests of clarity or brevity. A pilot version of the questionnaire was completed by and discussed with primary teachers attending in-service courses in the department during the autumn term of 1992. In the light of their responses, the order of items was changed to minimise various kinds of response set, and the wording of a few of the statements was adjusted to remove apparent ambiguities.

During the spring term of 1993 copies of the questionnaire were sent in batches of fifty to named link-persons in a sample of fourteen LEAs together with detailed instructions on sampling and administration.

Collection of observation data

The 1986 observation data were collected in Leeds, Bradford and Calderdale as part of the project on primary teachers' professional knowledge drawn on in Chapter 2, and took the form of videotapes of these teachers in action in their classrooms. The 1988 data were from a sub-sample of the sixty Leeds schools which featured in the PRINDEP classroom practice study described in Chapters 3 and 4, specifically in the Level Three phase of that study presented in Chapter 4. The 1992 data were gathered during CICADA fieldwork in primary schools in Wakefield and Bury. A programme of observation was mounted in the classrooms of twelve teachers, using the radio-microphone techniques developed in the two earlier projects.

In each of the three years, the sample was selected to ensure a proportion of men and women teachers similar to the national average, and a full and balanced spread of pupil age range. The 1992 sample was matched as closely as possible with those of 1986 and 1988. In each classroom the observer monitored the activity of the teacher and the pupils with whom she was involved. The teacher wore an unobtrusive radio microphone so that throughout the observation session all her utterances and those of the children with whom she was immediately concerned could be clearly heard by the observer through headphones, and also tape-recorded for detailed analysis later. The observers prepared qualitative accounts of the sessions to augment the tape-recorded data and clarify those situations where the tape recording on its own would not be enough to indicate precisely what was happening and who was involved. The original video-tapes were available from 1986, as well as detailed parallel notes from both 1986 and the 1988 studies, and because of this the number of uncodable utterances on the various analytical systems was negligible.

Analysis of observation data

The transcripts of the observation sessions were annotated according to six different coding systems. These focused on the *discourse structure* and *syntax* of what was spoken during the session, the *pedagogical strategies* and *curriculum context* of the interactions, the *varying numbers of children* with whom the teacher was interacting, and the *overall lexical content* of the session. Coding of the 1986 sessions was based on the video-recordings and transcripts, and coding of the 1988 sessions on transcripts and systematic observation schedules. Changes during the 1992 sessions were noted by the classroom observers and coded as they occurred. Each of these analytical frameworks is now described in detail.

Discourse

The discourse analysis was concerned with the structure and purpose of what was said, but not with the form of words, or the actual words used. As devised by Sinclair and Coulthard, traditional discourse analysis divides and sub-divides classroom discourse into smaller and smaller component units until it comes to the simplest unit, the speech act, and it was at the speech act level that the CICADA transcripts were coded. The relevant coding schedule is described in full by Sinclair and Coulthard (1975). In coding the CICADA material, some slight modifi-cations were made to the original schedule. Some categories were based on non-verbal elements of discourse and had to be omitted since much of the CICADA analysis was based on transcripts of sound recordings. CICADA also made use of a *narration* and a *reading* category which do not feature in the Sinclair and Coulthard scheme and which appeared in the CICADA analyses in situations where the speaker was using someone else's words.

In all, twenty-two different categories of speech act were coded over the sixty transcripts. However, five of these speech acts accounted for 84 per cent of all utterances, while none of the other speech acts accounted for more than 3 per cent of utterances. The five categories which occurred most frequently in the CICADA material are defined below in terms taken verbatim from Sinclair and Coulthard (1975).

- *Accept* 'Realized by a closed class of items – 'yes', 'no', 'good', 'fine', and repetition of pupil's reply, all with neutral low fall intonation. Its function is to indicate that the teacher has heard or seen, and that the informative, reply or react was appropriate.'
- *Directive* 'Realized by imperative. Its function is to request a non-linguistic response.'
- *Elicitation* 'Realized by a question. Its function is to request a linguistic response.'
- *Informative* 'Realized by statement. It differs from the other uses of statement in that its sole function is to provide information. The only response is an acknowledgement of attention and understanding.'
- *Reply* 'Realized by statement, question, moodless and non-verbal surrogates such as nods. Its function is to provide a linguistic response which is appropriate to the elicitation.'

Syntax

The syntax analysis was concerned with the syntactic structure used to achieve the purpose of the discourse. Teacher and pupil utterances were subjected to a simplified version of a syntax analysis originally devised by John Willcocks as part of an ongoing PhD project at the University of Leeds. The principal concern here was to determine the complexity of the teachers' classroom language, but the opportunity was also taken to examine its directness (for example, the extent to which commands were disguised as questions or statements). For the purposes of the syntax analysis, utterances were broken down into clauses, each clause being annotated at its end with a code letter indicating its status as a statement, question, command and so on, and, where appropriate, one or more other letters indicating the nature of its syntactic relationship to the immediately preceding clause. Coding was carried out purely in terms of syntactic structure, without reference to the imagined intention of the speaker. The four categories which occurred most frequently are listed below with examples.

- *Abort* The current clause is abandoned before completion. It may be followed by an attempt to reformulate the idea which the speaker wishes to express or it may simply be left incomplete – e.g., *What did it* . . . ?
- *Command* The verb of the clause is in the imperative mood. For the purposes of the present analysis, the various types of command in the original categorisation system have been amalgamated into a single broad category – e.g., *Come on Lee.*
- *Question* The operator is placed immediately before the subject (1, below), or the clause begins with an interrogative word (2, below), or

both (3, below). For the purposes of the present analysis, the various types of question in the original categorisation system have been amalgamated into a single broad category – e.g., 1: *Will you wash these brushes?* 2: *Who's talking?* 3: *What else did we do?*
- *Statement.* The current clause offers an account of fact or opinion. Its subject is followed by a finite verb – e.g., *We had a look round the museum.*

Pedagogy

An analysis was conducted to indicate teachers' use of various interaction strategies, and to track the ways in which their emphasis fluctuated between task content, procedure, accuracy and presentation. The system was devised on the premise that in many primary classrooms the children are not simply recipients of the teacher's pedagogy but are also participants and partners in it. For purely practical reasons, in the observation sessions it was always the teacher who wore the radio microphone and who was therefore the constant focus of the enquiry while individual children moved into and out of the picture in a way which was often entirely unsystematic. Consequently the teacher was always the central character in the recordings of observed sessions. Nevertheless, in each case she was involved in interactions with children for virtually the whole of the time; and the categories in the system of analysis were designed to be, in principle, equally applicable to the utterances of teachers or pupils (even though some kinds of utterance were very much more likely to come from the former than the latter). Pedagogic interactions were coded into eleven different categories of which the most frequently occurring are listed below with examples.

- *Evaluative feedback* Praise or criticism, for ongoing or completed work, with no information of a kind that furthers the child's understanding and/or satisfactory performance of the task. Evaluative feedback is always related to the pupil's work or utterance, never to the task itself – e.g., *That's not very good, is it?*
- *Explain/explore.* A comment, question or conversation about the nature of the current task. (This category is broadly equivalent to Bjorkman's *feedforward.*) E.g., *Once we really get started, though, we're going to have to find a way of sorting them out and storing them properly, so we can find them quickly when we want them.*
- *Formative feedback* A response to a child's work or utterance containing information of a kind that furthers the child's understanding and/ or satisfactory performance of the task. Formative feedback is always given as a direct response to a pupil's work or utterance. In any other circumstances, formative comment or discussion is coded as

exploration/explanation – e.g., *It's not really tight enough, James. It'll fall to bits in no time.*

- *Task direction* A comment, question or instruction in relation to the performance of the current task (except an instruction to think about or otherwise explore the task and its options, which would be coded as exploration/explanation) – e.g., *Hold it firmly so it doesn't slip while you're drawing the line, Rachel.*

Curriculum

The subject area was recorded under six headings: *English, Mathematics, Science, Other curricular, Non-curricular* and *Unknown*. Codings referred to individual utterances rather than to whole teaching sessions, and in some classrooms where the teacher moved rapidly from group to group, curriculum changes were very frequent.

Participants

The fluctuating number of participants in the teacher's interactions was monitored throughout and coded under five headings: *Individual child, Group(s) of children, The whole class, Another adult* and *Other/unknown*.

Lexis

In the lexical analyses, consideration was given to the actual words used. The transcripts were processed using the Oxford Concordance Program (OCP) by Hockey and Martin (1988). This program was used to provide lists of all the different words used by the various participants in the sessions observed and the frequency of use of each word. The lexical analysis also provided a measure of the relative numbers of words used by each kind of participant in the sessions – teachers, other adults and children.

RESULTS

Teacher interviews

Three of the themes in the interview schedule drew comparatively little response: school management and contact with LEAs were usually brushed aside with the comment that the respondent personally had very little to do with them, and answers to questions on general morale tended to be both stoical and succinct. Throughout the summaries of the remaining four themes which follow, direct quotations from the transcripts are italicised.

Assessment

Assessment was variously described as *never-ending, a burden* and *a major problem*. It was said to take up more time than teachers had available, partly because they realised that they must be more rigorous and less *intuitive*, and partly because there was *more and more to assess*. Some teachers were finding that they needed to enlist the help of ancillary staff. Grave doubts were expressed about assessing the youngest children, *5-year-olds who had maybe only had a term in school*, and there was a widespread feeling that no *real surprises* had emerged from *all this teacher assessment*.

However, some teachers said that their own assessment procedures had been changed for the better, that it was *all more focused down*, and that they were now insisting on *a lot more concrete evidence* before making an assessment.

Teachers' views on National Curriculum attainment targets (ATs) echoed those on assessment generally. The time taken was a particular problem: *the children would need to be in school for fourteen hours a day to cover all this*. The targets were changing classroom practice: *I've got to teach attainment targets; it's not a natural way of teaching*. However, ATs were also seen as agents for beneficial change: *it has tightened up practice*, and *you've got to be more precise*. Some respondents thought that the targets themselves had changed for the better, being *clearer and more organised than the old ones*.

Record-keeping

Record-keeping had changed dramatically since the implementation of the National Curriculum: several teachers mentioned *whole-school* and *formal systems*, contrasting these with old record cards which *had been filled in, but didn't actually tell us anything*. Current records were seen as *user friendly*, and frequent mention was made of their value either to the class-teacher who could *see immediately an overview of everything that we've done*, or in the longer term, when they might *be of some use to other teachers*.

There were, however, some reservations, for example that *you don't get much picture of a child simply through ticking in attainment targets*, and that other things *much harder to quantify* were not being recorded, but most schools had tackled this by including some *more formal kind of profile writing* in a child's folder. A minor worry was that the sheer volume of records (*eight million ticks for everything*), had *created all sorts of storage problems*, but on the whole the teachers welcomed tighter systems of recording.

Curriculum

On the curriculum itself, two comments were made again and again: its range was too great and some of its content was inappropriate for the younger children. Some respondents *used to be able to put a much higher emphasis on teaching basic literacy skills* while others felt that *you're so busy doing science, maths and language that other things have had to go*. This combination of unrealistic range and inappropriate content was forcing them into a superficiality they resented: *I don't want to skim over the top: I don't think the children learn a thing that way*. On the other hand, some respondents acknowledged that they could now *be more precise*, and *allow continuity as children move about classes*.

With regard to English, teachers of younger children particularly felt that pupils *still need to do more reading and writing because without a good English foundation they can't achieve in history, geography, science*. It was commonly held that *reading standards will suffer*, although one respondent placed the emphasis somewhat differently by praising the National Curriculum for raising *speaking and listening as skills to a level with reading and writing*.

In science, even more than in other subjects, the amount of content was thought *ridiculous* for younger children: it was *difficult to make sure you've covered in breadth for all levels*. On the positive side, however, *it has made you have to . . . teach things that were left*, and *I've had to do a lot of work on my own scientific knowledge*. Some teachers found that the problems they were facing with science were exacerbated by severe shortages of equipment.

Classroom management

Although some respondents reported *a change towards more whole-class teaching* since the introduction of the National Curriculum, for the most part they believed that classroom management had remained much the same. The most common view was that *the best teaching practice in a classroom is a mixture*, with the children working in groups for *the majority of the time*.

In practice the managerial style was often dictated by specific and fluctuating constraints: by the subject itself *(in things like maths, there's no way you could do a class session*, while *RE is done as a whole class)*, by the presence or absence of ancillary staff *(that would be perfect if you could have an extra person in your class)* or by the amount of equipment available *(we've had to look really hard at our school resources, particularly books*, and *you can't teach history and geography without books and posters and visits)*.

Questionnaire survey

The analysis

A computer analysis was conducted to provide simple descriptive statistics relating to the teachers and their responses. Questionnaire items were first treated individually and then grouped for the exploration of underlying attitudes. The significance of differences between the responses of different groups (for example,. men and women) was determined by analyses of variance or t-tests as appropriate.

With two exceptions, the probability of the differences mentioned in the analyses which follow was comfortably beyond the .01 level, and in some cases well beyond the .001 level. The two exceptions were differences with a probability of .013, and these are clearly identified in the text.

The sample

The overall response rate from the fourteen participating local authorities was 77 per cent. As a check on the representativeness of the sample, respondents were asked to indicate whether they were male or female, how many years primary teaching they had done, and the age group(s) they were currently teaching. In spite of the usual assurances about anonymity and confidentiality, a number of respondents left one or more of these items blank. Of the 536 respondents 94 per cent indicated their sex, and of these, 84 per cent were women (compared with 82 per cent in public-sector primary schools nationally, according to the most recent figures available).

Among the 91 per cent of the sample who indicated the length of their primary school teaching experience there was a wide range, from those who were still in their probationary year to one who had clocked up thirty-eight years in the classroom. For the purposes of the analyses which follow, teachers were divided into four groups on the basis of their experience:

- *Group 1* consisted of the 138 teachers who had been teaching in primary schools for less than five years. Their training and experience had thus for the most part all taken place in a National Curriculum context, although there is inevitably an element of arbitrariness about this cut-off point because of the gradual way in which the National Curriculum was introduced, and the fact that some of the teachers would have done a four-year and some a one-year training. In the discussions which follow, the teachers in this group will be identified as recently qualified.
- *Group 2* consisted of 121 teachers whose experience ranged from five to twelve years. These teachers would have completed their training and had some (but not necessarily very much) experience in the classroom before the introduction of the National Curriculum, and they can be conveniently characterised as established teachers.

- *Group 3* consisted of 114 teachers with more than twelve but less than twenty years' experience in primary schools. These were, by any standards, very experienced teachers by the time the National Curriculum came along, and they are given this label in the discussions which follow.
- *Group 4* consisted of 117 teachers with at least twenty (and in some cases nearly forty) years' experience in the classroom. For want of a better term it is proposed to identify these teachers as veteran practitioners.

On the basis of this grouping, then, 28 per cent of the sample were recently qualified teachers, 25 per cent were established teachers, 23 per cent were very experienced teachers, and 24 per cent were veteran practitioners. No comparable national figures are available, but the sample includes a wide and evenly balanced spread of teacher experience. Among respondents 95 per cent indicated which year group(s) they were teaching, and for the purposes of analysis they have been divided into three groups:

- *Group A* consisted of 201 teachers working with one or more of the following groups: reception, year one, year two. They accounted for 40 per cent of the sample and are described in what follows as teachers of infants.
- *Group B* consisted of 137 teachers working with year three and/or year four. They accounted for 27 per cent of the sample and are described in what follows as teachers of lower juniors.
- *Group C* consisted of 170 teachers working with year five and/or year six. They accounted for 33 per cent of the sample and are described in what follows as teachers of upper juniors.

Responses to the questionnaire

The questionnaire item which attracted the strongest support from the largest number of people was:

> I really think that the number of different curriculum subjects is too many for the youngest children.

This item drew a response from 98.9 per cent of the sample, and more people strongly agreed with it than with any other item on the questionnaire, even though the sample included teachers of all year groups from reception to year six, so that the reference to *the youngest children* might well have meant different things to different people. There was some evidence that the very experienced teachers and veteran practitioners agreed more strongly than their less experienced colleagues with this proposition; the differences were not extreme but they were large enough to reach statistical significance (p=.013).

The two other statements for which there was very strong and widespread support were the assertion that:

it has certainly made everyone think very deeply about what they were doing and why they were doing it,

and the claim that:

the staff certainly help and support each other more than they used to.

In relation to the second of these propositions, there was some evidence that the teachers of lower juniors (years three and four) were rather more tentative in their views than teachers of other age groups (p=.013).

On only two items were there marked and statistically significant differences between the responses of men and women. As a group, the women tended to agree with the proposition that:

I like to be able to follow an idea that just springs to mind, but I can't do that so much with the National Curriculum.

The men, however, were very evenly divided between those who tended to agree and those who tended to disagree with the proposition, and the difference between the mean score of the two groups was too great for it to be likely to have occurred by chance. On the other hand, women respondents tended to disagree with the proposition that:

these days I stick to one activity at a time. If they're all doing the same thing I can focus in on what I'm supposed to be looking at.

Once more, however, the men were very evenly balanced between those who tended to disagree and those who tended to agree with the proposition, and the difference between the mean scores of the two groups was again too great for it to be likely to have occurred by chance.

On this particular item there were other highly significant differences between groups. On the whole, respondents tended to disagree with the statement – that is to say, they tended to assert that they still encouraged several different activities in their classrooms at the same time. Within this climate of opinion, the recently qualified teachers and the veteran practitioners were those most likely to express the opposite view, and it is tempting here to see a striking example of a wheel coming full circle. However, the age of the pupils was also a factor, for the older they were the more tentative was their teachers' rejection of the proposition, and among the teachers of upper juniors there were many who did not reject it at all.

Pupil age seems also to have been a powerful influence on teachers' attitudes to three other questionnaire items. The younger the pupils were, the more likely were their teachers to have groups in the classroom doing different subjects for most of the time, to feel that the records they passed on would be of some use to other teachers, and to be interested in teaching reading, writing and basic numeracy to the exclusion of all else.

Length of experience was apparently an influence on one item which has not yet been mentioned: with increasing experience teachers were more and more likely to agree that the science component of the National Curriculum had been the hardest thing for them to come to terms with because they didn't understand some of it properly themselves, and the major difference here was between the veteran practitioners and all the other groups.

The single item on the questionnaire which yielded the most forceful response from the largest number of people was one of those deliberately included because of its seemingly provocative nature:

> I think it's OK for a mum who comes in voluntarily to do quite a bit of the assessment for me.

Five respondents strongly agreed with this statement, and twelve more tended to agree. Two respondents left the item blank, and the remaining 96 per cent of the sample all disagreed with it, three-quarters of them strongly. There was no significant difference between the responses of men and women, nor between those of teachers of different year groups. However, there was a highly significant statistical relationship between teachers' attitudes and the length of their teaching experience. Among all but the veteran practitioners (where the disagreement moderated a little) there was a marked tendency for the more experienced teachers to disagree more strongly with the proposition than their less experienced colleagues. Thus, the respondents who were most likely to involve parent helpers in the assessment process were among the recently qualified teachers, although even in this group the prevailing attitude was a tendency to disagree with the proposition rather than to accept it. The strongest rejection came from the very experienced teachers.

Factor analysis

Although they address a good many different issues, the questionnaire items are certainly not entirely unrelated, and there was consequently a strong tendency for respondents who agreed with some of the individual statements also to agree (or disagree) with certain other statements which in some way tapped the same underlying attitudes. For example, although the two items below are by no means synonymous, respondents who agreed with one of them generally agreed with the other.

> These days I stick to one activity at a time. If they're all doing the same thing I can focus in on what I'm supposed to be looking at.

There has been a definite shift towards more whole-class teaching.

To group such associated items together and build up a picture of the respondents' attitudes to major aspects of the National Curriculum, the data were subjected to a factor analysis which yielded four principal factors, relating to:

- the usefulness of assessment and record-keeping,
- the manageability of the National Curriculum,
- co-operation and reflection in school and classroom,
- curriculum and classroom organisation.

Factor One: the usefulness of assessment and record-keeping   Factor One had high negative loadings for questionnaire items 28 and 31:

> Now at least I feel that the records I pass on will be of some use to other teachers.

> The assessment has helped me personally to know where the children are at.

and high positive loadings for items 7, 12 and 15:

> Nobody ever looks at ticked boxes on a record card. It's just a way of covering yourself if anyone comes into the school.

> We've got plenty of records but they're actually of no use.

> I don't particularly feel that I've learned anything I didn't know already from all this teacher assessment.

It might therefore be said to measure the extent to which people found National Curriculum assessment and record-keeping helpful and informative. The issues involved in this factor are well illustrated in an extract from the interview with a year two teacher in the 1992 fieldwork sample:

> I don't particularly feel that I've learnt anything different that I didn't already know about. I mean, even in the short space of time that I was with them, there were no real shocks in the results that came out. Most, I think most of them I would have put there anyway. [The records] had been filled in, but they didn't actually tell us anything. . . . I felt I couldn't give the child a score or a mark on the basis of what I found in the records. It wasn't fair. . . . They should tell me about the children and where we're at. I should be able to pass those on to the next person who can then work from that. That would be valuable, yes; otherwise we found they were useless.

Only 11 per cent of respondents strongly agreed that National Curriculum assessment and record-keeping procedures in general were helpful and informative, and a slightly larger proportion – 17 per cent – strongly disagreed. The rest – not far short of three-quarters of the sample – fell somewhere near the middle of the range of views, for the most part because they tended not to agree or disagree strongly with any of the items which went to make up the factor, but also because when they did, their agreement with one item tended to cancel out their disagreement with another.

There were no systematic differences between the responses of men and women, short- and long-serving teachers, or teachers of older and younger children on this factor.

Factor Two: the manageability of the National Curriculum Factor Two had high positive loadings for items 14, 13, 17, 3, 16 and 24:

> I really think the number of different curriculum subjects is too many for the youngest children.

> The amount of content that's expected in science is ridiculous: you're skimming the surface rather than doing anything in any great depth.

> I like to be able to follow an idea that just springs to mind, but I can't do that so much with the National Curriculum.

> All this planning is quite unrealistic because I'm never able to fulfil my plans.

> I'm so busy doing science, maths and language and all the curriculum subjects, that other things have had to go.

> Before, non-teaching assistants just did the more mundane tasks, but now you have to involve them in the actual learning process.

This factor might therefore be said to measure the extent to which people found the demands of the National Curriculum manageable (or, to put it another way, not unduly burdensome and disruptive). It is illustrated here in two extracts from the 1992 interviews, the first with a year three/four teacher, and the second with a teacher of years five and six:

> A lot of my best work has come from incidentals that have happened whilst I've been doing a topic. I like to be able to be flexible like that, to follow something that happens in the classroom or to follow an idea that just springs to mind because of something I'm doing, and I've found more constraint really with the National Curriculum because you've got to get through x, y and z.

> [The balance of the curriculum has changed] totally as far as I'm concerned. You don't have time for little bits and pieces. I find you're so busy doing science, maths and language and all the other curriculum

subjects that other things have had to go. I think music to a certain extent [and] some of the crafty things children will never do. It's not an important thing, but it is one thing I remember doing when I was a child and doing before the National Curriculum, things like sewing and making things. Unless you actually sort of put it into a project you're doing there's no time for that.

Almost a quarter of the sample (23 per cent) expressed strong negative attitudes about the manageability of the National Curriculum: they were finding its demands both burdensome and disruptive. One in ten (9.9 per cent) expressed strong positive attitudes and were finding things manageable.

Within this general picture, the National Curriculum was perceived as presenting more of a management problem by women than by men, and more of a management problem by teachers of infants than by teachers of juniors. The recently qualified teachers were very evenly divided over the manageability of the National Curriculum, and less burdened by it than any other group. Apart from them, the less experience the teachers had, the more of a management problem the National Curriculum was found to be.

Factor Three: co-operation and reflection in school and classroom
Factor Three had high positive loadings for items 4, 2, 8, 11, 18 and 5:

The staff certainly help and support each other more than they used to.

There's a lot more working together and a lot more talk amongst children in my classroom than ever before.

We get a lot of support, help and back-up from the school's adviser in getting to grips with the National Curriculum.

It has certainly made everyone think very deeply about what they were doing and why they were doing it.

It has made me think much more carefully about what you say about children when you're assessing them.

The National Curriculum has raised speaking and listening, as skills in their own right, to a level with reading and writing.

This factor might therefore be said to measure the extent to which people had found the National Curriculum a catalyst for serious reflection, mutual support among teachers and an increase in talking, listening and co-operative groupwork among pupils. It is illustrated in three short extracts from the 1992 interviews, the first two from teachers of reception and year one, and the third from a deputy head with a year five/six class:

The advantage, it has to be said, is that it has raised speaking and listening as skills to a level with reading and writing, whereas previously it was difficult to justify spending the time on the speaking and listening skills which we all know are important.

When it was first mooted I must admit I was a little bit nervous and reticent about what it would do to education, but to be honest I don't think it has changed dramatically the way teachers actually work on the chalk face. It has made us perhaps clarify our aims more than we did previously, and it has made us think much more about the actual progression from one stage to another, so in that respect it has been a very good thing.

Talking from senior management level, I actually think the National Curriculum has been a good thing, has allowed myself and the Head to be in a position to help guide the teachers and give them something that they can work with.

A quarter (24.8 per cent) of the sample strongly agreed that the National Curriculum had been a catalyst for serious reflection, mutual support and co-operation. Only one in forty (2.6 per cent) rejected all the elements in this factor.

There were no systematic differences between the responses of men and women, short- and long-serving teachers, or teachers of older and younger children on this factor.

Factor Four: curriculum and classroom organisation   Factor Four had a high positive loading for item 25:

I still find that for most of the time there are groups in the classroom doing different subjects.

and high negative loadings for items 19 and 10:

These days I stick to one activity at a time. If they're all doing the same thing I can focus on what I'm supposed to be looking at.

There has been a definite shift towards more whole-class teaching.

The factor might therefore be said to measure the extent to which the National Curriculum was thought to have forced a shift in two fundamental aspects of primary curricular and pedagogic organisation: away from a multiple curriculum focus of the kind characterised (and questioned) in Mortimore *et al.* (1988) and OFSTED (1993a, 1993b) to a focusing on one subject at a time; and from group and/or individual work towards more whole-class teaching. Though these two facets of pedagogy are theoretically distinct, in practice there has been a historical tendency for multiple curriculum focus teaching to be associated with a high incidence of groupwork (it is difficult to organise it any other way). In contrast, though many primary teachers have tended to treat single-subject organisation and whole-class teaching as inseparable, sometimes indeed equating or even confusing them, they are in no necessary respect contingent, and in practice some teachers have used a great deal of groupwork when teaching one subject at a time, while others have used much whole-class teaching, and others again have used a mixture of strategies.

However, there is no doubt that teachers see single/multiple curriculum focus and whole class/group/individual strategies as joint components of an overall pedagogical package which the National Curriculum has called into question. This view is illustrated here in two extracts from the 1992 interviews, the first from a year one teacher and the second from a teacher of year two:

> To an extent, I think there has been a change towards more whole-class teaching. I used to do far more groupwork. I still do some. I like a mixture, and I think the good, the best teaching practice in a classroom is a mixture. For some lessons – I emphasise for some – there might be some vital information I want to get over, but I might be distracting somebody who might want some help with something in another group. That has been quite a problem.

> It has almost become subject-based, I feel, to, to, you know, some of the teachers feel they've actually got, they've actually covered everything. They're almost having sub ... having lessons: 'We'll do geography now. We'll do history now,' which is more a junior and secondary idea. We should be integrated.

Yet, despite the sense that these strategies had become more of a dilemma than hitherto, only a few teachers (3.2 per cent) claimed to have made a major change in their curriculum and classroom organisation in response to the requirements of the National Curriculum, while over two-fifths (43.5 per cent) were adamant that no such changes had been forced upon them.

Observation study

The CICADA interview and questionnaire analyses, as well as the other studies quoted above, all relied for their evidence on teachers' accounts of what they believed was happening in their classrooms. The observation study, on the other hand, recorded in as objective a way as possible the minute-by-minute interactions of teachers and pupils, and accumulated a wealth of such data from everyday classroom practice both before and after the introduction of the National Curriculum.

Analysis of all the coded utterances from 1986, 1988 and 1992 revealed differences between individual teachers which far outweighed any group differences which might be attributed to the introduction of the National Curriculum or to any other effects of either time or location. In all of the characteristics tapped by the instruments used in the study, teachers who had been observed in different years and different local authorities were neither more nor less likely to resemble one another than were teachers observed on the same day in the same school. This finding raises important issues. First, given the general perception that the period since 1989 has been one of radical change, it can be suggested that the real extent of such change may have been less than many teachers and commentators believe. Second, it is clear that there are several levels of teaching on which studies of change can usefully focus, and among these the fine detail of pedagogy is both significant, and – in studies of change, at least, relatively under-explored.

On average, a little over a quarter of all teacher utterances concerned the kind of classroom management that has no overt curriculum content (although individual sessions differed widely from one another in the amount of management they involved). There was no significant correlation between the proportion of such utterances in each teacher's two sessions, as can be seen in Figure 5.1 where the proportion of non-curricular management utterances in the two teaching sessions is charted separately for each teacher.

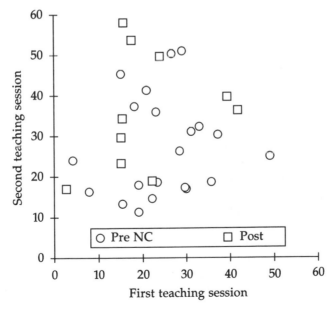

Figure 5.1 Percentage of non-curricular management utterances in two teaching sessions

Through the use of different symbols for the sessions observed before and after the introduction of the National Curriculum, Figure 5.1 also illustrates the fact that there was no systematic difference between the proportion of non-curricular management utterances under the two conditions. On the whole, the teachers were not tending to spend more (or less) of their time engaged in such matters in 1992 than they had been in 1986 or 1988.

Turning from non-curricular classroom management to the more overtly subject-related sections of the teaching sessions, a variety of analyses were conducted on the observation data. The first of these analyses sought to chart the most common patterns or sequences of pedagogical utterance in the teaching sessions. It was a straightforward matter to isolate the most commonly occurring interaction variables from the *discourse, syntax* and *pedagogy* analytical frameworks (and indeed these have already been listed with definitions as part of the exposition of the research instruments used in the study).

To discover the extent to which individual teachers' practice in one teaching session differed from their practice in another, a cluster analysis was conducted on the basis of these thirteen variables together with a fourteenth drawn from the lexical analysis; namely, the ratio of teacher talk to pupil talk in each session.

The preliminary analysis yielded two clear-cut and widely differing clusters – that is to say, two basic and different ways in which the observed sessions had been conducted. To investigate the stability of this clustering over time, the analysis was conducted separately on the data from each of the three years in turn. The striking feature of this analysis was that the two distinct clusters reappeared in remarkably similar form in each of the three years. Table 5.1 shows the proportions of utterances in each cluster in each year for those variables where there was a significant difference in at least one of the three years. The remaining six of the fourteen variables used in the cluster analysis (abort, statement, task direction, evaluative feedback, informative, and ratio of teacher talk to pupil talk) did not significantly differ between clusters in any of the three years.

It will be seen from Table 5.1 that, except for the variable *reply*, which showed a significant difference only in 1988, the differences between the two clusters were in the same direction in each of the three years: consistently, year by year, Cluster 2 was always characterised by more examples than Cluster 1 of some of the categories listed, and by fewer of others. Thus the clustering was stable over the three years, and this being so, the discussion of the characteristics of the two clusters which follows is based on a cluster analysis of all sixty sessions together. It should be noted here that the coding category *reply* did not differ significantly between clusters when the cluster analysis was conducted

Table 5.1   Percentage of utterances in each of the main categories where there was a significant difference in at least one of the three years

| | 1986 | | 1988 | | 1992 | | All | |
	Cluster 1	Cluster 2	Cluster 1	Cluster 2	Cluster 1	Cluster 2	Cluster 1	Cluster 2
Command	13.5	11.8	17.5	9.6	13.0	9.5	14.2	10.3
Question	19.6	23.9	20.0	28.9	22.6	24.7	21.2	25.9
Accept	12.5	17.9	8.6	13.5	12.6	16.9	11.5	16.1
Directive	15.8	14.7	25.1	13.1	18.8	12.7	19.1	13.7
Elicitation	15.8	21.6	15.9	24.0	19.9	22.7	17.6	22.9
Reply	2.3	2.6	4.3	2.0	3.5	2.4	3.4	2.3
Explain/explore	13.2	34.0	10.4	31.5	10.4	37.6	12.0	34.3
Formative feedback	34.3	13.6	38.4	13.9	37.1	18.4	36.3	14.7

over all sixty sessions, and that consequently this category is not considered further.

Figures 5.2 and 5.3 make use of data from Table 5.1 to give two purely visual representations of the statistically significant differences between the two clusters. While the main emphasis of Figure 5.2 is the comparative strength of each variable *within* each cluster, Figure 5.3 highlights the balance of each variable *between* the two clusters.

Cluster 1 involves very much more formative feedback and more directing and commanding than the second cluster. It seems to represent a way of teaching characterised above all else by setting tasks, and then

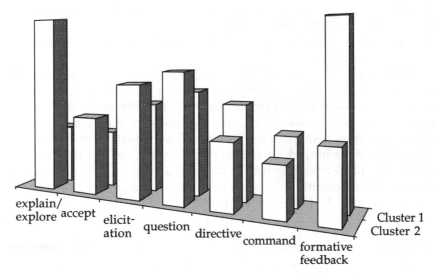

Figure 5.2   Defining characteristics of the two kinds of teaching session

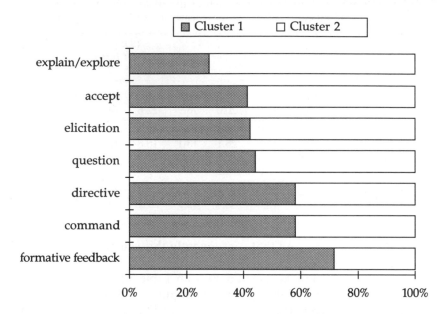

Figure 5.3 The balance of the defining characteristics of the two clusters

intervening where necessary to promote individual children's under-standing or satisfactory performance of the tasks set. The important feature of formative feedback is that it is always given or solicited as a direct response to a pupil's work or utterance, unlike the kind of inform-ative comment which is offered without reference to work currently being undertaken by the children (and which was coded as *explain/explore* in the pedagogical analysis).

Cluster 2 involves a very high level of explanation compared with the first, as well as more accepting, questioning and eliciting. It will be recalled that questioning refers to the *form* of an utterance and eliciting to its *intent*; on both counts Cluster 2 sessions were of a more overtly enquiring nature than those in Cluster 1. Thus, Cluster 2 seems to repre-sent a way of teaching characterised by classroom conversation in which the teacher plays a leading role. It involves a good deal of question and answer, not necessarily in relation to children's ongoing tasks but often for its own sake. In fact relatively few specific tasks are set and, for the most part, the talk is not merely *about* the work; it *is* the work. Instead of remaining outside the work as a facilitator, overseer or consultant, the teacher participates in it with the children.

Although the sampling ensured that the subject focus of the interac-tions in each teacher's pair of sessions was different, there was a strong tendency for the two sessions to be in the same cluster. Only one of the ten teachers who were observed in 1986 had one teaching session in one cluster and the other teaching session in the other cluster. In 1988 there were two teachers whose teaching sessions followed this pattern, and in 1992 there were three. Overall, 24 of the 30 teachers (responsible for 48 of the 60 sessions) taught in such a way that both of their observed sessions were in the same cluster. The probability of this occurring by chance is extremely remote (P<0.002), and the tendency for teachers to stick to the same general teaching tactics, regardless of what they were teaching, must therefore be considered highly significant.

Although at first glance this might seem to indicate a tendency for teachers to prefer one mode of interaction and stick to it, we stress that it should not be taken to imply a new typology of teachers as *outside the task* (Cluster 1), *inside the task* (Cluster 2) or *mixed*; such an exercise would require a study involving many repeated observation sessions with the same group of teachers, each involved in a very wide range of classroom activities.

Whole-class, group and individual interaction

Overall in the sessions observed, teachers interacted with individual children far more frequently than with the whole class or groups, and, as Table 5.2 and Figure 5.4 show, there were many more individual interactions than whole-class and group interactions combined.

Table 5.2 Whole-class, group and individual interaction in the two clusters

	Pre-NC		Post-NC		Overall	
	Cluster 1	Cluster 2	Cluster 1	Cluster 2	Cluster 1	Cluster 2
Class	1.7	11.0	4.3	14.7	2.7	12.1
Group	23.0	20.6	4.5	6.4	15.8	16.4
Individual	75.3	68.5	91.2	78.8	81.5	71.6

This was especially the case where Cluster 1 sessions were concerned and the contrast between the substantial majority of individual interactions and tiny minority of whole-class interactions was particularly striking. In Cluster 2 sessions the minority pursuits of whole-class and group interactions together constituted a more sizeable counterbalance to the individual interactions.

The *individualisation* of interactions in Cluster 1 sessions, bearing in mind the general discourse characteristics of these sessions as we described them above – especially the heavy emphasis on feedback – tends

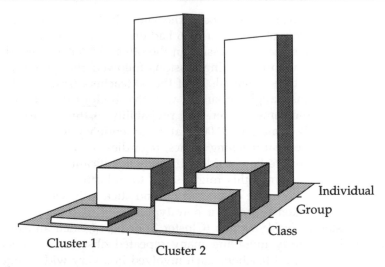

Figure 5.4   Proportion of whole-class, group and individual interaction
categories in the two clusters

to suggest a productive comparison with the ORACLE 'individual
monitor' teaching style, in which interactions tended to be 'largely
didactic, concerned with telling pupils what to do, while their questioning
[was] mainly factual rather than probing or open-ended' (Galton *et al.*
1980b: 37). In the same way, the marked difference in the proportion of
whole-class interactions between the two CICADA clusters mirrors the
way explaining, questioning and other techniques generally associated
with 'direct instruction' in subject matter tended in the ORACLE study to
be associated with whole-class and group-dominated interactions.

   With this in mind, one might expect the marked content-mastery orien-
tation of the National Curriculum to be reflected as a shift away from
individualised to whole-class and/or group interactions in the CICADA
data. In fact, as Figure 5.5 shows, the introduction of the National
Curriculum made the dominance of individualisation in Cluster 1 interactions even more marked, and reduced group as well as whole-class
interactions to an even smaller minority than previously: in the 1992
Cluster 1 sample, the conjunction of feedback-dominated discourse and
individualised interactions is very striking. Cluster 2 sessions showed a
corresponding increase in individualised interactions and a decrease in
group interactions, but also an increase in those between the teacher and
the whole class.

   In these respects, the observation data reinforce this project's survey
finding that teachers claimed not to have changed their mix of individual,
group and whole-class teaching as a consequence of the requirements of
the National Curriculum. However, this contrasts with the conclusion

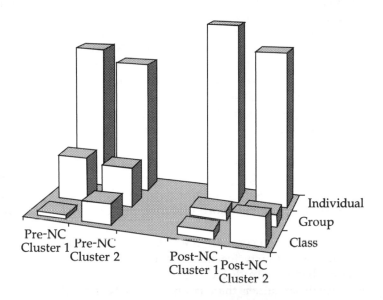

Figure 5.5   Proportion of whole-class, group and individual interaction
categories in the two clusters, before and after the introduction
of the National Curriculum

from the somewhat earlier PACE project data (Pollard *et al.* 1994) that
teachers believed that 'pressure of National Curriculum requirements'
had forced them to emphasise 'more traditional methods, including
whole-class teaching'. If anything, CICADA shows the traditional primary
attachment to individualisation becoming even more marked with the
introduction of the National Curriculum. However, this may well represent a rather different concept and manifestation of 'individualisation'
than the 1960s archetype, the loss of which the PACE teachers so strongly
regretted.

Subject matter and pedagogic discourse

At a common-sense level it is to be expected that different areas of the
curriculum will require different teaching methods. Thus, the ORACLE
process-product data indicated a relationship between direct teaching
involving 'higher-order cognitive interactions' and successful learning in
basic aspects of English and mathematics, especially the latter (Galton
et al. 1980b: 43–98). The PRINDEP process data plotted relationships
between curriculum area and aspects of classroom practice such as use of
space and resources, pupils' use of time, pupils' task-related behaviour,

and the balance of the generic curriculum activities of writing, reading, collaborating, using apparatus and so on (see Chapter 4, Tables 4.15 and 4.16). In the present project we were particularly interested to discover how far the codification of the primary curriculum resulting from the introduction and implementation of the National Curriculum Orders – that is to say, the translation of loose and often largely implicit knowledge structures into highly explicit subject requirements – had sharpened such subject-related pedagogic contrasts as had emerged in the earlier studies.

The observation data allowed us to compare what in 1989 became the three core subjects of the National Curriculum: English, mathematics and science, concentrating on the first two (the limited proportion of time devoted to science in the project classrooms, especially in 1986 and 1988 when science was still very much a novelty in many primary schools, force us to be rather more tentative in our conclusions about science).

Table 5.3 and Figure 5.6 compare the balance of interaction in English and mathematics in all sixty teaching sessions observed. To undertake this analysis we have reintroduced the full range of categories from the Pedagogical Analysis rather than confine ourselves to the two most prominent items (*explain/explore* and *formative feedback*) which featured in the cluster analysis discussed above. This allows us to present comparative profiles of the pedagogic discourse associated with the teaching of these two subjects in the sessions observed.

Table 5.3 The balance of pedagogical interaction categories in English and mathematics

	English	*Maths*
Evaluative feedback	14.1	12.9
Explain/explore	30.4	24.4
Formative feedback	23.4	22.7
Introduce task	1.3	3.3
Reiterate	1.8	1.5
Task direction	27.6	33.4
Other pedagogy	1.5	1.9

In one view, the proportions are much as commonsense knowledge of teaching would suggest. Thus, the small showing of *introduce task* simply reflects the small proportion of time, typically, teachers devote to this, while the dominance of task-in-hand interactions (*evaluative feedback, explain/explore, task direction* and *formative feedback*) is similarly what one would expect. More significant is the comparison between the profiles of English and mathematics.

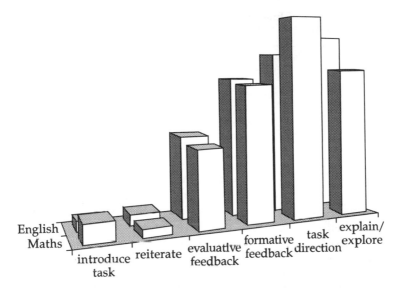

English
Maths

introduce
task

reiterate

evaluative
feedback

formative
feedback

task
direction

explain/
explore

Figure 5.6 The balance of pedagogical interaction categories in English and mathematics

In the teaching of most of the curriculum, there was no strongly marked, subject-linked tendency for teachers to veer towards the approaches encapsulated in Clusters 1 and 2. However, our comparison using the full range of items from the Pedagogical Analysis shows that although *task direction, explain/explore* and *formative feedback* predominated in both English and mathematics, there were noticeable differences between the two subjects in respect of each of these categories. Thus in mathematics *task direction* predominated, while the corresponding dominant category for English was *explain/explore*. Indeed, the somewhat more instrumental, less exploratory character of mathematics interaction was reflected throughout its profile in Figure 5.6, right down to the admittedly small difference between *introduce task* in the two subjects.

A clear explanation for this difference will have to await the detailed *qualitative* scrutiny of the sixty session transcripts with which our present account does not deal. At this stage, however, we can venture the suggestion that the English/mathematics difference seems to reflect the well-established tendency for primary mathematics teaching to be more dominated by published schemes, materials and tasks than is any other subject (DES 1978; Bennett *et al.* 1984; Alexander 1992). This results in many teachers concentrating less on the *inside the task* exploration and explanation of Cluster 1 than on giving children sections of the mathematics text to work from and then monitoring or intervening (*outside the task*, or Cluster 2) as they consider necessary (Table 5.4).

Table 5.4   Distribution of English, mathematics and other curricular interaction
between the two clusters

	Pre-NC		Post-NC		Full sample	
	Cluster 1	Cluster 2	Cluster 1	Cluster 2	Cluster 1	Cluster 2
English	22.5	26.9	33.4	38.6	26.8	30.4
Maths	33.0	22.1	21.6	9.5	28.5	18.3
All other	44.5	51.0	45.0	51.9	44.7	51.3

The further shift towards Cluster 1 in the post-National Curriculum mathematics discourse suggested by our data (Figure 5.7) would tend to reinforce this interpretation, especially given the extreme pressure that primary teachers experienced in attempting to implement what was in fact a very crowded and complex Order, demanding far more of teacher time than most felt able to provide while they were simultaneously attempting to meet requirements in nine other subjects and to achieve some kind of coherence and balance in respect of the whole (Campbell 1993).

The balance of clusters was not significantly different before and after the introduction of the National Curriculum, and there was no perceptible shift towards (or away from) either approach as the years went by.

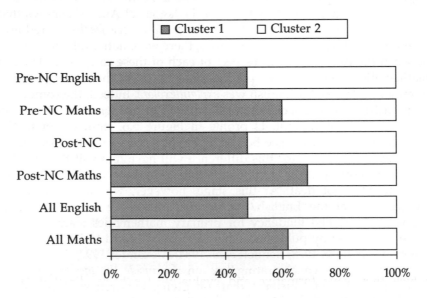

Figure 5.7   Distribution of English and mathematics interaction between the two clusters, before and after the introduction of the National Curriculum

Nor was either approach systematically related to sessions involving infants, lower juniors or upper juniors.

Towards greater heterogeneity in primary classroom discourse?

There is one further analysis to be reported here. An examination of the mean percentages of the main coding categories before and after the introduction of the National Curriculum (Table 5.5) revealed at least the possibility of a somewhat intriguing trend.

Table 5.5 Standard deviations of the mean percentages of the most commonly occurring coding categories

Category	Pre-NC	Post-NC	Significance of difference*
Syntax analysis			
Abort	1.94	2.18	.50
Command	4.40	5.21	.57
Question	5.99	6.90	.39
Statement	6.25	7.82	.65
Discourse analysis			
Accept	4.48	5.10	.53
Directive	6.54	6.82	.78
Elicitation	5.38	7.58	.06
Informative	7.45	6.45	.52
Reply	1.67	1.44	.35
Pedagogical analysis			
Evaluative feedback	5.08	6.04	.57
Explain/explore	12.81	6.16	.08
Formative feedback	13.13	14.12	.80
Task direction	10.13	14.65	.10

* Levene's test for the homogeneity of variance

As Table 5.5 shows, in all but two of the thirteen coding categories there was more variability after the introduction of the National Curriculum than before. None of these differences was large, and some of them were very small indeed; certainly none of them was statistically significant in itself. However, eleven of the thirteen differences were in the same direction, and this general trend *was* significant (P=0.023). For some reason, in the teaching sessions observed after the introduction of the National Curriculum teachers were slightly more heterogeneous in the extent to which they gave formative and evaluative feedback, directed tasks, asked questions, gave commands and so on. They simply differed more from one another in the extent to which they did these things than did teachers who were observed before the introduction of the National Curriculum (even though there were twice as many teachers in this latter group, and hence twice as much scope for differing behaviour).

THE MAIN FINDINGS SUMMARISED

The CICADA project was one of a number of studies undertaken in the wake of the 1988 Education Reform Act to examine the impact of ostensibly far-reaching education policies on professional and educational practice. As originally conceived it included the advantage of a longitudinal study of classroom practice. This should have involved our revisiting in 1992 the classrooms of those teachers who were involved in Level Three of the intensive 1988 observation study which formed part of the Primary Needs Independent Evaluation Project (PRINDEP). However, the project was confronted with a methodological crisis of some severity when, several months into CICADA's programme, and as a result of damaging fall-out from the political and media exploitation of the final PRINDEP report, the LEA in question withdrew permission for these classrooms to be used.

The CICADA team attempted to offset this reverse by identifying a new sample of teachers to match the 1988 PRINDEP sample, and at the same time buttressing the longitudinal element by introducing data from a 1986 project which itself had been a precursor of PRINDEP. The 1986, 1988 and 1992 data were comparable in that they consisted of a set of full, unedited transcriptions of lesson samples of primary teachers, using the identical data-collection technique in each case. There was also continuity of personnel and theoretical perspective through the three projects. Thus, although this methodological adjustment undoubtedly weakened the project as originally conceived, it also enabled an alternative kind of longitudinal study to be pursued. In any event, the project's two other strands – a set of interviews with the teachers in the 1992 sample, leading to a national survey of primary teachers' views of the impact of the National Curriculum on professional and educational practice – remained intact and provided an essential reference point against which to set the intensive local data. The results of the project as modified can be summarised as follows.

The interviews highlighted four areas in which the National Curriculum was proving problematic for teachers: *assessment, record-keeping, the curriculum* and *pedagogy*. Comment centred on issues of manageability as much as substance.

The national questionnaire survey elicited a 77 per cent response. Factor analysis of the responses yielded four principal factors, as follows.

- *Factor 1 the usefulness of assessment and record-keeping.* A minority of respondents found the requirements helpful and informative. Most either found them unhelpful or had mixed feelings.
- *Factor 2 the manageability of the National Curriculum.* A substantial proportion of the respondents found the National Curriculum, at both Key Stages 1 and 2, both burdensome and disruptive. There were notable differences, however, as between KS1 and KS2 teachers, men and women, and new and experienced teachers.
- *Factor 3 co-operation and reflection in school and classroom.* A substantial proportion of the respondents noted the positive impact of the National Curriculum on the professional climate of the school – as a catalyst for debate, reflection and mutual support – and on pupil–pupil collaboration in the classroom.
- *Factor 4 curriculum and classroom organisation.* Teachers saw single/ multiple curriculum focus and whole class/group/individual teaching strategies as joint components of a pedagogical package which the National Curriculum had called into question. Despite this, the majority of teachers believed that they had neither narrowed the curriculum focus of their teaching nor shifted significantly towards a whole-class pedagogy. (Though no significant differences between the teacher categories in the sample emerged for the factor as a whole, we noted elsewhere that on the specific item of curriculum focus there were significant differences between (1) early and later years teachers, (2) more and less experienced teachers, (3) women and men. By and large, multiple curriculum focus teaching was favoured more by the early years teachers, by those in mid-career rather than those recently or long qualified, and by women.)

The observation study provided the focus for the larger part of CICADA's programme and yielded its richest data. Computer analysis of the discourse, coded according to six category systems (*lexical, syntax, discourse, pedagogy, participant* and *curriculum*) is being supplemented by qualitative analysis. This chapter has reported on the former only.

The analysis used a three-stage procedure for focusing on the most commonly occurring and therefore statistically most viable items in the category systems, also bearing in mind CICADA's principal concern with *curriculum-associated* discourse. This is not to say that the discourse categories and sub-categories which did not feature in the cluster and related analyses were unimportant, and we are fully alive to the dangers of making the realities of teaching fit the methods available for studying them rather than *vice versa*. We return to this matter in the discussion below.

Analysis of all the coded utterances from 1986, 1988 and 1992 revealed differences between individual teachers which far outweighed any group differences which might be attributed to the introduction of the National Curriculum. Put another way, longitudinal observational analysis of *pedagogic discourse* may reveal some of the fundamental continuities in classroom practice which policy changes concerned with *curriculum* and *assessment* do not or cannot affect, despite the fact that it is through pedagogy that curriculum and indeed much assessment are mediated. Moreover, observational study tends to offer a more neutral assessment of the extent of change than can be obtained by trawling teacher opinion, especially when such opinion is offered against the background of stress, curriculum overload and low morale.

The analysis revealed two clear-cut and widely differing clusters. *Cluster 1* comprised teaching which involved much more formative feedback, directing and commanding than the second cluster. That is to say, it tended to involve the teacher first setting tasks, then monitoring them and intervening where necessary, but generally staying outside them as overseer or consultant. *Cluster 2*, in contrast, involved high levels of explaining, exploring, questioning and eliciting, both about the task and about other matters. The teachers themselves were a component of the task set, and participated in it with the children. The clusters do not represent a new teaching typology (*outside the task, inside the task* and *mixed*) but they do represent fundamentally different approaches to teaching which will repay further study. They were stable over time and, in the main, between each pair of each teacher's observed teaching sessions.

No strongly marked shift in the balance of whole-class, group and individual teaching was noted over the six-year period. Teaching in all the classrooms, both before and after the arrival of the National Curriculum, was dominated by individual interactions, especially in Cluster 1, though Cluster 2 sessions showed a small shift from group to whole-class interactions.

The paucity of science teaching in the dataset as necessarily modified made it impossible for us to pursue our originally intended comparison of change in English and science. However, we were able to compare English and mathematics. Here, reintroducing the full range of items from the Pedagogical Analysis (rather than the two which featured in the clustering), we noted that English teaching tended to be associated with a slightly more open, exploratory discourse than the more task-directed mathematics.

Notwithstanding our finding that the differences between teachers on each of the analytical categories and clusters were greater than differences attributable to the arrival of the National Curriculum, we found the hint of a trend to greater pedagogical heterogeneity in as far as the 1992 sample differed more from one another in their quantified discourse profiles than did those in the 1986 and 1988 samples combined.

DISCUSSION

Studying change post-ERA: a cautionary note

Quite apart from the methodological adjustment we were forced to make after this project had started, there are three other reasons why we would wish to open our discussion by characterising our work here as exploratory rather than definitive.

First, and most importantly, CICADA dealt with change and the impact of change – a notoriously difficult area to research, and one especially problematic in the present circumstances. At the time of writing, the National Curriculum is still young, and – Dearing's defusing efforts notwithstanding (Dearing 1993a, 1993b) – it remains a highly charged phenomenon, professionally as well as politically. In the course of the battle for hearts and minds in state education there has been a great deal of ideological fallout. England and Wales have moved almost overnight from curriculum *laissez-faire* to an exceptionally high level of central direction and control, backed by sanctions. For government, the credibility of its high-stakes, high-profile educational policies hangs partly on their being implemented, at whatever the cost, so that government rather than the despised educational establishment can be seen to be in control of the system for which it is responsible; and partly on their delivering the improved standards which feature so prominently in the surrounding rhetoric.

At the same time, within the primary professional community, the hegemony of its liberal, progressive wing, which remained relatively unchallenged within the profession and among contingent groups like advisers and teacher trainers for nearly three decades (at least at the levels of public affiliation and espoused theory) has become far less secure. This is due only in part to the depredations of the political right – in the face of which teachers have naturally tended to close ranks. Research on children's learning and teachers' teaching, and the changing consciousness of teachers themselves, have chipped steadily away at the old certainties.

For reasons such as these it will probably be several years before it becomes possible to assess the impact of the National Curriculum dispassionately and reliably, just as it was a long time before the character of primary schools and classrooms in the wake of the 1960s progressive 'revolution' could be portrayed with a reasonable expectation of accuracy (Simon 1981, 1992). Ideological fall-out, vested interests and the sheer immediacy of events, then as now, have made the impact-assessment enterprise in education and public policy a hazardous one. This is not to say that researchers should not attempt such assessments, for the *dynamics* and *culture* of change are as important to our understanding of the policy–practice interface as are the *outcomes*.

The other two reasons for treating the CICADA material as exploratory rather than definitive are particular to the project itself. CICADA developed and used a methodology which was in some respects novel and in any event will benefit from further refinement. The interviews and survey were of course relatively straightforward, though none the less essential to our analysis for that. However, the analysis of classroom talk is a different matter. We defined six analytical frameworks, each with multiple categories, and proceeded to code all the transcript data in accordance with these prior to subjecting them to various kinds of computer analysis to see what patterns and relationships emerged. The implications of the fact that we ended up using a relatively small proportion of the total number of category items need to be teased out. In the case of the two clusters which emerged from our analysis, warnings should be posted about the need to avoiding treating models *of* practice as models *for* practice.

In any event, much of the analysis itself dictates tentative treatment. Some of the findings were by no means clear-cut, they were not in every case absolutely consistent, and there were some examples of outcomes which we had to suggest rather than confirm (like the shift to greater heterogeneity in kinds of classroom discourse). Apart from this, we have yet to complete the qualitative analysis which necessarily complements the quantitative treatment of the discourse data on which we have reported here.

With these notes of caution in mind, we can now draw together the main threads of the project findings to date.

Change in school and classroom

CICADA has confirmed a scenario of considerable change in the areas of curriculum planning, curriculum management, assessment and record-keeping taking place against a backdrop of relative continuity in pedagogy; or of change in the collective culture of schools contrasting with continuity in the privacy of classrooms. Curriculum and assessment are now *managed* in primary schools to an extent – or on a scale – that they rarely were before the 1988 legislation, though it is important to note that the seeds of this shift go back rather further. The 1988 Act did not so much initiate the growth of managerialism as rapidly accelerate a process which was already under way. That much the HMI surveys and reports of the 1980s make very clear, and as early as 1984 one of this chapter's authors was urging caution about the dangers of 'superficiality, mechanisation and bureaucratisation' which attended the management strategies eagerly being fostered in primary schools by LEAs, management units, HMI and certain higher education institutions during this period (Alexander 1984: 204–9).

Current requirements do nothing to diminish these dangers. The weight of formal requirements placed on schools in the wake of, for example, budgetary delegation, National Curriculum implementation, assessment, recording and reporting, school development plans and the OFSTED inspection cycle, all dictate a rapid and efficient response. In the face of such pressure, autocracy and bureaucracy are tempting solutions.

At the same time, the weight of these requirements also prompts action at the more fundamental level of staff relationships, and to this extent the CICADA data confirm the leavening impact of collaboration and collegiality (Nias *et al.* 1989 and 1992; Webb 1994). The National Curriculum was not just another external directive to prompt a simple managerialist response of the kind illustrated in the proliferation of checklists, schemes and policy documents – and the blind faith in documentation generally – which characterised the 1980s. Its scale and complexity demanded the fullest possible deployment of each school's professional resources, and a response which was more genuinely collaborative than the management rhetoric's easy deployment of 'delegation' and 'participation' could encompass, for such rhetoric was still predicated on a model of management as something one group does to another, rather than on the kind of collective problem-solving which has been essential to survival since 1988.

When we turn to the classroom, however, the picture is one of self-evident transformation of curriculum content contrasted with resilience at the deeper levels of pedagogy. The primary curriculum, only partly codified up to 1988, and then only on a voluntary and consensual basis, is now stipulated as a set of Orders which specify in considerable detail what is to be taught. Yet pedagogy is the means by which a paper curriculum becomes a set of learning encounters, and the pedagogic process is one of content *transformation* as well as *translation* (not that translation is ever an exact science).

For this reason, study of the impact of the National Curriculum needs to chart and compare the versions of knowledge, understanding and skill which teachers create for pupils, and which pupils create from themselves out of the learning tasks teachers provide, with those specified in the Orders. Because teachers inevitably draw on what they know and have done before, and because the policing of the National Curriculum through reported testing and the vigilance of OFSTED is at best limited in scope and frequency, it would be realistic to expect considerable divergence between the various versions of curriculum – as intended and as transacted, and between one classroom and another.

The CICADA data support this proposition, though the current analysis cannot illuminate it in the full detail needed. Thus, if the clustering of discourse has validity, the remarkable feature is its persistence over time, from 1986 to 1992, from well before the National Curriculum to some time after its introduction. Equally, though we noted small shifts in the balance of whole-class and group interactions in the Cluster 2 sessions, the more striking figure was that claims that the National Curriculum had produced a dramatic switch to whole-class teaching seem, on the strength of these data at least, to be for the time being unfounded.

However, in the category of the suggestive rather than the definitive, we also noted a greater heterogeneity in the teaching interactions of the 1992 sample than in either of the 1986 or 1988 groups, and we believe that this trend could well become more pronounced.

We argue this for two reasons. First, the National Curriculum itself, as specified, cannot be reduced to the relatively simple pedagogic formulae which characterised some classrooms in the days when the basics were taught as single subjects in the morning and the rest of the curriculum could be loosely subsumed within the post-prandial pursuit of topics and/or creative activities. Although the amount of detail specified in the Orders for each subject diminishes the further away from the three core subjects one moves – graphically reflecting government's view of their relative importance – the extent of subject codification, even for art, music and physical education, is far greater than was available in most schools during the period when HMI noted that schools had schemes of work for mathematics and reading, if that (DES 1978, 1982), but not for other curriculum areas.

Second, the professional climate is increasingly one which encourages teachers to devise their own responses to the imperatives of teaching in primary schools. The progressive/liberal hegemony of the 1970s and 1980s has given way to what some see as unprincipled pragmatism or technicism (Carr 1994), but which we prefer to view as a liberation of teachers from the pressure to conform to beliefs, theories and versions of 'good practice' which they are not permitted to question and to which they may not necessarily subscribe. Indeed, the PRINDEP study itself offered powerful evidence of this kind of political correctness and its impact, and prompted the argument for an approach to good practice which, while recognising the primacy of values and the need for a clear underpinning of beliefs and principles, also takes full account of empirical, pragmatic, political and conceptual considerations (Alexander 1992: chap. 11). The 1992 primary DES discussion paper encapsulated this idea, in a deliberate echo of the craft principle of the seamlessness of the ethical, the aesthetic and the practical, in the phrase 'fitness for purpose' (Alexander, Rose and Woodhead 1992: para 101).

Thus, we anticipate that the growing heterogeneity in primary pedagogy to which the CICADA data tentatively point will become a quickening trend as primary teachers and the National Curriculum accommodate themselves to each other, and as the established power structures of primary education are modified or dissipated.

Change in professional dilemmas

One bonus of the enforced change in CICADA's methodology was that it allowed us to compare certain critical aspects of class-teachers' consciousness over a longer period. The 1986 data yielded and illustrated the idea that professional development is in part a deepening conscious-ness of and response to the problematic nature of teaching, represented in the form of 'competing imperatives'. This book's second chapter expressed the situation thus:

> Teachers are confronted on a day-to-day basis not only by 'practical' choices of a more or less resolvable kind, but by more fundamental dilemmas and tensions which have their roots partly in the diverging and competing values which constitute primary education as a whole, partly in each teacher's particular school and classroom situation – and partly within teachers themselves, as unique and changing individuals.

This idea was carried forward into both the PRINDEP and CICADA projects and, for each of the teachers whose classrooms yielded the discourse data in the CICADA project, we also have in-depth interviews in which such dilemmas are explored.

As we saw in Chapter 2, the 1986 interviews revealed a recurrence of four such concerns:

- The tension between the progressivist commitment to flexibility, openness, spontaneity and choice on the one hand, and the teacher's need for structure and predictability on the other.
- The tension between incremental and comprehensive planning – that is to say, planning one step at a time, with broad goals but no detailed objectives or strategies in mind, and planning in full and for the longer term, anticipating as many eventualities as possible, well in advance.
- The problem of deciding when and how to intervene in a child's learning, and of reconciling the principle of teacher as non-intervening facilitator who allows children to learn at their own rate with the need, dictated by particular classroom circumstances, to prompt and accelerate this process.
- The dilemmas of grouping: how to reconcile basic classroom manage-ment pressures with the expectation that children should be grouped

and at any one time each group should be working in a different curriculum area; and how to distribute one's time and attention between groups – on the basis of what teachers called 'equal' or 'unequal' investment.

By 1988, as we showed in Chapter 3, the PRINDEP teacher sample used in the CICADA study highlighted the following areas of dilemma:

- Classroom organisation issues, especially in respect of the physical layout and use of space and resources, the number of curriculum activities to be undertaken at any one time, and the tension between thematic/integrated and separate subject treatment of such activities.
- Management of learning issues, especially (as in 1986) the challenges of grouping and groupwork and the dilemma of how best to distribute the time and attention of one teacher among, say, twenty-five children.
- School issues, especially the tension between the kinds of practice which are consistent with the ideas, beliefs and circumstances of the individual teacher and those expected, encouraged or required by the head and/or adopted as school policy.

The 1992 interviews, as we have seen in the present chapter, highlighted four problem areas, as perceived by the primary teachers in question:

- The massive burden, but dubious utility and suspect conceptual basis, of National Curriculum assessment.
- The problem – expressed in similar terms to that of assessment – of record-keeping.
- The unrealistic range and quantity, and the not necessarily appropriate content, of the National Curriculum, especially at Key Stage 1.
- The perceived pressure to modify classroom practice and in particular to introduce more whole-class teaching.

As we have also seen, the national survey data replicated these concerns.

If dilemma-consciousness is an important aspect of professional life, then the changes here are revealing and instructive. In 1986 and 1988 neither of the two main foci of the National Curriculum – curriculum content and pupil assessment – was mentioned, despite the fact, of course, that the teacher's task has always involved critical decisions about these matters. Instead, the earlier interviews showed teacher dilemmas to be largely concentrated within the one area with which the post-1988 legislative programme was *not* concerned, overtly at least: pedagogy.

Moreover, the comparison shows in a dramatic way how a dilemma can be transformed into a certainty. Thus, while comprehensive planning, predictability and structure were areas of professional activity which provoked strong ambivalence in the 1986 interviews, by 1992 they had all become viewed as essential features of teaching properly conducted. Some dilemmas, then, are intrinsic to teaching, while others are induced by the climate and fashion of the times.

The other point to note about the dilemmas is that while all the teachers voiced a sense of being under the pressure of expectations and requirements of some kind, not only had the *nature* of these changed, but also the *source*. In 1986 and 1988 the teachers were conscious of a pressure to conform to certain versions of good practice which combined generalised ideals like openness, spontaneity, integration, flexibility and non-intervention (what tend to be defined as features of 'informal' practice) with specific operational requirements like grouping and multiple curriculum focus teaching. These pressures emanated from heads and advisers, were sometimes, but not always, internalised by the teacher, but in event were a fundamental part of the professional culture of primary education. The requirements of the National Curriculum, in contrast, and the values it reflected, both emanated from outside the world of primary education and were generally perceived as foreign to it.

This difference in the source of the pressures from which classroom dilemmas are generated makes for important differences in professional response. Unreasonable and inappropriate demands from outside the school or the profession, inconvenient, burdensome or unpalatable though they may be, have the virtue of engendering professional solidarity and redirecting frustration and stress towards an external scapegoat. In contrast, those pressures which come from within the profession, especially when they are passed down from above and are seen to relate critically to the individual's career prospects, are much more difficult to handle and tend to be resolved – or not – by the individual rather than collectively. In practice, on the two previous projects we found teachers unable to vent or discuss dilemmas such as those exemplified (except with researchers) and being forced to live with them as well as they could, which in some cases made for acute personal stress and practical difficulty. Put at its simplest, the problems and dilemmas of implementing the National Curriculum could be attributed to government NCC, SEAC and SCAA; but the problems and dilemmas of primary teaching before 1988 were 'in the situation', and those teachers who did not blame the children, the parents or the head tended to attribute difficulties which were often not of their own making to their own inadequacy. This component of self-laceration, among some of the teachers in the 1986 sample, was very pronounced. In extreme cases that we know of (though not in this particular group) teachers of talent, intelligence and sensitivity have found this characteristic of the professional culture of primary education more than they could bear and have left the profession.

Change in pedagogy?

We have emphasised that the two discourse clusters which emerged from computer-analysis of the sixty teaching sessions should not be represented as a new typology of teaching: *Outside the Task* or *Directive* (Cluster 1), *Inside the task* or *Exploratory* (Cluster 2) and *Mixed*, though it is of course tempting to set them against typologies by now familiar in the primary classroom research literature: Bennett's (1976) *Formal, Informal* and *Mixed*; HMI's *Didactic, Exploratory* and *Mixed* (DES 1978); ORACLE's *Individual Monitors, Class Enquirers, Group Instructors* and three types of *Style Changer* (Galton *et al.* 1980b). The contrasts are interesting in as far as we see family resemblances between, for example, ORACLE Individual Monitors and CICADA's Cluster 1, or between ORACLE Class Enquirers and CICADA's Cluster 2: but only up to a point, for in each case the link between interactive style and unit of interaction (whole class, group or individual) was more tenuous in the CICADA data than in ORACLE.

Similarly, the parallels with the 1978 HMI typology must not be pressed too far, for teachers in the HMI Exploratory mode tended to adopt not the engaged, interventive stance of the CICADA Cluster 2 *explain/explore* teachers, but the more directive, outside-the-task style of Cluster 1. It thus becomes very difficult to characterise the CICADA clusters in terms of the HMI Didactic/Exploratory typology.

Moreover, though both CICADA and ORACLE, together with Mortimore *et al.*'s (1988) further application of the ORACLE observation procedures, highlighted teacher–pupil interaction, they did so in very different ways and the latter two projects encompassed the participants and dynamics of the interactions much more comprehensively than did CICADA, which concentrated more on the utterances themselves.

Nevertheless, certain propositions can be offered, tentatively, on the basis of considering the CICADA categories and discourse clusters in the light of earlier studies of pedagogy:

- There does seem to be some basis here for a legitimate typological contrast between teaching which involves an emphasis on open, responsive, challenging and exploratory teacher–pupil dialogue as an intrinsic aspect of the learning task, and teaching which involves setting up a learning task, standing back while children undertake it, intervening only where necessary, and providing *post-hoc* feedback.
- This contrast resonates strongly, though not precisely, with tendencies charted in a number of recent primary classroom studies, notably those of Bennett, Galton, Mortimore and their colleagues. Further, they seem to bear directly on the core classroom dilemma of when and how to intervene in children's learning, which emerged from the 1986 and 1988 interview data referred to above.

- There is no necessary or inevitable connection between such emphases in teaching and the balance of whole-class, group and individual interaction. Both pedagogical tendencies can be associated with all three interaction strategies. Thus, discourse mode and organisational strategy are to some extent independent variables in teaching. This tends to undermine the popular view that whole-class teaching is necessarily didactic and closed while groupwork is necessarily exploratory and open.
- Though research studies tend to show many teachers tending to favour particular styles and strategies, and though there was a high level of consistency in the CICADA clustering between the two teaching sessions observed, there is insufficient evidence to support the view that teachers adopt the same strategy or combination of strategies in all their teaching. However, it is possible that at the deeper levels of discourse tapped by CICADA, the tendencies may represent fairly pervasive habits for each teacher involved.
- No typology of teaching, or clustering of teacher–pupil discourse, can be more than a representation of general tendencies discernible in the complex web of behaviour of which teaching is constituted. The notion that such devices constitute 'models' of teaching, let alone the idea that they offer models *for* teaching, cannot be sustained.
- If the character and quality of teacher–pupil (and pupil–pupil) interaction are indeed as pivotal to learning as both learning theorists and classroom researchers assert, then much more detailed exploration of a qualitative kind is needed. In this matter, we freely acknowledge that this project's statistical treatment of the mass of discourse data from the sixty teaching sessions needs now to be supplemented by qualitative analysis of the same material.
- In the search to apply the lessons of classroom research to the improvement of teaching and learning, the CICADA material may help to shift attention from the general preoccupation with what the 1992 primary discussion paper called *organisational strategy* (the pros, cons and balance of whole-class teaching, groupwork and individual attention) to the generic, interactive *teaching techniques* which underpin all such strategies.

NEXT STEPS

CICADA is one part of a larger endeavour. It has picked up and developed themes from earlier research in which two of this chapter's authors were involved, notably the focus on classroom interaction, and the idea of teaching as a process of confronting and resolving certain basic dilemmas. It connects with other recent research, especially the sequence of studies of primary pedagogy from the late 1970s onwards and the more recent studies of the implementation and impact of the National Curriculum. It has identified a scenario of change in curriculum planning, content, management, assessment and record-keeping taking place against a background of continuity in teacher–pupil interaction; and of change in the collective culture of schools and the dilemma-consciousness of teachers contrasting with continuity in the privacy of classrooms.

In doing so it has suggested that the changes produced by the 1988 Education Reform Act at the level of the curriculum as transacted in classrooms and experienced by children may not be so far-reaching as proponents claim or critics fear – or at least (an important caveat) not yet. For at the time of writing we are still only six years into these reforms, and while our research demonstrates familiar historical truths about surface change and deeper continuity, it also offers a tantalising glimpse of what may well turn out to be more fundamental longer-term change, in as far as dilemma-consciousness and pupil–teacher discourse are both undoubtedly central aspects of those 'deeper' layers of teaching to which study of educational change ought now to be directed.

Equally tantalising is the way that, though pedagogy is the central means of realising the curriculum intentions of the post-1988 reforms, teachers' preoccupation with the Act's focus on curriculum content and assessment seems to have pushed pedagogy further into the background of their professional concerns than it was before 1988. Thus, though the core professional dilemmas of primary teaching seem to be changing, primary pedagogy may not change substantially until it recovers its central position within teachers' dilemma-consciousness.

But in all this, CICADA, we freely admit – indeed, we insist – is but a beginning. Its methodology, for reasons we have explained, was problematic, its findings were often relatively tentative, and the analysis of its data is still incomplete. We end, therefore, by identifying the kinds of research we would hope to see building on our study.

Process-product research revisited

In general, recent pedagogic research has tended to concentrate more on classroom processes than their educational outcomes. At the same time, policy-makers and other commentators with ideological axes to grind are usually eager to take such outcome indicators as are available – like National Curriculum test results or GCSE passes – and claim that they demonstrate the effectiveness or otherwise of particular teaching methods. Yet notions like 'effective teaching' are conceptually complete only when criteria are explicated, and empirically sustainable only when such criteria are translated into viable outcome measures. Process-product research is methodologically highly problematic, and many in the research community view it with suspicion as well as understandable caution because of a historical tendency for the outcome measures to focus, regardless of the teacher's intentions, on those outcomes which are most readily and straightforwardly testable, that is to say, usually, aspects of mathematics and literacy. This means that the circle of conceptual validity and empirical sustainability is not really squared, and research tends not to provide the much-needed empirical rebuff to the political noise about 'trendy teachers' and 'back to basics'. Though finding a just and viable array of outcome measures which are consistent with the full range of learning goals being pursued is not easy, process-product research is necessary, and must continue to be attempted. Otherwise, claims about the impact on particular ways of teaching on what and how pupils learn will continue to be based on evidence which is to an excessive degree circumstantial.[3]

The role of the subject in teaching and learning

We need to know more about the relationship between subject structures, the teacher's conceptual grasp of subject matter, and the character and content of teacher–pupil interaction. On this point, despite its original intention, the CICADA data discussed here remain elusive. Qualitative analysis of the classroom transcripts, however, will allow us greater purchase on this problem.

The determinants of teachers' practice

It is important to understand more clearly why teachers teach as they do. The evidence of powerful continuities in teacher–pupil discourse tends to support the view that the National Curriculum Orders are probably a weaker influence than factors specific to the teacher, the classroom and the professional culture. The studies reported in this and the previous three chapters provide insights into each of these, but the question needs to be pursued further if we are to understand how generalised notions of pedagogical effectiveness of the kind referred to above can be applied meaningfully to the unique circumstances and dynamics of individual teachers, children and classrooms.

Levels of practice

We have asserted the need to probe change processes in education to deeper levels such as those discussed here. We now need more refined models of educational change in order to identify (1) the various levels or aspects of educational practice at which change can usefully be analysed, (2) the nature of those 'deeper levels' which tend to remain relatively resistant to change, and an understanding of why this is so, and (3) the aspects of educational practice which are most significant if change in educational policy is to yield corresponding change in educational outcome.

Some with a more jaundiced view of the policy process will no doubt argue that identifying (3) above would provide policy-makers with a weapon which they would almost certainly abuse and that it is the function of educational research to enhance professional skill, understanding and autonomous judgement rather than to facilitate social engineering by central government. However, we suspect that for the foreseeable future the policy–practice interface in education will remain as elusive as we have found it to be, and policy-led educational change will remain the patchwork portrayed here of the traumatic, the partial and the incipient, all offset, balanced or indeed subverted by apparently fundamental continuities.

NOTES

1 In 1991, Prime Minister Major and the education ministerial team launched an attack on what they saw as the continuing dominance of 'progressive' teaching methods in primary schools, drawing strength, as it happens, from the PRINDEP research, including the material reported in this book's second and third chapters. However, the document they commissioned to support this attack (Alexander, Rose and Woodhead 1992) both failed to support the government's one-dimensional characterisation of the problem and argued that decisions about how to teach must be left to teachers. Since then, attempts to revive the 'trendy teacher' rhetoric of this period – for example, to accompany the publication of OFSTED's two follow-up reports on this initiative (1993a, 1994a) and after HMCI Woodhead's 1995 lecture at the Royal Society of Arts – have failed, though the issue will almost certainly return, as it has with monotonous regularity since the war. The last of these excursions was notable for the way that those concerned were able to blur the boundaries between Woodhead's personal opinions as expressed at the RSA lecture (Woodhead 1995) and the evidence gathered during the OFSTED inspection process and presented in his HMCI annual report (OFSTED 1995), thus suggesting that all of his assertions about the state of English primary education were grounded in OFSTED evidence. They were not.

2 For an account of this period which explores the relationship between published research, government policy and the media, see Wallace (1993). For an analysis of the way in which the 1992 DES primary discussion paper became a battleground for competing political, professional and academic interests, see P. Woods and P. Wenham, *Politics and Pedagogy: a Case Study in Appropriation* (forthcoming).

3 The debate about class sizes is a good example of a process-product issue on which the running tends to be made more strongly by politicians than the educational and research communities. The evidence, as Mortimore and Blatchford (1993) and Bennett (1994) show, is problematic. In some respects it does tend to support the proposition that large classes are detrimental to learning. At the same time, it is incomplete or open to question on methodological grounds – in Bennett's words (1994: 2), 'The British evidence is

... sparse, flawed and ambiguous', a deficiency which successive governments readily exploit while, naturally, refusing to support research of a more thorough and systematic kind than is currently available. For of course the matter is doubly charged politically: if detriment can be proved, then government can be culpable to the extend that class sizes are tied to the level of resource; and rectifying the problem is extremely expensive. These factors produce the consistent and predictable response of ministerial stonewalling whenever the matter is raised, most recently, at the time of writing, in the government's evidence to the Commons Select Committee enquiry on primary school funding (House of Commons 1994a) and its subsequent response to the report of that enquiry (House of Commons 1994b).

Chapter 6

Innocence and experience

*From the day-to-day life of primary classrooms to broader questions again:
this chapter looks at versions of primary education past, present and
future, and to primary education's construction, deconstruction and
reconstruction. It traces the roots of our modern system, examining the
continuing legacies of elementary and progressive education and how these
intertwine with the purportedly radical alternative version embodied in
the National Curriculum. It looks ahead to the millennium and identifies
a number of key areas where choices must be faced and resolved: the
structure of primary education, funding, teaching roles, teaching methods,
the curriculum, and, above all, values and purposes. On the way, the poet
William Blake provides a starting point for our reassessment of progressivism. He also provides the metaphor for some of British education's
most pervasive tensions: the two main primary traditions and the very
different values they embodied; the contrast between the broad consensus
of the 1960s and 1970s and the conflict of the 1980s and 1990s; the
dilemma about where education for childhood ends and education for
adulthood begins; and the tension between a primary agenda defined in
terms of the preoccupations of the classroom here and now and one which
looks to the future and to wider cultural and global imperatives.*

The duty of a state in public education is ... to obtain the greatest
possible quantity of reading, writing and arithmetic for the greatest
number.

A school is not merely a teaching shop, it must transmit values and
attitudes. It is a community in which children learn to live first and
foremost as children and not as future adults.

The principal task of the teacher at Key Stage 1 is to ensure that pupils
master the basic skills of reading, writing and number.

Though, as I suggested in Chapter 2, it is possible to identify at least
seven distinctive traditions which have been influential in shaping

modern primary education, two of these have been particularly prominent: the elementary tradition of a minimal basic education for the masses, which emerged in the nineteenth century, and progressivism, whose roots go back further still, but which had its strongest impact from the 1930s onwards, especially during the 1960s and 1970s. Much that has happened in post-war primary education can be illuminated by exploring the interplay between the values and practices which each of these traditions embodied. Hence the three essentially emblematic quotations above. They come from the 1861 Newcastle Commission Report on elementary education, the 1967 Plowden Report on primary education, and the 1993 Dearing Interim Report on the National Curriculum.[1] The close affinity between 1861 and 1993 is of course striking. More on this as we proceed: but first, let us remind ourselves of primary education during its formative years, using the device of the historical snapshot, taken at intervals of roughly a generation.

ELEMENTARY TO PRIMARY: SNAPSHOTS OF SIX GENERATIONS

We start in 1839. The great Victorian economic boom is under way, but it rides on the back not just of the industrial revolution but also of an unbridgeable gulf between rich and poor. For the latter there is a motley array of charity schools, Sunday schools and industrial schools, supplemented by the now large number of monitorial schools run by the (Anglican) National Society and the non-conformist British and Foreign School Society. In these establishments the monitorial principles of their founding fathers, Andrew Bell and Joseph Lancaster, deliver instruction in the 3Rs and religion as cheaply as possible, using the services of 10–11-year-old senior pupils to teach the groups into which the large number of children in the single schoolroom have been divided. Thus is elementary education born. But there is another tradition already established, that of the infant school, owing its less mechanistic and more humane regime, and its more liberal curriculum, to industrialist and proto-socialist Robert Owen, to Samuel Wilderspin and the London Infant School Society, and to the ideas of Pestalozzi, imported from Switzerland. Also in this year a Committee of Council for Education has been set up to oversee public education – the ancestor of the DFE, in fact – with Dr Kay (later Sir James Kay-Shuttleworth) as its first secretary and a small team of inspectors beginning the long march of Her Majesty's Inspectorate through educational history and into OFSTED. The scene is set for state intervention in education (though in this respect England is, and for decades remains, well behind Prussia, France, Holland and Switzerland) (Green 1990). At this stage, however, the task for elementary education is clear and unambiguous:

to confer upon the children of the poor the inestimable benefit of religious instruction, combined with such acquirements as may be suitable to their stations in life, and calculated to render them useful and respectable members of society.

(Quoted in Lawson and Silver 1973)

Let us move on a generation, to 1870. The Elementary Education Act has just been passed in order to plug the many gaps in the patchwork of public education. Its architect – Bradford local hero and brother-in-law of the most famous HMI of them all, Matthew Arnold – is W. E. Forster. Though elementary education is not yet compulsory (it will become so for children aged 5–10 in 1880), and though the Act is very much a compromise to pacify Church opinion and leave voluntary schooling untouched, elected school boards are being formed to provide education in areas where voluntary provision is inadequate. A major school building programme begins (many of these seemingly indestructible edifices will still be in use at the end of the twentieth century). In the schools themselves, the 1862 Revised Code, the system of 'payment by results' – the despair of John Ruskin, Sidney Webb and, especially, Matthew Arnold – is successfully containing educational expenditure while impoverishing the curriculum. Children between the ages of 6 and 12, divided into six 'standards', attract a grant on the basis of attendance and examination in reading, writing and arithmetic, though the 1867 Code has recently extended this list to include some other subjects. The system has been justified, notoriously, by Robert Lowe, who, scornful of the previous method of allocating grants to schools, has proposed what he called 'a little free trade' and asserted that if the system 'is not cheap it shall be efficient; if it is not efficient, it shall be cheap.' However, the separate development of infant education is encouraged by the exemption of children below the age of 6, though such children have nevertheless to be prepared for the Standard 1 examination. Moreover, the 1870 Act has itself enabled infant schools and departments to become an integral, though still distinct part of public elementary education – witness those signs visible above the doorways of many primary schools whose buildings date back to this time: 'boys', 'girls' and 'infants'.

On again a generation to 1902. Payment by results has finally disappeared, in 1898, to be replaced in 1900 by the single block grant. On the other hand, the extension of elementary education and the improvement in school attendance have produced, as well as a school building boom, a steady improvement in literacy levels, especially among girls, and have made the question of what lies beyond elementary education an urgent one. Indeed, the national educational agenda now begins to be increasingly dominated by secondary education. The curriculum of elementary schools has expanded from its narrow base to include, by 1896, a core of the 3Rs plus object lessons or a 'class subject', needlework for girls and drawing for boys, and the possibility of subjects like science, history, geography, singing, and so on. In many schools, particularly those of the larger school boards like London, separate classrooms have replaced the hall of the now long-abandoned monitorial regime, and desks have replaced benches. In London, too, the idea of infant education, and indeed infants schools, is generally accepted. The 1902 Balfour Education Act has tidied up the local administration of elementary education so that the Board of Education now deals with 318 local education authorities instead of 2,500 school boards and 14,000 voluntary schools.

Our next snapshot is from 1931. The climate for elementary education, if not its actual practice, is now somewhat different. The 1904 Elementary School Code, and the efforts of the LEAs and schools themselves, have begun to erode the stigma of pauper education which has marked elementary education since its inception, though R. H. Tawney (1923) still insists that 'the hereditary curse of English education is its organisation along lines of social class', and he will certainly not be the last to level this charge. The 1918 Education Act has enforced compulsory school attendance to age 14 and has made the provision of universal secondary education inevitable. But the most significant event of this year in the present context has been the Hadow Report's legitimation of 'primary education' as both idea and legal entity. This report is in fact the second of three. In the first, dealing with the education of the adolescent, published in 1926, the Consultative Committee has argued strongly for a 'break at age eleven' between the junior and senior stages of elementary education, and for the establishment of separate primary and secondary schools, thus making the Labour Party's dream of 'secondary education for all' a reality. Tawney, the editor of the Labour Party's 1922 policy document which coined that slogan, is also a member of the Hadow Committee. But Hadow also heralds and indeed endorses features of English state education which are to prove extremely contentious three decades or so later: the tripartite secondary system, selection at 11 plus, and streaming. Meanwhile, the 1931 Report goes well beyond structural concerns to present a view of primary education which is very close to that in our next snapshot: it is grounded in principles of child development offered by the now well-established discipline of psychology, and argues – famously – for the curriculum 'to be thought of in terms of activity and experience rather than knowledge to be acquired and facts to be stored' (Board of Education 1931: para 75). Progressivism has at last come in from the cold, though it must be stressed that in commending the ideas of John Dewey in this way Hadow is offering an ideal rather than portraying the reality, for in many respects primary schools in 1931 are not very different from a generation before.

On, then, to 1967 and another report, that of the Plowden Committee, commissioned in 1963 by Minister of Education Edward Boyle. The Hadow reorganisation is now nearly complete: there are still some 7,000 pupils in all-age schools, but 4.5 million pupils in primary schools, and by 1970 the modern system of primary education will be fully in place. But this new system, endorsed by the 1944 Butler Education Act, is now beset by other pressures. For the consolidation of secondary education has washed back into the primary phase the effects of selection at 11 plus. During the 1940s and 1950s most primary schools large enough to have parallel classes within an age group have streamed children by ability (as they perceived it) – a system which had been endorsed by Hadow, on the advice of that committee's psychological consultant, Cyril Burt (Simon 1992). Streaming commands a loyalty from primary heads in the early 1960s whose fierceness is matched only by their opposition to it ten years later (Simon 1991; Jackson 1964): a fickle thing is professional opinion. But because Plowden in 1967 comes out against streaming – though not without a certain ambivalence – and because as a result of the Labour Government's Circular 10/65 selective secondary education is on its way out anyway, streaming in primary schools crumbles fairly rapidly. But Plowden is about much more than this. Taking its cue from Hadow, it argues that the most fundamental reality in primary education is the nature of the developing child. It argues strongly for universal nursery education. It builds on post-war social research showing the consistent educational under-achievement of working-class children. It highlights the particularly damaging consequences for the child's educational and life chances of social disadvantage and urban decay, and it proposes a programme of positive discrimination to compensate for these. It paves the way for the three-tier structure of first, middle and upper schools as an alternative to the two-tier structure of primary and secondary.

But especially, in celebrating the child as child rather than adult in the making, in commending learning by doing and an open and integrated curriculum in relation to which the teacher adopts a facilitating and heuristic role, and in arguing the virtues of freedom, spontaneity and affectivity, Plowden finally closes the door on elementary education. Or does it? Plowden also reports that only 10 per cent of schools conform to this vision, while the largest single group are 'run of the mill' or worse (CACE 1967: chap. 8).

Finally, to 1995. Economic boom has been replaced by recession and high unemployment. The broad educational consensus of the Plowden years has been replaced by a 'discourse of derision' (Wallace 1993) directed at 'trendy' teachers but especially at the so-called 'educational establishment' of LEAs and – as pedlars of the 'barmy theory' responsible for the claimed fiasco of English primary education – teacher trainers.[2] The balance of responsibility between government, LEA and school has been replaced by the uneasy counterpoint of government control of curriculum and assessment and school control of budgets. But the main change, at least as far as children are concerned, is that the primary curriculum is now a National Curriculum of nine mandatory subjects, plus RE, with testing of pupils' attainment at age 7 and 11. OFSTED, successor to Arnold's inspectorate, has identified the following achievements of this National Curriculum: greater consistency in curriculum content; clearer lines of progression in each subject; improved planning; a more secure place for science, technology, history and geography; and better assessment and record-keeping (OFSTED 1993d). Meanwhile, the ideas and practices celebrated in Plowden have come in for close scrutiny by a succession of university-based research studies and HMI surveys,[3] and the Plowden Committee itself has had to suffer a sustained campaign of vilification from the right which continues unabated a quarter of a century after their report was published.[4] Though primary education is in structural terms now well-established, in terms of rationale it is floundering. Where next?

ELEMENTARY AND PROGRESSIVE: CONTINUITIES AND CONFLICTS

The elementary legacy

I have briefly traced the transformation of elementary into primary, but how complete has that transformation really been? There are, in fact, significant continuities. Here are some of them.

Continuity number one: the funding of primary education still very clearly reflects the 'cheap or efficient' principle of Robert Lowe and, indeed, the primary sector's pauper origins more generally. Primary schools have significantly larger classes than secondary (an average of twenty-seven per class compared with twenty-one, though it should be noted that a quarter of primary pupils are in classes of more than thirty) (DFE 1992a). Primary per capita funding is much lower than secondary: a 1993 national comparison of age-weighted pupil units (AWPUs) across all LEAs shows an average AWPU of £992 at age 7, and £1,675, or a 67 per cent difference, at age 14.[5] Primary teachers have more limited prospects for advancement above the basic salary scale than their secondary colleagues, and much less non-contact time. They also endure the status consequences of the assumption that the younger the pupil the less complex and demanding is the task of teaching that pupil – an assumption which pervades the education world itself as well as government and society.

Continuity number two: the primary curriculum has been consistently and continuously dominated by the 3Rs, not least during the 1960s – those 'trendy' 1960s which were the bane of Rhodes Boyson, John Patten, Sheila Lawlor, John Major, the Black Paper authors and sections of the press. In fact, commitment to the so-called 'basics' has been one of the most remarkable constants of both elementary and primary educa-tion,[6] and indeed, few people have seen fit to challenge the assumption that what was 'basic' in the Revised Code should remain basic in 1994. Though the core subjects of the National Curriculum now include science alongside English and mathematics, the pre-eminence of reading, writing and computation in primary schooling remains absolutely secure. Indeed, the Dearing report hinted that at Key Stage 1 science, newly graduated to basic status, might once again have to give way to the 3Rs (Dearing 1993b: para 4.20). Some may find it baffling that in general educational discourse arithmetic – however important – is given parity with language. To explain this we need to remind ourselves that the scope of the language curriculum in elementary education was extremely narrow, and to equate the basic skills of reading and writing with those of computation seemed therefore not unreasonable. The idea that the language curriculum should engage with culture in its broadest sense, that it should include the critical study of literature and media texts, a wide variety of forms and processes of writing and above all that powerful (but, to the Victorians, subversive) skill of engaging with others through the spoken word – all this came much later.[7] Our problem, however, is that the portmanteau term '3Rs' – like so much else from our elementary legacy – is embedded so deep in our collective consciousness that questioning it has become, for some at least, unthinkable.

Continuity number three: the remainder of the primary curriculum, beyond the basics, is – as it always has been – rather less secure. The 1988 Education Reform Act gave every pupil an entitlement to all nine National Curriculum subjects at Key Stages 1 and 2, and this ostensibly secured the place in primary education of previously vulnerable subjects like science, history and geography, art and music, whose treatment during the 1960s, 1970s and early 1980s was often found by HMI and others to be superficial. However, this new-found security was immediately compromised, partly by assessment requirements which concentrated on the basics, and partly by the overcrowding and unman-ageability of the whole package: hence Dearing. On this it is worth noting that Dearing (1993b: paras 4.12–4.19) proposed solving the problem of unmanageability by the familiar device of pruning the non-core subjects. The nineteenth-century view that the curriculum for the masses should consist of mandatory basics and dispensable trimmings is alive and well. Elementary habits die hard.

Continuity number four: the dominant teaching role in primary schools remains that of the class-teacher – one person teaching the whole curriculum to a large class. Though the overall scope of the primary curriculum has remained remarkably consistent in terms of the subjects taught, the character and complexity of each such subject, and therefore the sophistication and professional demands of the whole, have all vastly increased. Yet it is still presumed that the model which worked when primary teaching involved little more than drilling children in the 3Rs remains adequate. And though the limits of the class-teacher system in respect of a modern curriculum have been under discussion for a good fifteen years now, the deep professional loyalty that this system inspires legitimates government resistance to increased funding for primary education. For most people, then, the class-teacher system *is* primary education, just as it *was* elementary education.

Continuity number five: though infant education is less detached from primary than it was from elementary – indeed, the largest single category of primary schools today is the 5–11 – the old infant–elementary distinction still has considerable resonances in the professional culture of primary education. This has been consolidated by the National Curriculum's separation of Key Stages 1 and 2 (5–7 and 7–11), and further strengthened by Dearing's fairly sharp differentiation of the purposes of each of these key stages.

Our final continuity, and ultimate testament to the abiding influence of Victorian values, is 'back to basics'. In 1993–94 this call to arms for those nostalgic for the days of empire, class and elementary education briefly became the touchstone for the entire spectrum of government policy – before foundering on the rock of Tory sleaze.

The progressive legacy

So: six continuities from nineteenth-century elementary education in today's primary schools – and fundamental ones at that. What, now, of the progressive legacy? Characterising elementary education is relatively straightforward, for it was embodied in legislation, regulations, codes and, most durable of all, structures. The nearest progressivism came to acquiring that kind of status was its endorsement at the level of principle in the Hadow reports of 1931 and 1933, and in Plowden and the HMI handbooks of suggestions for teachers. Otherwise, it was defined and transmitted in the popular professional literature and on courses; in open meetings for the aspiring and in closed and highly selective gatherings of the faithful; in writing and by word of mouth; through inspectors, advisers, heads, training college lecturers and various other enthusiasts. If elementary education was disseminated by statute, progressive education was disseminated by homily and the grapevine (Selleck 1972; Cunningham 1988).

In any case, progressivism is not so much one idea as a package of many, some of them at best loosely connected. These ideas have come from different sources, and indeed different countries, and concern themselves with various aspects of the task of primary education. There are two possible ways to unravel this package. One is to identify the cast of characters and what they stood for: Rousseau; Robert Owen; Pestalozzi; Froebel; Dewey; Montessori; Rachel and Margaret Macmillan; Susan Isaacs and Dorothy Gardner; Jean Piaget; Alec Clegg, Stewart Mason and John Newsom; Christian Schiller, John Blackie and Robin Tanner; Edith Moorhouse and Marianne Parry; Arthur Stone and Sybil Marshall; Len Marsh and John Coe. Though such a list – and there are other principal characters, not to mention the hundreds of walk-on parts and thousands of understudies – is itself instructive in confirming that we are dealing with something fairly complex and elusive here, the more useful task, I suggest, is to tease out the core *ideas*.

It is generally accepted that the key text for an understanding of progressivism is Rousseau's *Emile*, and that the *leitmotif* of *Emile* is this:

> Nature would have children children before they are men ...
> Childhood has its own ways of seeing, thinking and feeling: nothing
> is more foolish than to try and substitute our ways.

But Rousseau goes on, and primary teachers will recognise the resonances:

> Your scholar ... should be taught by experience alone.

And:

> I will be told that Emile needs to read. I agree. He must be able to
> read when he needs to read.

And:

> Let us lay down as an incontrovertible rule that the first impulses
> of nature are always right: there is no original sin in the human
> heart. [8]

This takes us to the first principle, or image, of progressivism, that of *innocence*, and here at last I come to the title of this chapter and to William Blake. Blake, like Rousseau, rejected the eighteenth-century enlightenment and its elevation of reason above feeling. But the forms and images of his *Songs of Innocence and Experience* seem more germane to our discussion than the more usual references to Rousseau's *Emile*, even though *Emile* is without doubt the seminal and more influential text, because Blake engages with the actual political and social circumstances which produced English elementary education in a way that Rousseau could not. With Blake, childhood innocence is corrupted not just by rationalism and Newtonian physics, but also by the poverty and degradation of the industrial revolution for which working-class children and their parents were so much factory fodder, by the loss of connection with the natural order as a consequence of urbanisation, and by the joylessness and repressive power of organised religion, especially as represented in the established Church (Coveney 1967). In this connection, we should note that elementary education, in which the Churches had a monopoly until 1870, embodied an unmistakable presumption of original sin: 'The primary object of early education', asserted one of the voluntary school societies in 1846, is 'to cultivate religious principles and moral sentiments; to awaken the tender mind to a sense of its evil dispositions and habitual failings'.[9]

But for Blake, these 'religious principles and moral sentiments' had little to do with what the Romantics understood by 'awakening' –

> And the gates of this Chapel were shut,
> And 'Thou shalt not' writ over the door.[10]

– while the 'evil dispositions and habitual failings' were those not of children but of the industrial England into which they were born and whose rapacious and corrupting interests they were forced to serve –

> I wander thro' each charter'd street,
> Near where the charter'd Thames does flow,
> And mark in every face I meet
> Marks of weakness, marks of woe.[11]

– and in which the Christian virtue of charity had been subverted or redefined to buttress the rich, the powerful, and the respectable –

> Is this a holy thing to see
> In a rich and fruitful land,
> Babes reduc'd to misery,
> Fed with cold and usurous hand?[12]

Blake, then, inverts the main assumptions about childhood and society which underpinned mass elementary education, and highlights the same elements of self-interest, greed, exploitation and hypocrisy which Dickens was to portray fifty years later.

The first of my Blake extracts was from *The Garden of Love*, and it takes us to one of progressive education's most pervasive metaphors – and to the starting point of this book's second chapter. Indeed, for Froebel, later, the idea of a 'kindergarten', or children's garden, stretched the metaphor about as far as it would go. The children were plants, the teacher was the gardener, and the skill of teaching lay in finding the child's 'budding points' and nurturing its natural growth through an organic curriculum rich in stimulus. Throughout the history of primary education, 'growth' itself, though obviously amenable to physiological and psychological

treatment, more commonly acquires botanical or horticultural connotations. But the 'garden' metaphor is triply suggestive – of Rousseau's
child in its 'natural' state, of the rural simplicities which had been
devastated by the industrial revolution, and, most fundamentally, of
Eden before the fall. For Blake made his stance on formal education very
clear:

> There is no use in education. I hold it wrong. It is the great sin. It is
> eating of the tree of the knowledge of good and evil.[13]

Innocence, childhood's untarnished vision and humankind at one with
nature were of course pervasive themes in the Romantic movement,
especially in Blake, Coleridge, Wordsworth and Keats, before they
dissolved into late-Victorian sentimentality. Despite rough treatment at
the hands of Freud, these themes were also a powerful stimulus to later
progressives like Alec Clegg, Christian Schiller and John Blackie, all of
them pre-war graduates (though only one of them in English) from a
Cambridge in which F. R. Leavis (1930) was forcefully asserting the
'supremely civilising' function of English literature, not just in education
but also as a means to explore 'the most fundamental questions of human
existence'. In this, another link is traced back, via English literature,
between the post-war progressive movement and that poet, essayist,
HMI and arch-critic of payment by results, Matthew Arnold, especially
his *Culture and Anarchy* (Arnold 1963). However, in as far as it celebrates
the 'high culture' of the arts and humanities, this is a tradition somewhat at odds with the rejection of a priori knowledge and the anti-subject
rhetoric of much progressive discourse. I shall come back to this apparent
paradox later.

The belief in childhood innocence, education as growth and development, and the imperative of respecting and conforming to the natural
order have all retained their potency in primary education to the present
day, as Ronald King's research in infant and junior classrooms shows
(King 1978, 1989). Indeed, his studies also suggest a strong belief among
early years teachers that the dividing line between childhood innocence
and experience (in the sense of culpability) is age 7, when primary
children move from the infant to the junior stage – resonances again of
the separateness of infant education within, and its resistance to, the
mainstream elementary tradition. By the early 1990s this belief had
coalesced into an increasingly articulate and coherent early years movement which drew its strength from an alliance of early years researchers
and teacher educators, practitioners in pre-school, nursery and primary
education and the contingent caring professions, and organisations like
the National Children's Bureau. The agenda for this movement had
moved well beyond the doctrine of innocence to espouse a broad agenda
in part concerned with a holistic approach to young children's health,

welfare and education, and in part seeking to resist what it perceived as the secondary-orientated hegemony of the National Curriculum.

The concern with the fact and imperative of *growth* in primary discourse, albeit botanical as much as human, provided fertile ground for the planting of emerging psychological theories of child development (note how hard it is to escape from these metaphors). Like no psychologist before or since, Jean Piaget was annexed lock, stock and barrel by the primary community. His was a theory which conveniently fitted progressivism rather than challenged it. His 'sensori-motor', 'pre-operational', 'concrete' and 'formal' stages of cognitive development came to dominate teacher training courses and teacher texts and materials – especially in the 'new' mathematics and science of the 1960s, while the over-rigid application – by others, not himself – of the ages he attached to each stage consolidated the principle of wait-and-see 'readiness' which Rousseau had first propounded in 1762. Indeed, the ages and stages proved doubly convenient since the transition from pre-operational to concrete and from concrete to formal coincided with the transfer from infant to junior and junior to secondary, thus giving the whole structure of primary education the ultimate Rousseau-esque seal of approval – oneness with the natural order.

In turn, Piagetian theory was used to endorse another key progressive principle, that of learning by doing – again one having a respectable pedigree which included Pestalozzi, Froebel, Rousseau and of course John Dewey. Dewey it was who inspired the Hadow Committee to their most famous dictum (Board of Education 1931: para 75): 'The curriculum is to be thought of in terms of activity and experience rather than knowledge to be acquired and facts to be stored.'

The principle of 'learning by doing' and the Rousseau/Dewey rejection of culturally transmitted knowledge have proved powerful and durable. Of course, Hadow's celebrated assertion soon collapses under analysis. The opposition of knowledge and activity, and of knowledge and experience, for example, and the equating of knowledge with a Gradgrindian image of fact-transmission, are all clearly untenable. But then such statements, bearing in mind their anti-rationalist origins, never really sought to *argue* their case, only to *assert* it.

But what is particularly interesting about this Hadow dictum is that, as originally drafted, it conveyed a very different message, for instead of the opposition invited by the 'rather than' ('activity and experience ... rather than ... knowledge ... and facts') there was 'and': 'the curriculum is to be thought of in terms of activity and experience *and of* knowledge to be acquired and facts to be stored'.[14] The change to 'rather than' was made after intense pressure from the Froebel Society, thus providing a credo for several generations of teachers and legitimating an exclusive and adversarial mode of discourse in primary education which is still with us: 'children rather than subjects', 'topics rather than subjects', 'spontaneity versus planning', 'groupwork versus whole-class teaching', 'teaching versus assessment', 'class teachers versus specialists', 'formal' versus 'informal', and even 'learning versus teaching'. None of these polarities, needless to say, is conceptually tenable, empirically sustainable or professionally helpful, and it is interesting to speculate on how things might have developed had Hadow not let the Froebelians have their way.

And yet, of course, the problem for the progressives was that knowledge and facts – indeed, the very idea of a curriculum devised by adults – were 'unnatural', and this view, taken to extremes, led them to false dichotomies like those I have just listed. The natural order, at one with 'the child's view of the world', demanded that knowledge be seamless rather than divided into subjects and that it be the unique outcome of each child's interaction with its environment rather than imposed by adults. It demanded, too, that pedagogy be facilitative rather than directive, heuristic rather than didactic. This position was without doubt a necessary and long-overdue corrective to the dismal practices of elementary education at its worst: the rigid curriculum canon of the 3Rs combined with a debased digest of some of the other disciplines; the repressive and repetitive pedagogy of rote learning and drill; the goal of fitting the child for its station at the bottom of society, and keeping it there.

Yet this line of argument could have unsatisfactory consequences, for the principle of naturalness in curriculum and pedagogy could imply a refusal to engage with social and economic realities and with the distinct forms of understanding – notably, in this context, science – which are an important part of the fabric of Western culture. This is not to say that these are, or should be, the sole basis for the primary curriculum; rather, that by turning its back on ways of making sense of and engaging with the world as deeply embedded in Western thought as are the arts, sciences and so on, there was a risk that an education which claimed to *liberate* might in fact do the opposite, and confine the child to an intellectual and occupational ghetto as surely as the 3Rs elementary curriculum was intended to. But at root, the principle of naturalness was flawed in one obvious and fundamental sense: the presumptions about the seamlessness of knowledge, the nature of the child and so on were simply constructs, cultural creations no more 'natural' and no less 'artificial' than the subject-based curriculum of secondary schools and universities. In the same way, the quintessential primary image of the garden betokened not nature untamed, and certainly not the savage free-for-all of the jungle, but the imposed order of humankind. It was the gardener, that is to say the teacher, who constructed the environment in which learning according to 'natural' principles was to take place. It was the teacher whose values, knowledge and skill facilitated the child's learning. It was the teacher, in short, who defined childhood.[15]

So far, allusively rather than by presenting a list, I have tried to suggest some of the central ideas of the progressive tradition: childhood innocence; growth and development; the principle of nature and naturalness; the seamless, reflexive curriculum; heuristic and facilitative teaching; active rather than passive learning; and the conscious opposition to everything elementary education was thought to stand for. There were of course enlightened and stimulating elementary school teachers, as Burnett's autobiographies show (Burnett 1974, 1982), and their work needs to be rescued from the progressives' caricatures as surely as the majority of modern primary teachers deserve to be rescued from the stereotype of egg-boxes and anarchy, and indeed from everything else that is implied by ministers' somewhat profligate use of terms like 'trendy teachers' and 'barmy theory'.

There is one further element. It is the influence of the arts and crafts movement, especially as mediated by individuals like Robin Tanner, an HMI who worked briefly in Leeds but spent most of his life in Wiltshire and Oxfordshire. Blake, with whom we started this exploration of progressivism, was an engraver as well as a poet and polemicist. Tanner, too, was an artist and a craftsman: an etcher whose subject matter was the quiet countryside of unmechanised farming, vernacular architecture, and nature minutely observed. He was profoundly influenced by the 1926 London exhibition 'Drawings, etchings and woodcuts by Samuel Palmer and other disciples of William Blake' (Tanner 1987: 41), and his work combined the luxuriance of Palmer (though without Palmer's disturbing inner vision) with the craft principles of William Morris. Tanner carried his ideals and his skills into primary classrooms, placing art and craft firmly at the centre of the curriculum and insisting that the school and classroom offer a visual environment for learning of the highest order. Like Blake he was a non-conformist, and like Morris, a socialist: for him the craft principle was no mere aesthetic dalliance, but was of a piece with his politics. He was enormously influential in Oxfordshire, and through Alec Clegg and Woolley Hall, in the West Riding and well beyond. He stands in direct line of succession, therefore, through Fabianism, Tawney, Sidney Webb and William Morris back to Blake and Rousseau, and it seems to me worth using the example of Tanner to point out that it is the *politics* of progressivism as much as its practical substance that makes it the target of right-wing vituperation and scorn, for its most fundamental roots lie not so much in the naïve pastoralism and folksiness of classrooms festooned with teasels and drapes as in the English radical tradition of political and religious dissent.

At the same time, Tanner's vision *was* deeply nostalgic and romantic, not to say Luddite, and his account of the countryside (Tanner 1987;

Tanner and Tanner 1939) was utterly cleansed of the grinding toil, poverty and exploitation of pre-mechanised farming captured by, say Ronald Blythe (1969), whose clear-eyed and unsentimental Akenfield contrasts sharply with the somewhat cloying imagery of the Tanners' Kington Borel. For Tanner, technology and creativity were implacably opposed, and it was thus all too easy for his disciples to find in his work support for a view of primary education which simply turned its back on the problems of the twentieth century.

Through this last example, too, we can begin to make sense of the progressives' rejection of subject knowledge. Blake was, in a formal sense, uneducated, though he was of course immensely well-educated through his own labours. He was one of a number of influential figures in the late-eighteenth and early nineteenth century who constituted a vigorous alternative intellectual tradition to that embodied at this time in Oxford and Cambridge, rejecting the university nexus of rationalist thinking, Anglican conformity, inherited wealth and political power and patronage, and who celebrated instead artistic insight, practitioner knowledge and the world of feeling (Thompson 1993). To the progressives in primary education, who – somewhat presumptuously in some cases – saw themselves as heirs to this tradition, the academic subject represented an unacceptable level of intellectual and political hegemony. This legacy is still with us – for example, in the separation of academic education and vocational training, and of study and performance in the arts; in the combination of romanticism and anti-intellectualism which were the hallmark of the old primary teacher training colleges (Taylor 1969); and in the residue of this latter culture, still extremely powerful and not infrequently strident, in many primary schools and some teacher training establishments today. Equally, these divisions, with their strong Cartesian overtones, mark the school curriculum as a whole – and certainly the National Curriculum, within which the arts have the lowest status.

Partly working against this, for progressivism is a broad church, was the passionate advocacy of the arts and humanities disciplines provided by Matthew Arnold and *his* heirs – the inspectorate generally (in the nineteenth and early to mid-twentieth centuries HMI were recruited mainly from Oxbridge rather than the elementary system), together with figures like Clegg, Blackie and Schiller, and some of the post-war generation of professors of education like Bantock, Peters, Ford, Walsh and – especially important in the primary context – Alan Blyth. This tradition never sat comfortably with grass-roots anti-rationalist progressivism, and indeed for Black Paper authors like Cox and Bantock, grounded firmly in the Leavisite canon, progressivism was as big a threat to civilised values as was technocracy (Cox and Dyson 1971; Bantock 1963). These tensions resonate loudly in primary education, still.

What, then, can one say about the impact and fate of progressivism? Whatever one might venture by way of reservation, progressivism offered a vision for primary education whose power could transcend the narrow utilitarianism of the elementary system. It commanded attention to the belief that this was a stage of education worthy of the name 'primary' – a foundation both for learning and for life. At best, its practices transformed primary schools at every level, from the physical setting, the content of the curriculum and teaching methods to the climate of teacher–pupil and teacher–teacher relationships. At best, it generated a palpable sense of excitement and purpose among children and teachers alike which translated itself into high standards of educational attainment across the whole curriculum, not just in the 'basics'. At best, it broke down the barriers between home, school and the community. Considering how primary schooling had originated, these were – and they remain – formidable achievements, and those who criticise primary schools would do well to acknowledge this.

As we have seen, progressivism also represented a fusion of ideas from different sources – literature, the visual arts, psychology, humanism, radical politics – all brought to bear upon the challenge of educating young children. But perhaps its most unique achievements were in the areas of affectivity and the arts. Without feeling obliged to coin the National Curriculum's banal label of 'PSE' (Personal and Social Education), primary schools made human relationships central rather than incidental to their work, while the quality of children's activities in art, craft, drama, dance, movement and creative writing attracted justifiable international attention.

Nothing, as I have said, can detract from these achievements. Nor can the right-wing attacks on progressive beliefs in the 1970s and 1990s, or the problems in implementation I note below, be deemed to invalidate what it stood for. I shall return to the question of its continuing relevance towards the end of this chapter.

Meanwhile, given the tendency of the critics of progressivism to portray it as some kind of plague which infected the entire system, it is important to emphasise the disparity between word, or image, and deed. Thus, Plowden in 1967 and HMI in 1978 recorded only a minority of teachers adopting fully fledged progressive practices (CACE 1967: chap. 8; DES 1978), and this picture was sustained in the several subsequent classroom studies to which we have referred at several points in this book, even though – and this is important – to the casual observer the widespread adoption of devices like grouping, and the general air of informality and busyness, might suggest otherwise. In this sense, the images of classrooms which are usually evoked to contrast elementary and primary education, and – in particular – to commend or attack progressive teaching methods, are bound to be misleading, for in capturing the externals of organisation, activity and behaviour they cannot elicit what matters much more: the structure of the learning task, the fine detail of interaction between the teacher and the child, and of course the child's cognitive processes.

In any event, the impact of progressivism was geographically somewhat patchy. It had a number of centres of gravity – Oxfordshire, the West Riding, Leicestershire, London, Hertfordshire and Bristol in particular. Within these areas one could identify many schools whose practice was true to progressive principles. Elsewhere in England the range more typically included, at one end, barely updated elementary practice, at the other, the trappings of progressivism without the flair, coherence or understanding, and in between – perhaps the majority – a pragmatic and reasonably successful mix.

Moreover, progressivism was promoted in a way which effectively guaranteed this uneven distribution. In each of the areas I have mentioned there were influential and frequently charismatic advocates of progressive ideals: Robin Tanner and Edith Moorhouse in Oxfordshire; Alec Clegg in the West Riding; Stewart Mason in Leicestershire; Christian Schiller, John Blackie, Marion Richardson and Mollie Brearley in London; John Newsom in Hertfordshire; Marianne Parry in Bristol. These were all figures of authority who could command resources as effectively as they could command allegiance – chief education officers, inspectors and advisers. Moreover, they mostly knew one another and constituted an effective network of the converted. Into this network were drawn advisers, heads and teachers, mainly from the LEAs in question. They nurtured and explored progressive ideas and practices, and fed off one another's enthusiasms.[16] Away from the network, however, things could be very different. Practices were adopted, but not necessarily comprehended; key texts – like Plowden and many others since then – were read, if at all, not in the original but in digests produced by LEAs, teacher trainers, the unions and the educational press; complex ideas were thus over-simplified or misunderstood; practice was diluted and bowdlerised. Above all, progressivism, without constant prompting and feeding by its leaders, lost the intellectual engagement with the core educational questions that it begged – and which its leaders, at least, had been so keen to explore.

This lack of intellectual engagement could be greatly exacerbated by the authoritarian climate with which the dissemination of progressivism was sometimes associated, notwithstanding its celebration of freedom for the child. Being about unquestioning belief rather than equivocating knowledge it laid itself open to zealotry. It tended to exploit the habits of professional deference and dependence that the primary teaching profession had inherited from the elementary system; and to induce in many teachers a powerful sense of guilt if their practice was not conforming to the required ideal. At worst it smothered dissent under the cloak of pseudo-consensus, projecting primary teachers into a politically correct culture which was the antithesis of what was advocated for children. But then, these characteristics are not unlike those associated with the opposing ideology of 'back to basics'.

Some progressive principles were in any event theoretically or empirically questionable. For example, notions like 'needs', 'development', 'interests', 'enquiry', 'discovery', 'freedom', not to mention the epistemology of themes, topics and integration, all required careful conceptual unpicking; while, as Donaldson's seminal studies showed (1978, 1992), the psychological models of human development which came to underpin and legitimate the progressive philosophy were too vulnerable to criticism on both methodological and theoretical grounds to justify the deference they received.

There was also the vital matter of the practicability of some of the teaching methods commended in the name of progressivism. In the hands of the convinced, the self-evaluative and the competent they could work, sometimes triumphantly. For those under pressure to adopt practices to which they were not fully committed or which they did not fully understand, or who were working in difficult classroom circumstances, or whose personal style happened not to match the professional image, the progressive ideal could be highly problematic as practice, particularly in respect of principles like individualised attention, group-work, the integrated day and topic work. At its worst, the result was by no definition of the word 'progressive' – simply mediocre.

Despite the gap between progressivism in its pure form and what was actually going on in the majority of England's primary schools, primary teachers as a profession had to endure a barrage of media and political misrepresentation as progressivism, and therefore they themselves, became the scapegoat for the country's educational and economic ills. This started shortly after Plowden, with the publication of the Black Papers (Cox and Dyson 1971), reached a peak in 1974–76 with the William Tyndale affair,[17] Bennett's apparent demonstration that traditional methods were more effective than progressive (Bennett 1976) and Callaghan's 'Great Debate', and then resurfaced in response to the publication of the Leeds report in 1991.[18] It was also recycled to justify the exclusion of higher education institutions from teacher training.[19] Primary education had become politicised: and truth, as always, was the first casualty.

Time, geography and – above all – the arrival of the National Curriculum have combined to create an ever-widening gap between those current primary school practices which have their roots in the progressive movement and the ideas which originally sustained them. Most of the key players have moved into the wings, and for many primary teachers Plowden means little or nothing (after all, most newly

appointed teachers today were not even born in 1967) – despite continuing to feature in the demonology of the right. And yet the outward
signs remain intact: the emphasis on display; the abundance of materials
and apparatus to encourage learning by doing; the commitment to
topic work; the organisational and pedagogical device of grouping; the
preference for teaching several subjects simultaneously.

Indeed, as we saw in Chapter 5, research charting the impact of the
National Curriculum is beginning to show that the radical transformation
since the 1988 Act hoped for by government and indeed perceived by
teachers themselves may reach less deeply than we think. Just as we can
now see the elementary legacy alive and well in the continuing dominance
of the nineteenth-century definition of 'the basics', the class-teacher system and the low level of funding, so, beyond the elaborate apparatus of
National Curriculum attainment targets, statements of attainment, levels
and programmes of study, we can also see the practices created from the
ideals of progressivism proving remarkably resilient in teachers' habits of
classroom organisation and pupil–teacher discourse. Progressivism, like
the elementary legacy, is now part of the basic fabric of primary education.

THE THIRD REVOLUTION?

The dates chosen for the snapshots with which this chapter started –
1839, 1870, 1902, 1931, 1967, 1995 – were not wholly arbitrary. It is true
that they conformed roughly to what used to be defined as a generation
– thirty years or so – and in terms of the way ideas come into and out
of the collective consciousness, and their proponents achieve and lose
influence or power, that may or may not be significant, for the dates
also marked significant *political* events in the evolution of our current
system of primary education. Thus, choosing 1839 as our starting point
allowed us to capture both the free-for-all of pre-universal elementary
education and the roots of subsequent reform. The 1870 and 1902 Acts
signalled the achievement of universal elementary education. Hadow in
1931 and Plowden in 1967 expressed the growing unease at the limited
educational vision which was the price paid for this achievement
and offered a richer alternative; they also legitimated 'primary' as a
distinctive part of a longer endeavour to replace 'elementary' as the
sum total of that endeavour. Finally we saw, and are still experiencing,
the rejection of progressive ideals and their replacement, riding
triumphantly on the tide of Thatcherism from 1988 or so, by an updated
version of the earlier instrumentality, consolidated in 1995 for the
remainder of the century, or so at least Dearing hoped.

In this chapter I have tried to identify some of the ideas and events
which have proved particularly influential in shaping our current system
of primary education, ideas and events which have their resonances in

all four of the empirical studies in this volume. In doing so I have confronted a choice about how these matters might be portrayed and explained. To some – notably, the dominant political group of the 1980s – educational history is a tale of constant transformation and progress, not to say revolution, as the elementary archetype is ousted by progressivism which in turn gives way to economic pragmatism and enlightened common sense. This view tends to generate an inflated faith in current achievements and future intentions, a dismissive attitude towards the recent past and an unquestioning presumption of consensus: means may be debated, but not ends. To others, the history of this phase of education is more properly seen as a pendulum which swings back and forth between the poles of 'traditional' and 'progressive', leaving in its wake the polarisation and adversarialism that these two terms connote. In contrast to both, the hybrid model espoused here and in Chapter 2 highlights continuity rather than transformation, conflict, paradox and dilemma rather than consensus, and it invites a more cautious evaluation of what has been and what might be achieved because of the inertia thus generated.

The weakness of the hybrid model is that in looking forward it becomes weighed down by its sense of the problematic, seeing no answers, only questions (while in the other models there tend to be no questions, only answers). Neverthless, albeit unfortunately, the current case of primary education seems indeed sufficiently problematic to justify this stance, and the four empirical studies in this volume lend support to this view.

Thus, we have the persistence of the elementary legacies of grossly discrepant funding, adverse pupil–teacher ratios, an inflexible and possibly outmoded model of staffing, a narrow view of what is 'basic' to education at this stage, and an over-sharp gulf between these 'basics' and the rest of the curriculum, all embedded within an educational culture in which paternalism/maternalism, deference, dependence and a fair measure of anti-intellectualism continue to exert what some may regard as a surprisingly strong influence over the lives and outlooks of many primary teachers. Neither of the two recent revolutions (or quasi-revolutions) in primary education, progressivism and Thatcherism, has done much more than chip at the surface of legacies such as these – and indeed each has to some extent reinforced them – and the tensions and dilemmas for those teachers who seek to pursue an agenda more comprehensive than simply doing what others require remain as sharp as ever.

Thus, therefore, the considerable achievements of progressivism – transformed physical and interpersonal contexts for learning, heuristic approaches to teaching, reduced curriculum boundaries, a focus on the affective and the creative – have by and large left intact, or have been diluted by, the more fundamental institutional and curricular structures inherited from the nineteenth century. If we turn now to the Thatcherite revolution, if that is what it will turn out to be, or the period since the 1988 Act, we see a similar tendency. Questions have been raised about the structure, content and manageability of the curriculum, but not its longer-term rationale. The curriculum thus restructured combines the partial modernisation of science, technology and information technology with the reaffirmation not just of the elementary curriculum but also its grammar-school counterpart, as the various subject lobbies extend their hegemony from secondary to primary education. Assessment is defined in the traditional form of the test, and – significantly – the test points (7, 11, 14 and 16) are exactly those proposed in the anti-progressive Black Papers of the 1960s and 1970s (specifically, Cox and Boyson 1975). Indeed, the extent to which the 1980s policy agenda was in part a final and comprehensive assault on progressivism is manifested almost daily in the political rhetoric of the time, from Prime Minister Major's gauntlet-throwing 'The progressives have had their say, and they've had their day' to his triumphalist Eastbourne litany of 'Knowledge. Discipline. Tables. Sums. Dates. Shakespeare. British history. Standard English. Grammar. Spelling. Marks. Tests. Good manners' (Major 1992) – all of them, according to the right-wing demonology, despised and rejected by the progressives. At the same time, Dearing uses the device of the Key Stage to confirm the rigidity of the traditional infant/junior/primary/secondary structure, and the government underscores this by refusing to intervene in the matter of secondary/primary funding discrepancies, thus making it difficult to explore more than marginal staffing alternatives to the class-teacher model, and by continuing to stonewall on the matter of primary pupil–teacher ratios and class sizes.

I have used the word 'revolution' to describe what has happened since 1988, though cautiously. Clearly, the Conservative governments of the 1980s and 1990s would have their policies and legislation rated as nothing less. In reality it is far too early to form a judgement about this, especially as the price politicians have to accept for politicising education to this extent and imposing reform with such cavalier ruthlessness is that their policies can be overturned, equally ruthlessly and equally quickly. In any case, the other studies in this book should indicate the need for caution in such matters.

Moreover, there is no simple measure for assessing the impact of a major educational initiative or movement. In the 1970s and 1980s there was pretty widespread espousal, within the primary professional community at least, of progressive *ideas*; yet at the levels of school and classroom *practice* and in the curriculum as experienced by primary children, the picture was far less convincing. Similarly, though by the mid-1990s a national curriculum of nine subjects was in place in every primary school, together with attendant procedures for assessment, budgetary delegation and school governance, such empirical research as by that time was beginning to examine the working-out of the National Curriculum in the classroom – for example, the CICADA study reported in Chapter 5 – suggested an emerging picture of complexity and unevenness which could eventually match that of the 1970s and 1980s, notwithstanding the surface uniformity which the imposition of the National Curriculum Orders produced.

This is probably just as well. Though neither group would wish to acknowledge the similarity, the government which introduced the 1988 reforms and many of the key figures in the post-war progressive movement had one characteristic in common: the unshakeable belief that they, and they alone, were right, and that being so they could legitimately expect teachers in primary schools to conform to their views. Such hubris should never go unchallenged and in any case usually carries the seeds of its own downfall.

The challenge to the 1988 reforms has come on a number of fronts. The manner of their introduction provoked widespread opposition at its apparent disregard for democratic principles and the extent to which it shifted the balance of power towards central government and eliminated the system's checks and balances (for example, Simon and Chitty 1993). The National Curriculum was challenged on empirical grounds in respect of the viability and manageability of its content (for instance, Campbell and Neill 1994a) and the validity of its contingent assessment programme (for example, Gipps 1993). It was criticised on fundamental ethical and conceptual grounds (for instance, Kelly 1990; O'Hear and White 1993). At the same time, both commentators and practitioners have demonstrated a fair measure of ambivalence towards the changes. Thus, to some, the prescriptions of national government were a much-needed corrective to the local culture of patronage and political correctness; in place of confusion about exactly what the primary curriculum should constitute, there was relative clarity; instead of the hand-to-mouth improvisation which often characterised curriculum planning in other than historically codified areas like mathematics there was a welcome degree of structure and guidance at the levels of both overall framework and operational detail; and even the least popular provisions, those concerning assessment, had their supporters.

In this respect, the comparison of professional dilemmas and dilemma sources which emerged from comparison in Chapter 5 of teacher interview data from 1986, 1988 and 1992 may have added significance. We noted there that the main source of the pressure to conform to particular values and practices, to which primary teachers, one way or another, have long been subject, has shifted in certain important areas from inside the profession to outside it. We suggested that this could make the handling of such dilemmas more rather than less straightforward in as far as they might generate collective solidarity rather than individual *Angst*. By the same token, though in matters like curriculum content teachers obviously have less autonomy than in the days when decisions about curriculum and assessment were left to LEAs and schools, in less obvious respects they may actually have greater autonomy than hitherto. For within the new framework of legal requirements there may be a greater-than-anticipated room for manoeuvre at the level of the curriculum as transacted in classrooms now that the locus of power and influence has shifted from the LEA to the school, and from the head as keeper of ethos, curriculum and pedagogy to the staff as collective decision-makers and problem-solvers.

TOWARDS THE MILENNIUM

Not only is a perspective on the past a prerequisite for understanding the present – in primary education no less than in other aspects of this country's culture – but it also conditions one's view of the future. If a study of the emergence of our present system of primary education teaches us to be cautious in our claims about what has been achieved so far, then we need to be equally careful in how we approach the period to come.

Means or ends?

Despite this slightly pessimistic sentiment, nothing in education should be taken as given or predetermined, and I want to end this chapter by tentatively identifying those aspects of primary education where choices are both necessary and possible. These fall into two contingent groups, a set of questions about *means*, and a set of questions about purposes or *ends*. The latter are in a fundamental sense of far greater importance, and indeed should properly speaking be resolved before one considers the manner in which primary education should be presented. Nevertheless, it is with the means that I wish to start, because it can fairly be argued that the structural, organisational and pedagogical context of schooling does not merely reflect educational values, it also shapes them, and in this sense educational means and ends are inseparable. If, therefore, so much about the future is unknowable we need above all to define structures for primary education which will *enable* rather than constrain, and it is to this principle that I now turn in identifying what seem to be some of the dilemmas to be confronted and resolved as we seek to construct a version of primary education which will meet the demands of the twenty-first century.

Schooling continuous or divided?

How far are the established divisions between infant, junior and secondary still valid? The divisions are rooted in the pre-war rationalisation of the muddled administrative legacy of the nineteenth century; but they were reinforced by the 1988 Education Reform Act's delineation of Key Stages and sharpened up in the interim and final Dearing Reports. The tension here, it seems, is between preserving what is seen as the distinctive but vulnerable ethos and agenda of pre-adolescent education, especially early years education, and addressing notions of educational continuity, progression and coherence (these latter being, perhaps, among the more important contributions of HMI before it was subsumed within OFSTED). The tension is acute because of the historical tendency for primary schools to be subservient – in terms of status, finance and power – to secondary, and for secondary imperatives to shape primary decisions on curriculum, assessment and organisation, most notably during the period of 11-plus selection, but also, in the view of some, after the arrival of the National Curriculum. Such subservience was paralleled among teachers themselves, until the demise of the training colleges (where until the 1970s nearly all primary teachers were trained), and the shift in the balance of undergraduate and graduate training, began to erode the double divide of culture and professional qualification. Awareness of these legacies, and the ever-present threat of secondary hegemony in respect of values, curriculum, assessment and pedagogy, prompt many in primary education to opt for separatism – and indeed for the erection of defensive barriers to resist any dilution of what is thought to be most distinctively and vulnerably 'primary'. However, separatism, whatever its benefits, also produces isolation and parochialism. Separatism, moreover, legitimates discrepancies in funding.

The same dilemma is becoming increasingly prominent within the primary phase itself. I showed earlier in this chapter how the first stage of primary education has always been a distinctive and even a semi-detached one, and how the 1988 Act's Key Stages legitimated and consolidated the division between 'infants' and 'juniors'. The Act has had another consequence, that of marshalling early years commentators against the established holistic notion of primary education. This has happened because the idea of a subject-based curriculum, let alone a curriculum of nine such subjects, was much more alien to early years thinking and practice than to that of later years, being seen as diametrically opposed to prevailing developmental models of learning. Moreover, some of the more prominent classroom research in which recent critiques of primary pedagogy have been grounded (for example, the influential ORACLE and ILEA studies of Galton *et al.* 1980a, 1980b and Mortimore *et al.* 1988) have focused on the 7–11 age range. Some in the early years movement have felt their values threatened further by the apparent acquiescence shown by their later years colleagues, and this has since been heightened by gender-consciousness as a mostly female early years community sees in later years education, and more generally in the professional hierarchy of primary education and indeed the academic study of primary education, the dominance of male agendas, values, language, realities and of course power.[20] In the face of such a double betrayal – by government and by others in primary education – the establishment of early years education as an institutionally as well as philosophically separate stage of education becomes increasingly attractive to some of its proponents, especially when the growth of pre-school and nursery provision and its increasing political prominence provide those working in the Key Stage 1 area (5–7) with both an alternative and perhaps more appropriate reference group to Key Stage 2 (7–11) and a more promising power-base.[21]

The choices to be confronted, therefore, are several. Is unity of purpose throughout compulsory education appropriate? If so, should it be reflected in unity of structure (bearing in mind, for example, that the separation of primary schooling from secondary is by no means a universal practice outside Britain)? If structural separation is appropriate, where should it come – at age 11 as argued by Hadow, at age 13 as postulated by Plowden; and within the phases so organised, is further division appropriate, and if so at what points: age 5, age 7 or age 9? What should be the relationship between what are currently defined as statutory and non-statutory early years provision – that is to say, Key Stage 1 on the one hand and pre-school and nursery provision on the other? How far should such subdivisions be taken: to the extent of an appropriate level of age-range differentiation within a common structure and a common framework of purposes and values, producing a unitary phase of pre-adolescent education; or to the extent of a sharper differentiation between, say, autonomous and distinct early years schools or centres catering for children aged 2 or 3 to 7 and truncated 7–11 schools sandwiched between the contrasting structures and philosophies of early years and secondary education?

Personally, I believe that fragmentation of the primary phase would be disastrous, for it would not only militate against coherence and progression in the young child's education and consolidate the current debilitating funding discrepancies, but it would also greatly weaken the impact of the primary community as an effective lobby just at the point when its influence is beginning to be felt in National Curriculum deliberations, in teacher education, in the Commons Education Committee, and even, up to a point, in government. I understand the growing sense of frustration among early years experts at the continuing failure of policy-makers, and indeed others in primary education, to acknowledge – let alone to speak to – their condition. The charge of secondary hegemony in respect of the National Curriculum in primary schools is well merited, especially as it bears on children in Key Stage 1 and those 4- and 5-year-olds not yet subject to the National Curriculum but already inevitably affected by its provisions. However, the solution to these problems is not secession from the primary 'union' but a much more strenuous effort by both early and later years practitioners and researchers to understand and accommodate to each other's perspectives and reach a shared and coherent definition of the purposes and character of pre-secondary education.

Funding: historical precedent or future need?

At the time of writing it is generally accepted – except by central government – that primary schools are seriously underfunded in respect of the tasks they are required to undertake, and this is true whether their tasks are defined narrowly, as in the Dearing Report, or more generously, as is actually implied in the first chapter of the 1988 Education Reform Act from which the National Curriculum, and hence Dearing's revisions, stem. The range and complexity of the learning agenda for primary schools as currently conceived cannot adequately be delivered by the combination of large classes and the singularly inflexible class-teacher system which primary schools have inherited from their elementary forebears. The evidence presented to the 1994 enquiry of the Commons Select Committee on Education strongly supports this proposition. At the same time we know that any significant easing of the current financial climate is unlikely, and that the economic and political risks of a policy commitment to activity-led funding for primary as well as for secondary schools are considerable. There are, after all, some 20,000 primary schools in England, compared with 4,000 secondary; some 4.5 million primary pupils compared with under 3 million secondary. But this does not weaken the argument as such. Even on a forward projection of the current National Curriculum, the notion that schools delivering the first two Key Stages of a nine- or ten-subject compulsory curriculum need up to half the resources given to schools delivering the second two Key Stages of the same curriculum is difficult, if not impossible to defend. The question to be confronted here, therefore, is whether primary education should continue to be funded on the basis of historical precedent allied to suspect claims about the relative 'needs' of younger and older pupils or on the basis of a proper reassessment of the tasks which primary and secondary schools have to undertake and the kinds and quantities of expertise and other resources which these require. Since many of the needs-based claims are essentially circular – that is, to say that a 16-year-old needs specialist teaching in small classes while a 9-year-old does not is simply to say that because history has thrown up such discrepancies then they have *ipso facto* educational validity – and since it is manifestly the case that the tasks of primary schools are now considerably more complex and diverse than they were when the current funding discrepancies first emerged, then the argument for a total reassessment of the relationship between tasks and resources in the two phases of compulsory education is irresistible. At the time of writing, the government has just announced that it is not prepared to undertake such a reassessment (House of Commons 1994b).

Teaching roles: the whole or the parts?

The origins of the prevailing teaching role in primary schools – the class teacher who teaches the whole curriculum to all children in his or her class for a year or more – are economic rather than educational, as we have seen. However, generations of primary teachers have not only come to terms with the challenges and constraints of the class-teacher system, but have also identified in the system considerable advantages both for them and their pupils, most of which can be encapsulated in the notion of holism.

I do not wish to rehearse here my earlier and fairly substantial critique of the class-teacher system (Alexander 1984: chaps. 2 and 3); nor, however, do I wish to imply that the holistic concern with the child's development, learning and curriculum is misplaced. Rather, I wish to argue that here, too, there are dilemmas.

Thus, for example, we must confront the question of how far the scope and complexity of the modern primary curriculum exceeds what it is reasonable to expect the professional knowledge of the one-class teacher to encompass. The 1992 DES primary discussion paper (Alexander *et al.* 1992: paras 146–9), drawing on the Leeds research (Alexander 1992: 204) identified a continuum of four teaching roles (as opposed to the existing two of class teacher and subject co-ordinator) which between them could accommodate the requirements of a modern primary curriculum, in both its early and later years manifestations: *generalist, consultant, semi-specialist* and *specialist*. It did not argue – as some claimed – for the abandoning of the class-teacher system any more than it argued that this system should at all costs be preserved. Nor did it say – as, again was claimed – that children in years five and six should be taught by specialists. Instead it proposed an approach to primary staffing which takes no primary teaching role – generalist, specialist or other – as given and starts instead with each school analysing its range of educational tasks, identifying the kinds of expertise these require, and constructing a profile of professional roles which match them as closely as possible.

What is now clear is that the primary discussion paper's continuum, novel though it was at the time, conceals an even greater range of variants on the themes of both full and partial responsibility (Richards 1994), and that the notions of generalist/specialist can apply to aspects of the work of primary schools other than the curriculum. Some of these variants, though subject to the severe constraints of historical funding formulae, have been explored by primary schools in the period since the 1992 primary discussion paper. The debate on this matter remains open, though for as long as funding is tied, as it currently is, to an assumption that the class-teacher role is the sole or dominant one in primary schools, there will be limited room for manoeuvre.

Pedagogy: fitness for what purpose?

The larger part of this book is concerned with the character and challenges of teaching in primary classrooms: the decisions and dilemmas teachers face on a day-to-day basis as they seek to reconcile values, expectations and circumstances; the strategies they adopt in response to these; the tasks children encounter as teachers translate curriculum goals and requirements into pupil learning experiences; the way children and their teachers use the time at their disposal, both globally in respect to the balance of the curriculum, and at the minute-to-minute level of the structure and sequence of lessons and their constituent activities; and the nature of those interactions between teacher and pupil which are such a prominent feature of classroom life and such a vital element in learning.

From being 'historically neglected' in Britain (Simon 1983), pedagogy has assumed much greater prominence in recent years as a field for research, study and debate. The studies in this volume are part of a much larger domain of enquiry into primary teaching which has grown extensively in the years since Bennett's lone and controversial foray of 1976. By 1992 it was possible for the DES primary discussion paper to bring together a set of propositions about the likely prerequisites for improved classroom practice (Alexander *et al.* 1992: 37–41) based on a synthesis of what by the winter of 1991 was a considerable body of empirical material. The specific propositions related to the following themes:

- teacher professional knowledge: of children, individually and collectively, of subject matter, of pedagogical practices and of the social, institutional and cultural contexts of teaching and learning;
- curriculum planning: at the levels of the whole school and the individual class; for pedagogy broadly defined rather than content alone; and for the long, medium and short term;
- curriculum balance as a multifaceted concept, encompassing curriculum areas and subjects; parity in quality among these; the way

content is conceived and encountered (subjects, themes and topics); and the cross-curricular generic activities of which learning tasks are constituted;

- the context of classroom values, norms and relationships;
- expectations of individual children and assumptions about particular groups of children;
- the deployment of teacher time in the classroom, particularly relating to pupil diagnosis and assessment;
- the construction of learning tasks which promote different kinds and levels of learning: revision, practice, new skills and understanding; creative and imaginative activity;
- assessing children's learning, both formative and summative, and focusing on learning processes as well as their outcomes;
- providing pupils with constructive and informative feedback;
- the nature and application of a pedagogical repertoire for primary education, and the judgement to deploy this appropriately, on the basis of 'fitness for purpose';
- the specific strategies of whole-class teaching, groupwork, including collaborative groupwork, and teaching one to one;
- the generic teaching techniques, underpinning all broad teaching strategies, of observation and listening; asking different kinds of questions; explaining; instructing; providing oral and written feedback; managing space, time and behaviour.

The propositions in this section of the primary discussion paper were grounded in an extensive trawl of the classroom research undertaken in the previous decade or so, mainly in the United Kingdom, and with reference to both published and unpublished material from HMI. Lest that imply that the list offered was simply an atheoretical 'best buy' based on a random and not necessarily compatible collection of research studies, let it be stressed that the propositions also had a consistent theoretical perspective grounded, in part, in a reassessment of the dominant pedagogical ideas of the 1960s and 1970s, particularly the influence on these of Jean Piaget, the Swiss zoologist-turned-psychologist whose massive output provided much of the theoretical core of the training received by that generation of primary teachers for whom, in turn, the Plowden Report of 1967 provided both inspiration and legitimation.

Because the Piagetian model isolated in considerable detail the stages, characteristics and approximate ages of cognitive *development*, together with attendant stage-independent processes like assimilation and accommodation, the theory of *teaching* derived from this was essentially applied child development rather than pedagogy in its broader sense; and since Piaget's studies had been of individual children interacting with materials and/or with adults on a one-to-one basis, the derived theory of teaching sought to replicate this individualisation in settings – large classes – where clearly this was difficult if not impossible, and had little guidance to offer on the practice of teaching other than that it should provide an environment and stimulus for such individualised and essentially self-directed learning. In contrast, where this theory focused on the interaction of learners and their environment, its revaluation highlighted the interaction of learners with one another and with the teacher, stressing the social nature of learning and the critical role of talk. Where the earlier model implied that the learning task should be matched to the child's existing stage of development and legitimated the notion of 'readiness', the alternative argued that the function of teaching was to accelerate development rather than merely keep pace with it (and indeed this counter to the 1960s/1970s view, a paraphrase of Vygotsky, was offered as the final proposition in the 1992 primary discussion paper's list referred to above). Where earlier models of teaching had tended to encourage a 'hands-off' role of teacher-as-facilitator, the alternative presented the teacher as intervener, fulfilling a critical role in mediating between pupil and task. Where the earlier model saw developed knowledge structures as incompatible with the developing child's ways of making sense of the world, its successor viewed these as a continuum, able to be bridged, and needing to be bridged, by 'scaffolded' learning tasks provided by the teacher which carry the child's understanding forward across the 'zone of proximal development'.

Such ideas were not new: Vygotsky, the key figure in what Bruner and Haste (1987) called the 'quiet revolution' in developmental psychology which generated these ideas, died as long ago as 1934, and though his work was for many years banned by the Soviet authorities it has been available in the West since the 1960s (Vygotsky 1962, 1978), the era during which the very different perspectives of Piaget were beginning to exert their maximum influence on primary education in the United Kingdom, especially through teacher training courses and published schemes in mathematics. Bruner himself had presaged the 'revolution' in his seminal texts arguing the essentially social nature of learning and the accessibility of knowledge structures 'to any child at any stage of development' subject to the teacher's ability to provide a 'courteous translation' of the knowledge to be encountered (Bruner 1963, 1966), ideas which were influential in several of the Schools Council curriculum projects in the 1970s. This raises the interesting question, which I have explored in detail elsewhere (Alexander 1984: chaps. 2 and 4) of why Piaget's work was adopted with such uncritical enthusiasm (while Vygotsky's and Bruner's was relegated to textbook footnotes) during an era when, generally, theory and research bearing on education were viewed by many teachers as largely irrelevant to their task.

Be that as it may, by the late 1980s an alternative, 'constructivist' learning paradigm was emerging and, equally important, the now substantial body of observational data on primary teachers and children at work in classrooms, ethnographic, qualititative and quantitative, provided evidence from several different starting points to support the new paradigm's emphasis on the context of social interaction. It therefore seemed to offer the prospect of squaring the circle of pedagogical theory, for the time being at least. The 1992 primary discussion paper's synthesis of pedagogical propositions referred to above reflected these developments as they were documented by late 1991.

In looking ahead, we have now to ask where the pedagogy of primary education should be heading. For some, the key questions about learning and effective teaching are now largely settled and the most important – and difficult – task now is to translate these into strategies for helping teachers currently in post to develop their pedagogic skill and understanding, and for training the next generation of teachers more effectively than the last (which of course is a comment on teacher training, not on teachers). Thus, Bennett, Wragg and their colleagues at Exeter have produced a succession of texts and training manuals on some of the generic teaching skills like questioning, explaining and organising collaborative groupwork (Dunne and Bennett 1990; Bennett and Carré 1993; Wragg 1993a, 1993b; Wragg and Brown, 1993; Brown and Wragg 1993; Wragg and Dunne 1994).

Work such as this not only focuses on the core interactions of which teaching is constituted, but is also premised on the importance of knowledge of curriculum subject matter (Shulman 1986, 1987), in turn grounded in a comprehensive 'map' of the subject as a whole, thus underscoring the constructivist view that the gap between the child's developing understandings and developed subject structures can and should be bridged. Behind such a view is a concept of education as being concerned with cultural engagement and cultural transmission, so that learning in schools requires the interaction of the learner and the world of ideas, not merely the learner and the physical environment.

Others are less sanguine. Galton (1989, 1994), another leading figure in the primary classroom research movement of the 1980s, sees primary teaching as in a continuing state of crisis and is strongly critical of the models of pedagogy which he believed underpinned the Leeds research and the 1992 primary discussion paper, though rather ignoring the fact that his own ORACLE project (Galton *et al.* 1980a, 1980b) itself exemplified some of the conceptual and empirical weaknesses of which he was so critical in the work of others. For Kelly (1990) a model of teacher education which makes subject matter pre-eminent – as had government requirements since 1984 (DES 1984, 1989c; DFE 1992b, 1993a) – was simply taking as given the subject-led version of the primary curriculum espoused for party-political reasons by central government, and distorting or denying the developmental imperatives which should be at the heart of the early years teacher's task. For Drummond (1993), the burgeoning teacher-effectiveness industry carried dangers of presenting pedagogy as mere technique, disembedded from questions of educational value and purpose.

The debate, therefore, is far from over, and in any event, even if one distances oneself a little from the quest for unitary pedagogical paradigms there remains a formidable list of problems in primary classrooms which need to be addressed, by both researchers and practitioners. Thus, on the basis of the Leeds research, extrapolating from the two studies in this book and the project's other investigations, we identified the following agenda (Alexander 1992: 195):

Improving our understanding of the children we teach:

- Raising teacher expectations of all children
- Eliminating stereotyping
- Focusing on the full range of pupil needs
- Looking at children's potential as well as their problems
- Sharpening the skills of diagnosis and assessment
- Adopting classroom strategies which maximise teachers' time to exercise these skills

Promoting children's learning:

- Shifting the thrust of debate about classroom practice from teacher style and physical context to interaction, learning processes and outcomes
- Rethinking groupwork
- Rethinking multiple curriculum focus teaching
- Maximising opportunities for productive teacher–pupil and pupil–pupil interaction
- Making teacher–pupil talk task-focused and cognitively challenging
- Balancing encouragement with informative, and formative, feedback
- Managing time in the classroom as economically as possible
- Matching learning task and child
- Matching learning task and classroom context

Defining and organising the curriculum:

- Addressing curriculum balance as a system-wide issue
- Ensuring that all subjects, regardless of their time allocation or perceived importance, receive the attention and resources they need in order to secure quality in their teaching
- Examining curriculum balance in the classroom in terms of the mix and balance of cross-curricular generic activities as well as subjects and the hours and minutes these are allocated

The wider school context:

- Exploiting and developing each teacher's specialist skills
- Extending the cross-school roles of teaching staff, especially in relation to curriculum support, review and development
- Delegating responsibilities and securing participative decision-making
- Addressing management as a whole-school rather than a merely hierarchical issue – all teachers are, or can be, managers
- Making questions of management strategy contingent on prior questions of educational purpose
- Giving professional development high priority and securing a mixed INSET economy

Schools and parents:

- Developing parent–teacher relationships which reconcile the rhetoric of partnership with the distinct responsibilities of each

Of course, much of the latter part of this list is not about pedagogy as usually defined, but I have left it intact to remind us that, however coherent and convincing a theory of teaching, its successful application in classrooms cannot ignore the wider school context within which the teacher works, and the power of this context (as we saw in Chapters 2, 3 and 4) to influence and/or constrain what the teacher does within what some perhaps erroneously call the 'privacy' of their classrooms. In this respect, it is perhaps offering the note of caution that a model of teaching defined too exclusively in terms of classroom interaction may be as likely to founder in its application as one which focuses too exclusively on processes of child development.

However, though the Leeds research portrayed and sought to explain classroom action not just in its own terms but also as a response to the culture of the school and LEA, it – like all pedagogic research – was constrained by the limitations of the methods it employed, and, even more fundamental, by the model of teaching which informed these methods and the particular aspects of teaching it selected for study. Thus, for example, systematic observation tends to atomise classroom action and divest it of the meanings it has for the actors; qualitative research may be both in obvious senses highly subjective (though of course subjective judgement plays a part in every single research paradigm yet identified or likely to be identified) and over-restricted by the small number of cases used; much research on pedagogy focuses far more – and perhaps to excess – on the teacher rather than the learner, thereby neglecting, for example, the extent to which pedagogy is a function of the child's strategies as well as the teacher's, the considerable diversity of understandings which members of a class or group of children bring to, and take from, a given teaching encounter, and the element of negotiation which characterises the whole enterprise. Nor is the broader debate about whether teaching is an art, a craft or a science as pointless as some suggest, since the dominant research paradigms tend, often tacitly, to opt for the latter and therefore to impose adult scientific rationality on activities which may be shaped – and therefore best explained – by entirely other means, and indeed may be more subtle than any such paradigm is able to encompass.

All this any researcher knows well enough, and it is standard fare in critiques of classroom research. Unfortunately, what some such critiques offer, however, is not so much a constructive nudge towards a better balance in the studies they criticise, born of a shared recognition that none of us in this business can do more than provide an incomplete picture of that which we seek to portray, as an insistence that their own bias, their own methodology, and their own definitions of what teaching is about are somehow more comprehensive, more neutral, and more correct than anybody else's. In fact, the best they can offer is a different picture, a different shot at the truth, a different selection of pieces from the vast and complex jigsaw that is teaching: it may be better, it may be worse, or it may just be different. Galton's surprisingly virulent and misinformed attack on the Leeds research and the 1992 primary discussion paper (Galton 1994) seems to display just this lapse in consciousness.

These sorts of considerations lay behind the choice of *Versions of Primary Education* as this book's title. The five studies are 'versions' of primary education in as far as each of them focuses on some aspects of primary education rather than others, employs a particular perspective or combination of perspectives, and applies its own research procedures. The five versions do not combine to form a whole, in the way that, say, a five-stage process of colour printing does, but instead represent attempts to reach a destination by different routes. Other routes are equally worth trying, or perhaps more so.

Thus the task ahead for those involved in the study of pedagogy is essentially one of continuing the journey in the hope that each attempt will add to the sum of our collective insights and contribute to the task of improving the quality of teaching and learning. In particular, I would like to see the common ground between radically different approaches to classroom study – for example Bennett *et al.* (1984), Pollard (1985) and Armstrong (1980), to cite three which are very different yet in their different ways equally illuminating – more carefully, and less aggressively, explored than hitherto. Especially, though the 1970s and 1980s saw a movement away from child study towards a focus on the teacher and the strategies the teacher deployed (a necessary corrective, as argued above, to the 'applied child development' model of pedagogy), the balance needs now to be tilted back, especially now that study of the learner can apply a wider range of perspectives than was on offer during the developmentalist 1960s. Moreover, the legal reality of the National Curriculum makes it essential that we build up our understanding of how the young learner engages with versions of curriculum which were peripheral to the concerns of the earlier studies.

Perhaps even more important, though we can and must isolate the processes and skills which a teacher needs in order successfully to promote learning, pedagogy is not simply a technical matter, reducible to some ostensibly value-free science. Pedagogy is perhaps the most powerful and pervasive way in which a school expresses and helps the child engage with the values and purposes which drive and shape both the curriculum in the classroom and the wider community of the school. The 1992 primary discussion paper's use of the craft principle of 'fitness for purpose' was taken by some (such as Drummond 1993; Carr 1994) to invite an unprincipled and narrowly pragmatic approach to teaching. This was certainly not its intention (though the political climate of the time may have encouraged such an interpretation). On the contrary, it sought to make precisely the opposite point, that the most basic test of the rightness of one's teaching is the degree to which it is true to the educational values which the teaching claims to manifest. It is to these matters, therefore, that we should now turn.

Curriculum: what basics, whose balance?

In December 1993, the final Dearing Report argued that after the trauma of implementing a new and in some respects unmanageable national curriculum, teachers and children were entitled to a period of stability, and that, once implemented, the 1995 statutory orders should remain unchanged for five years. While for battle-scarred primary teachers such a cease-fire was undoubtedly welcome, Dearing – in this recommendation and throughout his two reports – presumed, in my view both wrongly and dangerously, that the more fundamental questions about the character of the primary curriculum should now be regarded as settled. If there *is* to be a period of relative stability, therefore, I would wish to see it used, in part, to look to the next century and address the kinds of questions which government educational policy from 1987 so effectively pre-empted.

Thus, if we take the principles of 'breadth' and 'balance' which emerged first in HMI documents during the 1980s and were subsequently offered as guiding principles for the National Curriculum, we should note immediately that the ineffable blandness of what Kelly and Blenkin (1993) have called 'breadthandbalance' (like 'aimsandobjectives' in the sixties one portmanteau term to elide and make meaningless two concepts which are related yet also quite distinct) conceals value questions of profound importance. Since 1987, the *breadth* or scope of the primary curriculum has been defined in terms of a canon of nine subjects, and its *balance* has been conceived quantitatively in terms of time notionally allocated to each of these. The result is a curious definition of 'balance': three subjects get the lion's share of the time available, the nine are arranged in a temporal pecking order (as they always have been, of course), and the vital questions about the educational values which inform these arrangements are avoided. The rationale goes, tautologously, as follows: every child is entitled to a broad and balanced curriculum; the National Curriculum is every child's statutory entitlement; therefore the National Curriculum is a broad and balanced curriculum. From 1988, then, curriculum breadth and balance became non-negotiable concepts: they meant what government and its agencies said they meant. For schools, therefore, breadth and balance became *logistical* rather than *philosophical* imperatives – the challenge of fitting all that was required by law into the time available.

The Dearing moratorium – if it is observed (and five years is an exceptionally long time in educational politics) – allows us to consider alternative notions of breadth and balance. Elsewhere (Alexander 1994) I suggested three of the several possible starting points for this alternative analysis. The first was to develop and apply the notion of generic curriculum activities which emerged from the Leeds research and is explored empirically in Chapter 4. For example, we noted there that the large amounts of time devoted to mathematics and language seemed to be the least efficiently used and that those curriculum activities which most successfully maintained children's attention were those which involved interaction with other people. This prompted us to question not just the assumption that by allocating large amounts of time to these subjects one ensures their quality, but also the more fundamental supposition that apportioning time is all that curriculum balance is about. Beyond this, the notion of generic activities allows us to ask another question: which 'reality' of curriculum – as conceived by government and teachers or as experienced by children – matters most when we are debating questions of curricular breadth and balance? It also prompts us to examine the extent to which the questions concern pedagogy more broadly defined rather than content alone. For the importance we attach to the generic activities of, say, structured talk and collaboration, must in part be conditioned first by our knowledge that they both happen to be essential tools of learning – any learning, in any subject – and in part by the practical realisation that well-organised collaborative work can help the teacher manage time more effectively. Thus, regardless of broader assumptions about the place in the National Curriculum of speaking and listening (English Attainment Target 1) there could be an overriding *pedagogical* imperative to ensure that it features more prominently and pervasively than its presentation as a component of one subject allows.

The second starting point for reassessing breadth and balance which I proposed was also grounded in the Leeds research, though not just in the material included in this book. In the final report on the Leeds project we noted

> At each level of the system we found claims to breadth and balance liable to be undermined by countervailing policies and practices: by LEA special projects favouring some curriculum areas at the expense of others; in INSET provision; in funding allocations; in the distribution of posts of responsibility in schools; in the status of postholders and the time they had to undertake their curriculum leadership responsibilities; in the areas of the curriculum subjected to curriculum review and development; in teacher expertise; and above all in the quality of children's classroom experiences. In the end, curriculum breadth and balance are less about time allocation than the diversity and challenge of what the child encounters; and *if the goals of breadth and balance are to be achieved in the classroom they must be pursued at every other level of the system as well.*
>
> (Alexander 1992: 141, my italics)

Curriculum balance, then, is a product of decisions taken across the system as a whole, not merely within the school and classroom. It is a matter for policy-makers as well as teachers.

Thirdly, I proposed that we should cease to treat the important and universal notion of a core curriculum as synonymous with English, mathematics and science, and instead conceive of the core in more comprehensive and less bounded terms. In few other countries is the core curriculum defined so narrowly, and the commoner approach is to have a more generous notion of core which at the same time is specified in rather less detail. The problem with defining the core of the curriculum as core subjects is the 'winner takes all' effect on the curriculum as a whole: every aspect of mathematics, for example, however peripheral in relation even to political objectives like the country's economic vitality it actually is, becomes by this inclusive formula more important than aspects of other subjects which by any reasonable definition are of much greater significance.

We have this country's historical 3Rs fixation to thank for this somewhat restricted concept of a core curriculum, and perceptions will be slow to change. On this Dearing appeared at first to provide a window of opportunity. In recommending (Dearing 1993a) that each of the original subject orders be revised to divide its existing content into a statutory core and optional studies, he appeared to allow for the possibility of moving to a notion of a core curriculum which includes a far wider array of critically important knowledge, understanding and skill, drawn from the curriculum as a whole, than the idea of core subjects allows. This interpretation was soon scotched as it became clear that the core/options idea was simply a device for consolidating and securing the more effective delivery of the National Curriculum as first conceived, and that this was to be achieved by strengthening the three-subject core at the expense of the other six subjects. However, treating core curriculum and core subjects as synonymous is so palpably suspect, on conceptual as well as educational grounds, that it requires reappraisal. In practice, too, it might be argued that the core/non-core distinction has proved as damaging to curriculum coherence and consistency (two more 1980s HMI watchwords neutralised by adopting them as policy) as the old but perennially powerful basics/non-basics distinction traced in this chapter and Chapter 2.

Nor can the long-standing notion of 'the basics' continue to escape scrutiny. We have to ask how far a nineteenth-century preoccupation with a narrow spectrum of literacy and numeracy provides all that should be implied by a notion of 'basic skills' for the twenty-first century.[22] What, beyond this, is implied if we accept that tomorrow's adults will have needs, every bit as pressing, for the broader skills which will enable them to cope with the complexities and tensions of life in a pluralist and divided society, with the challenges of living in a fragile democracy set within an overcrowded world, with the need to relate to other people constructively and with empathy, with the need to engage with and benefit from imaginative and creative endeavour, with the need to find common cause with the rest of humanity, and with the need to invest life with meaning and purpose?

To argue for a reassessment of the basics is not to assert that the perennial commitment to the 3Rs is wrong. Oracy and literacy, in particular, seem to me to retain an unshakeable case for being accorded the highest priority, for they not only underpin the rest of the curriculum and therefore enable the child's learning across a wide spectrum of activities, but they are also vital ingredients in human discourse and the individual's meaningful participation in society. Rather, it seems reasonable to ask whether as a judgement of what is 'basic' to a modern education the 3Rs definition can be regarded, after over a century of continuous and unquestioned use, as adequate. In any event, it rests on unexamined but suspect assumptions about the separation of cognition from affectivity and skills from their application. It is also worth reminding ourselves that the 3Rs view of the basics was directed not at the social and cultural plurality which is typical of today's primary schools, but at the working classes alone; and it was devised not to enable or liberate those working classes, but to contain and control them.

There are, therefore, two kinds of question to ask about the received definition of the basics in relation to future models of the primary curriculum and their relationship to life in the twenty-first century. First, even if this definition is seen to retain its validity, what can be said about the particular understandings and skills which it incorporates: for example, the heavy emphasis on computation, reading and writing and the relatively lower value placed on other aspects of language, notably the spoken word, and other forms of literacy – for example, in respect of information technology, film, television and other audio-visual media?[23] Second, how far are its boundaries too sharply drawn when one looks to the claims of other skills and understandings necessary for learning and for life?

Primary education for what?

It will be understood that none of the questions I have posed so far can be adequately addressed without prior or simultaneous consideration of questions of value and purpose. It will also be recognised that the centralisation of key educational decisions on curriculum and assessment from the late 1980s allowed such questions to be annexed and pre-empted as part and parcel of educational policy. On that basis the electoral system was deemed to have given government a monopoly over the enterprise of raising educational value-questions as such and a mandate for imposing on the schools the answers it alone gave to the questions it alone asked. The only question which was regarded as open to those in the education service was how, through the curriculum, these values should be transmitted.

Such a view is of course both presumptuous and dangerous, and it is to the credit of the independent National Commission, set up in 1991 with the blessing but not the tangible support of government, that it sought to define afresh a value-orientation for the British educational system, grounded not in political or technocratic determinism but a careful analysis of future trends and needs. On that basis (National Commission 1993), the Commission identified the main global and national problems this country faces over the next few decades and urged a drive to use education and training to improve the country's economic performance. It argued that the tendency of our education system to educate a minority extremely well but fail the majority must be reversed and showed how this might be done, and that the debilitating divisions between education and training, and between the academic and vocational should be eliminated. The report deserves, and repays, careful study. Yet, apart from arguing for universal nursery education and the reduction of primary school class sizes, its recommendations for the primary stage were not particularly radical. Indeed, given the Commission's concern about the extent of under-achievement in English education, the modest attention they gave to the substance of primary education was somewhat surprising, for, of course, underachievement does not start at age 11. The core curriculum at Key Stage 1 (age 5–7), argued the Commission, should consist of English, mathematics, science and technology together with 'other areas of study chosen at the discretion of the school' – in other words, a slightly modified version of the National Curriculum. At Key Stage 2 (age 7–11) the curriculum should include a widened core, taking about 70 per cent of the available time, which includes English, mathematics, science, technology, citizenship and a modern foreign language, together with a minimum of one subject from the arts and one from the humanities.

Apart from the upgrading of technology, the addition of a foreign language and the emphasis on citizenship – modifications which would bring our primary curriculum more into line with those of some other countries – the diet is a familiar one. It accepts without question the division of compulsory education into four Key Stages along the historically established lines which we questioned above. It accepts the concept of a curriculum divided into a high-status core and a lower-status residue. It accepts the notion that the curriculum, for primary as for secondary, for early years as for later, is best defined as a canon of subjects. Like the National Curriculum, it is at the same time modernising and conservative. Like the National Curriculum, it implies that the challenges and tasks ahead are technical more than they are moral. Like the National Curriculum, it sees the humanities and arts as peripheral to the main thrust of education, especially in the early years. Like the National Curriculum, it does not really engage with the fundamental educational challenge of achieving a balance between meeting societal needs and fostering individual autonomy; though unlike the National Curriculum the National Commission does at least underpin its definition of 'citizenship' with principles like 'community' and 'democracy', even if they do look more comfortable in print than they are in practice. Perhaps, in the end, the Commission's understandable desire to achieve a broad consensus frustrated the need to be genuinely radical, about primary education at any rate. Or perhaps the Commission's report simply demonstrates this chapter's thesis about the immense durability of the structures and values which underpinned elementary education.

Comprehensively redefining the purposes of primary education for the twenty-first century demands a range of understanding and skill beyond the scope of one person; indeed, in a pluralist society it can only be undertaken by many people, working both separately and together. That of course was the unachieved promise of the National Commission. All an individual like myself can do is to assert the urgency of the task and nominate some of the key questions to be addressed.

Primary education as preparation

Being the first stage of education primary education constitutes, however it is defined and structured, a preparation. The question is, for what? For subsequent education, especially secondary? For the world of work? For the rounded life, of which work, paid work at least, is but a part? In considering these questions it is salutary to note current predictions that advances in medicine will ensure longer life expectancy for more and more people; that people can expect to change their jobs more frequently and radically than hitherto, and that the combination of these factors may therefore produce a situation in which for many people the longest phase of their lives is that spent in what, currently, we call 'retirement'. Should primary education attempt to provide a foundation for all this? Should it set itself more modest goals? Or should it eschew the social determinism that all notions of 'preparation' imply and reassert instead the progressives' belief in the value of education, for its own sake, here and now.

Primary education and culture

Education is one of the most important manifestations of, or mirrors to, a culture. But what version of culture should primary education reflect? One which is static, monolithic and consensual? One which is changing, pluralist and characterised by tension? One which is local? One which is national? One which is international or global? Having gained a purchase on the notion of culture, what particular aspects of culture should primary education engage with: for example, economic, political, intellectual, ethical, artistic, scientific, technical, spiritual, material? And what should be the character of that engagement: to depict; to transmit faithfully as heritage, generation to generation; to examine critically on the basis that culture must be actively shaped and reshaped?

Future and past

We have the lessons and the images of the past before us: universal, but uncompromisingly instrumental, elementary education; progressivism's attempt to provide an individually liberating alternative. How far do these provide pointers to the future? To what extent can the efforts to revisit and update the elementary model, which is arguably what government policy has invested some at least of its energies in since 1979, be regarded as appropriate for the twenty-first century? To what extent is a reassessment and reconstruction of the progressive model both useful as a counterbalance and viable as a version of primary education in its own right? Or can neither of these historical paradigms, however modified, provide a basis for the future and is it more appropriate to try to devise a version of primary education which – if this is possible, which I doubt – is totally new?

Coda

As I come to the end of this text I am in the middle of collecting material for a comparative study of primary education in five cultures which I hope will help me understand and more successfully address some of the problems of purpose and practice in British primary education, and especially the broader questions of value with which this book has ended. So far this project has taken me to four countries very different from Britain, where I have talked with those who make and enact national educational policy in general, and primary education policy in particular, and those who implement it in schools. I have spent many hours observing, filming and making notes in primary classrooms in these countries and in talking with children, their teachers and their parents. I have also observed and spoken with the some of the next generation of primary teachers currently undergoing their training. The project has taken two years to plan and negotiate; it will be several months before the data-gathering stage is completed, and, I suspect, several years before I have made sense of all that I have seen and heard and have translated it into publishable form. But the longer I spend in these countries the more convinced I become of the truth of four deceptively simple propositions.

First, in international terms much of what we do in our primary schools is both educationally ambitious and operationally impressive – often exceptionally so. This is no mere paternalistic platitude of the kind politicians give us before delivering yet another blow to educators' self-esteem, but an observable and testable truth, and one worth putting on record. Second, though wholesale educational transplants are not to be recommended, we can learn a great deal from other countries in our quest for alternative versions of primary education, at every level from policy to practice, and from the identification of broad purposes and values to the fine detail of classroom transactions. Third, in Britain we are sometimes extraordinarily parochial and insular in our thinking about primary education, and far too ensnared by the powerful historical legacies which have featured in this chapter, and the values, ideas, habits and practices which they carry in their train: somehow we have to escape from them, or at least stand back somewhat and view them for what they are. Fourth, the historical tendency of British primary education to stand outside the mainstream of the nation's intellectual life has been, and remains, a serious handicap.

We know why this last is the case. Elementary education set out to provide basic skills but under no circumstances to offer intellectual or cultural enfranchisement. Progressivism was rooted in anti-enlighten-ment values, and though it had roots, too, in political dissent and religious nonconformity of an often invigorating kind, these were soon diluted by a more generalised and unfocused romanticism which turned its back on the social and ethical issues which fed early progressive thinking. Primary teacher training for long reflected both these strands: at first primary teachers were given no more than a low-level appren-ticeship, later it became an induction into progressive ideas and practices; but in neither context were intellectual engagement or critical dialectic fostered or for that matter countenanced. Even when primary education, and primary teacher training, began to end its professional and intellectual isolation, there was the more general problem of the marginalisation of educational study as a whole within the universities to contend with. In the face of this, secondary teachers were at least part of the wider communities of subjects and subject study central to the university tradition which for many was the defining intellectual spring-board for adult life. Finally, it is only relatively recently that primary education became part of the personal experience of those with power and influence, political, intellectual and cultural.

Those of us interested in reconstructing a system of primary education for the twenty-first century must, for better or worse, end our isolation, look outwards to cultures other than our own, and engage the shapers of ideas and opinions in this country on their own ground and in their own terms.

NOTES

1 The extract from the Newcastle Commission's report was quoted, scathingly, by Matthew Arnold (1960). The several references to Dearing and the Dearing Report in this chapter are to the review of the National Curriculum commis-sioned in April 1993 from Sir Ron Dearing, first Chairman of the School Curriculum and Assessment Authority (SCAA), by the then Secretary of State John Patten. This gave particular attention to ways of 'slimming down' the National Curriculum to make it more manageable, to the future of the ten-level scale, and to ways of simplifying the assessment arrangements. Dearing's interim report (Dearing 1993a), from which this particular quotation comes, identified a number of possible strategies for achieving these objectives and these were the subject of a consultation exercise during the autumn of 1993. Dearing's final report (Dearing 1993b) was published in January 1994, and the resulting draft of the 1995 version of the National Curriculum Orders (SCAA 1994) was released in November 1994.

2 The terms 'trendy teachers' and 'educational establishment' were frequently used during 1991–93 by Secretaries of State Kenneth Clarke and John Patten, Minister of State Baroness Blatch, and Prime Minister John Major. The term 'barmy theory' was first used by Kenneth Clarke at the AGM of the 1991 Headmasters' Conference.

3 See, for example, references elsewhere to Bennett (1976 and 1984), Galton *et al.* (1980a and 1980b), Mortimore *et al.* (1988), Tizard *et al.* (1988), Alexander (1991), DES (1978 and 1982), etc.

4 See the 'Black Papers' published between 1969 and 1975, and newspaper headlines and reports of that period and 1991–93; also Alexander (1992) and Wallace (1993).

5 Information supplied by the Office for Standards in Education, October 1993. However, the funding position is rather more complicated than this, because it has several components. Thus, the Commons Committee enquiry into primary school funding identified an average *Standard Spending Assessment (SSA)* difference between primary and secondary schools, across all LEAs in 1994–95, of 39.3%, or £1,967 for primary as against £2,741 for secondary. However, comparison of *current expenditure* shows an even greater disparity – 46.3% in 1991–92, or £1,470 for primary and £2,150 for secondary. At the same time the *LEA LMS formulae* are calculated by using weightings for different age-bands, and the extent of variation is masked by national averages, though for what the latter are worth, the Commons Committee reported the following sample average weightings for 1993–94: £1,255 (under 4); £1,106 (age 5); £1,044 (age 7); £1,054 (age 9); £1,432 (age 11); £1,436 (age 13); £1,781 (age 15); £2,308 (age 18), producing a difference between the average allocation for all the ages 5 to 10 and 11 to 15 of 45–50% (House of Commons 1994a). What is beyond dispute, however, is the scale of the disparity between primary and secondary funding, and the fact that it exists for reasons which are essentially historical and unargued.

6 See Chapter 4, note 3.

7 As an example of a more comprehensive view than that sanctioned by central government of the kind of English curriculum needed for the twenty-first century, see the report of the 1993 independent enquiry into English sponsored by the British Film Institute and *The Times Educational Supplement* in 1993 (Bazalgette 1994).

8 All extracts here from J-J. Rousseau, *Emile*, translated by Barbara Foxley, Everyman, 1963.

9 Quoted in Lawson and Silver (1973: 282).

10 William Blake, *Songs of Experience: The Garden of Love*.

11 William Blake, *Songs of Experience: London*.

12 William Blake, *Songs of Experience: Holy Thursday*.

13 Quoted in Thompson (1993: 87).

14 B. Simon, Review in *Curriculum Journal* 3:1, 1992. Simon in turn cites the former Chief Inspector of Primary Schools, Miss A. L. Murton, as quoted in Liebschner (1992).

15 For a development of this thesis, see Alexander (1984: chap. 2).

16 For an account of these networks, and a case study of Oxfordshire, see Cunningham (1988). Also see Griffin-Beale (1984) for an important example of the way the network sustained and nourished itself by celebrating its leading figures (in this case Christian Schiller).

17 The highly publicised case of a London primary school which implemented its own extreme brand of progressivism in the face of opposition from the LEA, many parents and some of its staff, and became the subject of a public enquiry (Auld 1976).

18 Alexander (1991, 1992). The massive press coverage of this report and its aftermath, from late July 1991 to March 1992, are at the time of writing the subject of a Leverhulme-funded research project (*The Role of the Mass Media in the Education Policy Process*) based at Bristol University and directed by Michael Wallace.

19 Lawlor (1990), DFE (1993b). See also the contributions of Blatch, Skidelski, Pearson and Cox to the debate about the 1993 Education Bill, *Hansard*, 550:11. On the more general use by government of mythologising as an instrument of educational policy, see the papers by Bolton and Thornton in Chitty and Simon (1993), and Fred Jarvis's revealing correspondence on educational matters with the Prime Minister's office (Jarvis 1994).

20 Sometimes the charge that early years realities and needs are neglected is overstated and the early years and gender issues can be invoked needlessly and gratuitously. For example, when David, Curtis and Siraj-Blatchford (1992) wrote their riposte to the 1992 primary discussion paper of Alexander, Rose and Woodhead (1992), their fundamental criticism that it ignored early years rather missed the point that its remit was to concentrate on Key Stage 2. Their – valid – objection to the lack of a woman among the paper's authors and their exploitation of the 'three wise men' label ignored the fact that the discussion paper's authors were not self-selected, had themselves unsuccessfully questioned the wisdom of an all-male team, and had vainly tried to resist the epiphanic silliness of 'three wise men'.

21 It is the fate of nursery education to be more frequently advocated yet more frequently ignored than any other phase of education. At the time of writing, a new head of steam appears to be building up, following the Rumbold Report (DES 1990b), the strong endorsement of the principle of universal nursery education provided by the 1993 National Commission Report, and the Labour Party's acceptance of this position. The government's initial reaction, voiced by Secretary of State Patten, was to reject the National Commission proposals as far too expensive. However, Prime Minister Major soon contradicted this with a strong expression of support for nursery education. However, as on previous occasions, no commitments were given as to timing or funding.

22 It is interesting to note an apparent shift from the hard-line 3Rs position taken by Dearing in his 1993 interim report (quoted at the beginning of this chapter) to the more extended definition of 'basic skills' in his final report (Dearing 1993b): reading, writing, speaking, listening, number and information technology. In this respect the final Dearing position is close to that of the National Commission. The government view of the basics, however, remained unreconstructedly elementary, as Prime Minister Major repeatedly exhorted teachers to concentrate on getting children to 'read, write and do sums'. Dearing's revised definition was clearly a response to views expressed within the education profession, but the Prime Minister was targeting the more powerful constituencies of backbench and public opinion.

23 The question of the boundaries of English, as one of the traditional basics, was explored by participants in the 1993 Commission of Enquiry into English sponsored by the British Film Institute and *The Times Educational Supplement* (Bazalgette 1994).

Appendix 1
Primary teachers' professional knowledge in action (Chapter 2)

The fieldwork for this project was undertaken in 1986–87 with financial support from the University of Leeds. It was essentially an exploratory study, on a small scale, which sought to promote, through joint study by researchers and teachers, a shared understanding of aspects of primary teachers' day-to-day professional thinking. The project was directed by Robin Alexander, with Kay Kinder as Research Assistant.

Twelve teachers were involved in the project. They worked in primary schools in Bradford, Calderdale and Leeds. Half the group were previously unknown to me, having been nominated by LEA advisers as exemplifying what they deemed to be good classroom practice. The other half I already knew well as former secondees to an advanced diploma course in primary education for which I was then responsible, and these were chosen in part for their capacity and willingness honestly to articulate their thinking. The final selection was made from a considerably larger list of nominees with a view to ensuring that the proportion of women and men corresponded to the then ratio for the primary sector (about 80:20) and that there was at least one teacher for each pupil age-range from 5 to 11. Each teacher in the group provided biographical information and notes on what they counted as central to their teaching and distinctive about it.

The research had four stages. Stage 1 consisted of the observation and video-recording of one or two teaching sessions, nominated by the teacher as being representative of their practice. Researcher 1 operated the video camera, which was linked to a radio microphone worn by the teacher in order to catch all his or her utterances and those of the children with whom he or she was interacting, however quietly spoken these might be. Apart from panning out for contextualising shots at the beginning and end of lessons and at various points in between, the camera stayed with the teacher as the main target of the study. Researcher 2 made field notes using a simple open schedule which plotted the teacher's moves and all changes in the focus and/or content of his or her interactions, noting the time and duration in each case. To assist in this process, Researcher 2 wore earphones linked to the radio microphone receiver. Thus the transactions were both recorded and simultaneously monitored.

Immediately after the observation session, while still in the school, the researchers reviewed the video-recording and the field notes to check for a shared understanding of what they had observed and to identify extracts for discussion at Stage 2.

Stage 2 was the first of three interviews grounded in the observation and usually took place later the same day when the lesson observed and recorded was still fresh in the minds of all concerned. At this interview, which was recorded, as were all the project interviews, for transcription and later analysis, the teacher was invited to discuss their lesson intentions, the extent to which they were realised, and any problems encountered. Relevant sections of the video-recording were played to facilitate this discussion, and the extracts previously chosen by the researchers were also played in order to probe the nature of, and reasons for, decisions taken at what were believed to be key junctures in the observed lesson. The Stage 2 interview was transcribed, then photo-reduced for copying onto the left hand side of lengthways A4 sheets, thus leaving the right hand side free for comments. The transcription in this form was then sent to the teacher with an invitation to comment freely on what had been discussed. On its return to the researchers, the annotated transcript was photocopied for the teacher to keep.

Stage 3 was grounded in the Stage 2 transcript, as annotated by the teacher, and in the biographical information supplied at the start of the project. It sought to move from the particular lesson observed to the general question of the character of the teacher's practice and the reasons and influences which shaped it. Each interview followed a common format, but each was also different in that within this format the questions related specifically to what was by now known about the interviewee. The interview ranged over values, planning, classroom organisation, teaching methods, diagnosis, assessment and the teacher's underlying views of children's development and learning; together with the impact on these of biography, training, career, the context of the LEA and the school, reference groups and other influences. Once again, the interview was transcribed and returned to the teacher in a form which allowed him or her to write comments and also to correct or modify responses given at the time, before a copy of the transcript thus annotated was retained by both parties.

Some weeks elapsed between Stages 3 and 4. During this period, the researchers reviewed all the material gathered to date: the biographical notes, the video-recording, the lesson field notes, and the annotated transcripts of the Stage 2 and 3 interviews. They also completed an extensive literature review on teacher thinking – a field which at that time was only just opening up. Out of this combined analysis of the literature and the data, but especially from the latter, came the theory of 'competing imperatives' referred to and illustrated in Chapter 2. Preparation for the final, Stage 4, interview then consisted of attempting to identify and articulate the main 'knots', pressure points or dilemma areas in the teacher's professional thinking, as revealed in the data, and the specific competing imperatives to which the teacher was attempting to respond in each case. By this stage it was clear that some dilemmas were unique to each teacher, but many more were shared.

At the Stage 4 interview these dilemma areas, and the imperatives, were presented to the teacher for comment and discussion. By then, of course, researchers and teachers knew each other very well, and the interview benefited – as indeed had earlier stages – from the mutual trust which had been established and an open, conversational style of discussion. The teachers responded to the nominated dilemma areas by agreeing, disagreeing, modifying and extending, and by adding their own. The interview then reviewed the evidence by now available on the particular values, theories and beliefs underpinning the teachers' practice, their source, the main imperatives which these produced, and how these related to the imperatives arising from the practical circumstances of school and classroom. The interview, once again, was transcribed and returned to the teacher for comment and annotation before further photocopying for both parties.

At various points before, during and after the fieldwork programme, researchers and teachers met as a group. Initially, these meetings were planned to ensure a shared understanding of the project and its purposes and to enable the teachers to identify any problems or anxieties about the fieldwork, but it soon became clear to all concerned that the research methodology had, as a major spin-off, a powerful in-service development role. Thus, teachers and researchers met before the fieldwork programme to discuss the purposes and conduct of the project and to agree on procedures and ethical matters. They met half-way through to share views on the issues which were emerging and how they found the experience of being involved in this kind of activity. Finally, each was given a copy of their own data – the video-recording and, as the programme progressed, the annotated transcripts of the interviews from Stages 2, 3 and 4. At the request of the teachers, this material was used as the basis for a full-day meeting. Each teacher prepared for this by identifying extracts from their videotapes which they wished to share and during the meeting these were viewed and discussed before a plenary session reviewed the value and potential, for the teachers themselves, of their being involved in the project.

Appendix 2
The classroom practice studies
(Chapters 3 and 4)

The studies of classroom practice reported in Chapters 3 and 4 formed part of the Primary Needs Independent Evaluation Project (PRINDEP), funded from 1986-90 by Leeds City Council and commissioned to provide a formative and summative evaluation of the Council's Primary Needs Programme (PNP) which had started in 1985. The project was directed by Robin Alexander, with John Willcocks as Senior Research Fellow, Kay Kinder as Research Fellow, Steve Conway, Martin Ripley and Val Carroll as successive Research Assistants, together with twelve Leeds teachers seconded, usually for two terms at a time, over the four-year project period.

A detailed description of the project, and of the programme it evaluated, appears in Alexander *et al.* (1989) and Alexander (1992).

The Primary Needs Programme was a £14 million initiative aimed at improving the quality of primary education in the city's then 230 primary schools. It had one major aim – to meet the educational needs of all children, especially those experiencing learning difficulties – and three specific goals through which this broad aim would be realised: to develop a broadly based curriculum within a stimulating and challenging learning environment; to develop flexible teaching strategies and provide specific help for individuals and groups within the context of general classroom provision; and to develop productive links with parents and the community.

The programme's main reform strategies were the appointment of some 530 additional staff, with particular prominence given to 101 experienced 'co-ordinators' and 213 'support teachers'; increased capitation for equipment; a programme of minor works and refurbishment in the school buildings most in need; and a major programme of in-service support delivered by a strengthened advisory service and backed by the facilities and staff of a purpose-designed Primary Centre.

Schools entered the Primary Needs Programme in three phases, with priority given to those with greatest educational and social need as measured by their pupils' performance in the LEA's 7 plus and 9 plus reading screening tests and the incidence of free school meals. There were 71 Phase One schools which received the largest share of the programme's resources from 1985, 56 in Phase Two (1987), and 103 in Phase Three (1988).

The themes, procedures and ethical basis for the evaluation were negotiated between the project team at Leeds University and senior representatives of the LEA. A series of interim reports on various aspects of the Primary Needs Programme was to be provided at regular intervals to inform the programme's development and a final report providing firm conclusions and recommendations was to be submitted at the end of the evaluation. All reports were to be regarded as open to all interested parties, and copies were to be sent to schools, their governing bodies, local libraries, elected Council members, officers and advisers.

The six foci or themes for the evaluation related to the main aims of PNP and contingent enabling aspects of the work of schools and the LEA. They were: (1) children's needs: identification, diagnosis and provision; (2) the curriculum: content, development, management and evaluation; (3) teaching strategies and classroom practice; (4) links between home, school and community; (5) staff roles and relationships, and the management context of PNP schools; (6) professional support and development, with particular reference to the LEA. Chapters 3 and 4 of the present book relate to themes (2) and (3), but mainly the latter.

The project drew on seven main kinds or strands of evidence: (1) annual surveys of total populations in the city's primary schools – heads, PNP appointees, advisory staff and others; (2) fieldwork undertaken on an annual basis from 1986 to 1990 in a computer-generated representative sample of thirty of the city's primary schools, using observation and interviews and covering all six evaluation themes to provide both depth and a longitudinal study of change and development; (3) fieldwork in a separate sample of sixty schools, selected as exemplifying interesting or significant practice on the basis of a combination of self-selection, advisory staff recommendations and project information; (4) the study of classroom practice in sixty schools discussed in Chapters 3 and 4 (ten of these schools were from the main sample); (5) observation and interviews in connection with contingent roles and activities – advisory staff, LEA officers and members, programme support staff and so on; (6) analysis of school and LEA documentary material; (7) analysis of all 7 plus and 9 plus reading scores for the period 1983–89.

The project methods included: (1) twenty-five separate sets of questionnaires administered to all PNP co-ordinators, support teachers, primary heads, members of the LEA's advisory and support staff, and participants at the INSET courses monitored by the project; (2) thirty-six separate programmes of interviews undertaken in connection with each of the evidential strands listed in the previous paragraph apart from the final two; (3) eleven separate programmes of observation: of collaborative teaching; of PNP co-ordinators at work; of INSET courses; of school staff and curriculum meetings; and of teachers and children at work in the classrooms included in evidential strands (2), (3) and (4) in the previous paragraph; (4) analysis of documentary and test score data as indicated above.

The evaluation project's reports were issued over the period 1986–91. Eleven interim reports appeared between November 1986 and May 1990, and the final report was published in July 1991. Each report was sent in draft to the advisory service for comment before being modified as necessary and then submitted to the project's steering group (on which LEA officers, advisers and all three main political parties were represented) for decisions on dissemination and action. The process of negotiating the wording of the final report was considerably more protracted, with four months elapsing between presentation of the draft and agreement on the version to be published. In this case, following steering committee approval, a joint Leeds LEA/Leeds University press release was prepared.

The classroom practice study which forms the subject of Chapters 3 and 4 was undertaken in sixty (about one-quarter) of the city's primary schools. The study's aim was to conduct a programme of interviews and observation to explore the character of teaching and learning in schools within the Primary Needs Programme, and in particular to examine the relationship between the LEA's policies and recommendations on practice and practice as undertaken. The fact that this was an *evaluation* project, examining the implementation and impact of a policy and its four main aims, made it necessary for our working definition of pedagogy to encompass, as a minimum, all those aspects central to LEA thinking rather than impose on what we studied a model of pedagogy which might be incongruent with this thinking.

The study was conceived as having three 'levels', each one more detailed than the last. Level 1 (forty schools) consisted of a single school visit in each case, to observe a classroom and then to interview the teacher about its organisation and daily use. Level 2 (ten schools, all of them from the evaluation project's representative sample of thirty schools) combined the examination of data gathered over the previous three years with, in each case, a single visit to observe a nominated classroom, an interview with the teacher about its organisation and daily use, observation of the teacher in action, and a further interview to discuss the teaching session observed and the teacher's longer-term ideas and strategies. Levels 1 and 2 form the subject of Chapter 3 in this book.

Level 3, discussed in Chapter 4, consisted of a two-week programme of observation and interviews in each of a further ten schools. Here, using two observers per school, and with the aid of a radio microphone worn by the teacher so that everything he or she said could be clearly heard and tape-recorded, we conducted over each fortnight twenty one-hour sessions of systematic observation: ten of the teacher and, simultaneously, ten of a sample of six pupils, each pupil observed on each occasion for ten consecutive minutes. We conducted interviews about the teaching sessions beforehand and afterwards with the teacher and their support teacher(s) if any. At the end of the fortnight we interviewed the teacher and the school's head on more general matters of philosophy, policy and practice. All the interviews were tape-recorded and transcribed.

The forty teachers at Level 1 were chosen from the attendance lists of the LEA's courses on classroom organisation. These courses were the subject of an an earlier PRINDEP evaluation study (Alexander et al. 1989: chap. 6) and the teachers chosen for the Level 1 enquiry were drawn from those whose reactions to the courses appeared in the report on that study. The selection of the sample from this source ensured that all its members had been exposed to the same account of the LEA's thinking on some important aspects of the Primary Needs Programme, long enough beforehand for them to have been able to incorporate these ideas into their practice if they intended to do so. This explains some of the emphases in the interviews and observation sessions. For example, the importance attached in the courses to the display of children's work and other materials is reflected in the detailed attention to display in the observation schedules.

The ten teachers at Level 2 were drawn from the same lists of names, but an extra criterion here was that they should each be from a school in which we had already had an extensive involvement through our longitudinal study of development in the project's representative sample of thirty schools.

The schools at Level 3 were selected on the basis of their known enthusiasm for the LEA's primary education policies, the level of the LEA's investment in them within the Primary Needs Programme, recommendations received about the quality of their work, usually from the advisory service, and the need to secure an appropriate balance of different school sizes and locations. Seven were from PNP Phase 1, and three from Phase 2. The teachers in question had, like those at Levels 1 and 2, all attended the LEA's classroom organisation courses and their classrooms represented a positive response to the messages of these courses. The main criterion, therefore, was that teachers and schools at Level 3 should all have been clearly affected by LEA thinking and support. From the larger number initially identified, a sample of ten was drawn to include the gender balance of primary teachers as a whole and at least one of every age group of children from 5 to 11.

Six pupils were selected from each of these ten classes for detailed observation during ten one-hour stints over a period of a fortnight. The identity of the target pupils was unknown to both the pupils and their teachers. During each one-hour stint of observation the target pupils were observed one at a time for ten minutes each. The order in which they were observed was decided in advance and changed for each separate stint of observation. Alongside the pupil observations, a second observer monitored the activity of the teacher (or, if there were several teachers present, of one of them). The target teacher wore a radio microphone so that all his or her interactions with children during the observation stint could be clearly heard by the observer and also recorded for detailed analysis later.

The actions of the pupils and the target teacher were coded in accordance with specially devised systematic observation schedules, and subsequently subjected to computer analysis. The details of this aspect of the methodology are given in Chapter 4.

Appendix 3
Changes in curriculum-associated discourse and pedagogy in the primary school

Chapter 5 gives an account of the first three stages of data analysis from the project Changes in Curriculum-associated Discourse and Pedagogy in the Primary School (CICADA). The project was funded from 1991 to 1993 by the Economic and Social Research Council (ESRC ref. R000232904) and directed by Robin Alexander and John Willcocks, with Nick Nelson as Research Fellow and Elizabeth Willcocks as Research Assistant. The project's aim was to conduct a further programme of observation and interviews with the teachers from the PRINDEP Level Three study of classroom practice reported in Chapter 4 and through a rather different methodology from that adopted earlier to subject both sets of data to analysis in order to chart changes in the style and substance of teacher–pupil discourse over the period of the introduction of the National Curriculum (1988–92). A further objective was to set the observation study in the context of a national survey of teachers' attitudes to the National Curriculum and its impact on their work.

As explained in Chapter 4, the first objective was partly frustrated when the LEA withdrew permission for access to the schools in question, following the publication of the final PRINDEP report. A modified research design was negotiated with the ESRC which involved the analysis of pedagogical discourse recorded during observation sessions with primary teachers in 1986 (Chapter 2 of this book) and 1988 (Chapter 4), and the attempted isolation of those features which were relatively independent of time or location but sensitive to major curriculum changes. Data gathered in two different LEAs in 1992 would then be analysed, using the techniques thus developed, to identify any significantly different features of pedagogical discourse which had appeared since the introduction of the National Curriculum.

The twelve teachers who took part in the 1992 programme of classroom observation were all interviewed at length about the impact of the National Curriculum on their teaching. A hierarchically focused interview schedule allowed these teachers to take the lead in the choice and ordering of the topics under discussion while ensuring that nothing which the project team considered important was omitted altogether. After extensive piloting, the interview focused on seven main areas: assessment, record-keeping, classroom management, school management, contact with the LEA, the curriculum and professional morale.

Next, a national survey was undertaken to explore the attitudes of primary teachers more widely to the demands and impact of the National Curriculum in terms of the themes above. The questionnaire consisted of thirty-one items selected from the interview transcripts with which respondents were invited to signal their level of agreement/disagreement. A pilot version of the questionnaire was completed by, and discussed with, primary teachers attending in-service courses at the university. In the light of this piloting, modifications were made to the wording and order of the items. The questionnaires were administered by link-persons in fourteen LEAs, who were also responsible for sampling schools and teachers in accordance with instructions from the project team. Sampling covered school size, type, location and teacher sex, length of experience, and age-range of pupil taught. The responses were subjected to computer analysis, as described in detail in Chapter 5.

The observation data were collected from the classrooms of twelve teachers in primary schools in Wakefield and Bury LEAs. The observation procedure used the same technology as with the two earlier groups of teachers: that is to say, each teacher wore a radio microphone linked via the receiver to a tape-recorder (or video-recorder in the case of the first project) so that the target of observation remained identical: the utterances of the teacher and the pupils with whom he or she interacted. However, because the focus of concern in CICADA was more specific than in the other two projects – discourse as opposed to teacher thinking and decision-making (1986) and classroom practice generally (1988) – there was no parallel observation schedule as in those projects, and one observer rather than two. Instead, this observer prepared qualitative accounts of the sessions observed to augment and contextualise the transcript material.

The transcripts of the observation sessions in all sixty classrooms were annotated according to six coding systems dealing with *discourse structure, syntax, pedagogical strategies, curriculum content, participating pupils* and *overall lexical content*. These analytical frameworks are described in detail in Chapter 5, as are the methods of data analysis. It will be noted that this chapter deals only with the quantitative analysis. It is hoped to publish an account of the parallel qualitative analysis in the near future.

Bibliography

Alexander, R.J. (1984) *Primary Teaching*. London: Cassell.
—— (1988) 'Garden or jungle? Teacher development and informal primary education', in W.A.L. Blyth (ed.) *Informal Primary Education Today: Essays and Studies*, London: Falmer Press.
—— (1991) *Primary Education in Leeds: Twelfth and Final Report from the Primary Needs Independent Evaluation Project*, University of Leeds.
—— (1992) *Policy and Practice in Primary Education*, London: Routledge.
—— (1994a) *Innocence and Experience: Reconstructing Primary Education*, Stoke-on-Trent: ASPE/Trentham Books.
    (1994b) 'What primary curriculum? Dearing and beyond', *Education 3–13*, 22(1).
Alexander, R.J., Rose, A.J. and Woodhead, C. (1992) *Curriculum Organization and Classroom Practice in Primary Schools: A Discussion Paper*, London: DES.
Alexander, R.J. and Willcocks J. (1990) *Teachers and Children in PNP Classrooms (PRINDEP Report 11)*, University of Leeds.
Alexander, R.J., Willcocks, J. and Kinder, K.M. (1989) *Changing Primary Practice*, London: Falmer Press.
Argyris, C. and Schön, D. (1974) *Theory in Practice: Increasing Professional Effectiveness*, San Francisco: Jossey-Bass.
Armstrong, M. (1980) *Closely Observed Children*, London: Writers and Readers.
Arnold, M. (1960) 'The twice-revised code', in R.H. Super (ed.) *The Complete Prose Works of Matthew Arnold*, University of Michigan Press.
—— (1963), *Culture and Anarchy*, Cambridge: Cambridge University Press.
Ashton, P.M.E., Henderson, E.S., Merritt, J.E. and Mortimer, D.J. (1982) *Teacher Education in the Classroom: Initial and In-service*, London: Croom Helm.
Auld, R. (1976) *The William Tyndale Junior and Infants Schools: Report of the Public Enquiry*, London: ILEA.
Ausubel, D.P. (1968) *Educational Psychology: A Cognitive View*, New York: Holt, Rinehart & Winston.
Ball, S.J. and Goodson, I.F. (eds) (1985) *Teachers' Lives and Careers*, Lewes: Falmer Press.
Bantock, G.H. (1963) *Education in an Industrial Society*, London: Faber & Faber.
Barnes, D., Britton, J.N. and Rosen, H. (1969) *Language, the Learner and the School*, Harmondsworth: Penguin Books.
Bazalgette, C. (ed.) (1994) *Report of the Commission of Enquiry into English: Balancing Literature, Language and Media in the National Curriculum*, London: BFI Publishing.
Bennett, S.N. (1976) *Teaching Styles and Pupil Progress*, London: Open Books.

—— (1978) 'Recent research on teaching: a dream, a belief and a model', *British Journal of Educational Psychology*, 48.

—— (1982) 'Time to teach: teaching processes in primary schools', *Aspects of Education*, 27.

—— (1987) 'The search for the effective primary teacher', in S. Delamont (ed.) *The Primary School Teacher*, Lewes: Falmer Press.

—— (1992) *Managing Learning in the Primary School*, Stoke-on-Trent: ASPE/ Trentham Books.

—— (1994) *Class Size in Primary Schools: Perceptions of Headteachers, Chairs of Governors, Teachers and Parents*, University of Exeter.

—— (1995) 'Managing time', in C. Desforges (ed.) *An Introduction to Teaching*, Oxford: Blackwell.

Bennett, S.N. and Carré, C. (1993) *Learning to Teach*, London: Routledge.

Bennett, S.N., Desforges, C., Cockburn, A. and Wilkinson, B (1984) *The Quality of Pupil Learning Experiences*, Hove: Erlbaum.

Bennett, S.N. and Dunne, E. (1992) *Managing Classroom Groups*, London: Simon & Schuster.

Berlak, A. and Berlak, H. (1981) *Dilemmas of Schooling: Teaching and Social Change*, London: Methuen.

Bjorkman, M. (1972) 'Feedforward and feedback as determiners of knowledge and policy: notes on a neglected issue', *Scandinavian Journal of Psychology*,13(3).

Blake, W. (ed. J. Bronowski) (1958) *Songs of Experience*, Harmondsworth: Penguin Books.

Blyth, W.A.L. (1965) *English Primary Education: A Sociological Description*, London: Routledge & Kegan Paul.

—— (1984) *Development, Experience and the Curriculum in Primary Education*, London: Croom Helm.

—— (ed.) (1988) *Informal Primary Education Today: Essays and Studies*, Lewes: Falmer Press.

—— (1989) 'The study of primary education in England: retrospect and prospect', in *Primary Education and the National Curriculum: papers from the First National Conference of the Association for the Study of Primary Education*, Cambridge: ASPE.

Blythe, R. (1969) *Akenfield: Portrait of an English Village*, Harmondsworth: Penguin Books.

Board of Education (1931) *Report of the Consultative Committee on the Primary School* (Hadow Report), London: HMSO.

Brophy, J. (1983) 'Research on the self-fulfilling prophecy and teacher expectations', *Journal of Educational Psychology*, 75(5).

Brown, G. and Wragg, E.C. (1993) *Questioning*, London: Routledge.

Brown, S. and McIntyre, D. (1993) *Making Sense of Teaching*, Buckingham: Open University Press.

Bruner, J.S. (1963) *The Process of Education*, New York: Random House.

—— (1966) *Toward a Theory of Instruction*, Cambridge, Mass.: Harvard University Press.

Bruner, J.S. and Haste, H. (1987) *Making Sense: The Child's Construction of the World*, London: Methuen.

Burnett, J. (1974) *Useful Toil: Autobiographies of Working People from the 1820s to the 1920s*, London: Allen Lane.

—— (1982) *Destiny Obscure: Autobiographies of Childhood, Education and Family from the 1820s to the 1920s*, London: Allen Lane.

Calderhead, J. (1984) *Teachers' Classroom Decision-making*, London: Holt, Rinehart & Winston.

Campbell, R. J. (1993) 'A dream at conception: a nightmare at delivery', in R. J. Campbell (ed.) *Breadth and Balance in the Primary Curriculum*, London: Falmer Press.

Campbell, R.J. and Neill, S.R.St J. (1990) *Thirteen Hundred and Thirty Days: Final Report of a Pilot Study of Teacher Time in Key Stage 1*, London: AMMA.

—— (1992) *Teacher Time and Curriculum Manageability*, London: AMMA.

—— (1994a) *Curriculum Reform at Key Stage 1: Teacher Commitment and Policy Failure*, Longman.

—— (1994b) *The Meaning of Infant Teachers' Work*, London: Routledge.

—— (1994c) *Primary Teachers at Work*, London: Routledge.

Campbell, R.J., Evans L., Neill, S.R.StJ. and Packwood, A. (1991) *Workloads, Achievement and Stress: Two Follow-up Studies of Teacher Time at Key Stage 1*, London: AMMA.

Carr, D. (1994) 'Wise men and clever tricks', *Cambridge Journal of Education*, 24(1).

Central Advisory Council for Education (England) (CACE) (1967) *Children and their Primary Schools* (Plowden Report), London: HMSO.

Chitty, C., and Simon B. (eds) (1993) *Education Answers Back: Critical Responses to Government Policy*, London: Lawrence & Wishart.

Coveney, P. (1967) *The Image of Childhood*, Harmondsworth: Penguin Books.

Cox, B. and Boyson, R. (1975) 'Letter to MPs and parents', in B. Cox and A.E. Dyson, *The Fight for Education: Black Paper 1975*, London: J.M. Dent.

Cox, C.B. and Dyson, A.E. (eds) (1971) *The Black Papers on Education*, London: Davis-Poynter.

Csikszentmihalyi, M. (1975) *Beyond Boredom and Anxiety: The Experience of Play in Work and Games*, San Francisco: Jossey-Bass.

Cunningham, P. (1988) *Curriculum Change in the Primary School Since 1945: Dissemination of the Progressive Ideal*, Falmer Press.

David, T., Curtis and A., Siraj-Blatchford, I. (1992) *Effective Teaching in the Early Years: Fostering Children's Learning in Nurseries and Infant Classes*, Stoke-on-Trent: Trentham Books.

Dearden, R.F. (1968) *The Philosophy of Primary Education*, London: Routledge & Kegan Paul.

Dearing, R. (1993a) *The National Curriculum and its Assessment: Interim Report*, York and London: NCC and SEAC.

—— (1993b) *The National Curriculum and its Assessment: Final Report*, London: School Curriculum and Assessment Authority.

Department for Education (1992a) *Statistical Bulletin*, London: HMSO.

—— (1992b) *Initial Teacher Training (Secondary Phase)* (Circular 9/92), London: DFE.

—— (1993a) *The Initial Training of Primary School Teachers: New Criteria for Courses*, London: DFE.

—— (1993b) *The Government's Proposals for the Reform of Teacher Training*, London: DFE.

—— (1994a) *Our Children's Education: The Updated Parent's Charter*, London: DFE.

Department of Education and Science (1978) *Primary Education in England: A Survey by H.M. Inspectors of Schools*, London: HMSO.

—— (1981a) *A Framework for the School Curriculum*, London: HMSO.

—— (1981b) *A View of the Curriculum*, London: HMSO.

—— (1982) *Education 5 to 9: An Illustrative Survey of 80 First Schools in England*, London: HMSO.

—— (1983) *9–13 Middle Schools: An Illustrative Survey*, London: HMSO.

—— (1984) *Initial Teacher Training: Approval of Courses* (Circular 3/84), London: DES.

—— (1985a) *The Curriculum from 5 to 16: Curriculum Matters 2*, London: HMSO.

—— (1985b) *Education 8–12 in Combined and Middle Schools: An HMI Survey*, London: HMSO.

—— (1988) *The 1987 Primary School Staffing Survey*, London: DES.

—— (1989a) *Aspects of Primary Education: The Teaching and Learning of Mathematics*, London: HMSO.

—— (1989b) *The Implementation of the National Curriculum in Primary Schools*, London: HMSO.

—— (1989c) *Initial Teacher Training: Approval of Courses* (Circular 24/89).

—— (1990a) *Aspects of Primary Education: the Teaching and Learning of Language and Literacy*, London: HMSO.

—— (1990b) *Starting with Quality: Report of the Committee of Enquiry into the Quality of Educational Experience Offered to 3- and 4-Year Olds* (Rumbold Report), London: HMSO.

—— (1991a) *The Implementation of the Curricular Requirements of ERA: An Overview by HM Inspectorate on the First Year, 1989-90*, London: HMSO.

—— (1991b) *Assessment, Recording and Reporting: A Report by HM Inspectorate on the First Year, 1989–90*, London: HMSO.

Donaldson, M. (1978) *Children's Minds*, London: Fontana.

—— (1992) *Human Minds*, London: Allen Lane.

Drummond, M.J. (1993) *Assessing Children's Learning*, London: David Fulton.

Dunne E. and Bennett, S.N. (1990) *Talking and Learning in Groups*, London: Routledge.

Edwards, D. and Mercer, N. (1987) *Common Knowledge: The Development of Understanding in the Classroom*, London: Methuen.

Eischers, R., Greist, J. and Meluvaille, T. (1977) *Run to Reality*, Milwaukee: Madison Running Press.

Erikson, E.H. (1963) *Childhood and Society*, Harmondsworth: Penguin Books.

Galton, M. (1989) *Teaching in the Primary School*, London: David Fulton.

—— (1994) *Crisis in the Primary Classroom*, London: David Fulton.

Galton, M. and Simon, B. (1980) *Progress and Performance in the Primary Classroom*, London: Roultledge.

Galton, M., Simon, B. and Croll, P. (1980) *Inside the Primary Classroom*, London: Routledge.

Galton, M. and Williamson, J. (1992) *Groupwork in the Primary School*, London: Routledge.

Gipps, C. (1988) 'The debate over standards and the uses of testing', *British Journal of Educational Studies*, 36(1).

—— (1992) *What We Know about Effective Teaching*, London: University of London Institute of Education.

—— (1993) 'The structure for assessment and recording', in P. O'Hear and J. White (eds) *Assessing the National Curriculum*, London: Paul Chapman Publishing.

Golby, M. (1986) 'Microcomputers and curriculum change', in R Davis (ed.) *The Infant School: Past, Present and Future*, Bedford Way Paper 27, University of London Institute of Education.

Graham D. (1993) *A Lesson for Us All: The Making of the National Curriculum*, London: Routledge.

Green, A. (1990) *Education and State Formation: The Rise of Education Systems in England, France and the USA*, Basingstoke: Macmillan.

Griffin-Beale, C. (ed.) (1984) *Christian Schiller in his Own Words*, National Association for Primary Education.

Hockey, S. and Martin, J. (1988) *Oxford Concordance Program*, Oxford: Oxford University Press.

House of Commons (1986) *Achievement in Primary Schools: Third Report from the Education, Science and Arts Committee*, London: HMSO.

—— (1994a) *The Disparity in Funding Between Primary and Secondary Schools: Education Committee Second Report*, London: HMSO.

—— (1994b) *Education Committee Third Special Report: Government Response to the Second Report from the Committee, Session 1993–4 (The Disparity in Funding Between Primary and Secondary Schools)*, London: HMSO.

Jackson, B. (1964) *Streaming: An Education System in Miniature*, London: Routledge & Kegan Paul.

Jackson, P.W. (1968) *Life in Classrooms*, New York: Holt, Rinehart & Winston.

Jarvis, F. (1993) *Education and Mr Major: Correspondence between the Prime Minister and Fred Jarvis*, London: Tufnell Press.

Jenkins, D. (1975) 'Classical and romantic in the curriculum landscape'. in M. Golby, J. Greenwald and R. West (eds) *Curriculum Design*, London: Croom Helm.

Kelly, A.V. (1990) *The National Curriculum: A Critical Review*, London: Paul Chapman.

Kelly, A.V. and Blenkin, G.V. (1993) 'Never mind the quality, feel the breadth and balance', in R.J. Campbell (ed.) *Breadth and Balance in the Primary Curriculum*, Falmer Press.

King, R.A. (1978) *All Things Bright and Beautiful: A Sociological Study of Infants' Classrooms*, Chichester: John Wiley.

—— (1989) *The Best of Primary Education? A Sociological Study of Junior Middle Schools*, Lewes: Falmer Press.

Lawlor, S. (1990) *Teachers Mistaught*, London: Centre for Policy Studies.

Lawson, H. and Silver, H. (1973) *A Social History of English Education*, London: Methuen.

Leavis, F. R. (1930) *Mass Civilization and Minority Culture*, Cambridge: Minority Press.

Liebschner, J. (1992) *Foundations of Progressive Education: The History of the National Froebel Society*, London: Lutterworth Press.

Lortie, D.C. (1975) *Schoolteacher: A Sociological Study*, Chicago: University of Chicago Press.

Major, J. (1992) Speech to the Conservative Women's Conference, Eastbourne.

Mortimore, P. and Blatchford, P. (1993) *The Issue of Class Size*, NCE Briefing No. 12, National Commission on Education.

Mortimore, P., Sammons, P., Stoll, L., Lewis, D. and Ecob, R. (1988) *School Matters: The Junior Years*, London: Open Books.

National Commission on Education (1993) *Learning to Succeed*, London: Heinemann.

National Curriculum Council (1991) *Report on Monitoring the Implementation of the National Curriculum*, York: NCC.

—— (1993) *The National Curriculum at Key Stages 1 and 2: Advice to the Secretary of State*, London: NCC.

Nias, J. (1984) 'The definition and maintenance of self in primary teaching', *British Journal of Sociology of Education*, 5(3).

—— (1985), 'Reference groups in primary teaching: talking, listening and identity', in S. Ball and I.F. Goodson (eds) *Teachers' Lives and Careers*, Lewes: Falmer Press.

—— (1992) *Primary Teachers Talking: A Study of Teaching as Work*, London: Routledge.

Nias, J., Southworth, G. and Campbell, P. (1992) *Whole School Curriculum Development in the Primary School*, London: Falmer Press.

Nias, J., Southworth, G. and Yeomans, R. (1989) *Staff Relationships in the Primary School*, London: Cassell.

Office for Standards in Education (OFSTED) (1993a) *Curriculum Organisation and Classroom Practice in Primary Schools: A Follow-up Report*, London: OFSTED.

—— (1993b) *Well-managed Classes in Primary Schools: Case Studies of Six Teachers*, London: OFSTED.

—— (1993c) *The New Teacher in School*, London: OFSTED.

—— (1993d) *The National Curriculum: Possible Ways Forward*, London: OFSTED.

—— (1994a) *Primary Matters: A Discussion on Teaching and Learning in Primary Schools*, London: OFSTED.

—— (1994b) *Framework for the Inspecton of Schools (Revised May 1994)*, London: OFSTED.

—— (1995) *Standards and Quality in Education 1993–4: the Annual Report of Her Majesty's Chief Inspector of Schools*, London: HMSO.

O'Hear, P. and White, J. (eds) (1993) *Assessing the National Curriculum*, London: Paul Chapman Publishing.

Pollard, A. (1985) *The Social World of the Primary School*, London: Holt-Saunders.

Pollard, A., with M. Osborn, D. Abbott, P. Broadfoot and P. Croll (1993) 'Balancing priorities: children and the curriculum in the nineties', in R. J. Campbell (ed.) *Breadth and Balance in the Primary Classroom*, London: Falmer Press.

Pollard, A., Broadfoot, P., Croll, P., Osborn and M., Abbott, D. (1994) *Changing English Primary Schools: The Impact of the Education Reform Act at Key Stage One*, London: Cassell.

Richards, C.M. (ed.) (1982) *New Directions in Primary Education*, Lewes: Falmer Press.

—— (1994) 'Subject expertise and its deployment in primary schools: a discussion paper', *Education 3-13*, 22(1).

Rousseau, J-J. (1963) *Emile*, translated by B.Foxley, London: Everyman.

Scheffler, I. (1971) *The Language of Education*, Springfield, Ill.: Thomas.

Schön, D.A. (1982) *The Reflective Practitioner: How Professionals Think in Action*, London: Temple Smith.

School Curriculum and Assessment Authority (1994) *The National Curriculum Orders 1995: Draft Text*, London: SCAA.

Selleck, R. J. W. (1972) *English Primary Education and the Progressives, 1914–1939*, London: Routledge.

Shulman, L.S. (1986) 'Those who understand: knowledge growth in teaching', *Education Researcher*, 15(2).

—— (1987) 'Knowledge and teaching: foundations of the new reforms', *Harvard Educational Review*, 57.

Sikes, P.J., Measor, L. and Woods, P. (eds) (1985) *Teacher Careers*, Lewes: Falmer Press.

Simon, B. (1981) 'The primary school revolution: myth or reality?' in B. Simon and J. Willcocks (eds) *Research and Practice in the Primary Classroom*, London: Routledge.

—— (1983) 'The study of education as a university subject in Britain', *Studies in Higher Education*, 8(1).

—— (1992) *Education and the Social Order 1940–1990*, London: Lawrence & Wishart.

Simon, B. and Chitty, C. (1993) *SOS: Save Our Schools*, London: Lawrence & Wishart.

Sinclair, J. McH. and Coulthard, R. M. (1975) *Towards an Analysis of Discourse*, London: Oxford University Press.

Tann, S. (1981) 'Grouping and group work', in B. Simon and J. Willcocks (eds) *Research and Practice in the Primary Classroom*, London: Routledge & Kegan Paul.

Tanner, H. and Tanner R. (1939) *Wiltshire Village*, London: Impact Books.

Tanner, R. (1987) *Double Harness: An Autobiography by Robin Tanner, Teacher and Etcher*, Impact Books.

Tawney, R.H. (1923) *Secondary Education for All: A Policy for Labour*, London: Allen & Unwin/The Labour Party.

Taylor, W. (1969) *Society and the Education of Teachers*, London: Faber & Faber.

Thompson, E. P. (1993) *Witness Against the Beast: William Blake and the Moral Law*, Cambridge: Cambridge University Press.

Tizard, B., Blatchford, P., Burke, J., Farquhar, C. and Plewis, I. (1988) *Young Children at School in the Inner City*, London: Lawrence Erlbaum.

Tomlinson, P. (1989) 'Having it both ways: hierarchical focusing as research interview method', *British Educational Research Journal*, 15(2).

Vygotsky, L.S. (1962) *Thought and Language*, Cambridge, Mass.: MIT Press.

—— (1978) *Mind in Society: The Development of the Higher Psychological Processes*, Cambridge, Mass.: Harvard University Press.

Wallace, M. (1993), 'Discourse of derision: the role of the mass media within the education policy process', *Journal of Education Policy*, 8(4).

Webb, R. (1993) *Eating the Elephant Bit by Bit: The National Curriculum at Key Stage 2*, London: ATL.

—— (1994) *After the Deluge: Changing Roles and Responsibilities in the Primary School*, London: ATL.

Woodhead, C. (1995) 'Education: the elusive engagement and the continuing frustration'. Royal Society of Arts HMCI Annual Lecture, London: OFSTED.

Wragg, E.C. (1989) *Classroom Teaching Skills*, London: Routledge.

—— (1992) *Primary Teaching Skills*, London: Routledge.

—— (1993a) *Class Management*, London: Routledge.

—— (1993b) *An Introduction to Classroom Observation*, London: Routledge.

Wragg, E.C. and Bennett, S.N. (1990) Leverhulme Primary Project: Occasional Paper, Spring 1990, University of Exeter School of Education.

Wragg, E.C. and Brown, G. (1993) *Explaining*, London: Routledge.

Wragg, E.C. and Dunne, R. (1994) *Effective Teaching*, London: Routledge.

Index